STATE-SPONSORED INEQUALITY

STATE-SPONSORED INEQUALITY

The Banner System and Social Stratification in Northeast China

Shuang Chen

STANFORD UNIVERSITY PRESS
STANFORD, CALIFORNIA

Stanford University Press
Stanford, California

Printed in the United States of America on acid-free, archival-quality paper

Library of Congress Cataloging-in-Publication Data

Names: Chen, Shuang, 1977– author.
Title: State-sponsored inequality : the banner system and social stratification in northeast China / Shuang Chen.
Other titles: Studies in social inequality.
Description: Stanford, California : Stanford University Press, 2017. | Series: Studies in social inequality | Includes bibliographical references and index.
Identifiers: LCCN 2016043178 (print) | LCCN 2016044315 (ebook) | ISBN 9780804799034 (cloth : alk. paper) | ISBN 9781503601635 (ebook) | ISBN 9781503601635 (e-book)
Subjects: LCSH: Social stratification—China—Manchuria—History—19th century. | Landowners—China—Manchuria—History—19th century. | Land grants—China—Manchuria—History—19th century. | Wealth—China—Manchuria—History—19th century. | Manchuria (China)—Social conditions—19th century. | China—History—Qing dynasty, 1644–1912.
Classification: LCC HN740.M35 C44 2017 (print) | LCC HN740.M35 (ebook) | DDC 305.5/1209518—dc23
LC record available at https://lccn.loc.gov/2016043178

Typeset by Newgen in 10/14 Sabon

To the memory of my mother and to my father

CONTENTS

LIST OF ILLUSTRATIONS

Figures

Maps

Tables

ACKNOWLEDGMENTS

This book represents an intellectual endeavor to integrate quantitative and qualitative methods and produce a holistic understanding and history of human experience. It would not have been completed without the many teachers, colleagues, friends, and family who sustained my efforts across the years of research, writing, and rewriting. My first thanks go to the research group led by James Lee and Cameron Campbell. The book has benefited greatly from their collective work. I especially thank James Lee for his unfailing support of my career as a scholar. A great mentor and enthusiastic teacher, he broadened my horizon by guiding me to the field of social scientific history and constantly pushing me to reflect on methodological issues. It was James who first located and acquired the microfilm version of the Eight Banner household and land registers for Shuangcheng County and suggested them to me as a potential research topic. These registers were later transcribed into the China Multi-Generational Panel Dataset, Shuangcheng (CMGPD-SC). The three coders, Sun Huicheng, Jiyang, and Xiao Xing, diligently worked on transcribing the household and land registers into machine-readable form. Cameron Campbell wrote the original code used to process the raw data into a form that was amenable to analysis. A wonderful teacher, Cameron also taught me the techniques of data analysis through individual tutoring and spent enormous amount of time reading and commenting on the manuscript. Chen Weiran, Eric Li, Ren Yuxue, and Matthew Noellert provided me with companionship in studying the history of Shuangcheng and generously shared with me the materials they collected. Ren Yuxue, a specialist in the institutional history of the Qing dynasty Northeast China, also helped me with her knowledge of the larger institutional background as well as her focus on spatial patterns. Matthew Noellert, a historian on Land Reform and communist revolution, invited me to join his fieldwork in the former banner villages in Shuangcheng in summer 2013. Other colleagues and friends in the research group, Dwight Davis, Dong Hao, Liang Chen, Li Ji, Song Xi, Byung Ho Lee, Zang Xiaolu, Li Lan, Wang Linlan, and Lai Sze Tso, read and commented on various versions of the manuscript.

I am also indebted to the broader intellectual community in the United States, which offered me crucial support in the process of writing the book. Mark Elliott read the book manuscript and offered unwavering support when I needed it most. At the University of Michigan, Myron Gutmann opened my eyes by bringing me into a larger community of historical demography. Myron, Barbara Anderson, Pär Cassel, Ernest Young, and Kenneth Sylvester offered valuable comments and suggestions on the manuscript. Susan Leonard closely followed the project of CMGPD-SC and commented on my work. In the field of Chinese Studies, Joseph Esherick, Christopher Isett, Huaiyin Li, Daniel Little, Peter Perdue, Kenneth Pomeranz, William Rowe, Wang Feng, R. Bin Wong, Yunxiang Yan, and Elizabeth LaCouture read all or part of my work and had conversations with me at various stages of the project. Their insightful comments and thought-provoking questions greatly inspired my work. Various participants at my presentation to conferences such as the Social Science History Association and American Historical Association also offered valuable input on my papers, on which some chapters of the book are based. It is with deep gratitude that I acknowledge their help.

My teachers and friends in Asia also offered me unfailing support and companionship. The teachings of Luo Xin, Zhang Fan, and my other former teachers in Peking University shaped my passion for history and scholarly thinking. Li Bozhong, Ding Yizhuang, and Zhang Xiaoye helped me expand the scope of analysis in the book with their expertise in socioeconomic history, Eight Banners, and local histories. Qiu Yuanyuan and Yoshiki Enatsu inspired me with their works on manor lands in Beijing and Fengtian. Yoshiki Enatsu also graciously offered help in collecting Japanese scholarship on Shuangcheng. Lin Xingchen and Huang Yulin at the Academia Sinica helped me acquire archival sources from the collection of *Neige da ku dang'an*.

My appreciation also goes to my colleagues at the University of Iowa. The Department of History provides me a wonderful intellectual home. Stephen Vlastos, Alyssa Park, James Giblin, Michaela Hoenicke-Moore, and Jaki Rand from history department and Newell Ann Van Auken from the Department of Asian and Slavic Languages and Literatures commented on various parts of my manuscript and offered tremendous moral support during the publication process. Outside Iowa, my friends in other academic disciplines—Meina Liu, Huijuan Zhao, Lan Yang, Hao Zhao, Dengfeng Sun, Qian Yu, Jie Zhou, and Guorong Zhu—were a constant source of support and inspiration with their caring hearts and passion for research.

My heartfelt thanks go to the following institutions and individuals for their support of my research: The First Historical Archives in Beijing, especially Wang Jinlong; Liaoning Provincial Archives and Liaoning Provincial Local Gazetteer Office, especially Gao Jing; Shuangcheng Municipal Archives, especially Jiang Mingshan and Xue Qi; Jilin Provincial Archives. Yin Wenhua and Guan Guoqing in Shuangcheng and Zhang Baohui, my friend at the University of Michigan with a Shuangcheng origin, offered great help to Matthew Noellert and me during our fieldwork.

Cynthia Col copyedited an early draft of the manuscript. Jenny Gavacs and Kate Wahl at the Stanford University Press guided me through the publication process. The two anonymous reviewers helped me refine my thesis with their insightful comments and suggestions. Ren Yuxue and Robert Shepard offered great help in creating the maps in the book. Che Tailai and Yu Meide gave me permission to use the cover image, and Jiang Mingshan, Zheng Mengnan, and Du Yue provided me tremendous help in obtaining the permission. I am grateful to all of them.

For financial support, I am beholden to the International Institute, the History Department, the Rackham Graduate School, and to the Center for Chinese Studies at the University of Michigan for various fellowships. The research related to this book is also a part of the larger research project on population and demographic behavior in historical China and the project to publicly release the CMGPD-SC dataset. The two projects were supported by NICHD 1R01HD045695-A2 (James Lee PI), "Demographic Responses to Community and Family Context," and NICHHD 1R01HD070985-01 (Cameron Campbell PI), "Multi-

Generational Demographic and Landholding Data: CMGPD-SC Public Release." A Junior Scholar Grant provided by the Chiang Ching-Kuo Foundation of International Scholarly Exchange, the flexible-load assignment and the Old Gold Fellowship provided by the College of Liberal Arts and Science, and the research grant offered by the Center for Asian and Pacific Studies at the University of Iowa enabled me to take time off from teaching and to focus on the research and writing of the book.

Finally, my deepest gratitude goes to my family—my father, Chen Chaoxin, and my late mother, Si Zuqin, whose unfailing love gave me courage and confidence, and my husband, Tong Niannian, and my son, Thomas, my most faithful friends—for their patience, love, and support. Thanks are not enough.

CONVENTIONS

Weights and Measures

The following are the metric conversions of weights and measures used in Shuangcheng:

1 *li* = 576 meters = 0.58 kilometers

1 *shang* = 10 *mu* = 18,432 square meters = 1.84 hectares = 4.55 acres

1 market *shi* = 2.5 imperial *shi* = 320.75 kilograms

Unless otherwise specified, the *shi* used in this book refers to market *shi*.

1 *tael* = 38 grams

Ages

The age used in this manuscript refers to *sui*, a measurement of people's age used in late imperial China. An infant is counted as one *sui* at birth and two *sui* at age one.

According to the Qing government standard, the age range for adult males in Shuangcheng is twenty to fifty *sui*.

Currency

One string of cash equals one thousand copper coins.

The Names of Banner Villages

Banner villages in Shuangcheng are named after the banner administration they belong to. As an institutional reform in 1870 reorganized the banner administration, the village names changed accordingly. All references to the banner villages in the book use the village names before 1870, which are shown in Map 2.1.

The Name of Qing-dynasty Capital

The Qing-dynasty capital, Jingshi, is refered to as Beijing in the book.

Dates

Date information that includes the day, month, and year is cited by Western calendar year, lunar month, and day, for example, the twenty-first day of the third month of the seventeenth year of the Jiaqing reign is cited as 1812.3.21.

STATE-SPONSORED INEQUALITY

CHAPTER ONE

Social Formation Under State Domination in Modern China

An Introduction

Eleven days after the Chinese New Year, in 1824, a procession of fifty-three wagons left Beijing, the capital of the Qing dynasty (1644–1911), and headed northward to a remote settlement in Manchuria[1] called Shuangcheng (map 1.1).[2] Riding in the wagons were sixty men, fifty-four women, and seventy-two children—a total of fifty-three households.[3] These travelers had begun this journey because the government had told them that they were returning to their ancestral homeland, where fertile land, clean and spacious houses, and assistance in farming the land awaited them. Fifteen days later, they went through the Shanhaiguan Pass—the easternmost pass on the Great Wall—and entered Manchuria. Escorted by local officials, they traveled farther north, taking another sixteen days to cross the border into Jilin. After another ten days, they finally arrived at their destination. These fifty-three households were the first Beijing pioneers to settle in Shuangcheng, but others soon followed.

These settlers from Beijing would become the state-designated elites in Shuangcheng. They were descendants of the warriors who had helped the Manchu rulers of the Qing conquer China proper in 1644. As early followers of the emperor, those warriors had been organized under a system called the Eight Banners, and were referred to as *bannermen*. Because of this distinguished status, they and their descendants were to serve the state as soldiers and receive stipends from the state in perpetuity. But in the early nineteenth century, amid a fiscal crisis surrounding the support of the banner population, the state decided to relocate the

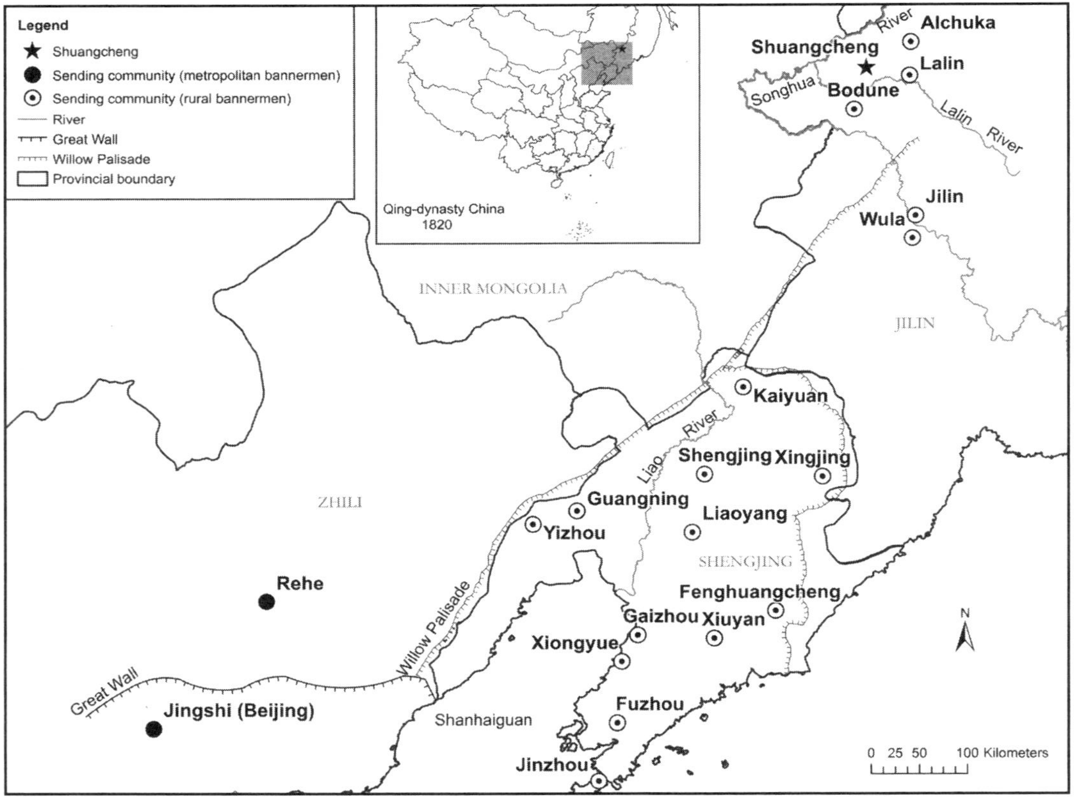

Map 1.1. Sending communities of banner immigrants to Shuangcheng.

SOURCES: Information of the sending communities is drawn from the CMGPD-SC. Location of the Willow Palisade is from Edmonds (1979, 602, fig. 1). Data for provincial boundaries and rivers are from "Datasets for 1820," CHGIS, Version 4, January 2007.

bannermen living in Beijing back to Manchuria, substituting state land for the state stipends. Over a period of two decades, a total of 698 such banner households arrived in Shuangcheng. To help them settle in their new homes, the state, between 1815 and 1820, also relocated three thousand households of bannermen from elsewhere in Manchuria (map 1.1) to Shuangcheng. The government's settlement of the banner immigrants triggered private migration into the area as well. By the 1860s, a total of 5,300 registered households had settled in Shuangcheng,[4] establishing a rural society divided into two segments: the *haves*—that is, the *jingqi*, or "metropolitan bannermen," from Beijing and Rehe and the *tunding*, or "rural bannermen," from other parts of Manchuria, who were supported by the state with land grants—and the *have-nots*, that is, the *fuding*, or "floating bannermen," and *minren*, or civilian commoners, who had moved into the area without the state's permission and thus did not receive land allocations. Among the haves, the metropolitan bannermen received land grants that were twice as large as those of the rural bannermen. These asymmetrical entitlements continued until 1906, by which time Shuangcheng had become a county with more than sixty thousand households, containing 440,000 people (SCXZ 1990, 829).[5] This legacy of social segmentation persisted in Shuangcheng far beyond the fall of the Qing in 1911.

This book explores the social and economic processes of inequality under a state-dominated system by providing a holistic, comprehensive view of the formation of the social hierarchy in Shuangcheng in the nineteenth and early twentieth centuries. The state created a social hierarchy from the top down by classifying people into distinct categories, each associated with differentiated entitlements to land. Under this system, the state directly intervened in wealth distribution and the determination of people's social status in order to fulfill its administrative goal: to maintain the elite status of the metropolitan bannermen. Eventually, the state-designated social hierarchy played out on the ground at the intersection of state policies and local practices.

As a well-documented case, the Shuangcheng story offers a historical perspective on the phenomenon of states using resource allocation to create structural inequality. Scholars who study social stratification pay increasing attention to the persistence of structural inequality in modern societies (Baron and Bielby 1980; Blau 1994; Diprete et al. 1997;

Tilly 1998). In his thesis of "durable inequality," Charles Tilly (1998, 1–40) points out that inequalities measured by acquired individual attributes that range along a scale from low to high—such as income level or education level—are open, fluid, and easy to change. However, when ascriptive characteristics, such as gender and skin color, become the basis of social differentiation and access to resources, the inequalities arising along these categorical boundaries interact with acquired individual attributes to become "durable" (ibid.). This is because boundaries between categories based on ascriptive characteristics are hard to change. In his study of the rising inequality in post-socialist China, Wang Feng (2008) reveals that the major sources of social inequality are the various categories created by the socialist state, based on household category, ownership type, industrial sector, and geographical location. The durability of structural inequality in a society raises two questions: Among the various ascriptive characteristics of an individual, how do certain ones become the basis of social differentiation? And, how are the boundaries corresponding to these characteristics created and maintained? The study of the Shuangcheng case shines a historical light on the role of one important actor—the state—in creating such boundaries, and on the social construction of these boundaries in an agrarian society.

This book focuses on structural inequality created by the state because such inequality is not only the foundation of the social hierarchy in nineteenth-century Shuangcheng but also a feature of the Chinese society after the foundation of the People's Republic of China ([PRC]; 1949–present). Among the many categories created by the socialist state, those created by the *hukou* household registration system most resemble the population categories in Shuangcheng. With its goal of industrialization, the PRC, established the *hukou* system and divided the population of the entire country into the "rural household" category or the "urban household" category (Wang 2005). This system has created nationwide inequality between the two household categories, with the urban households enjoying better entitlements to state employment and the associated benefits, such as housing and education. Numerous studies have highlighted the profound impact of the *hukou* system on social inequality in China and its connection with the socialist revolution (Solinger 1999; Wu and Treiman 2004; Wang 2005; Whyte 2010; Brown 2012). Yet people rarely recognize that the state-sponsored inequality in post-1949 China was not a socialist extension but a statecraft that had existed in history.[6] The Eight Banners registration system in Qing-dynasty Shuangcheng has many parallels with the *hukou* system in the PRC. Placing this phenomenon in the broader perspective of state-building and its social consequences renders an in-depth understanding of state-sponsored inequality in the past and present.

In a broad sense, both the state-dominated system in Shuangcheng and the *hukou* system in post-1949 China are state-initiated projects of social engineering, in which the state implemented policies to proactively design or plan the social order. The efforts to penetrate and control society go hand in hand with the emergence of the state. From time to time, these efforts culminate in projects of social engineering. In the twentieth century, government social-engineering projects garnered considerable attention because they were often carried out in an entire country and impacted the society on a massive scale. James Scott (1998) examines some of these large-scale social-engineering projects, such as Soviet collectivization and the Tanzanian forced villagization. He points out that the ways these projects were carried out are closely associated with the political system and ideology of the respective state; all the large-scale projects he studies were carried out by an authoritarian state with a "high-modernist ideology": "a strong version of self-confidence based on the development of science and technology and the expansion of production" (ibid., 4). Yet little attention has been given to social-engineering projects undertaken in the past. Although the Shuangcheng settlement and the *hukou* system were independent projects carried out under different ideologies, both grew out of a state belief in using resource allocation to create a social hierarchy among the population, and both were backed up by a political system that enabled the state to implement such policies. These parallels connect socialist China to its imperial past. By reconstructing the story of social formation under state domination in nineteenth-century Shuangcheng, this book offers a unique perspective on how historians and social scientists typically conceive modern phenomena.

In addition to the implications for the social stratification system in contemporary China, the Shuangcheng case also offers a special setting for the examination of some key issues in nineteenth-century China. The state-dominated system in Shuangcheng was special in two respects.

First, the Eight Banners institutionally distinguished Shuangcheng from many other local societies of the period. Although the Qing institutionalized the bannermen and created the Shuangcheng society from top down, it had only limited reach into local civilian society. For most of the Qing dynasty, the state did not establish formal government institutions below the county level. Only in the early twentieth century, the last decade of Qing dynasty, did the state begin to build government offices at the district level. State landownership and the level of state control in Shuangcheng were only seen in the Eight Banner farms in Manchuria, the manor lands in the areas surrounding Beijing, and Xinjiang (Wang, Liu, and Guo 1991; Diao 1993; Diao and Yi 1994; Guo 1997; Qiu 2014). Second, the ability of the state to carry out the Shuangcheng settlement and to design the immigrant society counters our general understanding of Qing history in this period. The received wisdom about nineteenth-century China portrays it as an age marked by the devolution of political power, a vicious cycle brought about by endless internal rebellions and foreign intrusions. At the societal level, the numbers of local elites greatly expanded, and they became more and more important in organizing local society.[7] Thus, the Shuangcheng society seems on the surface to be very different from other local societies. However, as this book reveals, Shuangcheng was still part of the China of the nineteenth century and experienced all the social and political changes of this period. Most importantly, banner officials in Shuangcheng adopted a style of local governance similar to that of the civilian system elsewhere in China. Therefore, despite the institutional difference, the ways in which the Shuangcheng immigrants responded to state policies, organized themselves, and carried out daily activities can serve as references to social behaviors of the time. The basic social dynamics—economic and demographic differentiation, social mobility, and social reproduction at the local level—are informative in understanding rural communities in nineteenth-century China.

By showing how the interaction of state policies, local politics, and customary practices gave rise to disparities in socioeconomic status among the Shuangcheng immigrants, the book illustrates in vivid detail the transformation of banner society in Manchuria in the late Qing. As the institutional foundation for Manchu's rule of China, the development of the Eight Banners has been key to understanding the history of the Qing. The political, socioeconomic, and cultural status of bannermen are important indicators of the vigor of this institution. Traditional views on the Eight Banners in the late Qing emphasize its decline, when it could no longer provide stipends to bannermen, and when the banner people lost their linguistic and military traditions. However, studies that have been done in the last thirty years shed new light on the ramifications of the fiscal and cultural crises of the Eight Banners. As their institutional support gradually dissolved, the banner people became embedded in the broader social fabric of Chinese society (Crossley 1990; Ding et al. 2004; Enatsu 2004; Qiu 2014). During this process, some bannermen were able to maintain their socioeconomic status and even became local elites (Enatsu 2004). At the same time, the banner people developed and preserved a distinct ethnic identity (Crossley 1990). While existing studies focus on either a select group of individuals or on a single aspect of the life of bannermen, the Shuangcheng story provides a holistic view of the banner people living in 120 villages in the last hundred years of the Qing dynasty. It confirms findings in the existing scholarship that "banner people" was not a simple, unitary category but a diverse group who interacted with and adapted to the larger society. It reveals that the Eight Banners significantly impacted the society of Manchuria, not only in terms of the identity of bannermen but also in terms of the social hierarchy in the region.

Moreover, the Shuangcheng story illuminates in particular the questions of to what extent and how the state was able to reach into and transform local society. Over the course of the development of the modern state, scholars have provided abundant documentation and theories about the complexity of state-society interactions and their perplexing consequences. Scott (1998, 2–3) highlights the inherent tension between state-building and local customs. Since myriad local customs are illegible to outsiders, state measures to govern a society, or make a society "legible," are ways to simplify that society. As such, the interactions between state policies and local society have consequences going both ways: on one hand, local people had the capacity to modify and subvert the state-imposed policies; on the other hand, despite resistance to the state's simplifications, state policies did shape social institutions and transform the society (ibid., 47–51). At the same time, the boundary between the state and society in everyday life is often blurred. As Joel Migdal (2001,

11–16) synthesizes in his "state-in-society approach," although the state has an image as "a coherent, controlling organization," in practice, both the state and society have multiple representatives, with different interests. These representatives formed "shifting coalitions and contended with one another over rules for everyday behavior" (Ibid., 11). This is also true in China. Because of the absence of a formal government structure below the county level, the state in the late imperial period relied on many agents to carry out its rule in local society (Hsiao 1960; Ch'ü 1962; Huang 1985, 219–48; Reed 2000; Zheng 2009). Some local elites helped to promote state policies and disseminate state ideologies to reinforce their own power and socioeconomic status (Wong, Huters, and Yu 1997; Faure 2007). Therefore, scholars studying local society in the late imperial period identify the influence of state ideology and policies everywhere. Whereas existing scholarship on state-society relations looks at how the state penetrates local society, the Shuangcheng case illuminates the boundary between the state and society by asking the question the other way: in a society created by the state, to what extent are local people able to exercise their agency, and how is this agency practiced?

Finally, by counting wealth as an indispensable variable in the process of social formation, and by using a non-Western case to illuminate the levers of wealth distribution in a noncapitalist setting, the book also contributes to comparative studies of wealth inequality. By revealing extremely unequal distributions of wealth, recent studies on global wealth distribution have sparked growing popular interest in this field (Lindert 2000; Davies et al. 2011; Piketty 2014).[8] Yet, most of the studies on wealth distribution that have been done so far focus on Western countries, where the patterns of wealth distribution were shaped by the interplay of the development of capitalism and state fiscal policies. Because of the scarcity of systematic data preserved from the early periods, our understanding of wealth distribution in preindustrial societies remains limited. The book offers one of the first empirical studies on the distribution of landed wealth in an entire county to show how wealth inequality in early modern China was produced and maintained in an agrarian society under a state-dominated system.

Above all, the socioeconomic process of inequality in Shuangcheng can be situated in a conceptual framework that encapsulates the question, how does a state-dominated system of social formation influence life opportunities? This framework integrates theories of both state-building and social stratification to provide a holistic view of the consequences of state-initiated projects of social engineering. It also illuminates the key factors that contribute to social stratification in agrarian societies in the nineteenth-century China. Theories of social stratification maintain that structural inequality is created in two steps: in the first, categorical boundaries are clearly defined; in the second, the various actors participate in the social construction of these boundaries to make them durable (Tilly 1998; Wang 2008). The Shuangcheng story illustrates both steps in detail. The institution of the Eight Banners and the frontier setting of Shuangcheng enabled the state to use registration and resource allocation to implement a social hierarchy according to its will. Yet, the customary practices associated with the property regimes in late imperial China and the style of local governance in the Qing gave immigrants considerable room to exercise their agency to pursue their interests. By creating their own patterns of upward and downward wealth mobility, local people simultaneously challenged and reinforced the state-mandated social hierarchy. Eventually, the strategies employed by both the privileged and underprivileged groups reinforced the boundaries defined by the state. Further, the interplay of state policies, the agency of the local people, and the economic and demographic conditions shaped the social hierarchy.

THE EIGHT BANNERS

The Eight Banners constitute the foundation of the Manchu state, the regime the Manchu rulers founded prior to their conquest of China proper. In the early seventeenth century, the founders of the Qing—Nurhaci and Hong Taiji—created the Eight Banner institution to organize all the people living in Liaodong,[9] transforming the various tribes into a bureaucratic state (Meng 1936; Elliott 2001; Liu 2001). Each banner represented an administrative division, and the banners were distinguished by eight different combinations of colors and patterns: plain yellow, bordered yellow, plain white, bordered white, plain red, bordered red, plain blue, and bordered blue. Bannermen, adult males organized under the Eight Banners, were farmers in times of peace and soldiers in times of war. On the eve of the Manchu conquest of China, three sets of the Eight Banners—Manchu, Mongol, and Han-martial (*hanjun*)—organized populations of their respective ethnicities.

After the Manchu conquest of China proper in 1644, the Eight Banners became an administrative system for organizing the conqueror's elite population, and the people of the Qing were divided into *bannermen* and *civilian commoners*. The emperors not only moved the Eight Banner population into the inner city of Beijing, but also established a national banner garrison system, stationing banner troops in garrisons located in important cities in China proper to police the civilian commoners (Crossley 1990, 47–73; Ding 2003). By serving the state, bannermen enjoyed economic and political privileges. The state provided banner officials and soldiers with two forms of material support based on their ranks: stipends, paid in silver and grain, and property grants, consisting of land and housing that was exempt from taxes and rent. Moreover, state regulations that reserved certain positions for the Manchu and Mongol bannermen increased their occupational mobility by giving them more opportunities to enter the state bureaucracy relative to those of civilian commoners.[10] Throughout the 268 years of Manchu rule, the Eight Banners maintained sharp boundaries between bannermen and Han civilian commoners (Rhoads 2000; Elliott 2001).

Although all bannermen belonged to the elite strata of society, the state created categories among them to define hierarchical entitlements to state support. The state classified the bannermen based on multiple sets of criteria—such as ethnicity and service location—and established a hierarchy along with each set of criteria. In terms of ethnicity, the Manchu bannermen, who shared the ruler's ethnicity, and the Mongol bannermen, who had an affinal relationship with the Manchu, enjoyed better material support and occupational mobility than did Han-martial bannermen, who were ethnic Han people.[11] In terms of service location, the court also treated the bannermen in Beijing, those stationed in the garrisons in China proper, and those serving in Manchuria differently. The bannermen in Beijing, the metropolitan bannermen, were at the top of the hierarchy, receiving larger state stipends and land grants; whereas those in Manchuria were on the bottom and received the least material support.[12] Compared to the metropolitan bannermen, the bannermen serving in the garrisons in the provinces had much more restricted occupational mobility.[13]

While the Eight Banners institution distinguished between bannermen and civilian commoners, over time, maintaining the system became more and more difficult because of changes in bannermen's lifestyle and the growing fiscal burden on the state of supporting them. The first challenge was to the state's banner-land system, one of the measures that maintained the economic privilege of the bannermen. In the beginning of the Qing dynasty, the state controlled a large amount of land in the areas surrounding both Beijing and the banner garrisons in the provinces, which it allocated to banner soldiers, officials, and nobles (Zhao 1999, 2001a, 2001b; Qiu 2014). The court granted bannermen permanent usufruct on their allocated land but prohibited them from selling their land to civilian commoners (Zhao 2001a). However, because the state stipends to bannermen in the form of cash and rice salaries weakened the importance of banner land as a material support, the majority of bannermen in Beijing rented their land out to civilian commoners. By working on the banner land as tenants, the civilian commoners gradually came to occupy the land. Private land transfers among bannermen and between bannermen and civilian commoners soon became frequent. These private land transfers not only impoverished some bannermen but also jeopardized the state's control of banner land and thus the Eight Banners as an elite institution. Moreover, as the banner population increased, the state could no longer provide a government post with a state stipend to every adult bannerman. The Qing court used the term "*xiansan*" to refer to all the bannermen who were not able to obtain a banner post and therefore unemployed. In the eighteenth century, the group of *xiansan* bannermen grew in size in both Beijing and the garrisons and across the Manchu, Mongol, and Han-martial Banners (Wei 1995; Liu 2008, 721–22).[14]

Since the 1730s, court officials had been embroiled in heated discussions over policies to solve the bannermen livelihood problem and save the Eight Banners. Among the various solutions that were suggested, moving the banner population to the state-owned lands and rekindling their attachment to the land was especially appealing, because it would relieve the state of the fiscal burden of supporting the bannermen with stipends, on the one hand, and ensure them a means to earn a stable income, on the other.[15] Since the state's banner land around Beijing was already occupied by rich bannermen and civilian commoners, many officials proposed relocating bannermen to frontier regions. In 1742, following a long-term policy discussion, the Qianlong emperor (r. 1736–1795) ordered the relocation of the metropolitan bannermen from Beijing to Lalin, a site southeast of Shuangcheng (Ding 1985; Diao 1993, 198–205; Wei Y. 2010). Between 1742 and 1758, the government settled three thousand banner households in Lalin and allocated land to them equally. However, having lived in Beijing for a century, these bannermen had become acclimated to the urban lifestyle and could not adapt to rural life. Many households failed to settle in, and soon abandoned their land to return to Beijing.[16] The failure of the relocation project during the Qianlong reign initially discouraged further attempts to relocate the metropolitan bannermen. However, as the Eight Banners crisis worsened, the new proposals for rusticating bannermen became increasingly attractive to the court.

By the early nineteenth century, relocating bannermen to the frontiers became both a practical solution and a symbolically meaningful move. Between 1796 and 1804, the White Lotus rebellion swept through Sichuan, Shaanxi, and Hubei provinces. The huge military expenditure needed to quell this rebellion created a new fiscal crisis for the Qing state. Moreover, in the process of suppressing the rebellion, local military forces had consolidated under the organization of local elites, which challenged the norm of centralization (Kuhn 1980). Solving the livelihood problem of the banner people became imperative for the Qing court. Practically, the central government relocated bannermen to frontier regions to ameliorate its fiscal crisis. Symbolically, relocation represents an effort by the state to restore the banner tradition and to sustain Manchu ethnic identity as a conquest elite.

SHUANGCHENG

Located on the alluvial plain of the Songhua River in today's Heilongjiang province, Shuangcheng in the early nineteenth century was a sparsely populated area with fertile land. In an area of approximately three thousand square kilometers, the relics of seventeen cities built during the Jin dynasty (1115–1234) were scattered on the peripheries (SCXZ 1990,

800–803).[17] The name Shuangcheng, meaning "twin cities," derived from two Jin-dynasty cities located in the southeast. After the fall of the Jin, the area was depopulated, and the cities were abandoned. In the Qing, the region belonged to a forbidden zone. Because the Qing rulers considered Manchuria to be the cradle of the Manchu people, for almost two hundred years, from 1668 through the 1850s, the government forbade free immigration beyond the Willow Palisade (map 1.1).[18] The purpose was to ensure Manchu privileges in this area. Even though the Qing government organized China proper under provinces, it always insisted on maintaining Eight Banners military control in Manchuria. Three banner generals (*jiangjun*)—Shengjing, Jilin, and Heilongjiang—administered Manchuria.[19] Shuangcheng fell under the administration of the general of Jilin. In addition to the military function, the general's office (*yamen*) in Jilin also handled civil affairs and collected taxes from the few registered residents and on products from the land.[20] Consequently, in the early nineteenth century, only a few civilian commoners entered the region without government permission and cleared land there.

The frontier setting and the state control in Shuangcheng allowed the Qing government to draw the blueprint of this immigrant society according to its ideal. Institutionally, the banner system in Shuangcheng had three features: the state intervention in land distribution, the assignment of differentiated entitlements across population categories, and an egalitarian distribution of land within each population category. These were based on principles that not only existed in the Eight Banners but also grew out of the long history of China. The historical precedents included the equal-field (*juntian*) system, which existed between 485 and 780, and the military farms (*juntun*) of Ming dynasty (1368–1644).[21] In fact, these features exemplified the ideal of imperial state's control over land and population. Practically, the egalitarian distribution of land at the household level ensured the absolute power of the emperor; it prevented the rise of large landholders who would compete with the emperor for control of the population and taxation. Yet, in most regions of Qing China, private landownership was the norm, and so the state was not able to maintain these ideals. Because Shuangcheng was sparsely populated, it provided the state a place to experiment with an "ideal" institution. For the Qing, the assignment of differentiated entitlements across population categories and egalitarian land distribution within each population category were equally important in preserving the political and economic privileges of metropolitan bannermen and, eventually, restoring the vitality of Eight Banners.

Yet, if the Qing was able to design an "ideal" institution, the political and social transformations in the nineteenth and early twentieth centuries challenged this system. The abundance of land and the shortage of labor in Shuangcheng attracted more and more unofficial immigrants, who moved there despite the state's prohibition. These unofficial immigrants—including both civilian commoners and bannermen—entered the area to make their livings as tenants or laborers. The growth of this unregistered population created a problem of control. Furthermore, to solve the deepening fiscal crisis and pressing border issues, in 1861, the central government eventually allowed free migration into northern Manchuria (Lee 1970; Diao 1993; Fan 2007). This move initiated mass immigration to Jilin; its population increased by a factor of thirteen, from 327,000 in 1850 to 4,416,300 in 1907.[22] Because most of the new immigrants were civilian commoners, their arrival dramatically changed the demographic and ethnic composition of the province.

In the second half of the nineteenth century, some of the banner generals' proactive efforts at state-building in Manchuria further challenged the Eight Banners; the generals initiated institutional reforms to transform the banner administration into a civilian government—with the goal of integrating Manchuria into China proper. The Manchu court continued to try to protect Manchuria as its backyard, but these banner generals already viewed the region as the northeastern provinces of China, and sought to protect it from invasion by Russia. Instead of considering civilian commoners the enemy of the Eight Banners, the banner generals advocated using them to strengthen the borders. To accomplish this, they also urged the court to develop a civil administration to enforce social control in the frontier regions. Consequently, in 1881 the court established an Intendant of Circuit (*fenxundao*) in Jilin to take charge of civilian affairs, and organized five local civilian governments in the province.[23] This institutional transformation was completed in 1907, as the state abolished the banner garrison system and established three provincial governments in Manchuria—Fengtian, Jilin, and Heilongjiang (Diao 1993, 274–79).

The reform resulted in a dual government system consisting of both banner and civilian administrations in Shuangcheng, which weakened the institutional support to metropolitan and rural bannermen's land entitlements. A civilian government was established in Shuangcheng in 1882.[24] In a related move, the state downgraded the local banner government, preserving it as the authority of the 120 banner villages and more than one hundred natural settlements called *wopeng*. Although the state planned to administer the bannermen and the civilian commoners separately, in reality, the two governments were not completely distinct because administrative areas overlapped. Both governments often adjudicated disputes that involved both bannermen and civilian commoners; and some bannermen also directly filed lawsuits with the civilian government. Because they were unfamiliar with the banner institution and its land-allocation policies, the civilian officials sometimes justified practices that transgressed the boundaries between the population categories. Moreover, in the first decade of the twentieth century, the Qing privatized the banner land and did away with the institutional support of the hierarchical land entitlements in Shuangcheng. In 1902, the court made the decision to open all land in Shuangcheng to private owners.[25] In 1906, the state allowed the free transfer of banner land between bannermen and civilian commoners.[26]

Along with these political and social transformations, Shuangcheng also developed into an economic center in northern Manchuria. As one of the earliest settlements in the region, Shuangcheng has been a major site of grain production since the nineteenth century.[27] The soil in northern Manchuria was rich in organic material, and both crop yields and the quality of the grains exceeded those in southern Manchuria (MMTKK 1909, 13). Located at the intersection of several transportation routes, Shuangcheng also became a center for grain distribution (ibid, 144). The high crop yields in northern Manchuria produced considerable surplus for farm households. In 1909, about 80 percent of the wheat and 70 percent of the beans produced in northern Manchuria were exported from the region. Merchants gathered grains purchased from villages of Shuangcheng and the surrounding counties to the Shuangcheng seat and then transported them to Yingkou, a treaty port in Fengtian (today's Liaoning province; ibid, 55-59). Shuangcheng's strategic position became even more prominent at the end of the nineteenth century. Because

Shuangcheng is close to Harbin, in 1899, Russia selected it to be the site of a station of the Chinese Eastern Railway and started to build the railway across the county (SCXZ 1990, 20). In 1903, the railway was put in operation. Thereafter, the grains were also transported from Shuangcheng to Siberia (MMTKK 1909, 57–58).

However, Shuangcheng remained a largely agrarian economy, with a low level of economic development.[28] Even in the early twentieth century, agricultural production in Shuangcheng and other parts of northern Manchuria was not specialized (Reardon-Anderson 2005, 169–251). Households were still the basic unit of production. Farmers, large landholders and tenants alike, made very limited investment in capital and technology. They used traditional technologies to cultivate land, alternating four types of grains: beans, wheat, sorghum, and millet. Harvests were used first for the consumption by family members and for the following year's production. Farmers then sold the surplus at the market (MMTKK 1909, 54–57). In other words, the commercialization of agricultural products did not advance the way of agricultural production.

At the same time, amid all the social and institutional changes, the banner administration and banner society in Shuangcheng showed considerable resilience. Even after the establishment of the civilian government, the banner government in the Qing remained powerful in that it administered the majority of rents and taxes from the land.[29] The banner government remained active even after the fall of the Qing in 1911. In 1912, the Office of the Banner Affairs (*qiwu chengban chu*) was established under the republican county government; it continued to be part of the local administration even under the Manchukuo (1932–1945).[30] Yet, the banner administration could no longer ensure the privileges of the banner people. The socioeconomic status of the bannermen, as indicated by the size of their landholdings, was especially crucial in determining their fate and fortune in the Republic of China (1912–1949). As Enatsu's (2004) study on the local elites in Fengtian shows, many Han-martial bannermen, who were already the de facto landlords of the Qing manor lands, purchased land during this political transformation. This also happened in Shuangcheng. The persistence of the social hierarchy in Shuangcheng after the fall of the Qing indicates that the state-designated elites were able to successfully convert the political and economic privileges granted by the Qing into social and economic capital that withstood the political revolution. Moreover, this transformation was accomplished through the long-term interactions between state policies and the efforts of local people during the one hundred years that followed the settlement.

STATE REGISTRATION AND SOCIAL ENGINEERING

Government registration of the population and property has been an indispensable component of bureaucratic states. Registration systems developed along with the state's growing capacity to gather information, organize its population, and perform routine tasks such as taxation. By registering people and property, the state established its authority over and defined the rights and obligations of the registered population. In Western Europe, the development of registration systems contributed significantly to the rise of the modern state (Tilly 1975; Szreter and Breckenridge 2012). In China, however, this "modern" feature of the bureaucratic state had emerged as early as the sixth century BC (Liang 1980; Song 1991; Xin 2007; Von Glahn 2012). By the first century, household registers in China recorded biographical information about not only the household head and his dependents—including name, occupation, residence, rank of nobility, and age—but also household property, including the house, land, slaves, and livestock. From then on, successive regimes continued to register their populations (Von Glahn 2012). Registration established a contractual relationship between the state and the people: the registered people paid taxes and provided labor to the state; in return, the state granted them entitlements and rights which the unregistered people did not have.

At times of social engineering, registration becomes an important tool for states in implementing the designated social hierarchy. Theories of social formation hold that for structural inequality to become durable, the boundaries between social categories should be clearly defined (Tilly 1998; Lamont and Molnár 2002; Wang 2008). Registration makes this possible because the systematic recording of the various ascriptive characteristics of individuals and households involves defining and standardizing these categories. As studies on registration and census show, local people's understanding of categories, such as ethnicity and race, vary dramatically from that of the government (Kertzer and Arel 2002;

Mullaney 2010). Therefore, the act registering these categories is an effort at state-building. When carrying out social-engineering projects, the state standardizes the characteristics that best manifest its desired social hierarchy and classifies the people into categories. For example, in Shuangcheng, a combination of institutional affiliation and place of origin was the basis of the social hierarchy. By recording these ascriptive characteristics and compiling separate registers for metropolitan, rural, floating bannermen, and civilian commoners, state registration institutionalized the boundaries between these groups and made them hereditary categories.

Once the boundaries of population categories are defined, the state assigns differentiated entitlements to each category to establish the hierarchy. This creates a system of exclusion in which people outside certain groups are excluded from access to resources.[31] The registers document an individual's membership in a certain category and serve as the official proof of eligibility to the entitlements associated with that category. In this sense, registration helps to produce what social psychologists call a "group-based social hierarchy," which means that an individual's power and privilege is derived from his or her ascriptive membership in a socially constructed group (Sidanius and Pratto 1999, 32). The unequal assignment of entitlements also renders people a sense of ranking associated with their group boundaries.

The above statecraft lays out the foundation for the social construction of the categorical boundaries among people. While the state registration and resource allocation define the boundaries that generate structural inequality, these boundaries are not clearly drawn until they go through the process of social construction by which individuals in a group develop a sense of belonging and agree on a collective identity (Wang 2008). Only then does the structural inequality become durable. The social construction of categorical boundaries is a complex process that involves the actions of various actors (White 1992, 127–28; Verdery 1994; Barth 1998), and the actions are based on the actors' perception of their socioeconomic statuses and interests. As the registration categories and the unequal entitlements largely shape people's understandings of their status and interests, actors consciously adapt their actions to the state-designated social hierarchy. The privileged groups use the power and privilege associated with membership in that group to maintain their status. At the same time, members of the disadvantaged groups, even when they manage to overcome categorical boundaries and promote their socioeconomic status, are constantly reminded of the barriers the state set on their access to resources. The long-term interactions between the registration categories and state policies give rise to collective identities, thereby transforming these registration categories into socially constructed groups. The Shuangcheng case illustrates the entire process of social formation, from the creation of boundaries by the state to the social construction of boundaries by the immigrants.

LANDOWNERSHIP AND LOCAL PRACTICES

In Shuangcheng, as in other agrarian societies, the pattern of land distribution and the actions surrounding it are key in understanding the process of social formation. In preindustrial rural societies, land was the most valuable family asset of farm families. Thus, the landholdings of a family are an important measure of its socioeconomic status in the community. Moreover, under the state-dominated system in Shuangcheng, land, especially, was central to both the state's effort to define the social hierarchy and the actions of immigrants that contributed to the construction of social boundaries. The state used land allocation to differentiate immigrants' entitlements. Yet, despite the state's land-allocation policies, immigrants created their own upward and downward wealth mobility, outside the state's purview: capable families increased their landholdings by clearing or buying more land, and incapable metropolitan and rural banner households lost their state-allocated land. While the patterns of land distribution per se reveal the consequences of this statecraft and social construction, the mechanisms that enabled immigrants to exercise their agency and influence land distribution also illuminate the question of how the state-designated social hierarchy finally played out on the ground.

To better understand the dynamics of wealth distribution, it is important to look at the incomplete nature of landownership in imperial China. In contrast to the "full and free" landownership in the Western capitalist world (Engels 2001, 205), in imperial China individual owners never had exclusive rights to their land.[32] Three parties—the landowner and the members of his immediate household, the state, and the owner's kin and fellow villagers—had ownership claims. Ownership was not evenly distributed among the three parties; there was a general trend toward granting a greater portion of the ownership to private owners and less to the state.[33] Understanding this provides a framework for interpreting complicated property regimes in the local societies. In imperial China, with only a few exceptions, property rights belonged to the household, not to individuals (Zhang 2002b; Zelin 2004; Yang 2009, 1–10). Even though land was registered under the name of the household head, his immediate family members and kin living in the household also had legitimate claims on the land. Second, people living outside the household, the kin and fellow villagers of a landowner, also had considerable influence on landownership. When selling land, the seller was required to give priority to buy to his kin and then to his fellow villagers whose land plots bordered the plot being sold. This custom recognized kin and fellow villagers' rights over particular land plots (Zhang 2002a; Yang 2009). This phenomenon has led Yang Guozhen (2009, 4–5) to conclude that "land ownership in historical China is a combination of private ownership and the ownership of state, village community, and kin groups"

The incomplete and divisible nature of landownership resulted in complicated property regimes in rural communities. On the one hand, officially registered landownership served as the most important indicator of the socioeconomic status of farm households. On the other hand, as a practical matter, tenants working on rented land enjoyed use rights that often eventually developed into partial ownership. Existing scholarship has revealed the prevalence of a two-tiered form of landownership during the Ming and Qing dynasties.[34] By investing their labor in increasing the value of the land, tenants as the de facto farmers and managers of land secured their use rights. They were able to preserve their control over land across several generations, even renting out their plots to other tenants. This custom is so prevalent that, in many regions, landownership was divided into ownership of "topsoil," which belonged to tenants, and ownership of "subsoil," which belonged to landlords.[35]

The fact that usufruct can develop into a form of landownership has two important implications for interpreting wealth distribution in Shuangcheng. First, the rights the official immigrant households had over their land was a form of ownership. Although the state owned all the land, metropolitan and rural bannermen had the right to manage their land and pass it down to their descendants. In theory, they could keep their rights so long as they maintained their registration status. Thus, in this book, I use the term *ownership* to describe the rights immigrants had over their registered land; the officially registered landownership is used to measure wealth status. Second, immigrants without registered land still had opportunities to enjoy partial landownership through customary practices. Despite the state control, local practices of land rental and conditional sale (*dian*), in which landowners sold their land at a price that reflected only the plot's partial market value and preserved the right to buy back the plot at this price within a stipulated period of time, were common in banner communities in Manchuria (Sudo 1941; Diao 1993, 133–38, 254–66; Isett 2004, 2007). In Shuangcheng, due to the low labor to land ratio and the metropolitan bannermen's limited knowledge of farming, a large number of "have-nots" worked on the land as tenants or laborers. As chapter 8 shows, their annual income per unit of land was actually greater than that of their landlords. Some tenants became affluent. Therefore, registered landownership indicated only one aspect of the socioeconomic condition of immigrant households.

While recognizing the complex property regime in Shuangcheng, the book highlights the importance of registered landownership in social formation. In this sense, it also sheds light on the different roles wealth and income played in the socioeconomic life in rural China.[36] Despite the financial well-being generated by income from the land, eventually, it was a combination of the political and economic rights associated with land entitlements that defined social conflicts and the formation of social groups. Not only did registered landownership indicate the elite status of metropolitan and rural bannermen, but the land entitlements also became a source of power, by which the metropolitan and rural bannermen could increase their landholdings. Those who successfully maintained their official landownership continued to be the upper class even after the regime changed from the Qing to the Republic of China.

AGENCY AND STRUCTURAL INEQUALITY

The process of social formation in Shuangcheng vividly illustrates the interplay of agency and structure. Here *agency* refers to the capacity of human beings to develop strategies and to shape their circumstances (Sewell 1992; Emirbayer and Mische 1998). This capacity includes both people deriving a perception of social relations from the existing schema and developing strategies to work with or work around that structure. Works by sociologists demonstrate that all humans not only have agency but also the capacity to exercise agency in everyday life (Goffman 1959, 1982). The agency of Shuangcheng bannermen could first be seen in the development of village communities and households as independent social units to organize everyday life. Due to the highly institutionalized nature of the Eight Banners and the background of the settlement as a social-engineering project, the state planned villages and households to be administrative units. Yet, after settlement, these administrative units soon developed into autonomous entities. Villages became independent communities, organizing land clearings and supervising land transfers outside the state's purview. Households, with rights equivalent to landownership, enjoyed the autonomy to make decisions regarding production, consumption, and the management of their lands.

The style of local governance in Shuangcheng, as elsewhere, gave immigrants considerable room to exercise their agency. It has been well established that in late imperial China the state intentionally kept the local government lean. Therefore, the organization of everyday life became largely the responsibility of various social organizations, such as village communities and families. While local elites made efforts to disseminate state ideology and laws to the local communities, customs played a major role in directing civil affairs, such as land transfer, land rental, marriage, and adoption (Scogin 1994; Huang 2001; Cohen 2004). Moreover, Melissa Macauley (2001, 332) points out that compared with that of the Ottoman Empire, the Qing government's effort to implement laws and policies before the twentieth century represents "an instance of legal simplification without the state-building dimension." Under the logic of limited administration, the officials had no intention of actually changing local practices but merely kept the state vision of local society in paper to facilitate tasks of local governance, such as taxation. Interestingly, although the Qing meticulously carried out the Shuangcheng settlement and built a state-dominated system, in governing civil affairs officials still followed the principle of indirect rule and kept state policies in paper. As chapter 5 shows, despite the state's prohibition, local officials accommodated land sales among bannermen, so long as they followed state policy and reported these cases as official land transfers. Therefore, despite the state-dominated system, village communities, households, and individuals in Shuangcheng enjoyed the same level of agency as residents in rural communities elsewhere in nineteenth-century China.

Shuangcheng immigrants lived in multiple structures. In addition to the state-dominated system and the unequal assignment of land entitlements, the general economic conditions and family demography also constituted the structural settings. These structures served as the schema for immigrants to develop strategies to cope up or change social relations. At the same time, these structures both provided resources for and constrained the agency of immigrants. Moreover, these structures affected the agency of immigrant groups differently, depending on their position in the social hierarchy and other characteristics.[37] When making important decisions regarding the fortune of their family, immigrants had to consider these constraints and opportunities and make use of available resources in pursuing their interests. In turn, these decisions affected family demography and socioeconomic status, thereby creating variations in the pattern of land distribution. Thus, the interplay between the agency of immigrants and the above structural settings underlay the process of social formation in Shuangcheng. Eventually, the subsequent economic and demographic differentiation, social mobility, and social reproduction shaped the social hierarchy.

The economic conditions in Shuangcheng—the low labor to land ratio and the low level of economic development—affected the wealth status of the Shuangcheng immigrants. As a newly settled area, Shuangcheng had abundant land and few people. Although the frontier setting created hardships for the settlers, it still offered most immigrants opportunities to become wealthy. Not only did the state allocate a large amount of land to metropolitan and rural bannermen, but the immigrants who moved there without a government order and therefore had no land entitlement had the leverage to acquire use rights of land. Moreover, in the initial years of settlement, the frontier setting also affected the formation of social organizations and social groups. Most of the immigrants moving into the area lacked the support of extended families and had to fight the wildness and clear land on their own. Only families that have enough laborers to farm the land could survive. This was true for both official and unofficial immigrants. Immigrant households organized to clear land, rented their land out, or hired laborers. Along with this process of securing laborers, immigrants also built village communities and formed other social networks, which then shaped the social organizations and hierarchy. Finally, the low level of development indicates that capital had very limited influence on land distribution in Shangcheng.

Family demography, because it affected production and consumption, had significant impact on the wealth status of immigrant households. Birth, marriage, and death are the major events in the life cycle of a household. The outcome of these events—fertility, timing of marriage and remarriage, and mortality—determines the household size, measured by the number of members and its gender and age composition. The household size and gender-age composition indicate the numbers of its available laborers and of the non-working-age members in need of economic support (Cain 1978). Since labor is an important factor in agricultural production, both conditions significantly affected the ability of a rural family to manage its land. A household with few laborers and a lot of non-working-age members had a shortage of labor in production and pressure in consumption. Without strategies for surmounting these difficulties, family members had to exchange land or other property for money, and potentially leading to downward wealth mobility. Existing studies on the demographic behaviors in preindustrial Europe and Asia have revealed a strong correlation between household socioeconomic status and the demographic success of families; families with higher socioeconomic status were likely to have more surviving children, better chances of entering into marriages, and lower risk of dying during a period of economic hardship (Harrell 1985; Campbell, Lee, and Bengtsson 2004; Clark and Hamilton 2006; Shiue 2008; Tsuya et al. 2010; Bengtsson 2014). This is also true in Shuangcheng (Chen, Lee, and Campbell 2010; Chen, Campbell, and Lee 2014). This correlation can be explained as a two-way effect: better economic conditions gave family members the resources to achieve demographic success; and, at the same time, the demographic circumstances of a household also influenced the direction of its wealth mobility.

In addition to its effects in production and consumption, the impact of family demography on the intergenerational transmission of wealth deserves special attention. Existing studies on wealth distribution in Western countries have demonstrated that intergenerational transmission of wealth, or inheritance, is a major cause of wealth inequality (Oulton 1976; Menchik 1979; Piketty 2000, 2014; Arrondel and Grange 2006; Harbury and Hitchins 2012). Since wealthier families have more assets to pass down to the next generation, inheritance results in the reproduction of the status of the family. At the same time, different principles of inheritance practice also affected wealth mobility. For example, in preindustrial Europe, wealth was transmitted through the right of primogeniture, through which a family passed down all of its property to the eldest son. The practice of primogeniture helped to maintain a concentrated pattern of wealth distribution. In societies in which families divide their properties among all the children, children from larger families tend to have much less wealth than their parents (Menchik 1979). In late imperial China, partible inheritance was the norm, and families divided their properties equally among all the sons. If families always had two or more sons in the next generation and the members did not acquire more land through other paths, the practice of partible inheritance resulted in the dissipation of family wealth in a few generations' time (Myers 1970, 159–66; Lavely and Wong 1992).

In Shuangcheng, family demography interacted with the state's land-allocation policies and inheritance practices to influence the wealth mobility of individual households. First of all, having at least one surviving male heir was crucial if immigrant households were to continue the family line and maintain the family's wealth. Families without a male heir would eventually become extinct. Once families successfully secured heirs, they could choose how to pass down their property. Under the Eight Banners, the state adopted the practice of primogeniture inheritance to regulate and register household landholding. Some families followed the state regulations, but others continued practicing partible inheritance (Chen 2009, 222–61).[38] The coexistence of primogeniture and partible inheritance rules gave immigrant households room to exercise agency and make choices based on the specific family situation. Often times, the choice reflected the power dynamics within the family. Thus, variations in inheritance practices and the number of heirs also resulted in disparities in wealth status.

Finally, one of the most important components of social formation in Shuangcheng was that immigrants actively used the structure of the state—the government institution and the land-allocation policies—to pursue their interests. The state-dominated system made state power conveniently available to immigrants. By differentiating land entitlements, the state created discrepancies in the agency of different immigrant groups. For the privileged metropolitan and rural bannermen, the state served as an important resource that gave them an advantage in the competition for wealth with other immigrant groups. As the book shows, metropolitan and rural bannermen actively maintained their boundaries and blocked other groups' access to land entitlements, through mechanisms that sociologists label "rent seeking" and "opportunity hoarding" (Tilly 1998, 74–116; Wang 2008, 18–21). Meanwhile, the groups that were excluded from land allocation faced tremendous constraints in exercising their agency. As chapter 3 shows, even though some floating bannermen and civilian commoners privately cleared land on their own, they lost the land to metropolitan and rural bannermen.

The interaction between the agency of immigrants and the state structure became even more complicated, because the different interests of state representatives provided immigrants multiple channels through which to appeal to state authority. Although the state had a strong presence in Shuangcheng, the central, provincial, and local governments often had different interests in governance. Thus, state power in local society was presented in various forms, which offered communities and individuals abundant choices. Aware of the multitude of state representatives, immigrants tactfully chose their allies, forming coalitions with some state authorities while resisting others. The different interests of state representatives not only offered the privileged groups more room to exercise agency, but also made state a source of power for the disadvantaged groups. For example, although the central government prohibited civilian commoners from settling and owning land in Shuangcheng, by acquiring the personal sponsorship of local officials, some civilian commoners were able to work as contractors to organize land clearing and thereby occupy a large amount of land. Thus, state power was so convenient to use that it became prevailing in local society.

Eventually, both social reproduction on the basis of population categories and social mobility at the household level helped to reinforce the state-designated hierarchy. In the long term, the interaction between general economic conditions, demography, and state policies gave rise to demographic and economic differentials at the household level. Capable households had opportunities to maintain their socioeconomic status or achieve upward social mobility, while incapable families were located at the bottom of the hierarchy. However, the majority of the members of the privileged groups were able to maintain their wealth status. The boundaries between population categories, especially, were fortified when the state served as a major resource for immigrants to exercise agency. As immigrants sought to use state power to maintain or promote their status, the state structure deepened their knowledge about the social relations. Ultimately, immigrants developed distinct identities based on the state-designated population categories.

DATA SOURCES AND ORGANIZATION

Shuangcheng has rich and comprehensive archival sources. Unlike the archival sources of most local societies during this period, which mainly center on local administration and legal cases, the archival sources available for Shuangcheng include edicts, court memorials, official correspondence, legal cases, and banner household and land registers. These voluminous documents provide information not only on local administration and socioeconomic life but also on the policies and the rationales of the emperor and the officials in the central, provincial, and local governments. The edicts and memorials preserved in the First Historical Archives in Beijing offer details about the motivation of the central government and the processes of Shuangcheng settlement from 1812 onward. The archives of the local banner and civilian governments in the Qing and the Republican periods provide continuous documentation of local life, beginning in 1852.[39]

The comprehensive archival sources are suitable for analyses using a mixture of qualitative and quantitative methods. Records from 338 volumes of household registers and twenty-three volumes of land registers for the period 1866–1913 constitute a uniquely rich dataset: the China Multi-Generational Panel Dataset-Shuangcheng (CMGPD-SC). With 1,346,826 annual observations on 107,890 individuals, the dataset covers all the official immigrants—metropolitan and rural bannermen—and the registered unofficial banner immigrants and their descendants living in Shangcheng's 120 banner villages (Wang et al. 2016). Moreover, with 37,187 plot inventories for 8,182 individual landowners, the dataset also includes farmland registered in Shuangcheng from 1866 to 1906. This dataset makes possible not only analyzing the overall pattern of land distribution but also tracing the upward and downward mobility of individual families throughout the time period.

These land and population data surpass the data used by existing studies both in scale, covering an entire county, and in depth, providing longitudinal individual- and household-level information on local socioeconomic conditions. Existing studies of land distribution in historical China are based on either aggregate county-level data or household-level data from a few villages.[40] The aggregate data omit details of the individual landowners; data collected from a few villages are likely to provide only piecemeal glimpses of a more complex agrarian society. In imperial China, the county was the lowest level of bureaucratic structure. Individual counties not only had a certain unity but also were large enough to include a variety of social groups with different socioeconomic statuses. Thus, taking a county as the unit of analysis generates a more comprehensive view of social categorization and wealth inequality.

The administrative documents and legal cases available in the traditional archives make it possible to explore in detail the socioeconomic processes that generated the patterns of land distribution. These documents complement the dataset by providing rich information on the interactions and tensions among officials and different immigrant groups and on the mentality of the local people. In other words, the book fleshes out the statistical patterns of social categorization and land distribution with vivid pictures of local practices of land accumulation and their interplay with government policy. Gazetteers, survey reports published by the Japanese Southern Manchuria Railway Company, and genealogies and oral histories collected during fieldwork supplement these sources to provide an account of Shuangcheng's history.

To present a complex picture of social formation under state domination across a long span of time, the narrative is organized thematically while maintaining a sense of the chronological unfolding of events. Chapters are grouped into two themes—"State-Building" (Part I) and "Social Development and Stratification" (Part II)—to address the two processes that formed this immigrant society. An analysis of how the development of each theme affected the distribution of land drives the narrative of each part.

Part I, which consists of chapters 2 to 4, provides an overview of the processes by which the state built institutions and consolidated its power between the 1810s and 1850s. Chapter 2 examines the implementation of Shuangcheng settlement to highlight the state's efforts to clear the existing boundaries among the immigrants: the state eliminated existing social organizations among the settlers by scattering households from the same place of origin or same descent group among different villages. This boundary-clearing procedure provided a foundation on which the state could build a two-tier hierarchy, with metropolitan bannermen at the top and rural bannermen on the bottom. Chapter 3 analyzes the population categories recorded in the state household registers and the unregistered population to explore the ways the state built new boundaries among immigrants. It shows that, by assigning differential land entitlements to the registration categories, the state created a new social hierarchy. Chapter 4 examines the issue of local governance in Shuangcheng to illuminate two processes of consolidation in this newly settled frontier society: the consolidation of the society per se, marked by immigrants reaching an agreement on a local identity, and the consolidation of the control of local government by the imperial court. Although the state built this society from the top down, it took the central government thirty years to embed the local government in the bureaucratic system.

Part II, which consists of chapters 5 to 8, explores the social construction of categorical boundaries from the 1840s to the 1910s. Chapters 5 and 6 examine the development of village communities and family, respectively, and explore immigrants' activities of wealth accumulation surrounding these two organizations. These two chapters show that, despite the state policies of land allocation and population registration, savvy immigrants strategically coordinated local practices with state policies to create their own upward and downward wealth mobility. By actively using the state as a source of power in land accumulation, immigrant groups reinforced the state-built boundaries. Chapter 7 analyzes the patterns of land distribution between 1870 and 1906 to explain why the state-mandated social hierarchy endured in Shuangcheng. It shows that land distribution among bannermen with land entitlements exhibited a pattern of stratification without concentration. This pattern of land distribution sustained a stable landowner class consisting of metropolitan and rural bannermen. Finally, chapter 8 shows that, by the end of the Qing, the unequal assignment of land entitlements had transformed the population categories into groups with distinctive identities. These identities continued to serve as the basis of social grouping and to define local conflicts in the early period of the Republic of China.

PART I

STATE-BUILDING

CHAPTER TWO

Clearing Boundaries

The Founding of Shuangcheng Society

When nations engage in frontier settlement, the state typically plays an aggressive role in sending migrants to particular destinations; this process transforms and integrates the peripheries with the center. This model describes the overseas colonies of Netherlands, Spain, the British Empire, the American West, and Canada; it also describes the frontier history of China's southwest, northwest, and even Taiwan.[1] China has a long history of government-organized migration projects, dating back to the eleventh century BC.[2] The Chinese state not only organized migrations to the frontier, but also invested considerable effort and revenue in settling and developing frontier societies.[3] Through these migration projects, the government developed a wealth of techniques for planning and financing migrations and settling migrants. To maintain the frontier developments, state revenue regularly flowed from the center to the periphery, a uniquely Chinese model of governance.

Yet despite the Chinese state's widespread reputation for organizing migrations, we still understand very little about the state's role in the development of settler communities. This is especially true when it comes to settlement on China's northeast frontier in the nineteenth century because the Qing court forbade free migration to northern Manchuria for over two centuries. Not until the 1860s, when the state was experiencing deep political and economic crises, did the Qing open up Manchuria for free migration. The scholarship on migration to this region describes this movement as primarily a voluntary migration by desperate Han Chinese who encroached on institutions established by a declining state.[4] This narrative, however, fails to recognize the role of the state in building and adjusting those institutions.

The Shuangcheng settlement serves as an exemplary case of state-organized migration and provides detailed documentation of the art of statecraft. The successful settlement of bannermen and the availability of exceptionally complete records of the process reveal that the Qing state not only actively organized migration to northern Manchuria but also built institutions that set the foundation of the social hierarchy in this region.[5] Compared to other frontiers, where the state had to confront indigenous populations outside its control, the relative emptiness of Shuangcheng gave the state greater control and more freedom to manifest its will there. In carrying out the entire process of settlement—from site selection, residence planning, and migrant recruitment to final settlement—the state successfully settled a mixture of urban and rural migrants. Moreover, during the settlement process, the state eliminated existing social organizations among the migrants as well as boundaries within them, an innovative practice that laid the groundwork for the creation of a state-mandated social hierarchy.

INITIATING THE RELOCATION

In 1812, the Qing court initiated the relocation of bannermen to Shuangcheng, an effort that ultimately engaged the emperor, central government officials, and the banner generals. In that year, the Jiaqing emperor (r. 1796–1820) issued an edict to establish a state settlement in Manchuria to relieve the state's fiscal obligation to support the metropolitan bannermen (JQCSYD, book 17, 110). This move was the culmination of long-term policy discussions and experiments that had started in the mid-eighteenth century,[6] and it was intended to shift the banner population from a condition of state dependency to one of self-support. The edict motivated several enthusiastic banner officials experienced in establishing settlements in frontier regions—notably, Fujun, the vice president of the Board of Works of Shengjing (today's Liaoning), and later the general of Jilin; Saichong'a, the general of Jilin (1809–1813; QSG, book 37, 11212); and Songyun, the minister of the Department of Personnel (1811–1812).[7] From 1812 to 1814, in search of an ideal place to settle the metropolitan bannermen, these officials investigated all the proposed sites (in today's western Liaoning and northern Jilin).[8] After each investigation, they sent back memorials discussing the conditions of the site and the feasibility of relocation. The emperor and ministers in the Grand Council discussed these official recommendations and, in 1815, settled on Shuangcheng as the relocation destination.

Fujun, the general of Jilin (1814–1817, 1818–1822, and 1824–1827), was the major figure who pushed through the entire relocation and organized the state settlement.[9] Fujun was born under the Mongol Plain Yellow Banner in Beijing, gained his *jinshi* degree in 1779 after taking the translation exam for bannermen,[10] and started his official career as the assistant secretary (*zhushi*) of the Board of Rites (Zhu 2002, vol. 6, 593). Like many of his contemporaries, Fujun had been trained in a tradition of statecraft (*jingshi*) that emphasized the pragmatic manipulation of institutions and organizations in the pursuit of wealth and good governance. Before becoming the general of Jilin, he had held a variety of other posts in frontier regions, including Xinjiang and Shengjing, and had gained a good reputation for maintaining order in local societies.

On receiving the Jiaqing emperor's edict in 1812, Fujun, as the vice president of the Board of Works in Shengjing, immediately devoted himself to the project of relocating the metropolitan bannermen. Together with Songyun and Hening, the commander-in-chief of Rehe, he proposed the banner pastureland, located in today's western Liaoning, as the site of relocation and even managed to obtain the emperor's approval to test farming in the area. Their foray into this region, however, impinged on the interests of earlier appointed authorities, including the pasturage director (*muzhang*), Lamas, and the Mongol banner officials who were in charge of the region. As a result, the emperor and the Grand Council decided to stop the test farming after just two years, and punished the three officials. Fujun, who by that time had advanced to the post of general of Jilin, insisted on continuing the project because he considered ending it a waste of the time and effort that had been put into it. His insistence, however, irritated the emperor and the Grand Council, resulting in Fujun receiving a punishment that downgraded his salary rank by three grades.[11]

Under Fujun's close supervision, the final planning and initial settlement of Shuangcheng took place over the next fourteen years, from 1814 to 1827. After accepting the post of the general of Jilin in 1814, Fujun continued the site investigation begun by his predecessor, General Saichong'a. Fujun recommended Shuangcheng as the relocation site in 1815 and obtained the approval of the Jiaqing emperor and the Grand Council.[12] In that same year, the first one thousand bannermen, from four garrisons in Jilin, were moved to Shuangcheng to prepare the land and housing for the eventual arrival of metropolitan bannermen. To ensure that the relocation proceeded smoothly, Fujun even moved his office to Shuangcheng. From then until 1827, he oversaw every important step of the relocation.

PLANNING THE LANDSCAPE

Fujun and the Jiaqing emperor had selected Shuangcheng because of its natural resources and political advantages. Shuangcheng surpassed other proposed destinations by virtue of its flat topology and fertile, uncultivated land. Shuangcheng is in the alluvial plain of two rivers, the Songhua and the Lalin. The area Fujun selected extended forty-three kilometers from north to south and seventy-five kilometers from east to west.[13] The Lalin and Songhua Rivers surrounded its southern, western, and northern borders (Map 2.1). When they were investigating possible sites, officials had found that proposed locations in Shengjing were either largely occupied by civilian commoners or controlled by other banner authorities;[14] whereas Shuangcheng was relatively unpopulated. Only about one hundred civilian settlements, each consisting of a handful of registered households, were scattered over the area.[15] Establishing the settlement in a relatively unpopulated area allowed the government to avoid the cost of driving settled residents off the land and the inevitable disquiet and discontent that would cause.

Moreover, to facilitate political control, the emperor emphasized that the site should be close to administrative centers. The most ideal site would be about ten *li* (5.8 kilometers) from both Jilin, the seat of the general of Jilin, and Ningguta, a major banner garrison in Jilin. As the Jiaqing emperor stated, "The site that accommodates the relocated bannermen has to be supervised by the general or vice commander-in-chief

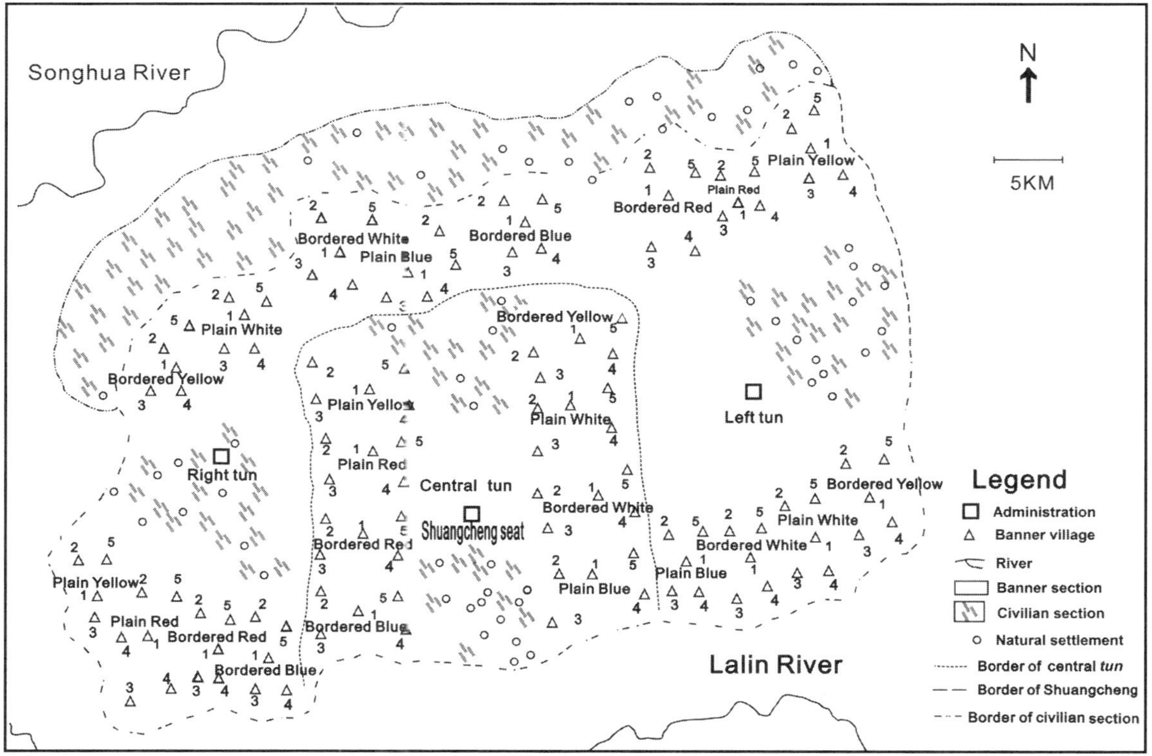

Map 2.1. The borders of Shuangcheng and distribution of villages, 1820–1822.

SOURCE: GIS data collected by Ren Yuxue. Also see Ren, Li, and Kang (2012, 526).

NOTE: In 1870 the state reorganized the twenty-four banners into eight banners. This reorganization did not change the residence of bannermen, but all the banner villages were renamed according to the new banner administration. For details of the reorganization and the new village names, see Wang et al. (2016, appendix A).

(*fu dutong*), so that bannermen would settle down and make their livings."[16] Shuangcheng was located forty-six kilometers from Alchuka and Lalin, two major banner garrisons in Jilin.[17] Although Shuangcheng's proximity to administrative centers was not as ideal as the emperor expected, based on the considerations of both emptiness and proximity, it was an optimal site.

In 1815, Fujun carefully laid out the boundaries of Shuangcheng and the banner villages. He first built several hundred sizable tamped mounds (*fengdui*) to mark the settlement's borders (Map 2.1).[18] With this move, Shuangcheng became a formal administrative area. The seat of Shuangcheng was situated in the south, eleven kilometers from the southern border and thirty-four kilometers from the northern border. Fujun established the first forty banner villages around the Shuangcheng seat. As Map 2.1 shows, these forty villages, known as the central *tun*, were grouped into eight banners, with five villages in each banner. The eight banners of the central *tun* were lined up in two columns. To the west of the county seat were, from north to south, the Plain Yellow, Plain Red, Bordered Red, and Bordered Blue banners, which made up the right wing (*yi*) of the banner administration. Opposite these to the east of the county seat were the Bordered Yellow, Plain White, Bordered White, and Plain Blue Banners, which made up the left wing of the banner administration. This distribution of the eight banners was standard in every banner city.[19]

In 1819, Fujun expanded the settlement and designed two more sets of banner villages, known as the right *tun* and the left *tun*.[20] As Map 2.1 shows, the right *tun* and left *tun* were located to the west and east of the central *tun*, distinguished by some small tamped mounds.[21] Like the central *tun*, both the right and the left *tun* contained forty villages, organized by the eight banners. In the center of both the right and the left *tun*, Fujun established corresponding banner administrations. Probably because of geographic constraints, Fujun aligned the wings of the right and left *tun* not vertically but horizontally; that is, looking out from the Shuangcheng seat in the central *tun*, one would find the right and left wings of either *tun* lined up to the right and left of the seat of either *tun*, in a configuration like that of the central *tun*. To establish these banner villages, Fujun also drove the few hundred civilian settlers who had been there out of the designated areas. This early planning laid out the basic landscape of Shuangcheng.

RECRUITING BANNER MIGRANTS

The Recruitment

Compared to planning the Shuangcheng landscape, recruiting banner migrants was a much more difficult and lengthier task. To prepare the land and housing in Shuangcheng for the eventual settlement of metropolitan bannermen, Fujun recruited banner migrants from the rural areas in Jilin and Shengjing to relocate to the area first and pave the way.[22] In 1815 he arranged to move the first one thousand bannermen, from four banner garrisons in Jilin, to the central *tun* of Shuangcheng.[23] The plan soon seemed to falter, however, because many of the Jilin bannermen abandoned the farms shortly after their arrival. Fujun attributed the departures to the fact that their families had not been allowed to follow them to Shuangcheng, and further blamed the inadequate material compensation provided by the government.[24]

Learning from this setback, Fujun then turned to Shengjing. In 1817, he accepted the post of general of Shengjing. Although the official history does not explain his reasons for doing so, it appears that he went to Shengjing to recruit more banner migrants for Shuangcheng. In 1818, Fujun proposed recruiting another two thousand banner migrants from Shengjing and Jilin to fill the empty land in Shuangcheng. In his memorial, Fujun claimed that 1,739 bannermen from Shengjing were already willing to move to Shuangcheng.[25] After the emperor approved this proposed relocation, Fujun returned to his post as general of Jilin, from which he would supervise the settlements of these bannerman in 1819 and 1820.

At the same time, Fujun revised the policy that had required the bannermen from other parts of Manchuria to move to Shuangcheng as individuals, and instead required them to move with their families. The Shengjing bannermen responded enthusiastically to the recruitment. As Fujun wrote in his memorial, "I checked on the bannermen who were relocated to [Shuangcheng] one by one. Many of them moved with their entire family. Some of them even moved their entire kin group, and, some even retired from active banner service in order to move."[26] For this recruitment effort, Fujun was not only able to fill the quota of two thousand households but also recruited more to fill the vacancies left over by the Jilin bannermen who had arrived in Shuangcheng in 1815 but abandoned the farm soon after the settlement. Ultimately, the quota of three thousand households was filled by bannermen from a total of twelve banner garrisons in Shengjing and five banner garrisons in Jilin (Map 1.1).[27] These banner households were classified as the "rural bannermen" (*tunding*). The success of the later settlement of metropolitan bannermen depended significantly on the contributions of this rural advance team.

Overall, the rural bannermen from Shengjing were better farmers than those from Jilin because they had prior farming experience. Although both groups served the state as soldiers, when their military service was not needed, the Jilin bannermen mainly worked as hunters and lumberjacks,[28] whereas the Shengjing bannermen mainly lived off the land as farmers (Ding 2003, 199–200). Notably, bannermen from Jinzhou, Fuzhou, and Gaizhou (Map 1.1), who accounted for a large proportion of those from Shengjing, were especially successful at farming. They responded favorably to the move because their original garrisons were mainly located in strategically important coastal areas, hilly land that was not ideal for farming.[29] Songlin, the general of Shengjing (1820–1822) and later the general of Jilin (1817–1818 and 1822–1823), describes the enthusiasm of the Shengjing bannermen for emigrating to Shuangcheng:

> [These bannermen] were originally farmers who could not find land to farm because there were many people but land was scarce. In Shuangcheng there were few people and land is abundant and fertile; once they arrived there they were all happy to work on the land.[30]

By the fifth month of 1820, three thousand rural banner households had settled in Shuangcheng.[31]

In 1821, with the settlement of the rural bannermen concluded, Fujun started to recruit the metropolitan bannermen. Six days after the New Year, Fujun submitted a memorial to the Daoguang emperor (r. 1821–1850), along with a well-planned task list and a timetable for relocating the metropolitan bannermen to Shuangcheng.[32] According to Fujun's plan, the court would move two hundred households every year, from 1824 on, so that in fifteen years, three thousand metropolitan banner households would have moved to Shuangcheng. The three-year interim between 1821 and 1824 would give banner officials time to recruit the metropolitan bannermen and the rural bannermen time to prepare their land and housing. Fujun expected that the rural bannermen would have developed enough land by 1824 to produce surplus crops, which could help subsidize the costs of relocating metropolitan bannermen. The relocation project would then be self-sufficient and self-sustaining—a major achievement both for the state and for the bannermen because "their relocation could relieve the burden of supporting the banner population in our interior; while it strengthens the frontier on our borders" (SCPTTJL, 43).

The recruitment effort, however, did not go as the emperor and Fujun had planned. The recruitment of metropolitan bannermen was carried out among the Manchu and Mongol bannermen. In early 1822, after a year of recruiting efforts, the emperor learned that only twenty-eight metropolitan banner households had volunteered. Two years later, at the end of 1823, the number of metropolitan banner volunteer households had only increased to fifty-three. As Table 2.1 shows, after these fifty-three households moved to Shuangcheng in 1824, another seventy-seven households volunteered to move in 1825. Disappointed with this result, the imperial court put more effort into recruiting bannermen who did not hold state posts, known as the *xiansan*. In a discussion at the court, Yinghe, the assistant grand secretary, proposed that banner captains in Beijing circulate an order among the adult *xiansan* bannermen who had no property (*jia wu chanye nian yi cheng ding zhi xiansan*); the order would list all the benefits of moving to Shuangcheng, and threaten them with cancellation of their banner registration if they refused to move.[33] Perhaps as a result of such efforts, 189 households volunteered to move to Shuangcheng in 1826, followed by another forty-nine households in 1827.[34]

The government's recruitment of metropolitan bannermen for Shuangcheng slowed down after 1827. In that year, Fujun advanced to the post of the assistant grand secretary and left Jilin.[35] Although he tried to continue the relocation project and to recruit more metropolitan banner households, the emperor and the court officials had by this time shifted their attention elsewhere. Consequently, the number of house-

TABLE 2.1

Number of metropolitan banner households that volunteered to relocate to Shuangcheng and household income (in taels *of silver) at the time of move*

Year of relocation	*N. of households*[a]	*Place of origin*	MONTHLY STIPEND[b]: *More than three* taels *(including three* taels*)*		*One or two* taels		*No stipend*		
	N.		N.	*Percent*	N.	*Percent*	N.	*Percent*	*Total percent*
1824	53	Beijing	31	58.5	11	20.8	11	20.8	100.0
1825	77	Beijing	37	48.1	31	40.3	9	11.7	100.0
1826	189	Beijing	111	58.7	54	28.6	24	12.7	100.0
1827	49	Beijing							
1828	28	Beijing							
1930	9	Beijing							
1831	120	Rehe							
1832	19	Beijing							
	68	Rehe							
1833	27	Beijing							
1834	14	Beijing							
1835	24	Beijing							
1836	10	Beijing							
1838	11	Beijing							
Subtotal of years 1824–1826	319		179	56.1	96	30.1	44	13.8	100.0
Total	698								

SOURCES: The memorial and attached name lists of the metropolitan banner immigrants in 1824 (NGTFDTYMDA, 52: 289 and 559), and in 1825 (JJCLFZZ, 03-3388-025); in 1828 (ZPZZ 04-01-16-0132-078); in 1829 (ZPZZ 04-01-01-0704-034); in 1830 (JJCLFZZ 03-3380-030); in 1831 (JJCLFZZ 03-3012-024); in 1832 (NGDKDA 203000-001); in 1833 (ZPZZ 04-01-22-0054-101); in 1834 (NGDKDA 130817-001); in 1835 (JJCLFZZ 03-2837-007); in 1836 (ZPZZ 04-01-22-0056-051); in 1838 (JJCLFZZ 03-2837-040).

NOTES: [a]The number of households that actually moved and arrived in Shuangcheng was slightly different in some years, as a few banner people died or escaped on the way.

[b]Information on the monthly stipend is from BQTZ, book 1, 549–51. This information is available only for bannermen who volunteered to move between 1824 and 1826, as the name lists of these years recorded their banner posts. The monthly stipends in 1825 and 1826 only reflect the income of the household head, as the name lists did not record the details of household members.

holds moving to Shuangcheng again dropped significantly, with only twenty-seven households moving in 1828.[36] Fujun proposed allowing the banner captains to use coercion to secure enough banner migrants to fill the annual quota of two hundred households.[37] But even this effort did not increase the number of volunteer households. As Table 2.1 shows, in the ten years from 1829 to 1838, the annual number of banner households moving to Shuangcheng from Beijing fluctuated between nine and twenty-seven. In 1831, Hengqing, the censor of the Fujian Circuit, described the situation:

> In recent years, few are willing to move [to Shuangcheng]. The number is especially low this year. Moreover, I heard that, in the Manchu Bordered Red Banner, all the members in the households selected by the commander-in-chief to move kneeled around him and asked to be excused. Not a single person is willing to go, even in the face of punishment for disobeying the orders of a supervisor.[38]

Clearly, the state's efforts to recruit more metropolitan bannermen could not surmount their unwillingness to move.

Metropolitan bannermen were unwilling to move because of their fear of the drastic change in lifestyle. By the 1820s, these descendants of the banner warriors had lived in Beijing for more than 150 years. Moreover, because of their state stipends, they were accustomed to the comforts of city life. Having no knowledge of farming, Shuangcheng to them meant a hard life in a cold and remote land on the wild frontier. As Fujun vividly depicted,

> [The metropolitan bannermen] are not willing to move for the following reasons. They think Shuangcheng lacks an opera house, tea house, or wine house. Therefore, there is no place to go for entertainment. Moreover, there is also no place for them to ask for loans. They have gotten used to a life of leisure and do not care about the sense of honor and the need for a livelihood, and consider farming drudgery.[39]

Alhough Qing officials described the *xiansan* bannermen as extremely poor people without property and occupation, they enjoyed a leisurely life style and were relatively well off.

In response to the low number of households recruited in Beijing, the court reduced the relocation quota of metropolitan banner households, and then started to recruit bannermen in Rehe, a garrison north of Beijing, to fill the lower quota. In 1829, Boqitu, Fujun's successor as the general of Jilin (1827–1829), submitted a memorial in which he recommended reducing the quota of metropolitan banner households from three thousand to one thousand, which the emperor approved. Then, in 1830, Yu'en, the vice commander-in-chief of Rehe, wrote a memorial recommending relocating some of the Rehe bannermen to Shuangcheng.[40] The Daoguang emperor approved the request, and thereafter the plans for the relocation moved quickly forward. By the fifth month of 1830, more than 180 households in Rehe had volunteered to move to Shuangcheng.[41] These 180 households arrived in 1831 and 1832.[42] Metropolitan bannermen continued to arrive sporadically in Shuangcheng, as well. By 1838, a total of 698 households of metropolitan bannermen had relocated to Shuangcheng (Table 2.1). The government effort of relocating metropolitan bannermen also ended.[43]

Migrants' Socioeconomic Profiles

Previous studies on the social status of the Shuangcheng migrants describe them as poor bannermen who had neither land nor the means to make a living. For example, Ding Yizhuang describes the metropolitan bannermen who volunteered to move to Shuangcheng, even those who had banner posts and government stipends, as "penniless" (*chipin*).[44] This view mainly derives from the languages used in the correspondence between the emperor and officials; in the edicts and memorials, the emperor and the officials identified the target population as "penniless" bannermen. In the past, at the occasions of sending bannermen out of Beijing, it had been a typical practice for the government to first choose those with lower socioeconomic status. For example, the Jiaqing emperor had stated, "When sending bannermen in Beijing to banner garrisons in provinces, there is absolutely no reason to first select those who are law-abiding and ambitious."[45]

The actual status of both the rural and the metropolitan bannermen recruited to Shuangcheng, however, reveals a different pattern. Initially, when recruiting the first one thousand bannermen in other parts of Jilin for relocation to Shuangcheng, the banner officials followed the traditional practice and selected lower-status bannermen.[46] In the first years of settlement, however, Fujun noticed that these migrants were more likely to abandon the settlement and return to their places of origin because they were incapable of farming. Therefore, during the second recruitment, of the Shengjing and Jilin rural bannermen, in 1819, Fujun focused instead on relatively higher-status households.

Fujun required banner officials to screen migrants according to their ages and family backgrounds, ordering them to "select those from a large and affluent descent group (*zu*) with many adult males, so that they will not escape."[47] Fujun also required that the bannermen recruited in Jilin and Shengjing obtain a signed guarantee from their descent group,[48] guaranteeing that they would not flee. Consequently, quite a few rural bannermen were from at least the middle of the social spectrum. The settlement experience later validated the wisdom of these screening policies. In 1822, when Songlin investigated Shuangcheng, he found that the most successful settlers and farmers were the migrants from the coastal areas of the Liaodong Peninsula. These households were generally large and affluent, having both estates and land in their places of origin: "Every principal adult male [household head] had one to three assistant adult males to help with the farming. Some of them even cashed in their estates [in their places of origin] and bought cows and horses themselves, so that [they] could cultivate more land."[49]

In recruiting metropolitan bannermen, Fujun also found that the bannermen with banner posts and state stipends were the ones more likely to move.[50] Originally, Fujun and the court planned to move unemployed *xiansan* bannermen to Shuangcheng. After a year of recruitment, however, Fujun found that the majority of the twenty-eight volunteer banner households were in fact headed by bannermen with such posts as tax preceptor (*lingcui*) and foot soldier (*bubing*); these bannermen received a monthly stipend of three or four *taels* of silver plus an annual grain salary.[51] In addition, some bannermen also held the post of supported soldier (*yangyubing*), which had a monthly stipend of one-and-a-half *taels* of silver but no stable grain salary.[52] Fujun attributed the relatively high status of these families to a regulation that unmarried bannermen could not qualify as households and thus could not move to Shuangcheng (*zhishen buzhun suan hu*). This excluded those who were too poor to get married from the recruitment pool.[53] To accommodate unmarried bannermen, Fujun moved to loosen the recruitment criteria to allow any combination of three relatives to move as a household. In 1825, Yinghe supported Fujun's proposal, believing it would help fill the annual quota of two hundred households.[54] For Yinghe, the ideal recruits were Manchu and Mongol bannermen with monthly stipends of less than three *taels* of silver.[55]

Despite the continuous efforts by these officials to recruit poor bannermen, relatively higher-status bannermen still accounted for the majority of metropolitan migrants. As Table 2.1 shows, in 1824, thirty-one of the initial fifty-three banner households (58.5 percent) from Beijing had banner posts with a monthly stipend of three or more *taels* of silver plus a grain salary. Eleven households contained a member with the post of supported soldier. Only another eleven households were *xiansan*, without any kind of state support. Among the thirty-one households with monthly stipends of three or more *taels* of silver plus grain salaries, the grain salary of the lowest rank alone could feed a family of two adults and two children, and that of the highest rank could feed a family of six adults and one child.[56] None of the metropolitan banner households who moved to Shuangcheng had more than seven members, so those banner officers and soldiers may well have used their salaries to support the entire family.

In addition to monthly stipends and grain salaries, metropolitan bannermen also received housing. In keeping with the standard banner-housing practice in the eighteenth century, the state allocated two rooms to each bannerman with a cavalry post or higher.[57] By the nineteenth century, some banner soldiers had sold their estates for money and become impoverished through extravagant spending. While most banner soldiers were still able to afford a fair standard of living in Beijing,[58] the supported soldiers with monthly stipends of only one-and-a-half *taels* of silver might have found it difficult to support large households. In the 1820s, one-and-a-half *taels* of silver could purchase 0.7 to 0.8 *shi* of wheat or millet in Zhili, which was enough to feed a family of three (two adults and a child).[59] Yet their situation was still better than that of unemployed *xiansan* bannermen without state stipends, who, nonetheless, accounted for only 20.8 percent of the first group of the fifty-three metropolitan banner households moving to Shuangcheng.

Even after the court revised the relocation regulation in 1825, the high-socioeconomic-status composition of the metropolitan migrants persisted. As Table 2.1 shows, in that year thirty-seven of the seventy-seven households (48.1 percent) had a monthly stipend of three or more *taels* of silver plus a grain salary, and thirty-one households (40.3 percent) had a monthly stipend of one-and-a-half *taels* of silver. Only nine households that year had no state stipend. In 1826, the socioeconomic composition of the migrants from Beijing remained the same as in 1824 and 1825; 111 of the 189 migrant households had a monthly stipend of three or more *taels* of silver plus a grain salary. Moreover, nine households had a total of thirteen servants. Thus more than half of the 389 households that moved to Shuangcheng between 1824 and 1827 could have continued to live a decent life in Beijing.

But these higher-status bannermen—comprising mainly middle- to low-ranking banner officials and soldiers—chose to move to Shuangcheng to take advantage of the opportunities to attain a higher socioeconomic status. Although they were assured a living in Beijing, the banner hierarchy and wealth stratification in the city significantly restricted their social mobility. Their socioeconomic status was not comparable to that of the high-ranking officials, imperial lineage members, and the rich families who owned several thousand hectares of land in the city's suburbs.[60] Life in Beijing was a golden cage for those lower-ranking bannermen who were ambitious and desirous of greater power and prestige. Moving to Shuangcheng provided them with opportunities to rise to the top of society. Although Shuangcheng was a backward rural frontier, they could enjoy life as landlords, with abundant land, state-supplied housing, and rural bannermen to work for them as laborers.

Thus when the recruitment effort ended in 1838, the 3,698 households of banner migrants to Shuangcheng included bannermen from a wide variety of origins, lifestyles, and social statuses. Their places of origin ranged from urban Beijing to rural Shengjing and Jilin. In terms of socioeconomic status, the metropolitan bannermen, who had enjoyed all the cultural and economic benefits a big city could provide, were better off overall than the rural bannermen. Despite the Qing documents that describe the unemployed *xiansan* bannermen in Beijing as destitute paupers who could not make ends meet, these bannermen were still able to lead leisurely city lives—if not with their own money—with borrowed money.

Differences in lifestyles and social status not only divided the metropolitan and rural bannermen, but also existed within each of the two population categories. For example, the Shengjing bannermen were often seasoned farmers, while most of the Jilin bannermen had no farming experience. Moreover, metropolitan bannermen included both former banner officials with a monthly stipend of four *taels* of silver plus a grain salary and *xiansan* without banner posts. The next challenge for Fujun and the court officials, then, was to settle this heterogeneous population in rural Shuangcheng.

SETTLING THE POPULATION

The work of settling the migrants in Shuangcheng lasted more than thirty years, from 1815 to 1844, and beyond. Beginning with the settlement of the first one thousand individual Jilin bannermen in 1815, the state closely monitored every stage of the process. Especially after the arrival of metropolitan bannermen in 1824, the Daoguang emperor frequently sent imperial envoys to Shuangcheng to make sure they were making a smooth transition to rural life. As late as 1844, court officials were still discussing policies to relieve the hardships faced by metropolitan bannermen in adjusting to their lives as landlords in rural Shuangcheng. Under the intense care of enthusiastic officials, the settlement of Shuangcheng included elements of both a state-organized frontier settlement and on-site innovation.

Financing

To settle the banner migrants, the state invested a huge amount of money on preparing the basics of housing, farming, and living, and paying relocation stipends. The two generals of Jilin, Fujun and Songning (also known as Songlin), carefully planned the relocation budget, which included not only the cost of building new houses, but also the cost of buying farm tools, draft animals, and such basic household goods as pots and bowls. Each metropolitan banner household was also given thirty *taels* of silver with which to hire laborers. By comparison, each Shengjing rural banner household received only eight *taels* of silver, and each Jilin rural banner household received just four *taels* of silver as a relocation stipend. As Table 2.2 shows, the total moving expenditure for a Beijing banner household was two hundred *taels* of silver, while expenditures for banner households from Rehe, Shengjing, and Jilin ranged from forty-five to forty-nine *taels* of silver. According to Fujun's budget, moving two thousand Shengjing and Jilin banner households in 1820 alone cost 94,090 *taels* of silver, and relocating all 3,698 households would cost the state about 252,000 *taels* of silver,[61] an amount greater than the budget of some of the populous provinces inside China proper.[62] In addition to these expenses, establishing the local government cost 14,060 *taels* of silver.[63]

The state counted on both government revenue and the rents collected from state land in Shuangcheng to finance the relocation. As Fujun

TABLE 2.2
Government budget (in taels *of silver) for relocation and settlement, per household*

	THE PLACES OF ORIGIN OF BANNER IMMIGRANTS			
Budget item	*Beijing*	*Rehe*	*Shengjing*	*Jilin*
Housing	120	6	6	6
Farming and living basics	50	35.045	35.045	35.045
Moving stipend	30	8	8	4
Total	200	49.045	49.045	45.045

SOURCES: The budget for rural bannermen attached to Fujun's memorials on 1818.12.6 (ZPZZ 04-01-22-0041-27); the budget for metropolitan bannermen from Beijing in Fujun's memorial on 1821.1.6 (SCPTTJL, 43); and the budget for metropolitan bannermen from Rehe in QSL (Daoguang reign), book 35, 587b.

had planned, the settlement and farming costs for the first ten years were paid for with taxes collected from ginseng merchants, a major source of revenue for the Imperial Household Agency (*Neiwufu*).[64] Three years after its opening, rural bannermen would begin to pay rent on some of the land they farmed. In ten years, rent income would offset settlement expenses; from the eleventh year on, the settlement would become self-sufficient and even generate a surplus.[65]

The importance of the Shuangcheng settlement is reflected in the size of the government's investment and the thoughtful planning that went into it. Compared to other Qing settlements, the Shuangcheng relocation was better financed. At the beginning of the Qing dynasty, the state had tried to establish a series of state settlements in the wastelands of north, south, and southwest China. In these projects, the government did not provide farmers with stipends, but only promised them loans to finance the start-up costs. The financial resources for these promised loans, however, relied on unstable revenue streams, such as fines on the salaries of the officials who violated state regulations or committed crimes. Moreover, in other sites of military rustication established in Xinjiang and Sichuan, the state only invested in one-time funding for the purchase of farming basics (Wang, Liu, and Guo 1991; Guo 1997). The settlement of Shuangcheng, in contrast, had solid financial support from the revenue of the Imperial Household Agency.

Moreover, compared to other Qing migration projects, the banner migrants to Shuangcheng received much better governmental care.[66]

In the government-organized migration to the southwest frontier in the eighteenth century, each migrant household had received only twelve *taels* of silver as a start-up fund. This twelve-*tael* stipend was expected to equip a family of four for over a year (Li 2012, 108). In Shuangcheng, however, the government provided migrants with housing and basic living and farming essentials, as well as transportation and accommodations on their journey to Shuangcheng.[67] They also received a separate relocation stipend with which to start their lives in Shuangcheng. The state treated the metropolitan bannermen especially well. The rural bannermen only had thatched houses, worth six *taels* of silver each; whereas the metropolitan bannermen lived in four-room houses with walled yards, each costing 120 *taels* of silver (Table 2.2). Similarly, every four households of rural bannermen shared a set of farm supplies, consisting of four cows and a plow; whereas each metropolitan banner household had its own set of these supplies. Moreover, each metropolitan banner household head received a relocation stipend of thirty *taels* of silver, with which he was expected to hire two rural bannermen as long-term laborers; whereas the relocation stipend allocated to each rural banner household was only four or eight *taels* of silver (Table 2.2).[68] In addition, for the first five years in Shuangcheng, each metropolitan banner household also received a stipend of twelve strings of copper coins with which to purchase clothes.

Settlement

The major settlement of all the banner migrants in Shuangcheng took place from 1815 to 1830. The rural banner households arrived in three waves, in 1815, 1819, and 1820. The first thousand individual rural bannermen from Jilin who arrived in 1815 were assigned to villages in the central *tun*; the two thousand rural banner households from Jilin and Shengjing, who arrived in 1819 and 1820, were assigned to villages in the left and the right *tun*, and some additional households arriving in these two years were also assigned to the central *tun* to fill the vacancies left over by bannermen who abandoned the farm. Upon arriving, each household received a plot of village land from the state. Fujun had sized the villages to accommodate either twenty-four or twenty-eight rural banner households each. Villages of twenty-four households covered about 0.25 square kilometers, and those of twenty-eight households covered 0.3 square kilometers. The bannermen built entrenchments around each village to mark its borders. From 1824 on, the government assigned metropolitan bannermen to the forty villages of the central *tun*. Rural bannermen ultimately settled in all 120 villages, while metropolitan bannermen settled only in the forty villages of the central *tun*.

Fujun had initially designed the villages to include both rural northeastern and urban Beijing banner migrants. Each of the forty villages of the central *tun* had three streets running east to west, transected through the center by another street running north–south.[69] The residences of bannermen were lined up along the three streets. Fujun paired rural bannermen households with those of metropolitan bannermen.[70] The land lot for each pair was about 4,400 square meters, of which the rural banner household had 2,000 and the metropolitan banner household had 2,400 square meters.[71] Fujun matched rural and metropolitan bannermen in this way because he hoped that the experienced farmers from Manchuria would help the metropolitan bannermen farm and settle down.[72]

The settlement process also reflected the government's effort to institutionalize the rural bannermen and undercut their previous social ties. Between 1819 and 1821, Fujun noticed that some of the large rural banner households had more than twenty members. He therefore adopted the *tuntian* system practiced during the Ming dynasty, dividing these large families into multiple households, each headed by a married adult male between twenty and fifty years old.[73] Each household head worked on one plot of land as the principal adult male (*zhengding*); the other males in the household—the single, the young, and the elderly—worked as assistant adult males (*bangding*). This way, the entire household became a unit of administration and production, and every male member filled a state position. This policy also scattered households from the same banner administration and descent group, producing a remarkable heterogeneity in the Shuangcheng banner villages.

The village-level distribution of the rural banner households by their original banner affiliation illustrates this designed heterogeneity. As Table 2.3 shows, in 1866, only three of the 120 villages were relatively homogeneous; the households of these three villages had belonged to the same banner captain at their places of origin. In contrast, the majority of the villages (61.6 percent) each contained households from eleven to

TABLE 2.3
The diversity of Shuangcheng banner villages, measured by rural bannermen's banner affiliation in their places of origin, 1866–1869

N. of banner captain in each village	*Number of villages*	*Percent*
1	3	2.5
2–5	17	14.2
6–10	26	21.7
11–15	58	48.3
16–20	15	12.5
21–22	1	0.8
Total	120	100.0

SOURCE: CMGPD-SC.
NOTE: The population data of the 1860s are analyzed because these are the earliest available household registers. The number of different banner administrations was identified by immigrants' place of origin, immigrants' original banner affiliation, and the name of the captain the household originally belonged to.

TABLE 2.4
Number of different surnames among the rural bannermen of each village, 1866–1869

Number of surnames in each village	*Number of villages*	*Percent*
3–5	3	2.5
6–10	22	18.3
11–15	57	47.5
16–20	36	30.0
21–24	2	1.7
Total	120	100.0

SOURCE: CMGPD-SC.
NOTE: The unique surnames were identified by the immigrant's place of origin, original banner affiliation, original banner captain, and surname. Thus one unique surname represents a unique descent group origin.

twenty-two different banner captains. The distribution of the surnames by village exhibited a similar pattern. As Table 2.4 shows, the most homogeneous of the 120 villages consisted of three descent groups, and the majority of the villages (77.5 percent) each consisted of eleven to twenty descent groups. In the extreme cases, the rural banner households in two villages came from more than twenty different descent groups. Given that each banner village consisted of only twenty-four or twenty-eight rural banner households, it meant that almost every individual household in the two villages represented a distinct descent group.

The designed heterogeneity of the banner villages distinguished the Shuangcheng settlement from most other resettlement projects, in which the government had usually settled migrants in homogeneous groups by place of origin, village, and descent group, using the authority of these organic units as a convenient way to organize and control migrants. Scholars studying resettlement processes have agreed on the importance of migrants' original social organizations in helping them adjust to their new environments (Scudder and Colson 1982; Guggenheim and Cernea 1993). According to Scudder and Colson's classic framework of resettlement processes, all migrants pass through a "transition" stage, during which they tend to behave conservatively and turn inward, to such social organizations as the household or lineage, for support. The whole community forms a closed social system. It is only in the next stage of "potential development" that the migrants adapt to the environment, seeking new opportunities and exhibiting more individualism.[74] The settlement of bannermen in Shuangcheng, however, followed an unusual path; it ignored not only migrants' previous kinship ties, but also their previous banner affiliations. Although none of the officials explained their rationale in extant sources, this design laid the groundwork for the Qing to carry out an ambitious plan: to settle urban dwellers in a rural society and simultaneously build a new social hierarchy on the site.

This heterogeneous pattern of settlement in Shuangcheng created a favorable environment for metropolitan bannermen. In contrast to the rural bannermen, who were used to a relatively homogeneous social environment, metropolitan bannermen had lived in a heterogeneous residential arrangement back in Beijing. The Qing government had initially assigned Beijing residents to live in particular zones on the basis of ethnicity and banner affiliation; however, those residential boundaries had been blurred since the early eighteenth century (Liu 1998b). By the early nineteenth century, the metropolitan bannermen in Beijing had grown accustomed to residing not only with bannermen of different banner affiliations but also with civilian commoners. This made the heterogeneity in Shuangcheng relatively easy for the metropolitan bannermen to adjust to.

Moreover, dismantling the preexisting social organizations among the rural bannermen was an indispensable step toward preventing their potential resistance to the state-created social order. As noted earlier, the state's purpose in creating the Shuangcheng settlement was not to simply transport migrants to the banner villages, but also to build a new social hierarchy based on state-designed population categories, with the metropolitan bannermen at the top and rural bannermen providing continuous support to these elites. The previous social organizations based on descent group and banner community represented potential threats to the hierarchy defined by the registration categories, because these organizations could stir up powerful resistance to the joining of metropolitan bannermen, who were neither familiar with the rural environment nor backed up by strong descent groups. Therefore, settling the rural bannermen was also a boundary-clearing process that paved the way for the state-mandated social hierarchy.

Contrary to this dismantling practice for rural bannermen, the government intended to strengthen the social ties among the metropolitan bannermen and smooth the transition to their new lives. When the second group of metropolitan bannermen arrived in 1825, Fujun reported that he had asked the newcomers whether they had relatives or friends who had arrived in 1824; if so, he settled them in the same villages, "enabling them to reunite and take care of each other."[75] Fujun's successors continued this practice until 1838.[76]

Despite the efforts of Fujun and his successors, however, due to their relatively small number and the slow progress of the land-clearing efforts, the metropolitan banner households were nonetheless scattered. In 1822, Songlin, the general of Jilin, found that not a single rural banner household in the central *tun* had been able to independently clear enough land to allocate to one metropolitan banner household.[77] Songlin thus wrote a memorial recommending that the first fifty-three metropolitan banner households be assigned evenly among the forty villages of the central *tun*, with one or two households in each village, so that all the rural banner households in that village could work together to clear the land needed to support the one or two metropolitan banner households. This initial distribution of the fifty-three pioneer metropolitan households established the pattern for the subsequent metropolitan migrants. In 1866, the metropolitan households in each village of the central *tun* came from at least five different banner administrations. In the majority of the villages (thirty out of forty) the metropolitan migrants came from six to ten banner administrations; in eight extreme cases, the metropolitan banner households in each village came from eleven to fifteen banner administrations.[78] Thus, the settlement of metropolitan bannermen was also heterogeneous.

By the same token, the banner villages also had a heterogeneous ethnic composition. The banner immigrants to Shuangcheng came from a total of six ethnic groups: the four common ethnicities in the banner system (Manchu, Mongol, Han-martial, and Xibe) and two small ethnic groups (Taimanzi and Baerhu).[79] The majority of metropolitan bannermen belonged to either Manchu or Mongol, whereas the rural bannermen had more diverse ethnic backgrounds. As Table 2.5 shows, the Manchu and Han-martial were the two largest ethnic groups; the Manchu accounted for 48.5 percent, and the Han-martial, for 32.2 percent of all the banner households. The Xibe and Mongol, which accounted for 11 percent and 7.5 percent of the banner households, respectively, were relatively smaller ethnic groups in Shuangcheng. In addition to the above four common ethnic groups, the two small ethnic groups of Taimanzi and Baerhu were represented by only a handful of households.

Although in other regions of China proper the banner administration organized bannermen of different ethnicities separately, the Shuangcheng settlement mixed different ethnicities in the same village. As Table 2.6 shows, most of the banner villages in Shuangcheng consisted of two or more ethnic groups. If we consider the four common ethnic groups, only

TABLE 2.5
Ethnic composition of the metropolitan and rural banner households, (indicated by household head's ethnicity), 1866–1869

	METROPOLITAN BANNERMEN		RURAL BANNERMEN		TOTAL	
Ethnicity	*Number*	*Percent*	*Number*	*Percent*	*Number*	*Percent*
Manchu	406	81.0	1,335	43.2	1,741	48.5
Mongol	91	18.2	178	5.8	269	7.5
Xibe	4	0.8	390	12.6	394	11.0
Han-martial			1,157	37.5	1,157	32.2
Taimanzi			4	0.1	4	0.1
Baerhu			16	0.5	16	0.4
Unkown			9	0.3	9	0.3
Total	501	100.0	3,089	100.0	3,590	100.0

SOURCE: CMGPD-SC.

TABLE 2.6
Number of ethnicities in the banner villages of Shuangcheng, 1866–1869

	THE FOUR MAJOR ETHNICITIES		ALL ETHNICITIES	
Number of ethnicities in each village	*Number of villages*	*Percent*	*Number of villages*	*Percent*
1	11	9.2	11	9.2
2	18	15.0	18	15.0
3	50	41.7	43	35.8
4	41	34.2	44	36.7
5			4	3.3
Total	120	100.0	120	100.0

SOURCE: CMGPD-SC.

eleven villages had a unitary ethnic component, accounting for 9.2 percent of the 120 banner villages. Fifty villages (41.7 percent) had three ethnic groups, and forty-one villages (34.2 percent) had four ethnic groups. Moreover, if we take Taimanzi and Baerhu into consideration, the number of villages with four ethnic groups increases to forty-four (36.7 percent). The heterogeneous ethnic composition of banner villages, if not a state design, at least indicates that ethnicity was not a principle in organizing bannermen in Shuangcheng, a departure from the Eight Banner tradition.

The heterogeneous settlement of Shuangcheng banner migrants exemplifies the state's efforts to clear the existing social boundaries among migrants and thereby to enforce the new boundary between the state-created categories of metropolitan and rural bannermen. In this regard, this designed heterogeneity in fact marked a process of homogenization. By mixing migrants from various origins, the state intentionally extenuated all previous social boundaries and delivered the message that in Shuangcheng the previous social categories—descent group, banner community, and ethnicity—were no longer important. Within the frame of the metropolitan-rural hierarchy, all migrant households were equal.

Governance

To complete the boundary-clearing process and successfully settle the banner migrants, Fujun focused on building new social organizations and institutions. When planning the banner villages, he intentionally built the five villages in each banner as new communities that would replace the migrants' old social organizations. Fujun distributed the five villages evenly in the land allocated to each banner. As Map 2.1 shows, the first village in each banner was located in the center; the other four villages surrounded the first village at the four corners. This distribution resembled the shape of a plum blossom. Fujun designed them this way to ensure that the distances between the villages were equal; each village was five *li* (about three kilometers) away from its neighbors. This even spacing facilitated both state control and self-surveillance between villages. The efforts of Fujun and subsequent officials enabled these banner villages to develop into new communities. Komekura (1941, 145) observes that some of these five-village communities still exhibited strong cohesion in the 1940s in that members of each community participated in sacrifice ceremonies together.[80]

In addition to creating new communities, Fujun worked hard to establish a reliable and capable local government. In 1819, four years after the first thousand individual bannermen from Jilin were relocated to Shuangcheng, Fujun found that the banner officials assigned to Shuangcheng were incapable of controlling the rural migrants, who had not yet either cleared enough land or built enough houses to accommodate themselves. He therefore asked the Jiaqing emperor to assign some cashiered Han-Chinese officials to Jilin to assist with the settlement. Fujun was especially partial to the former magistrate, Dou Xinchuan. Dou, a native of Shanxi province, was a Han-Chinese official who had attained his position by passing the civil service exam.[81] Since 1801, Dou had been the magistrate of several counties in Jiangxi, Shengjing, and Hebei provinces and was experienced in local governance. As the general of Shengjing, Fujun had worked with Dou and trusted his abilities. Fujun therefore requested that Dou be sent to Shuangcheng to supervise the settlement.[82]

With Dou's assistance, the settlement of rural bannermen made significant progress, ensuring that the settlement of metropolitan bannermen could move forward. Fujun, instead of assigning Dou to an official post in the local government, appointed him to work as the general representative. Dou took charge of all the basic settlement work, including the construction of migrants' housing, building the granary system, and recruiting merchants to Shuangcheng to produce construction supplies and thereby reduce government expenditure. Moreover, Dou also diligently visited all 120 villages to investigate and resolve any problems the migrants faced in living or farming. When the first group of metropolitan bannermen arrived in Shuangcheng in 1824, they found a total of 1,164 households of rural bannermen from Jilin and 1,836 households of rural bannermen from Shengjing.[83] These rural bannermen had already opened a total of 22,841 *shang* of land. In contrast to the barren landscape in 1815, by 1824 the three *tun* of Shuangcheng had seen the opening of forty shops, including four wineries and seven grocery stores. Moreover, the government also built one charity granary (*yicang*) in each *tun* and an additional public granary (*gongcang*) in the central *tun*.[84] These granaries loaned seeds to the farmers, ensuring timely planting in good times and providing famine relief in bad times.

The government offered even more attention and assistance to the settlement of metropolitan bannermen. In 1832, the government established a separate wing, the Metropolitan Banner Wing (*jingqi yi*), to administer them.[85] It took an especially long time for metropolitan bannermen to adjust to the rural environment. In 1844, Jing'ebu, the general of Jilin (1840–1848), completed a site investigation and reported varying economic conditions of the 598 metropolitan banner households living in Shuangcheng.[86] Since 698 metropolitan banner households had settled in Shuangcheng by 1838, the lower number six years later revealed that about one hundred metropolitan banner households did not survive the first twenty years of the settlement, either abandoning the land or becoming extinct. The government continued to provide economic support to the remaining metropolitan banner households.

Despite all the challenges, the state finally succeeded in settling a majority of the metropolitan bannermen. By 1869, 225 of the 698 metropolitan banner households had died out or abandoned the farm, and 473 households had survived and settled in for the long term. In the next year, 225 new households were created from the existing 473 households to fill the quota of 698. In 1878, another 302 households were created from those 698 metropolitan banner households. The descendants of metropolitan bannermen continue to live in today's villages in Shuangcheng.

THE STATE'S ROLE IN FRONTIER SETTLEMENT

The Qing state's ambitious plan made the founding of Shuangcheng a unique case in population-settlement history, as it created overwhelming difficulties for the settlement process. As urban-to-rural migrants, the metropolitan bannermen especially faced a hard adjustment to rural life and took a long time for them to adapt to their new environment. From 1870 to 1890, about a half-century after their initial settlement, beginning in 1824, male mortality rates were still higher for metropolitan bannermen than for rural bannermen in all age groups except the elderly (Chen, Campbell, and Lee 2005). The infants and children of metropolitan bannermen were especially vulnerable; the mortality rate for metropolitan banner children at ages one and two was three times that of their rural counterparts, and between the ages of three and ten, it was 1.7 times that of rural banner children. In the period 1890–1912, the long-term adaptation process closed the gap in infant mortality rates between metropolitan and rural bannermen; mortality rates for children aged one to five were eventually the same for both groups. The metropolitan bannermen's mortality deficit, however, persisted in other age groups.

Yet, in the long term, the settlement of Shuangcheng was indeed successful.[87] Although the state did not achieve its goal of settling three thousand households of metropolitan bannermen, the metropolitan and rural bannermen who survived the initial hardships stayed and prospered. The Shuangcheng community soon achieved a vibrant social life. Beginning in the 1840s, the immigrants privately cleared more land for themselves on top of what the state had allocated to them. Stratification emerged in the villages, indicating that these communities reached the "potential development" stage (Scudder and Colson 1982, 275; Scudder 1985, 164–67). Moreover, Shuangcheng has been an important locus of grain production and distribution in northeast China since the mid-nineteenth century.

The successful settlement of immigrants in Shuangcheng proves the Qing to have been a capable, experienced actor in organizing a society. Shuangcheng thus serves as an example of how much the state could do and had done in many places. Meticulous statecraft ensured the proper control of migrants as well as their transition to frontier life. Before the settlement began in earnest, the emperor and officials had carefully planned the site selection, residential arrangements, and financing. It took them three years

(1812–1815) to identify the relocation site and eight years (1815–1823) to get it ready for the metropolitan bannermen. The successful settlement of rural bannermen was a crucial step in the process. By the time the metropolitan bannermen arrived, Shuangcheng was no longer a barren wasteland; rather, it was a well-organized rural society with a constant supply of labor provided by the rural banner population. Of course, the timing of the settlement was also important to its success. Although the Qing started to decline in the early nineteenth century, it still had the ability to establish this settlement. In the 1880s, the Qing initiated another relocation project to settle more metropolitan bannermen in Hulan, another site in northern Manchuria, but it failed when only nine households responded (Wei 2011). In the late nineteenth century, as the political and fiscal crises deepened, the Qing no longer had the money to invest in another settlement.

In addition to the state's efforts, the geography of Shuangcheng and its fertile land made it a good site for settlement. Compared to other involuntary migrations, when migrants had been settled on barren land, the high quality of land in Shuangcheng provided migrants with an incentive to stay. The spacious landscape provided them with both the room and the raw materials necessary to prosper. Although the settlement experience was intimidating for the metropolitan bannermen, the government established them as the elite in Shuangcheng. The promise of life as landlords ensured their loyalty and the success of those who survived the initial resettlement stage.

Finally, the metropolitan and rural bannermen had one thing in common; they were highly institutionalized under the Eight Banners. The Eight Banners had played an active role in organizing bannermen and even institutionalized such social organizations as *zu*, or descent group.[88] Compared to non-banner populations, their highly institutionalized nature made bannermen more likely to adjust in a setting in which their original social ties became fragmented. Moreover, this characteristic of the bannermen enabled the state to achieve more in state-building in Shuangcheng, including creating new population categories among them. In fact, government's undermining of migrants' previous boundaries defined by ethnicity, place of origin, original banner affiliation, and descent group was only part of the statecraft. To accomplish its social-engineering goals, the state also built and maintained new boundaries among immigrants and establish the social hierarchy.

CHAPTER THREE

Building Boundaries

Land Allocation and Population Registration

Frontier settlement is full of competition and negotiation. Lured by opportunities for wealth and upward social mobility, various groups of people explore and tame the wild fields. The state is only one of the actors. Along with state-organized migration, aborigine peoples and voluntary settlers also organize themselves outside the purview of the state. State-building on frontiers means that state institutions compete and negotiate with nonstate institutions to include all the people under its administration. This process took place on all the frontiers of China (Shepherd 1993; Ke 2001; Perdue 2005; Li 2012). Frontier settlement in other countries, such as Russia, followed similar patterns (Treadgold 1957; Khodarkovsky 2002). Settlement in Shuangcheng, where the state claimed ownership of all the land, was no exception. Although there had been virtually no aborigine population in Shuangcheng, the state soon faced the problem of organizing the immigrants who were settling there without the government's permission. Not only had a few hundred immigrants settled in Shuangcheng prior to the state-organized migration in 1815, but an increasing number of voluntary migrants moved there after the government settlement was established. Given that the purpose of Shuangcheng settlement was to solve the bannermen's livelihood problem, state-building in Shuangcheng for the Qing meant not only administering all immigrants but also maintaining the elite status of metropolitan and rural bannermen.

The state's policies of land allocation and population registration in Shuangcheng serve as a well-documented example of state-building in a frontier region. In the history of frontier settlement, registration is the state's effort to standardize and simplify the existing institutions, making previously unknown frontier societies legible (Scott 1998) and thereby integrating the frontiers into state administration. During this process, it is common for the state to differentiate the settler population to achieve its goal of administration, either containing the groups it does not favor or empowering some groups and relying on them to carry out the state's administrative project.[1] Consequently, state policies and institutions also reshape the social hierarchy and local organizations. In Shuangcheng, because the state claimed ownership of all land, it took more aggressive steps to directly impose a social hierarchy. As early as 1814, the Qing decided to assign a total of ninety thousand *shang* of uncultivated land to the metropolitan and rural bannermen.[2] Designating this land *jichan*, or private property, the state allowed the metropolitan and rural banner immigrants to use their allocated plots for free; they paid neither rent nor taxes and could pass the land down to their descendants. Government household and land registers documented the membership of metropolitan and rural bannermen and their ownership of allocated land. Settlers not recorded on the metropolitan and rural banner household registers were not eligible for land allocations. Entitlement to *jichan* land, which accounted for more than half of registered farmland in Shuangcheng during the Qing dynasty, was an important marker of the socioeconomic status of settlers.[3]

The creation of population categories in Shuangcheng illustrates in detail how state registration and the associated policies initiated a complex process of social construction. The government's population registers classified the settlers into four categories: metropolitan bannermen, rural bannermen, floating bannermen, and civilian commoners (*minren*). The creation of these population categories was not a linear process. In the beginning, the state had only envisioned metropolitan and rural bannermen living in Shuangcheng. It was the presence of the unofficial settlers that caused the government to register floating bannermen and civilian commoners, out of the need to organize a growing frontier population. The state drew boundaries based on immigrants' institutional affiliations and official immigrant status. Although these are ascriptive characteristics, once the government began using them to differentiate land entitlements, they became markers of the different socioeconomic status of immigrants.

HOUSEHOLD REGISTRATION IN SHUANGCHENG

The Eight Banners registration system, to which the Shuangcheng household registration system belonged, elaborated the function of registration as a means to control people and resources. It especially emphasized resource allocation among the elite and the differentiation of entitlements based on heritable categories assigned at the time of settlement. By registering bannermen under the Eight Banners, the state distinguished them from civilian commoners registered under the *baojia* and *lijia* systems. Different from the *baojia* and *lijia* registration, which mainly functioned to control the population and collect tax, the Eight Banners registration was used in assigning banner posts and allocating stipends among the subject population. Instead of paying taxes to the state, bannermen provided service—either as soldiers or farmers. The Eight Banner population registers defined the particular membership of each bannerman and concurrently differentiated the obligations and privileges of banner populations (Ding 2009). As a result, inclusion in the banner registers became the single most important prerequisite for securing a banner post and its associated state stipend, land, and housing.

Because of its importance in resource allocation, the Qing state paid close attention to the maintenance of the banner household registration. When the Qing first began registering bannermen, it only recorded adult males, excluding children, the elderly, and the disabled. In 1727, the banner administration revised the system to register the population by households, and to record information on every male household member.[4] Every three years, each banner captain updated the register and sent the updated version to the banner commander. To enhance the recording of pedigrees, the banner administration stipulated, in 1729, that all bannerman had to register their newborns with their banner captains within one month of the child's birth (QDBQTZ, book 1, 540). Extant banner registers in north and northeast China show that, in the eighteenth and nineteenth centuries, the banner administration not only registered males, but also wives, widows, and some unmarried daughters.

As a means of organizing and controlling banner immigrants, the banner household registration in Shuangcheng was the most important instrument utilized by the state. During the recruitment stage, once a household volunteered to move to Shuangcheng, the banner captain would transfer its records to a separate register, listing in sequence each household's place of origin, banner affiliation, and ethnicity, and then each member's banner post, name, and age.[5] When these households set off for Shuangcheng, the banner governments in their places of origin would submit a copy of the register to the Shuangcheng banner government. The Shuangcheng banner government then recorded this information in the local register under their new residence and new banner affiliation, preserving all the information from their place of origin. Throughout the Qing, the state maintained separate registers for the metropolitan and the rural bannermen.

The household registers in Shuangcheng served as the only official reference for determining land allocations. The state used three criteria to define population categories in Shuangcheng: banner affiliation, official migration status, and place of origin. Civilian commoners were considered the have-nots because they were not members of the Eight Banners and thus recorded in the banner registers; the *fuding*, or floating bannermen, were likewise compromised because they had moved to Shuangcheng without state sponsorship and thus were not included in the original registers compiled for the official migrants. Among the haves, metropolitan bannermen were granted twice as much land as rural bannermen because they were from the capital. This strict association between membership in a specific category and entitlement rights made maintaining accurate records especially important; whereas the banner captains in other parts of China only updated household registers every three years, in Shuangcheng they did so annually. Thus, the four population categories in Shuangcheng also formed and developed along the lines of the state's policies of population registration and land allocation.

LAND ALLOCATION AND THE HAVES

Land Allocation

Fujun's original plan for the Shuangcheng settlement set out the land-allocation policy. Establishing the household as the basic unit for land allocation and production, he fixed the quota of households at six thousand: three thousand for rural bannermen and three thousand for metropolitan bannermen. Fujun planned to allocate twenty *shang* of *jichan* land to each metropolitan banner household, and only ten *shang* to each rural banner household. This meant that the three thousand planned metropolitan banner households would occupy two-thirds of the ninety thousand *shang* of *jichan* land. Moreover, to ease the transition of metropolitan bannermen to their new rural environment, the state required the rural bannermen to clear land for the metropolitan bannermen prior to their arrival. Consequently, all *jichan* land was first cleared and farmed by rural bannermen and then transferred to the later-arriving metropolitan bannermen.

In 1815, the government allocated the land in the central *tun* to the first one thousand rural bannermen from Jilin, dividing them into groups of four and assigning each group a thatched cottage and a set of farming tools and a draft animal. The government allocated equally sized plots of thirty *shang* of *jichan* land to each bannerman. In the eighth month of that year, the government issued a certificate to each bannerman to indicate his ownership status and obligations.[6] The certificate stated that each rural bannerman was required to clear twenty of the thirty *shang* of land within three years, keeping the remaining ten *shang* unfarmed. After three years, a rural bannerman would begin paying twenty imperial *shi* (*cang shi*) of grain as rent for the twenty *shang* of cultivated land, a rate of one imperial *shi* per *shang*.[7] When the metropolitan bannermen arrived in Shuangcheng, the rural bannermen would turn over twenty *shang* of land—fifteen *shang* of the cultivated land and five *shang* of the uncultivated land—to their metropolitan neighbors. The rural bannermen could then enjoy the remaining ten *shang* of land—five *shang* cultivated and five *shang* uncultivated—as their own property, exempted from rent. Rural bannermen could not, however, rent or sell their ten-*shang* plot to others; the government would confiscate the plots of those who violated this rule.

In 1820, after all three thousand rural banner households were settled in Shuangcheng, the government completed the allocation of all ninety thousand *shang* of *jichan* land. The central *tun*, right *tun*, and left *tun* contained one thousand households each. Each village consisted of twenty-four or twenty-eight plots, one for each settled rural banner household. To separate the plots, the government intentionally left a waste area of less than two meters (five to six *chi*) between them.[8] To augment these boundaries, rural bannermen constructed mounds along the borders of the plots and waste areas. Banner officials stuck a peg of wood on each plot denoting the banner and village affiliations associated with the property's provenance. The captain's offices then drew a map showing the location of each plot and assigned the plots to the rural bannermen in the order of the names on the household registers.[9]

After the initial allocations, the captain's office compiled land registers documenting the results, indicating which households had been assigned to which plots. The structure of the land register was similar to that of the household register. It recorded the principal bannerman (*zhengding*), or household head, as the owner of the plot; these landowners were organized based on their residential banner affiliation and village. Listed after the name of the landowner were the type and amount of land he had been allocated. In some instances, the register also recorded the location and boundaries of the plot.[10] Whereas the household register officially proved the eligibility of individuals to acquire state land, the land register officially documented the ownership of a specific plot. The land register superseded the land certificates the government had originally issued to the rural bannermen and became the only official proof of landownership.[11]

These different sizes of land allocations for the two groups reinforced the social difference that had existed between the metropolitan and the rural bannermen, and created the two-tier hierarchy in Shuangcheng. The metropolitan bannermen enjoyed not only more land but also government privileges and were therefore the dominant group. In accepting their land allocations, the rural bannermen simultaneously became landowners in their own right and laborers for the metropolitan bannermen.

Rural Bannermen and Metropolitan Bannermen

As the designated laborers, rural bannermen experienced remarkable hardship when clearing the land in the early years. In particular, because their allotted stipends and the available labor had been insufficient, the first thousand bannermen from Jilin sent to the central *tun* experienced more hardship than later arrivals. As Songning reported in 1818, the twenty-five *taels* of silver Fujun initially allocated to each bannerman was not enough to cover his expenditures for housing, farm tools, and draft animals. Moreover, because this first group of rural bannermen had to settle in Shuangcheng as individuals, not as households, they did not have family members to assist them (SCPTTJL, 86). By 1822, 209 of these original thousand rural bannermen had fled, and 241 had died or become disabled because of illness.[12] Although the rural banner households that arrived from Shengjing in 1819 and 1820 made up the loss, the hardship of settlement continued.

This hardship seriously delayed the progress of land clearing. By 1823, eight years after the arrival of the first Jilin bannermen and one year before the first group of metropolitan bannermen arrived, the rural bannermen had only cleared 19,675.6 *shang* of land (Table 3.1), which only accounted for less than one-third of the sixty thousand *shang* of *jichan* land Fujun wanted cleared in the first three years after all the rural bannermen were settled. The one thousand rural households in the central *tun* were the slowest; in eight years, they only cleared 7,006.5 *shang* of land—an average speed of 850 *shang* each year. The two thousand rural banner households in the right and the left *tun* who settled later in 1819 and 1820 were faster; in three to four years, they cleared 12,669.1 *shang* of land, with each thousand households annually clearing about 1,800 *shang*.

The delay in land clearing made it more difficult for the government to settle the metropolitan bannermen. When the first group of metropolitan bannermen arrived in 1824, officials found that, although each village was designed to accommodate twenty-four or twenty-eight metropolitan households, no single village had a sufficient amount of cultivated land to accommodate that many. Therefore, the government had to scatter this group throughout the forty villages in the central *tun*, to ensure that each household received a sufficient amount of cultivated land.

TABLE 3.1
The amount of jichan *land cleared by rural bannermen by 1823 (unit:* shang*)*

Year	*Central* tun	*Right* tun	*Left* tun	*Subtotal*
1821	5,552.1	3,796.5	2,931.9	12,280.5
1822	1,000.0	1,231.5	1,546.5	3,778.0
1823	454.4	1,122.0	2,040.7	3,617.1
Total	7,006.5	6,150.0	6,519.1	19,675.6

SOURCES: Songlin's memorials on 1822.5.15 (ZPZZ 04-01-22-0044-18) and 1823.6.5 (ZPZZ 04-01-22-007-2391).

After settling in Shuangcheng, the metropolitan bannermen soon became landlords, turning the rural bannermen into their tenants. The government urged the metropolitan bannermen to use their travel stipends to hire rural bannermen as laborers. In practice, however, many metropolitan bannermen simply rented their land to rural bannermen and lived on their rental income. As landlords, metropolitan bannermen had both symbolic and real power over their tenants. As Jing'ebu reported in 1844, some metropolitan bannermen

> treated their tenants like slaves, commanding them and shouting loudly to them. Moreover, these metropolitan bannermen also asked for loans from their tenants. If they were refused, they would deprive their tenants of land and look for somebody else to rent the land.[13]

This reveals that, having acquired greater power through the state allocation of *jichan* land, metropolitan bannermen held the superior position in the social hierarchy.

The state sought to maintain the privileges of metropolitan bannermen throughout the Qing. In 1829, given the unwillingness of metropolitan bannermen in Beijing to move, the court adjusted the quota of metropolitan banner households to be relocated in Shuangcheng from three thousand to one thousand. This two-thousand-household reduction generated an extra forty thousand *shang* of *jichan* and allowed both metropolitan and rural bannermen to increase their landholdings. The government granted an additional 8.33 *shang* to each of the three thousand rural households and an additional 15 *shang* to each of the anticipated one thousand metropolitan households. Each rural household then had a total of 18.33 *shang* of *jichan* land, and each metropolitan household had a total of 35 *shang*, which was still about twice the size of the plots held by the rural bannermen.

The metropolitan bannermen were also privileged in being exempted from service to the government. Although the state did not require regular labor service from the metropolitan and rural bannermen, when labor was needed for construction, the government turned to the residents. In 1866, the government extracted money and labor from residents to rebuild the city wall at the Shuangcheng seat. But whereas it took money from all Shuangcheng residents, it ordered only rural bannermen and civilian commoners to work as laborers.[14] The rural banner adult males not only had to provide the labor needed to build the city wall but also had to supply their own food and tools. Households without adult males had to hire laborers to fulfill their service obligation. In return, the government gave the laborers limited stipends. Since the government found new damage to the city wall every year, it extracted labor from rural banner households on a regular basis. This labor service lasted for several years, but metropolitan bannermen were spared.

At the same time, despite the metropolitan bannermen's superior position, they did not necessarily have more income than rural bannermen. According to Jing'ebu, in the early years, rural bannermen would pay 0.5 market *shi* of grain in rent for each *shang* of land they farmed for their metropolitan banner landlords, which was more than the original rent charged by the state.[15] Some other archival source indicates that the actual rent rural bannermen paid to metropolitan bannermen was one market *shi*.[16] Thus, metropolitan bannermen who rented out their full twenty *shang* of *jichan* land could collect ten to twenty *shi* of grain. Under this arrangement, the rural banner tenants took in even more income from the produce of the land they rented. According to Jing'ebu, in an average year, the yield of one *shang* of land could reach six *shi* of grain. Then, after paying the rent, a rural banner tenant could keep 5 or 5.5 *shi* of grain, more than 80 percent of the yield. Even after taking into consideration of the cost of farming, this income was high. Jing'ebu also reported that in the 1840s, metropolitan bannermen who rented out all their land were better off than those who did not. This indicates that, although rural bannermen held the inferior position in the two-tier hierarchy, their labor and knowledge of farming ensured them greater economic gain.

To control the official immigrants and their land, the government fixed the number of households of rural and metropolitan bannermen. For rural bannermen, the quota was three thousand households, corresponding to the number of land plots. Whenever a household became extinct because all the members died or left the area, the government created a new household from existing immigrants or recruited new immigrants, in order to maintain the quota. As a result, the number of registered rural banner households did not change significantly during the Qing. As Table 3.2 shows, the number of rural banner households reached 3,000 in 1820 and increased to only 3,140 in 1890. Despite

TABLE 3.2

Number of registered households under the Shuangcheng administration by population categories, 1816–1890

	METROPOLITAN BANNERMEN		RURAL BANNERMEN		FLOATING BANNERMEN		CIVILIAN COMMONERS		TOTAL	
Period	*Number*	*Percent*	*Number*	*Percent*	*Number*	*Percent*	*Number*	*Percent*	*Number*	*Percent*
1816–1820	0	0.0	3,000	94.0	0	0.0	190	6.0	3,190	100.0
1844–1847	598	8.3	3,000	41.7	3,026	42.1	565[a]	7.9	7,189	100.0
1864–1866	498	7.2	3,087	44.7	2,049	29.7	1,272	18.4	6,906	100.0
1890	1,000	12.5	3,140	39.3	2,023	25.3	1,831[a]	22.9	7,994	100.0

SOURCES: The banner government's orders to rural bannermen and civilian commoners, respectively, in 1816 (SCPTTJL, 194 and 197–98); Jing'ebu's memorial in 1844 (HCDXTGZY, book 14, juan 31, 6b); the government report on the establishment of *baojia* system in 1866 (SCPZGYMDA, 160: 636: 354–60); SCXZ 1990, 829; CMGPD-SC; local government's retrospective summary of floating bannermen registration in 1879 (SCPZGYMDA, 202: 838-3: 337–41).

NOTE: [a]The number of households was estimated based on various sources.

the fixed number of households, the size of the rural banner population significantly increased overtime. Based on available data, the population of rural bannermen was 14,670 in 1824 and increased to 27,028 in 1869, and then to 43,948 in 1910, an average annual growth rate of 2.3 percent.[17]

Although the government had set the quota of metropolitan banner households at one thousand in 1829, it was not actually met until 1879. While a total of 698 metropolitan banner households had settled in Shuangcheng, some households became extinct or abandoned the farm in the first two decades of settlement. By 1843, only 598 of these households remained in the area.[18] By 1870, the number of metropolitan banner households had dropped to 473. In that year, the government used 698 as the standard number and created 225 new households from among the existing metropolitan bannermen to reach it.[19] In 1878, in response to requests from some of the metropolitan bannermen living in Shuangcheng, the government allocated 302 additional plots of *jichan* land that had been reserved for this elite population category, resulting in the creation of 302 new households from the existing metropolitan banner households. This land allocation finally brought the number of metropolitan households up to one thousand.[20] Despite the fluctuation in the number of metropolitan banner households, the metropolitan banner population increased steadily over time. In 1824, the initial population of metropolitan bannermen consisted of 187 individuals. As a consequence of immigration and natural increase, the metropolitan banner population reached 2,324 in 1866 and increased to 4,838 in 1912, an average annual growth rate of 2.4 percent, which was slightly higher than that of the rural bannermen.[21]

THE "HAVE-NOTS"

The *have-nots* were immigrants who had settled in Shuangcheng without the government's permission and thus were not eligible to receive *jichan* land. In a broad sense, this was a residual category that included all the immigrants who were neither metropolitan nor rural bannermen. As such, the have-nots encompassed a wide range of socioeconomic statuses. Some of these immigrants were quite capable and resourceful. These included some of the civilian commoners who had already cleared land there before the government organized the bannermen settlement. Some of them even acted as agents who organized private settlement in this area. These unofficial settlers cannot be simply understood as impoverished people living on the frontier without support. In fact, they constituted a significant force that competed with state institutions. Therefore, their presence presented a challenge to the state: how to regulate them with state institutions and prevent them from interfering with the privileges of the metropolitan and rural bannermen.

Despite the challenge they represented, the shortage of labor in Shuangcheng also made these unofficial immigrants desirable to the government. The labor deficit among metropolitan and rural bannermen persisted for at least two generations. According to Songlin, an adult male in Shuangcheng could clear and farm six to seven *shang* of land, on average, and twelve or thirteen *shang*, at most.[22] At this rate, clearing and farming the full ninety thousand *shang* of *jichan* land would require the labor of about thirteen thousand adult males. In the early years, the migrant households were relatively small: in the 1820s the majority of rural banner households in the central *tun* had only one adult male; only some households in the right and the left *tun* had additional adult males, but none had more than four.[23] Thus, an estimate of the average number of adult males per household was two.[24] This suggests that there were approximately six thousand adult males in the rural banner population. Therefore, to farm all the *jichan* land required an additional seven thousand adult males. The arrival of metropolitan bannermen did not remedy this labor deficit, as these individuals had little if any farming experience. It would have taken at least two generations to fill the labor gap with metropolitan and rural bannermen. Consequently, the unofficial immigrants became important sources of labor.

To make use of unofficial immigrants' labor while also containing them, the state used the registration system to define their entitlements. It registered civilian commoners on civilian registers and created a separate register to record the unofficial banner immigrants, who were classified under the category of floating bannermen (*fuding*). Moreover, as more and more immigrants came to this area, the government stopped recording the growing population. The state excluded all the unofficial immigrants from land allocation; so, despite their varying economic statuses, these voluntary immigrants had no land entitlements. From the administrative perspective, they were the have-nots.

Civilian Commoners (Minren)

During the Qing, the division between bannermen and civilian commoners marked the most prominent categorical boundary, reflecting the court's priority of privileging the banner people. Bannermen enjoyed state stipends and housing for serving the state as officials and soldiers. Civilian commoners, in general, were not eligible for any of these economic and political privileges. By the mid-eighteenth century, when civilian commoners had encroached on more and more banner land inside China proper and in southern Manchuria, the state viewed them as a major threat to the Eight Banners (Sudo 1944; Diao 1993, 122–33). Thus as early as the planning stage of the Shuangcheng settlement, the state had prioritized preventing civilian commoners from occupying banner land and made careful plans to circumscribe their activities.

In Shuangcheng, the state first encountered the several hundred households of civilian commoners who had resided and organized land cultivation before the settlement of bannermen.[25] Although these civilian commoners had moved into this area outside the government's purview, the government had identified them and registered them under the administration of the vice commander-in-chief of Alchuka. On registration, these civilian commoners became legal residents (*ruding chenmin*), paying taxes and farming the land. For example, in 1816, Fujun identified 321 registered civilian farmers, who were farming a total of 8,250 *shang* of land in the area designated for the central *tun*.[26] On average, each of these registered civilian commoners farmed more than twenty-five *shang* of land, which exceeded an adult male's farming capacity of six to seven *shang* of land.[27] Thus, this amount of land indicates that these civilian commoners not only cleared land themselves but also had laborers, who were not registered by the government. Similar civilian settlements also existed in the areas of the right and the left *tun*. The presence of these civilian organizers of farming activities in this area threatened the government's plan to settle bannermen.

To ensure the smooth settlement of bannermen, the government went to considerable lengths to segregate the civilian commoners residentially from bannermen. It enclosed the area planned for banner villages as a banner section (*qijie*) and expelled the civilian commoners. The emperor and central government were especially concerned with ensuring that civilian commoners and their families did not occupy banner land. In 1822, when the Daoguang emperor learned from Songlin that some civilian commoners were living inside the banner villages together with their families, he immediately sent an edict to Fujun, admonishing him to strictly prohibit this arrangement.[28] In 1824, hearing that some civilian commoners were still residing in Shuangcheng, the emperor ordered Fujun to take a harder line, "only allowing the extra adult males from the bannermen to help farm the land and not hiring laborers from civilian commoners."[29]

Fujun, however, disagreed with the central government's policy. He and some of the local officials understood the importance of using civilian commoners as laborers and as a source of revenue in Shuangcheng—especially because the *jichan* land provided little rent income (Ren, Li, and Kang 2012). By the time Fujun established the right and the left *tun* in 1819, he had already decided not to expel all the civilian commoners from those areas; instead, he allowed them to stay and collected rent from their land for local use.[30] In 1822, the government officially registered 3,284 *shang* of land farmed by civilian commoners under the category of *gongzu*, or public rent, land, collecting a rent of 0.5 market *shi* for each *shang* of land.[31] This rental income helped to pay the local government's routine administration costs. Beginning in the 1820s, Fujun also allowed civilian commoners to farm the uncultivated land north of the border of the banner section, also using the rent money to run the local government (Ren, Li, and Kang 2012).

At the same time, to avoid civilian commoners interfering with the bannermen's livelihood, Fujun separated them residentially from bannermen. When designing the banner villages, Fujun set aside the area surrounding the seat of each *tun* to accommodate civilian commoners.[32] As Map 2.1 shows, while the 120 banner villages were distributed in an orderly way over the entire Shuangcheng area, the natural settlements of civilian commoners were scattered in the empty land around the Shuangcheng seat and the seats of the right and the left *tun*, and along the northern border of Shuangcheng.[33] The empty areas around the seats of the right and the left *tun* were especially large. The government later developed these areas as *suique* land—land allocated to individual officials and soldiers to subsidize their office-related expenditures—and civilian commoners worked the land as tenants.[34] These areas later developed into the civilian section (*minjie*) of Shuangcheng (Ren, Li, and Kang 2012; Ren 2013). Apparently, Fujun had intended this arrangement from the beginning. His early plan for the settlement established a boundary between the bannermen and the civilian commoners: metropolitan and rural bannermen residing in banner villages were designated as the "haves," while civilian commoners working as state tenants in the civilian section were designated as the "have-nots."

Although the central government gradually accepted the existing civilian commoners in Shuangcheng, it still tried to prevent more civilian commoners from arriving and thus to protect bannermen's privileges. In 1836, in his reply to Xiangkang, the general of Jilin (1835 and 1836–1840), regarding a proposal to allow floating bannermen to live in Shuangcheng, the Daoguang emperor articulated his hardline policy:

> Since [the floating bannermen from Jinzhou] are still bannermen and they neither occupied the land of metropolitan bannermen nor intervened in their livelihoods, I agree with your proposal [to allow them to stay in Shuangcheng]. However, with the passage of time, it is hard to prevent civilian commoners from surreptitiously going to Shuangcheng along with those floating bannermen. [Officials] should strictly prevent [civilian commoners from residing in the banner section]. Once [civilian commoners] are discovered, [I am] determined to blame and punish the general and responsible officials for what they deserve without pardon.[35]

After a careful survey, Xiangkang reported that, since 1822, the banner immigrants had recruited a total of 225 households of civilian commoners in the banner section.[36] To avoid punishment by the emperor, Xiangkang attributed this result to Fujun's ambiguous policies during the initial settlement stage and promised to expel all the civilian families living in the banner section. From then on, the government established a rule requiring local officials to check the banner villages annually and report any unregistered civilian commoners.

Despite the central government's hardline policy, Fujun's successors continued to use civilian commoners in Shuangcheng as state tenants. They did so not only to secure government revenue but also to reduce the likelihood of civilian commoners simply taking the land allocated to bannermen. In 1844, Jing'ebu justified this practice before the Daoguang emperor: "When we recruited tenants to clear land, the amount of land was fixed. Since they rent the land directly from the government, it is impossible for the civilian commoners to embezzle the land."[37] According to Jing'ebu, allowing civilian commoners to work as state tenants in fact reinforced the state's control over them.

Other than those state tenants, most of the civilian commoners who worked privately for bannermen as tenants lived in the natural settlements outside the banner villages. As Map 2.1 shows, these natural settlements, called *wopeng*, were scattered around the banner villages like satellites. Contemporary Shuangcheng residents still call the *wopeng* "tenant villages" (*dianhu cun*), a term marking the residential and social distinctions between the civilian commoners and the bannermen.[38]

Some civilian commoners gradually took advantage of these developments to acquire use rights, which could be considered a type of ownership, to state land. By 1876, government land registers reported that civilian commoners farmed 32,658 *shang* of land as state tenants, which accounted for 16.5 percent of the 198,326 *shang* of registered farmland in Shuangcheng.[39] The distribution of land among the civilian tenants was very unequal; this was in contrast to the equal distributions of *jichan* land among metropolitan and rural bannermen under the state's land-allocation policy. The 1876 civilian land register reveals that the amount of land held by individual tenant households ranged from 776.2 *shang* at the largest to 2.6 *shang* at the smallest.[40]

The large landholdings registered to individual civilian tenants reveals that some of the civilian commoners were also recruiting and organizing immigrants in Shuangcheng. Civilian commoners having several hundred *shang* of registered land were likely contractors; these contractors recruited tenants to clear large amounts of land and registered the land under the government, paying rents as a whole. This form of land cultivation characterized the settlement process of eastern Inner Mongolia and parts of northern Manchuria (Kong 1963; Zhao 1972; Wang 1999). In Inner Mongolia, the contractors were usually wealthy merchants and usurers who had developed certain connections with local officials or nobles. Local officials relied on the contractors to act as agents to recruit tenants and collect rents. In return, the contractors made profits by organizing farming and collecting rents. Some capable contractors at one time even claimed more than two thousand *shang* of land (Wang 1999). Although the wealthy civilian commoners in Shuangcheng had less registered land than the contractors in Inner Mongolia, the civilian commoners' landholdings were significant enough to indicate that they played a role in the civilian section similar to that of the contractors.

To gain access to large amounts of land, the civilian commoners in Shuangcheng also formed connections with local officials. For example, in 1819, when the government surveyed and collected rents from the land cultivated by civilian commoners, the assistant commandant, Mingbao, requested that the official in charge waive the rent on the 190 *shang* of land under a civilian commoner named Zhou Jin. Mingbao claimed that Zhou had already bought the land for "government-operated shops" (*guandian*).[41] This story shows that the coalition between local officials and civilian commoners in land clearing had started before the state registered these lands. The existence of this group of contractors also reveals that although civilian commoners had no land entitlements in Shuangcheng, they were not truly have-nots. Some capable civilian commoners had considerable power and wealth.

The state gradually established a civilian registration system in Shuangcheng to organize civilian commoners. As noted earlier, prior to 1866, the local banner government did not keep records for the civilian population; instead, civilian commoners were registered by tax-paying units (adult males, or *ding*) or rent-paying units (households) under the vice commander-in-chief's office in Alchuka (Ren, Li, and Kang 2012). As Shuangcheng gradually developed into an important settlement in Jilin, more and more civilian commoners entered the area and became involved in commercial activities. The population of Shuangcheng increased, especially at its seat. In 1866, in order to control the increasing population, the state organized all households that were not located in the banner villages into a *baojia* system, registering a total of 1,876 households, including merchants, civilian tenants, and some bannermen, into twenty *bao* and 185 *jia*.[42]

Despite the growth of the civilian population over the course of Shuangcheng's history, the registered civilian population remained smaller than that of the banner population. As Table 3.2 illustrates, from 1816 to 1820 the government registered about 190 civilian households in the Shuangcheng area. Therefore, when the three thousand rural banner households settled in Shuangcheng, the registered civilian households accounted for only 6 percent of total households.[43] The number of registered civilian tenant farmers did not significantly increase over the next twenty-five years; in 1844, there were 565 registered civilian households farming land in Shuangcheng, accounting for 7.9 percent of total households.[44] In 1866, the number of civilian tenant households increased to 668;[45] after taking the population residing in the seat of Shuangcheng into account, the estimated total number of civilian households was 1,272, comprising 18.4 percent of the total registered households.[46]

Even after the state permitted free migration to Jilin in the 1860s, the registered civilian population in Shuangcheng remained small. In 1890, eight years after a civilian government was established, the government surveyed the civilian population, which included those that had previously belonged to the administration of Lalin.[47] The civilian population that year was 1,831 households (Table 3.2).[48] By contrast, the rural and metropolitan banner populations recorded in the registers that year totaled 4,140 households, consisting of 36,398 people.[49] In addition, there were 2,023 households of 10,375 floating bannermen.[50] Therefore, by 1890, civilian commoners accounted for only 22.9 percent of the registered households in Shuangcheng.

Floating Bannermen (Fuding)

In general, the term *floating bannermen* (*fuding*) referred to any bannerman who was not listed on the metropolitan or rural banner registers because he had moved to Shuangcheng without a state order. Floating bannermen came mainly from Shengjing.[51] As early as 1820, when rural bannermen from Shengjing began moving to Shuangcheng, some of the bannermen not listed on the rosters moved along with the official migrants.[52] Between 1822 and 1829, the Liaodong Peninsula suffered harvest failures due to a drought, which forced more and more bannermen to move to Shuangcheng on their own.[53] In 1835, Yijing, the general of Shengjing, noticed the increasing number of Shengjing bannermen who had moved to Shuangcheng without state orders. He also pointed out that the majority of these bannermen were from Jinzhou, a garrison in the coastal area in the Liaodong Peninsula.[54]

By 1845, the unassigned banner population had grown quite large. To deal with this situation, the state formally accepted them as residents in Shuangcheng and gave them the designation "floating bannermen." In that year, each captain's office surveyed all the floating bannermen who resided in its administrative precinct and recorded them in separate registers. In 1847, the government followed up on its initial survey and identified more floating bannermen, to register a total of 3,026 households (Table 3.2).[55] After the initial registration, the captain's offices would check their administrative areas every three months to detect any additional floating bannermen who were not registered.

The registration of floating bannermen also followed a rigorous procedure. After the banner captains reported information associated with floating bannermen living in their precincts, the government would verify the self-reported information against the formal records in the bannermen's places of origin and then transfer the registrations to Shuangcheng. In 1870, the local banner government investigated twelve floating bannermen suspected of misreporting their original banner affiliations to determine the authenticity of their membership in the Eight Banners.[56] Consequently—like the registers for metropolitan and rural bannermen—the registers for each floating banner household recorded the head's place of origin and original banner affiliation, ethnicity, name, and age, followed by the records for each of his family members. Moreover, in each register, the government also classified floating bannermen according to their reasons to stay in Shuangcheng.[57]

The status of floating bannermen illustrates the fundamental inequality in land entitlements created by government's basing population registration on arbitrary boundaries. The floating bannermen not only shared places of origin with the rural bannermen but also were legal residents of the banner villages. Nevertheless, they were not eligible for land allocations. In fact, the majority of floating bannermen were relatives of rural bannermen. According to information recorded in the household registers, in terms of their relationship to rural bannermen, floating bannermen were thus classified into "kin," "non-kin," or "kin relationship unknown." In 1870, 67.4 percent of the floating-banner households were registered as "kin" of rural bannermen (see Table 3.3). Only 14.1 percent of the floating-banner households were registered as "non-kin." Thirty

TABLE 3.3
Types of registered floating banner households, by their reasons to stay in Shuangcheng and their relationship to rural bannermen, 1870 and 1901

Relationship to rural bannermen	*Types of floating banner households*	1870		1901	
		Number	*Percent*	*Number*	*Percent*
Kin	Close kin of rural bannermen	783	40.0	779	42.0
	Those who would like to stay to assist farming or as hired labor	537	27.4	442	23.8
Non-kin	Hired labor without relatives to depend on	277	14.1	253	13.6
Kin relation not specified	Those who were engaged in commerce	61	3.1	62	3.3
	Those who were vulnerable and looked after out of generosity	196	10.0	178	9.6
	Those who farmed land for the metropolitan bannermen	104	5.3	141	7.6
Total		1,958	100.0	1,855	100.0

SOURCE: CMGPD-SC.

years later, this composition remained the same; in 1901, 65.8 percent of the floating-banner households were kin of the rural bannermen and 13.6 percent were non-kin.

The only reason for refusing to allocate land to floating bannermen was that they were not considered official immigrants,[58] and this policy persisted even as their social status improved. Beginning in the 1850s, the state needed military manpower to suppress the various rebellions arising in China proper, and so the government gradually allowed registered floating bannermen to serve as soldiers or enter the examination system,[59] although clearly stating that "[floating bannermen] still shall not interfere with the livelihood of local bannermen (*bendi qiren*)."[60]

In 1879, a petition by Wulintai, a floating bannerman who had earned honorific titles for helping to put down local revolts, best illustrates the unfortunate situation of the floating bannermen. Wulintai's family had moved from Shengjing to Shuangcheng in 1843, registering under the Plain Red Banner. In 1866, he, together with other floating bannermen, had defended the city from a revolt led by a civilian commoner.[61] Because of Wulintai's significant contribution, his eldest son was allowed to enlist as a soldier, and his second son passed the entrance exam for the government school and became a student. Although

Wulintai's family had a decent occupational status, they had no land. He reflected on his situation in relation to that of metropolitan and rural bannermen and lamented:

> Although all my sons serve the state, my entire family has not even an inch of land to make a living. I am not a metropolitan bannerman who can [have family members] replace the extinct households [and take their land] to support their descendants. Neither am I a rural bannerman who at least has *jichan* land.[62]

Most floating bannermen could work in Shuangcheng only as tenants or hired laborers or could engage in commerce. Not only did individual metropolitan and rural banner households hire floating bannermen to farm their land, but the government also officially used them to farm land for the metropolitan bannermen. As Table 3.3 shows, in 1870, 104 floating-banner households made up a separate category, designated "floating bannermen assigned to farm the land of the metropolitan bannermen" (*chengzhong jingqi di fuding*). In 1901, although the number of households in the other types decreased, in this category, it increased to 141. The existence of this type of floating-banner household reveals that the government maintained stable supply of laborers to assist in the farming of the metropolitan bannermen's land.

Although floating and rural bannermen had drastically different entitlement rights to *jichan* land, the boundary between them was porous; kinship ties between the two groups provided floating bannermen with opportunities to enter the category of rural bannermen. For example, in 1819, the assistant commandant Tumin allowed twenty bannermen who had followed their relatives to Shuangcheng from Jinzhou, Fuzhou, and Xiuyan to become rural bannermen on the site to fill the quota of three thousand households; their relatives guaranteed that they were authentic bannermen.[63] After the quota of three thousand rural banner households was filled, a floating bannerman could still become a rural bannerman, by inheriting his rural bannerman relative's land in the event the principal adult male of the household died and none of the other male members in that household were capable of farming. In these cases, the general of Jilin would communicate with the general of Shengjing, obtaining a guarantee that the selected floating bannerman was married and capable of farming. Then the government transferred the bannerman and his immediate family's registration records, going back up to three generations, and formally entered their names in the rural banner registers.[64] Between 1866 and 1912, seventy-six registered floating bannermen changed their category to "rural bannerman."[65] Moreover, although the official regulation stipulated that only floating bannermen who had moved to Shuangcheng before 1842 could inherit *jichan* land and become rural bannermen, in reality some floating bannermen who arrived in Shuangcheng much later than that were still able to inherit their rural banner relative's land and status.[66]

At the same time, since floating bannermen did not own land in Shuangcheng, they were free to migrate away from the area. As noted earlier, after the 1840s, despite the fact that more floating bannermen had arrived in Shuangcheng, the state stopped their large-scale registration, referring to them instead as "floating bannermen not on the registers" (*bu zai ce fuding*). Beginning in the 1850s and 1860s, the state finally opened up land in Manchuria to free migration. Abundant land in areas in Jilin and Heilongjiang—including Bodune, Wuchang, Hulan and Bayansusu—attracted both banner and civilian migrants.[67] Whereas in the past, Shuangcheng was the only site that provided employment to floating bannermen, the opening of Manchuria allowed them more opportunities for both employment and landed property.[68]

As a result, Shuangcheng experienced a decrease in the registered floating-banner population. Between 1847 and 1866, the original 3,026 floating-banner households lost 977 households that had either moved to other places or died out, leaving only 2,049 households in the population registers (Table 3.2). Between 1866 and 1879, another 510 households moved out of Shuangcheng; of these, 243 listed their new destinations with the government, and 267 moved out without giving notice of their new destinations (*buzhi quxiang*). Therefore, in 1879, only 1,903 registered floating-banner households remained (SCPZGYMDA, 202: 838–83: 337–41). By 1890, the number of households in the floating-banner population register had increased slightly, to 2,023 (Table 3.2). By 1901, however, the number of floating-banner households in Shuangcheng had decreased again, to 1,855. Consequently, the overall size of the registered floating-banner population decreased from 11,364 in 1870 to 8,711 in 1901, and then to 4,359 in 1909.

The Unregistered Population

A 1910 Shuangcheng census conducted by the civilian government revealed a much larger population than the one previously recorded in the banner and civilian population registers. The 1910 census covered residents of both Shuangcheng and Lalin, and identified a total of 34,697 households of 227,321 Manchu and 27,950 households of 214,223 Han (SCXZ 1990, 829). Since this census identified households not by their banner affiliation but instead by their ethnicity, it is unclear how many households who reported themselves as Han were actually Han-martial bannermen. Nonetheless, the sizes of both the Manchu and Han populations far exceeded what we have observed in the population registers. Furthermore, a survey of the banner population in Shuangcheng in 1911 also indicated a much larger banner population; as of 1911, 161,946 banner people—87,671 males and 74,275 females—lived in the area of Shuangcheng and Lalin.[69] By contrast, around 1908, the registered banner population in these two areas totaled only about ninety thousand.

This apparent discrepancy in the size of the Shuangcheng population suggests the existence of a large, previously unregistered population of both bannermen and civilian commoners. For the banner population, three factors can explain the discrepancy: the expansion of the registration area from Shuangcheng to include both Shuangcheng and Lalin, the influx of migrants, and the prior underregistration of floating bannermen. For the Han population, since the 1890 data (Table 3.2) already included the civilian population of Lalin, the huge discrepancy can only be explained by the influx of migrants and the existence of an unregistered population. In fact, similar discrepancies existed in all of Jilin. According to Liang Fangzhong's (1980, 264 and 269) study, in 1897, the total registered population of Jilin was 779,000; by 1912, there were 5,393,744 people registered under the civilian government and 44,661 people registered under the banner government. These numbers suggest an almost eightfold increase since 1897 and an even greater increase since 1890. Alongside immigration, the prior population registration was also an obvious cause of this increase.

Lacking detailed data, we can only estimate the size of the unregistered population in the Shuangcheng area according to the land-labor ratio. By 1891, when all the land the government considered arable in

Shuangcheng was cultivated, the local government had registered a total of 225,473 *shang* of land.[70] If one adult male in the 1890s could farm ten *shang* of land,[71] it would have taken about 22,548 adult males to farm this land. In 1891, a total of 12,617 adult males were listed in the banner population registers, including metropolitan bannermen, rural bannermen, and floating bannermen. After excluding those with official posts and government student titles, as well as floating bannermen engaging in commerce, the total number of adult males dropped to 12,183. As for civilian commoners, since about half of the 1,831 registered households in 1890 resided in the seat of Shuangcheng,[72] the number residing in rural areas was probably around nine hundred. If the average number of adult males in each civilian household was two, the estimated number of adult males in these registered civilian households would be 1,800.[73] The total number of adult males in the registered banner and civilian populations was therefore probably about 13,983. Nonetheless, not all of these 13,983 adult males were engaged in farming. Those civilian commoners registering massive amounts of land were more likely to be managers, and some metropolitan bannermen acted as landlords.[74] Thus, to meet the minimum requirement of 22,548 adult males, at least nine thousand additional adult males had to work the land in Shuangcheng. If each adult male had one or two female family members or male dependents, the unregistered population would range from eighteen thousand to twenty-seven thousand.[75] Since this unregistered population of eighteen thousand to twenty-seven thousand meets only the minimum demand for labor, the actual number could have been even larger.[76]

It is clear that the government was aware of the existence of these unregistered bannermen and civilian commoners; as various government documents frequently mentioned "itinerant civilian commoners" (*liumin*) and "floating bannermen not on the registers." As noted earlier, every three months, the captain's offices were supposed to check for "itinerant civilian commoners" and "floating bannermen not on the registers" residing in the banner villages.[77] However, the large unregistered population revealed by the 1910 census indicates that these reports by the captain's offices amounted to routine paperwork and that the government did not actually track the unregistered populations.

In the last decade of the Qing dynasty, the government began to pay attention to the previously unregistered population. A *fuhu*, or floating-households register, compiled by the Plain Red Banner in 1909 reveals the state's interest in households that had yet to be captured in government registers (SCPZGYMDA, 165:392-1). Like the other banner registers, the *fuhu* register also organized households by village. However, unlike the other banner registers that recorded the detailed information of every household member, the *fuhu* register simply recorded the name, ethnicity, and occupation of the household head, and the number of household members of each gender. The *fuhu* register shows that, by 1909, a total of 1,148 households of 7,496 people lived in the twenty banner villages under the administration of the Plain Red Banner. The population size of the *fuhu* varied widely across the villages, ranging from twenty-three households of 204 people to 117 households of 820 people. Moreover, the household size of this *fuhu* population also varied greatly from the minimum of one to the maximum of thirty-five. This *fuhu* population had similar ethnic composition to that of the rural bannermen; about half (52 percent) of the household heads were Han, 37 percent were Manchu, and the remaining 11 percent belonged to Xibe, Mongol, and Baerhu. The *fuhu* were very likely to be unregistered floating bannermen who came from Shengjing and Jilin.

The existence of an unregistered population in Shuangcheng reveals the Qing state's inability to organize all the members of a growing frontier society. This is a common phenomenon throughout world history; even today, a significant proportion of the global population is not registered by any government system of civil registration. For example, in 2005, the United Nations Children's Fund estimated that an average of 36 percent of children were not registered by their fifth birthday (UNICEF 2005). Given that Shuangcheng was a newly settled society, it is not surprising that the Qing state was not able to track new migrants.[78]

At the same time, the unregistered population in Shuangcheng also illuminates the state's use of registration to manipulate the rights of its subject population. As Scott (1998, 2) points out in his study of various state efforts to re-engineer societies by manipulating the settlement patterns of their populations, the state's recording of its population and other aspects of the society resulted from a process of simplification: state bureaucrats often standardize complex social realities to make them legible. It is possible to interpret the state's reluctance to register unofficial immigrants in Shuangcheng in this light. Based on the ideal of maintaining banner privileges, the Qing state delayed the registration of "itinerant civilian commoners" and floating bannermen so as to deny them the right to own land. Doing so protected the landownership of metropolitan and rural bannermen because, as a consequence, the unregistered floating bannermen and civilian commoners could only work for Shuangcheng residents as private tenants and hired laborers. Through these efforts, the state proactively mandated a social hierarchy; because it did not register all floating bannermen and civilian commoners, metropolitan and rural bannermen were always the "majority"—at least in the official records.

ENTITLEMENT AND INEQUALITY

Although the state made a great effort to maintain the boundaries between the population categories and protect the privileges of metropolitan and rural bannermen, the complexity of social reality raised the question, how effective were these boundaries in differentiating the socioeconomic status of the immigrants? After all, the state's household and land registration system was a simplification of a more complex regime of land tenure in local society. In reality, many immigrants who had no land entitlements were wealthy. Some floating bannermen and civilian commoners, by working as tenants, enjoyed economic well-being and stable land-use rights that could be regarded as partial ownership. In 1891, in order to collect fees to subsidize the office expenditures of the civilian government, the captains of the Plain and Bordered Yellow Banners surveyed the economic conditions of the floating bannermen who farmed land for metropolitan bannermen, classifying their households into three grades according to the amount of land they farmed.[79] Of the 255 floating-banner households, forty belonged to the first grade (more than fifty *shang* of land); 105 belonged to the second grade (between twenty and fifty *shang* of land); the remaining 110 fell in the third grade (less than twenty *shang* of land). It reveals that their status as have-nots did not reflect their economic conditions but, rather, their entitlements to official landownership. They not only enjoyed economic benefits as tenants but also fulfilled government obligations associated with their land-use rights.

Nevertheless, the government's effort to "simplify" landownership in Shuangcheng did privilege metropolitan and rural bannermen in the accumulation of wealth. In the 1840s and 1850s, when the government started to register the land that the Shuangcheng immigrants privately cleared and farmed, the entitlement to official landownership empowered metropolitan and rural bannermen to claim more land. Although some itinerant civilian commoners and floating bannermen cleared and farmed land on their own, they had to register their plots under the names of these official immigrants, turning themselves into tenants through a process of "identifying a landlord" (*rendong*). Although the metropolitan and rural bannermen had to pay the government rent for these registered plots, they also automatically became landlords, collecting rents from the de facto farmers. Despite local customs that recognized the use rights of unofficial immigrants, when official immigrants proactively used their entitlement to seize land, the unofficial immigrants became vulnerable and were likely to lose their use rights.[80]

Thus, the state policies of land allocation and population registration created fundamental inequality in the distribution of registered landownership among Shuangcheng residents; throughout the Qing, the metropolitan and rural bannermen officially owned the majority of registered farmland. According to the land registers compiled in 1876, metropolitan and rural bannermen owned 72 percent of the registered farmland in Shuangcheng (Figure 3.1).[81] Civilian commoners, by working as state tenants, owned 17 percent of the registered land. A group classified as "banner tenants," bannermen who were not registered under the metropolitan or rural bannermen categories and were very likely floating bannermen, owned 9 percent of the registered farmland.[82] By 1876, the registered farmland in Shuangcheng not only included the allocated *jichan* land but also a category called *nazu*, or "rent-paying land," which was first privately cultivated by the immigrants and then registered by the state. Therefore, metropolitan and rural bannermen owned not only all the *jichan* land but also the majority of *nazu* land. The privileges of metropolitan bannermen were especially prominent. Although metropolitan banner households accounted for less than 10 percent of the registered households in Shuangcheng, they owned 23 percent of the registered land. Moreover, because of the state regulations

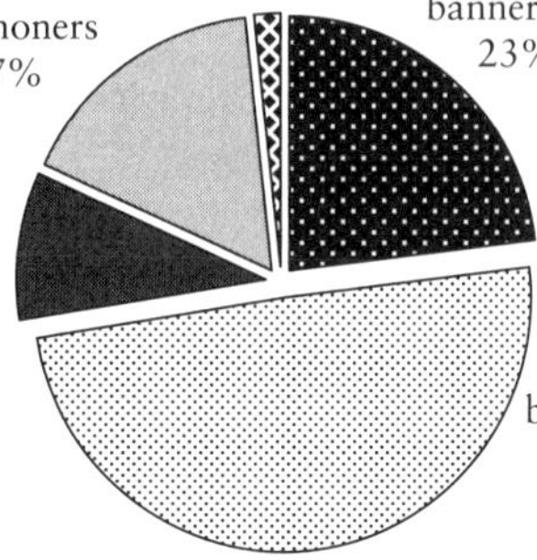

Figure 3.1. The distribution of all land among the population categories in Shuangcheng, 1876.

SOURCES: The 1876 land registers of the banner and civilian sections (SCPGBTDH-KDM, 1834696:285, 1834731:658 and 659, SCPZGYMDA, 160: 635: 147–295).
NOTE: The amount of *sanwanshang* land, a type of land located outside Shuangcheng, is included in the analysis.

that prevented land transfers between different population categories, the shares of registered landownership remained stable until the early twentieth century.[83]

Above all, despite the complexities existing in local society, the state's population-registration and land-allocation policies still created structural inequalities in landholding among the Shuangcheng immigrants. In subsequent decades, two concomitant processes at the state and society levels reinforced the structural inequality between the haves and the have-nots and between the metropolitan and the rural bannermen. The state population and land registration systems effectively maintained the boundaries between the different population categories. At the same time, metropolitan and rural bannermen proactively used their privileges to promote their wealth statuses. These processes interacted with each other over the course of the history of Shuangcheng.

CHAPTER FOUR

Consolidating Power

Banner Government and Local Control

During the process of settling bannermen and regulating the unofficial immigrants, tensions soon emerged between the central and local governments. In 1851 and 1852, two consecutive capital appeals[1] filed by Shuangcheng immigrants revealed the corruption of local officials and a tumultuous history of private land cultivation. In 1851, a former scribe in the Shuangcheng banner government named Taqibu filed a capital appeal charging local officials with having privately organized civilian commoners to cultivate land in Shuangcheng for the officials' own personal profit.[2] According to Taqibu, despite the court's prohibition against allowing civilian commoners to cultivate land in the banner section, local officials had recruited more than ten thousand households of civilian commoners to cultivate more than forty thousand *shang* of land. The officials pocketed the accumulated rent of more than ten thousand strings of cash as personal income.[3] The court ordered Guqing, the general of Jilin (1850–1853), to investigate the matter, with the assistance of the assistant commandant (*xieling*), Tuqing, the principal of the Shuangcheng banner government. However, the local officials denied almost all the charges, explaining or justifying their conduct in various ways. Failing to find solid evidence of corruption, the court only punished some of the officials for their violation of state orders.[4]

In 1852, another capital appeal finally uncovered all the stories of private land cultivation in Shuangcheng. Two plaintiffs—the widow of a metropolitan bannerman, woman Wu, and a bannerman named

Chenggui—filed the appeal, charging the local officials with having illegally organized civilian commoners to farm state land.[5] The general of Jilin, Jingchun (1853–1864) launched an investigation, sending officials to the villages to question the villagers door to door and measure their cultivated land. Eventually, Jingchun found that 2,670 Shuangcheng settlers had privately cleared more than forty-four thousand *shang* of unassigned land.[6] Moreover, except for three of more than one hundred local officials, all had either sponsored land cultivation by civilian commoners and bannermen or made profits as landlords.[7]

The discovery of this widespread corruption led the central and provincial governments to reflect on the nature of the Shuangcheng banner government. General Guqing attributed the corruption to the fact that all local officials, including the principals—the assistant commandant and the captains—were locally appointed:

> It is because all the officials of Shuangcheng are selected from the soldiers in the local area. Once they become officials, all their subordinates are their previous co-workers. With this familiarity and tie, the officials not only are unable to supervise their subordinates and rectify problems but [they] also protect one another. As this practice becomes a habit, even someone who has some conscience is forced to compromise with them.[8]

In other words, the official appointments in Shuangcheng contradicted the philosophy of local governance in the Qing, which followed strict rules of avoidance that forbade officials from taking posts in their native places to prevent corruption.

By the late imperial period, China's long tradition of autocracy with a centralized bureaucracy had established a normative model of local government. The county government was the lowest administrative level. The central government appointed magistrates as representatives to oversee local society. The magistrate was responsible for implementing policies promulgated by the central government, collecting taxes, and maintaining local order.[9] Since the political system was autocratic, there was no independent institution to check political power, and so the central government separated local officials from local society. The rule of avoidance is one such example. It forbade official candidates from taking posts not only in their native places but also in places in which they had a close connection.[10] The purpose of this policy was to prevent local officials from developing personal interests that would lead to corruption. This system ensured the state better control over bureaucrats.

The early history of the Shuangcheng banner government, however, represents an unusual case of local governance in late imperial China: a government in which all appointed officials were from the local area. This situation evolved from the mismatch between the military nature of Shuangcheng banner government and the oversight of civil affairs. The court designed the Shuangcheng banner government after the model of a banner garrison. Since the function of banner garrisons was to guard strategically important locations and to police the local areas, the court seldom applied the rule of avoidance to garrison officials; except for the positions of banner general and commander-in-chief (*dutong*), it was a common practice to appoint officials from within (Ding 2003, 145–52). Moreover, during the settlement stage, the court considered it important to appoint officials who were familiar with the local conditions to supervise particular settlements. However, the massive land area in Shuangcheng and its nature as a rural settlement determined that the local government also functioned like a civilian government in the supervision of the socioeconomic life of local society. As Guqing put it, "While [the function of] other banner garrisons is mainly to supervise and control the local place, the government of Shuangcheng specializes in settlement and land management, which is where profits come from. The corrupt practices involved are indeed a long story."[11] In other words, the case of Shuangcheng proved the court's concern that had led to the rule of avoidance: once political power merged with economic interests in local society, corruption arose.

As a story of the Qing consolidation of power in a frontier society, the early history of Shuangcheng offers an opportunity to examine the meaning of the late imperial state and its power in local society. While power was highly concentrated under the imperial political system, the Qing relied on local officials to act as representatives to carry out its rule. Thus, the success of imperial control of local society had two components: local officials represented the interests of the central government, on the one hand, and they were capable of implementing state policies, on the other. But the locally appointed officials in Shuangcheng had multiple interests based on their different roles: they represented the state, the immigrant group they belonged to, and themselves as individuals. Although they acted as state representatives in organizing the immigrants and maintaining order in Shuangcheng, their conflicting group and personal interests in power and wealth often called their authority into question. Officials often became embroiled in conflicts between different waves of settlers and between the metropolitan and rural bannermen. As a result, the Qing consolidation of power in Shuangcheng involved two interactive processes, at the administrative and the societal levels. At the administrative level, the state's consolidation of power meant incorporating the Shuangcheng local government into the imperial order. At the societal level, it meant a consolidation of the immigrant society: the different immigrant groups gradually developed common interests and agreed on a local identity.

The years between 1815 and 1852 were crucial for the consolidation of power in Shuangcheng. From 1815, when the banner government was established from scratch, to 1852, when the court finally carried out institutional reform, it took the Qing thirty-seven years to complete this consolidation. The consolidation process took place along with four developmental stages of the Shuangcheng banner government. From 1815 to 1823, before the arrival of the first group of metropolitan bannermen, officials from rural-bannerman families dominated the local banner government. Over time, a local identity gradually came into being. Then, between 1824 and 1829, upon the arrival of metropolitan bannermen, the tension between metropolitan and rural bannermen broke down the order of the young immigrant society. Problems of local governance surfaced. In the 1830s and 1840s, the immigrant society gradually consolidated, and private activities of land cultivation became widespread. Corruption arose as local officials began using their power to accumulate wealth. Finally, in 1852, the central government reformed local banner government to reassert its power and control.

THE EARLY BANNER GOVERNMENT, 1815–1823

Structure and Personnel

At the time of its founding, the Shuangcheng banner government was only a government prototype that lacked independent adjudication. When the state created the settlement in 1815, it established a small-scale administration, equipped with a provisional assistant commandant (*wei xieling*), two provisional captains (*wei zuoling*), and two provisional lieutenants (*wei xiaoqi xiao*), to administer the first one thousand rural bannermen from Jilin.[12] Fujun selected all these officials from the banner garrisons in Jilin.[13] The provisional assistant commandant acted as the principal official. Each provisional captain, with the assistance of a provisional lieutenant, supervised one wing—twenty of the forty villages—in the central *tun*. Their major task was to see that the rural bannermen settled in smoothly and cleared the land that had been assigned to them. The provisional assistant commandant had a staff consisting of two tax preceptors and twenty soldiers; and each provisional captain had a staff of two tax preceptors and fifteen soldiers. However, the provisional assistant commandant lacked the authority to adjudicate disputes. Instead, he had to report them to the vice commander-in-chief in Alchuka.

By 1820, after the settlement of the right and the left *tun*, the banner administration in Shuangcheng was formalized and significantly expanded to accommodate the two thousand additional rural bannerman households. Banner officers from various garrisons in Shengjing joined the local banner government. The 120 banner villages were then organized into three sets of Eight Banners. An assistant commandant supervised the entire area, and a captain acted as the principal official of a wing of four banners. As Table 4.1 shows, the Shuangcheng banner government had one assistant commandant and six captains. Each captain

TABLE 4.1
The staff of the Shuangcheng banner government, 1820

Title	*Number*	*Annual Salary (taels of silver)*	*Land (*shang*)*	*Housing (N. of rooms)*
Assistant commandant (*xieling*)	1	130	80	10
Captain (*zuoling*)	6	105	50	8
Lieutenant (*xiaoqixiao*)	6	60	30	6
Scribe (*bitieshi*)*	5	36 or 24	20 or 16	3 or 4
Ad hoc officer (*weiguan*)*	5	36 or 24	20 or 16	3 or 4
Tax preceptor (*lingcui*)	16	36	20	4
Soldier (*jiabing*)	120	24	16	3
Total number of officials	159			

SOURCES: The order from the general of Jilin to the local banner government in 1819.10 (SCPTTJL, 130–31). Salary information is drawn from BQTZ, book 2, 862 and the salary books in SCPZGYMDA.

NOTE: *The posts of scribe and ad hoc officer did not have separate rank and were filled by tax preceptors or soldiers. Therefore, the salaries of these posts were determined by the previous rank and salary of the specific official.

was assisted by a lieutenant (*xiaoqixiao*).[14] Following this expansion, the Shuangcheng government acquired the right to adjudicate civil disputes, though it still had to report criminal cases to the vice commander-in-chief in Alchuka. The assistant commandant's office was staffed with two scribes and two ad hoc officers (*weiguan*) to process paperwork and miscellaneous tasks that arose.[15] Similarly, each *tun* also had one scribe and one ad hoc officer. An additional sixteen tax preceptors and 120 soldiers staffed the various offices.

In Shuangcheng, these local officials enjoyed material wealth generated by their state positions. As Table 4.1 shows, they not only received monetary stipends but also enjoyed *suique* land and housing from the state. An assistant commandant received 130 *taels* of silver, eighty *shang* of land, and a ten-room house; a captain received 105 *taels* of silver each year, fifty *shang* of land, and a house with eight rooms; a lieutenant received sixty *taels* of silver each year, thirty *shang* of land, and a six-room house; a tax preceptor received a yearly stipend of thrity-six *taels* of silver, twenty *shang* of land, and a house with four rooms; a soldier received twenty-four *taels* of silver each year, sixteen *shang* of land, and a house with three rooms. The income from these lands was distributed to individual officials to be used at their discretion, with the understanding that it would be spent to pay office expenditures and business travel. Moreover, although they had to return their land allotment and house when they left their posts, these officials were also well-supported in retirement. In early 1822, Fujun reserved land in the northern part of Shuangcheng to be assigned to retired officials.[16]

The Shuangcheng banner government had both similarities and differences to a civilian county government. In terms of governance, the assistant commandant acted like a county magistrate to supervise the entire region, taking charge of adjudication and general administration. The tax preceptors, scribes, and soldiers acted like scribes and runners in a county government to handle the routine tasks, such as paperwork and rent collection.[17] Yet, compared to a county magistrate, who had very few subordinate officials (Ch'ü 1962, 9–13), the assistant commandant had captains and lieutenants who administered their respective banners and reported to him. This difference indicated that the banner government was still a military system, and therefore there was closer supervision of the banner immigrants. Moreover, unlike the civilian system, under which the scribes and runners were ineligible for promotion to official positions, the hierarchy of banner posts formed a ladder of success for bannermen. In theory, a bannerman could first become a soldier and then move up in sequence to the posts of tax preceptor, ad hoc officer, scribe, lieutenant, captain, and finally, assistant commandant. When the assistant commandant of Shuangcheng finished his term, he could advance to the posts of assistant commandant in other banner garrisons in Jilin.[18]

Tension with Provincial Officials

In the early years of settlement, both the court and the provincial government paid close attention to the progress of the land clearing efforts and the protection of banner land from civilian commoners. This created a tension between the provincial and local officials. Disappointed by reports of the slow progress in land clearing, the banner generals placed a great deal of pressure on the local officials, who were responsible for ensuring that the settlement and land clearing efforts went smoothly. As the principal official, the assistant commandant was the first to be blamed if the land clearance goal was not reached.

Moreover, the civilian assistants employed by Fujun to supervise the settlement also challenged the local officials. Although they did not hold formal official posts, these civilian assistants had power as representatives of the general of Jilin, and they watched the local officials closely. In 1820, Dou Xinchuan—Fujun's civilian assistant—reported that the local banner officials "did not properly direct the settlement."[19] In response to this report, Fujun demoted the major officials, citing the evidence that five years after the central *tun* was established, the immigrants had neither cleared enough land nor built enough houses.[20] Mingbao, the assistant commandant, was demoted to the post of captain in the central *tun*, and the two captains in the central *tun* were sent back to their places of origin and demoted to defense (*fangyu*) posts.

If the demotions of Mingbao and the captains were indicative of the tension between the different levels of state representatives, the suicide of Shujing'e—Mingbao's successor—was an even crueler sign of the heightened pressure on local officials. Prior to taking the post of assistant commandant in Shuangcheng, Shujing'e had served as a captain in the Bordered Red Banner in Jilin.[21] Fujun had appointed him assistant commandant of Shuangcheng based on a favorable review of his performance as a captain, which had included the comment that Shujing'e was "diligent and sharp in personality and serious in administration."[22] When Shujing'e moved to Shuangcheng in 1820, at the age of fifty-three, to serve as assistant commandant, his younger brother—Shuyi—had served as a lieutenant there for five years.[23] In addition to the replacement of major officials in Shuangcheng, 1820 also marked the completion of the relocation of all three thousand rural banner households. Now, the court in Beijing stepped up its efforts to recruit metropolitan bannermen, and the need to speed up the preparation of land and housing in Shuangcheng became even more pressing to the provincial and local officials. It was this heightened pressure together with the fear instilled by the imperial rule that eventually led to Shujing'e's tragic end.

Soon after Shujing'e had started to serve in Shuangcheng, Fujun showed his dissatisfaction with the new assistant commandant's inefficiency in managing the settlement. In the eighth month of 1820, Fujun learned from Dou Xinchuan's report that some rural bannermen had not only arrived as individuals but also had not yet received their farm tools.[24] Moreover, windows and doors had not yet been installed in some of the houses assigned to the newcomers. Fujun sent a reprimand to Shujing'e, urging him to take care of these problems and reminding him of what had happened to Mingbao.[25] For the next two years, Fujun repeatedly admonished Shujing'e for his inability to speed up the land clearing.[26]

The tension between the local and provincial officials escalated upon the arrival of another civilian assistant of Fujun, Wang Lütai. With the expansion of the settlement, Fujun submitted a memorial in 1821 proposing the use of more civilian assistants to help supervise the settlement, and subsequently assigned Wang Lütai to Shuangcheng.[27] Like Dou Xinchuan, Wang Lütai was a banished official. Prior to coming to Shuangcheng, he had served as the prefect (*zhifu*) of the Daming prefecture in Zhili. However, during the period of national mourning for the Jiangqing emperor in 1820, he indulged in entertainment and drank with courtesans and was banished to Heilongjiang for "violating the rules" (*wei zhi*).[28]

Because Fujun evaluated Wang's governing abilities highly, he asked the court to reassign Wang to Jilin and brought him to Shuangcheng.

Compared to Dou Xinchuan, who had served as a magistrate in various counties, Wang had had a more prominent position prior to his banishment. In the Qing, while a county magistrate was only ranked 7a, a prefect had a rank of 4b, which was two-and-a-half ranks higher. Moreover, Daming prefecture was one of the most populous prefectures in Zhili province, where Beijing was located. By 1820, the Daming prefect supervised one subprefecture (*zhou*) and six counties, and had the second-largest population—1,964,872—of all the prefect-level administrations in Zhili province (Liang 1980, 376, table 88; Niu 1990, 4–5). In Shuangcheng, Wang soon showcased his ability in shepherding the immigrants and documented all his activities in a work he compiled, *The Brief History of the Shuangcheng Settlement* (*Shuangchengpu tuntian jilue*).[29] According to the government correspondence collected in this book, he diligently went down to the villages and investigated the individual progress of each farm. During these trips, he also gathered the villagers together to admonish them about working harder, and even taught them proper farming skills.

Shujing'e, however, resisted Wang's proactive policies. In 1821, Wang tried to ask the Shuangcheng immigrants to grow cotton and raise silkworms to produce clothing materials. However, neither industry was suitable for Shuangcheng. In particular, Shujing'e viewed the raising of silkworms as a disruption of agricultural production, because one had to go as far as one or two hundred *li* away, to the forest, to raise them, which would result in a shortage of labor in the banner villages.[30] According to the account by Shuyi, Shujing'e had "earnestly persuaded" Wang Lütai to give up this effort.[31] In 1822, Shujing'e petitioned to Fujun to stop promoting silk production.[32] Fujun agreed with Shujing'e and decided to limit silk production to households that had cleared at least twenty *shang* of land.[33] According to Shuyi, Wang resented Shujing'e for interfering.[34]

Fear of Imperial Power

Wang Lütai soon sought revenge against Shujing'e, taking advantage of the central government's concern regarding civilian commoners' encroaching on banner land. In 1822, the court removed Fujun from the post of the general of Jilin and instead appointed Songlin, the former general of Heilongjiang, to the post. Very likely, this personnel change was due to Songlin's report that twenty-one civilian households lived in the banner section in Shuangcheng, working as hired laborers for bannermen.[35] Despite the small number of civilian households, the court still considered it a violation of the state policy. In 1823, Dou Xinchuan left Shuangcheng after fulfilling his term, leaving Wang as the only civilian assistant who was knowledgeable in administrative affairs.[36] Moreover, Songlin was in poor health, making Wang Lütai even more powerful; Wang fully represented the general of Jilin in handling the affairs in Shuangcheng and even drafted memorials and orders on Songlin's behalf.[37] In the eighth month of 1823, Wang drafted a memorial, impeaching Shujing'e and other local officials for allowing civilian commoners to live in the banner section and farm the land there.[38] Writing as of the general of Jilin, Wang made a specific request that Shujing'e be demoted to the post of captain and left the punishment of other local officials to the discretion of the Board of War.

The impeachment made Shujing'e panic. After submitting the memorial, Wang Lütai and Songlin did not file a copy at the provincial office, as was required by official protocol, leading to wild speculation and rumors about what had happened.[39] All the officials, including Shujing'e, knew about the impeachment but did not know the details. Shujing'e anxiously went to see Songlin, requesting to resign his official position. Songlin turned down the request and asked him to continue in the job. Perhaps having learned more information from Wang Lütai's friend, a civilian commoner named Jiang Shuhe, Shujing'e went to see Songlin again on the twelfth day of the ninth month, when the general was visiting Shuangcheng. During this meeting, Shujing'e tried to explain to the general that he in fact had been following Fujun's order in allowing the civilian commoners to live in the banner section.[40] Songlin refused to discuss it with him.

Feeling wronged and in tremendous fear of the possible repercussions, Shujing'e committed suicide. According to Shuyi, Shujing'e confided in his younger brother all the bitterness and fear he felt.[41] He told Shuyi that Jiang Shuhe said that the impeachment had contained the phrase "violating the edict" (*weizhi*). He cried, "How can our officials tolerate such a charge?" He even asked Shuyi, "What would you do if [the emperor] ordered me executed?" At dawn of the fourteenth day,

Shujing'e wrote an indictment to present to the gods in the other world (*yinzhuang*), which was full of the word "injustice" (*yuan*) and accusations against Wang Lütai and Muteng'e, the vice commander-in-chief of Alchuka, who had also clashed with Shujing'e over administrative affairs. Then he hanged himself.[42]

The death of Shujing'e provides a concrete example of the terror the Qing autocracy inspired among local officials. Ultimately, the reason for Shujing'e's suicide was his fear of the consequences of the accusation that he was "violating the edict." Under the imperial system, the emperor had absolute power, and all officials and subjects had to obey his edicts. The edict in Shujing'e's case was one issued in 1822 that forbade civilian commoners with families from living in the banner section in Shuangcheng. Although violating it was a serious enough infraction to cost his official position, it was not a fatal mistake. In fact, on the third day of the ninth month, the Daoguang emperor replied to Songlin's memorial and agreed with the proposed punishment that would have demoted Shujing'e to the post of captain while still allowing him the opportunity for future promotion.[43] Unfortunately, Shujing'e was not strong enough to wait for the emperor's reply to arrive in Shuangcheng. He interpreted "violating the edict,"—that is, challenging the absolute power of the emperor—as the equivalent of a death sentence. According to Shuyi, Shujing'e wrote on the indictment: "As humans, we all want to live, but one cannot live if he violates the edict."[44] This belief caused the mental breakdown that led to his tragic ending of his life.

Shujing'e's death also shocked Songlin and Wang Lütai. In fear of appeals from Shujing'e's relatives, they asked Shuyi to burn the indictment written by Shujing'e. Then they coerced Shuyi into writing a statement saying that his brother committed suicide out of dread of punishment and that there was no injustice involved. After some futile resistance, Shuyi followed the general's order. Fearing the emperor's investigation, on the seventeenth day of the ninth month, Songlin and Wang Lütai forged another charge against Shujing'e—they falsely accused him and other local officials of illegally renting the land in the Shuangcheng seat to civilian commoners to line their own pockets.[45] Because this charge involved corruption, it was much more serious than the previous one and made the suicide of Shujing'e seem well deserved. As usual, Wang

Lütai drafted the memorial in front of Songlin and a few other officials. However, events took a dramatic turn; Songlin, who was already very ill, died on the same day, right after the memorial was written.

After the death of Songlin, Shuyi finally appealed Shujing'e's case and accused Wang Lütai of manipulating his supervisor and taking personal revenge.[46] Shuyi first appealed the case in front of the vice commander-in-chief of Alchuka. Receiving no reply, in 1824, Shuyi submitted his accusation to Songyun, who was Songlin's replacement as general of Jilin (1823–1824). However, Songyun's priority was the settlement of the metropolitan bannermen and so he held off the investigation of the case.[47] Disappointed, Shuyi next submitted his accusation to Rongzhao and Qiying, the imperial envoys who had accompanied the metropolitan bannermen to Shuangcheng. Meanwhile, the court reappointed Fujun to the post of general of Jilin to replace the ineffective Songyun. Finally, in the fourth month of 1824, the two imperial envoys and the general of Jilin—Rongzhao, Qiying, and Fujun—adjudicated this case. Wang Lütai confessed everything; he admitted that he had drafted the impeachment in Songlin's name and that he had done so because of his personal grudges against Shujing'e.[48] The imperial envoys and Fujun suggested that Wang Lütai's sentence should be banishment in Ili, a remote garrison in northwestern China. In a related move, Fujun soon petitioned the emperor to drop all the charges Wang Lütai had filed in his impeachment against the local officials.[49]

The death of Shujing'e and its aftermath shed light on how the Qing power hierarchy operated in local society. The difficulty of frontier settlement, especially, dramatized the tensions between the multiple state representatives: the central, provincial, and local officials. Although officials at all levels prioritized the emperor's will, they had different interests in implementing state policies. As the principal of the officials, Shujing'e represented the interests of rural bannermen, who had experienced tremendous hardship in trying to build houses and clear land for the incoming metropolitan bannermen. But he was still subordinate to the provincial and central governments. And even though an official like Wang Lütai was able to manipulate the power of the general of Jilin to exact personal revenge on Shujing'e, the bureaucratic system had the mechanisms in place to check and rectify the wrongdoing.

LOCAL GOVERNANCE IN AN AGE OF CONFLICT, 1824–1829

When Shuyi was appealing his brother's case to the imperial envoys in 1824, the first fifty-three households of metropolitan bannermen arrived, turning a new page in the history of Shuangcheng. For rural bannermen who had been settled in Shuangcheng for a few years, the time was ripe to construct an identity in their new home. For metropolitan bannermen, however, it was just the beginning of their long-term adaptation to the frontier. Because the metropolitan banner population was small at that point, the court did not appoint officials to supervise them until 1826.[50] Therefore, the metropolitan bannermen who arrived in 1824 and 1825 were under the direct supervision of local officials appointed from among the rural bannermen. Without powerful representatives, the metropolitan bannermen found themselves aliens in Shuangcheng. They not only had to deal with the strange rural environment but also faced an overwhelming number of rural bannermen who had different lifestyles. The tensions and conflicts between the metropolitan and the rural bannermen were also reflected in the local administration.

Searching for Power and Identity

Following the court's rectification of Shujing'e's case, Shuyi and some immigrants promoted him to the celestial official of city god (*chenghuang*).[51] According to Shuyi, his subordinate, together with some immigrants, initiated this action. At first, a civilian commoner surnamed Huang erected a simple temple made of wooden boards, used for worshiping to Shujing'e's portrait. In 1828, a rural bannerman named Fucheng and a tax preceptor named Tuoyun sent a proposal to Shuyi for upgrading the temple. Fucheng offered to donate timber, and Tuoyun volunteered to collect money to pay for the construction. Shuyi adopted a half-declining and half-accepting attitude, answering, "What kind of virtue did my brother have [that he deserves you two to build a temple for him]?" Then, Shuyi encouraged the two by telling them that he dreamed of Shujing'e becoming the city god. With Shuyi's support, the construction of the temple began. Fucheng took charge of the logistics, and Tuoyun collected 1,070 strings of cash from local merchants and banner immigrants to cover the costs. Finally, they built a city god temple with a tiled roof. They also erected a statue of Shujing'e and performed a consecration ceremony that included staged dramas. Although the extant sources do not record the details of the ceremony, like most temple affairs in the country, it may well have been a large gathering.

Obviously, Shuyi built the city god temple to enhance his own authority and that of his brother. When Shujing'e's case was concluded in 1824, Shuyi was one of two captains in the central *tun* and was in charge of twenty villages. Moreover, after several personnel changes, he was the only official who had continuously served in Shuangcheng since the beginning of the settlement. This seniority gave him considerable authority and, at the same time, encouraged him to acquire more. By promoting his brother to a sacred position, Shuyi also benefited from being the blood relation of a deity and thus was able to enlarge his power.

However, backed by the cult of the city god, this event also carried cultural and social meanings that extended far beyond Shuyi's personal interest. The cult of city god emerged in China during the sixth and seventh centuries in walled cities in the Yangzi River region and spread throughout the country in the eighth to twelfth centuries (Johnson 1985; Atsutoshi 1992). City gods are anthropomorphic deities based on specific figures in local history. They are recognized as tutelary deities of cities and are considered local officials in the other world. People believed that the city god would protect the local area and respond to people's various needs. Not only did commoners worship the city god; many local officials considered worshipping the city god temple the first thing they should do on taking office in a particular area. In the Ming and Qing dynasties, the court institutionalized the cult of city god, turning it into a national system and highlighting the underlying imperial ideology; each city god was an official appointed by a central authority in the other world (Atsutoshi 1992). Therefore, in the Qing, almost every city had a city god temple. At the same time, the court also suppressed the anthropomorphism of the city gods; thus, not every city god figure was associated with a real person in local history.

In the context of the cult of city god, Shuangcheng officials and immigrants erected the temple to mark the beginning of Shuangcheng's history as a permanent settlement—a political and commercial center on a rural frontier. By 1828, the first group of rural banner immigrants had been settled for more than thirteen years, and even those who came in

1819 and 1820 had lived in this frontier society for about ten years. In the Shuangcheng seat, a small business area with shops also appeared. Over time, immigrants gradually recognized Shuangcheng as their new home and developed a sense of belonging. Shuyi's recounting of the history of the city god temple might not be a true story; nevertheless, it represents this consolidating social process in Shuangcheng; the fact that the three activists came from three respective backgrounds—civilian commoners, rural bannermen, and local officials—indicated that local officials and immigrants of different status demanded a deity to protect their new home, a symbol that could tie immigrants of all walks together, and a site that could convey the history of the new home to descendants.

The fact that immigrants promoted Shujing'e as the city god indicates that they perceived Shuangcheng to be an integral part of the imperial system. Shujing'e's official post in Shuangcheng justified him as city god figure under the imperial ideology. Although he had no legendary stories, extant records depict Shujing'e's loyal subordination to the emperor. As a captain in his place of origin, he was diligent and serious in carrying out administrative tasks. As the assistant commandant in Shuangcheng, he faithfully followed the policy implemented by the general of Jilin, was therefore accused of "violating the edict," and finally committed suicide because he could not tolerate the charge. Many city god figures in China proper had also died in office (Johnson 1985). The fact that Shujing'e committed suicide while still holding the post of assistant commandant lead people to believe that he would continue to be a principal official in the other world, and therefore deserved worship.

At the same time, the anthropomorphic features of the Shuangcheng city god represent an alternate view of the local history constructed by the central government; this alternate view features local officials and immigrants trying to promote the importance of a first-generation local official. The fact that the Shuangcheng settlement was the end result of an imperial project to relocate bannermen guaranteed that there would be strong intervention by the central and provincial governments. The narrative of Shuangcheng history created by the central government gave credit to Fujun and his Han-Chinese assistants for founding this frontier society, marginalizing the contributions of local officials. Fujun, as the banner general who laid the blueprint, is unarguably a legendary figure in local history. The edicts, memorials, and government orders collected by Wang Lütai in the *Brief History of Shuangcheng Settlement* also established the emperor and provincial officials as diligent supervisors who often admonished the local officials for ineffective governance. In this context, the promotion of Shujing'e by Shuyi and others was a way to draw attention to immigrants' efforts in founding Shuangcheng and to construct a local identity. The anthropomorphic city god was particularly helpful in creating personal ties between individual deities and local people. Because Shujing'e was a real person who had lived in the area and an official who had recently died, people knew his name and what he looked like, and had heard stories about him—many had even known him personally. Moreover, he had a living brother who served in the government. This closeness would give rise to close ties among local officials and the immigrants. Therefore, the city god temple represents the attempt by Shuyi and others to establish the centrality of local officialdom in the history of Shuangcheng.

The 1829 Capital Appeal

Later developments in Shuangcheng's history proved Shuyi and other immigrants' effort to construct a local identity premature; at the time, the Shuangcheng society was still far from being consolidated. Between 1824 and 1828, as the rural bannermen were gradually developing a sense of belonging, 319 metropolitan bannermen households arrived in Shuangcheng. As the upper stratum of the elite in Shuangcheng, the metropolitan bannermen changed the overall composition of the population and upset the balance of power that this immigrant society was about to achieve. Clashes between metropolitan and rural bannermen eventually suppressed the emerging local identity and led to Shuyi's downfall.

Extant sources show that three of the first 187 Beijing pioneers responded actively to the settlement and became the spokesmen for metropolitan bannermen in the early years: Dezhong, a forty-eight-year-old supported soldier (*yangyubing*); his forty-five-year-old wife, woman Wu; and Deqing'an, a cavalry (*mabing*) and *shengyuan* title holder.[52] These three represented two of the first twenty-eight households that volunteered to move when the government began recruiting metropolitan bannermen in 1821.[53] Upon arriving in Shuangcheng, Dezhong even approached to Fujun to request that the banner administration allow his older brother, Deliang, to resign his banner post in Beijing and move to

Shuangcheng, because "both the house and land were good."[54] In the fifth month of 1824, in response to Fujun's request that two chief village heads (*zong tunda*) and two assistant village heads (*fu tunda*) be appointed from among the metropolitan bannermen,[55] Dezhong became one of the village heads in charge of the metropolitan banner households living in one wing (twenty villages) in the central *tun*.[56] Deqing'an also served as an instructor at the government school.[57] In the first two years of settlement, these were probably the highest positions held by any of the metropolitan bannermen in Shuangcheng.

The honeymoon, however, was brief, and a few years later these spokesmen began to express dissatisfaction with the relocation and the farm work. In 1828, when Boqitu, the general of Jilin, visited Shuangcheng, Deqing'an approached him and complained about all the hardship the metropolitan bannermen had to deal with in managing their land. Deqing'an even petitioned the general to cancel his own banner registration and to take away his land and house, so that he could work in other occupations without worrying about farming.[58] In 1829, woman Wu traveled all the way to Beijing and filed a capital appeal charging Shuyi with abusing his power and victimizing the metropolitan bannermen.[59] Wu's accusation originated from her family's conflicts with Shuyi. Shuyi had assigned her family a house that had leaks and uncultivated land, and had refused to replace the unsatisfactory house. In adjudicating a financial dispute between Dezhong and a rural bannerman named Decang, Shuyi had favored the rural bannerman. Moreover, when Wu argued with Shuyi about the decision, Shuyi forced Dezhong to divorce Wu, threatening to remove Dezhong from the village head position if he did not.

Wu, however, soon went beyond personal conflicts, marshaling every bit of evidence she could identify as related to Shuyi's abuse of power.[60] The first act of misconduct Wu pinpointed was Shuyi's collection of money from the immigrants in order to build a temple for his deceased brother Shujing'e. The second charge concerned the social hierarchy in Shuangcheng. The metropolitan bannermen, inexperienced in farming, always rented their land to rural bannermen and collected an annual rent of one *shi* of grain for each *shang* of land. However, Shuyi had forbidden the rural bannermen from renting land from metropolitan bannermen. This order gave the rural bannermen bargaining power, since the metropolitan bannermen's income depended on the rural bannermen's labor. Consequently, rural bannermen, by privately agreeing to cultivate land for metropolitan bannermen, only paid 0.3 or 0.4 *shi* for each *shang* of land—a sum that represented 30 percent to 40 percent of the original rent. Shuyi's third act of misconduct was that he used the metropolitan banner immigrants as servants for his dinner parties and treated them abusively. Wu also charged Shuyi with ordering merchants to use containers that were larger than the regular *dou* to trade in grains from immigrants. He also was charged with cheating the provincial and central government by falsifying the crop yield in 1828.

Eventually, this capital appeal turned into an accusation against the major officials in Shuangcheng and revolved around two interconnected issues: the excessive extraction of the local officials and their hostility to metropolitan bannermen. Along with her own accusation, Wu also presented an indictment written by Deqing'an.[61] Besides Shuyi, the assistant commandant Tusa, and a captain named Minglu were two other major defendants. In all, Wu and Deqing'an made twenty-eight allegations against the local officials; seven of these allegations explicitly concerned tensions between rural and metropolitan bannermen, seven challenged the local officials' opaque property status and their unfair extraction of labor by the immigrants, and one concerned both. Other than the above two, Wu and Deqing'an also questioned particulars of policy implementation and official appointment.

Husong'e, the general of Jilin (1829–1830), adjudicated this case. After an investigation, the officials either found excuses to defend their behavior or confessed their misconduct. Witnesses' depositions and government documents disproved some of the allegations.[62] For example, Shuyi did not force Dezhong to divorce Wu. The local officials did not falsify the crop yield in 1828, and there was no evidence to prove that local officials used metropolitan bannermen as servants at dinner parties. Also, some of the charges Wu filed against Shuyi were actually committed by Tusa. At the same time, abuses of power did occur. For instance, despite the fact that Shuyi's son, Wuerxibeng'a, could neither read and write, nor did he excel at horse riding—a requirement for banner officers and soldiers—Tusa promoted him to the post of scribe. In another case, Tusa beat a rural bannerman named Liushijiu just because the latter had failed to stand up and greet the assistant commandant when he entered a shop.

Tension Between Metropolitan and Rural Bannermen

In their indictments, Wu and Deqing'an used the tension between metropolitan and rural bannermen strategically to solicit the central authority's protection of their interests. As metropolitan bannermen, they were aware of their upper-elite status in the state-mandated hierarchy in Shuangcheng. They were also acutely aware of the state's special interest in settling them. Wu had made up the story that local officials used metropolitan bannermen as servants and beat them at dinner parties in order to dramatize their miserable situation. Deqing'an also made up the story that local officials had replaced the instructors in the government school with people from Jilin and Fengtian, when in fact all the instructors in the government school were metropolitan bannermen. Moreover, when complaining about the local officials' management and control of the rents collected from the civilian tenants farming the newly encircled areas, Deqing'an emphasized that the rents "were all embezzled by officials from Jilin and Fengtian in a private capacity,"[63] highlighting the corruption of the rural-origin officials.

At the same time, the hostility of the rural-origin officials to the metropolitan bannermen was probably real. Having enjoyed city life in Beijing as urban dwellers for years, these metropolitan bannermen came across as aliens to the rural bannermen. The government's special treatment of the metropolitan bannermen imposed a division between the two population categories of the haves. If this state-mandated hierarchy had already placed considerable pressure on rural bannermen and officials before 1824, the arrival of metropolitan bannermen only increased this tension. Shuyi's ban on rural bannermen renting metropolitan bannermen's land was the focal point. In his deposition, Shuyi defended himself by claiming that he was actually implementing Fujun's policy, which was aimed at enabling metropolitan bannermen to farm independently and thus to enjoy the greatest yield from their lands.[64] Shuyi even referred to sixteen placards stamped with the general of Jilin's seal as evidence. Although extant sources do not have proof of this radical policy, it probably existed in Shuangcheng for at least a short period of time, because the state policies fluctuated considerably in the early years. However, once the policy was implemented, rural bannermen soon seized the opportunity to pursue their interests by negotiating the lower rent. As one of the major local officials, Shuyi very likely was aware that this was happening but did nothing to protect metropolitan bannermen's interests.

Moreover, the inattention of some of the local officials to the housing situation also exacerbated metropolitan bannermen's difficulties. This was the case with Dezhong and Wu. Depositions by Shuyi and other witnesses reveal that he had not intentionally assigned Dezhong and Wu to a house with leaks.[65] In fact, Dezhong and Wu had chosen their house and land. However, the dimension of the walls did not meet the building requirements. A captain named Yiketang'a, who had supervised the construction of the house, confessed that this was due to the carelessness of the artisans and a lack of supervision. This unpleasant settlement experience aggravated the relationship between metropolitan and rural bannermen. The metropolitan bannermen began to attribute everything they found unsatisfactory to the corruption and hostility of the rural-origin local officials.

Extraction and Fiscal Management

The tension between metropolitan and rural bannermen was exacerbated by local officials' excessive extraction and opaque fiscal management. Husong'e investigated every accusation that involved property and money, trying to find out whether the officials lined their own pockets. Interestingly, it turned out that, except for Shuyi's temple building, the purpose of all the other incidents of extraction—either collecting money from local people or confiscating residents' property—was to pay for office expenditures. For example, Tusa collected a total of 360 strings of cash from shops in Shuangcheng to produce the thirty-six grain containers used in trade as the official measurement. After spending nearly half of the funds to make the grain containers, Tusa used the remaining half to buy office furniture and supplies, to build a house for the archives, and to pave a path leading from the yamen building to the gate. In another instance, Tusa and Shuyi confiscated the house of a civilian commoner named Duan Fuyi because of his gambling. Then they rented the house out and used the rent to buy office supplies.[66]

These examples reveal that the shortage of local revenue was especially keen in the early years. The central and provincial governments had invested a huge amount of money in the settlement—including on immigrants' transportation and travel expenses, immigrants' housing and government buildings, and everyday living goods—but almost no money on office and other public expenditures.[67] Although in the early 1820s the provincial government had assigned the rental income from two types of land—*suique* and *hengchan*—to pay for the local government's expenditures,[68] a shortage of labor had left most of this land uncultivated in the early years. Even in the case of cultivated lands, tenants were not required to start paying rent until the fifth or sixth year after the initial cultivation. This meant that, in the 1820s, the local government of Shuangcheng had little revenue.

In fact, the shortage of funding and the opaque fiscal management plagued local administration of Qing China (Ch'ü 1962; Zelin 1984; Wei, G. 2010). Throughout the Qing the state maintained a relatively low rate of taxation. After the central government took revenue away from local government, the budget left for magistrates was tight and barely sufficient to cover the office expenditures.[69] Moreover, the magistrates were supposed to use their salaries to pay miscellaneous costs of running the government,[70] including paying their personal advisers and the various financial contributions assigned by the provincial treasurer when the government funds were inadequate (Ch'ü 1962, 24). This situation placed the local fiscal management in a gray area. Local officials used informal or extralegal means to collect funds for office expenses (Zelin 1984, 46–54; Wei, G. 2010, 331–44). Since these funding sources were not audited by the provincial government, local officials had total autonomy in how they spent the money. From the perspective of the governed, this blurred the boundary between public and private.[71] Thus, the corruption of local officials has been a persisting problem in late imperial China.

The fiscal management in Shuangcheng shared all the above features. That Shuangcheng was a frontier newly settled by immigrants of different backgrounds and interests intensified this problem. As Shuangcheng's local officials with rural-banner origins confiscated residents' properties, directly collected money from residents, and rented the land in the

Shuangcheng seat to merchants to build shops, metropolitan bannermen experienced local officials not as state representatives but as competitors for wealth and property. The opaque management of the rents collected from the above public properties provoked a particularly strong reaction from metropolitan bannermen. Therefore, in his indictment, Deqing'an complained that "the officials from Jilin and Fengtian embezzled all the rents from the 'newly encircled areas' in a private capacity." He also accused Shuyi and Tusa of disseizing immigrants of their properties and profiting from their actions.[72]

Because of their distrust of rural-origin local officials and their feelings of alienation in Shuangcheng, metropolitan bannermen rejected the identity constructed by local officials and other immigrants. The interpretation of Shuyi's temple-building activity as corruption reflects these feelings. Metropolitan bannermen clearly understood the different interests of the central and local officials; while the central government's main concern was the successful settlement of metropolitan bannermen, the local officials mainly represented rural bannermen's interests. Shuyi's temple-building activity and the associated extractions incurred particular resistance from the metropolitan bannermen; they had no connections to Shujing'e or any sympathy for his situation. In their view, this deceased local official was the brother of Shuyi—someone who represented the rural bannermen's interests. Therefore, Wu and Deqing'an actively sought support from the central government.

Wu and Deqing'an's charging of local officials' extraction appealed to the central and provincial authorities. While dismissing some of their minor mistakes, Husong'e found Tusa and Shuyi guilty of two of the twenty-eight charges. Tusa was found guilty of collecting money from the shops to make the grain containers, despite the fact that he did not use the money for personal purposes. Husong'e classified this behavior into the category of "collecting money for official use without explicit orders from a supervisor."[73] He suggested sending Tusa to the Board of Punishment to discuss the appropriate sentence. Shuyi was found guilty of allowing Tuoyun to collect money from the immigrants to build a temple for his brother without reporting it to the general of Jilin. Husong'e determined that Shuyi had violated two regulations in the Qing code. The first was a substatute that stipulated that anyone wanting to build a temple or erect a statue must first file a request for permission with the governor or governor general. Only after the emperor approved the request, could they proceed (DQLL, 194, substatute 311). Second, because of Shuyi's relation to Shujing'e, Husong'e considered his temple-building activity as an instance of an official committing a crime for personal reasons. The sentence for the first crime was a hundred beatings with a club; for the second, it was removal from his post. Husong'e also punished other officials who were involved in these cases and ordered the city god temple torn down.

The general of Jilin's ruling reveals that the provincial and central government was especially cautious about local officials' excessive extraction of the local society—whether for personal or public purposes. Despite the Chinese state's high level of centralization, the rulers of Chinese dynasties were also careful not to put rural societies under excessive government control. For example, in the Ming dynasty, the founding emperor Zhu Yuanzhang laid out the basic regulations of local government: local officials must live and work in the county government; without a justified reason, officials should not leave the county government (He 2006, 80–84). This principle continued to guide the rulers and governors throughout the Qing dynasty.[74] Therefore, in the emperor's view, an ideal local government should have officials who were from outside of the local society and who imposed as little harassment as possible on the local society. The Shuangcheng banner government deviated from the model local government in that the officials had close ties to local society.

CONSOLIDATION, CORRUPTION, AND CONFLICTS, 1830S AND 1840S

In the two decades following the 1829 capital appeal, Shuangcheng society gradually consolidated. Three signs indicated this development: the adaptation of metropolitan bannermen to Shuangcheng society, the erection of temples throughout the area, and immigrants' private activities of land clearing. During this process, conflicts were less likely to grow out of tensions between different immigrant groups; rather, struggles between individuals over wealth and power were more often a source of discontent. Local officials used power to pursue wealth. At the same time, official position was not the only source of power; wealth also gave large landholders power to manipulate local officials. Thus, two types of people—local officials and wealthy landholders—often became the main characters in conflicts.

Consolidation

With the passage of time, most metropolitan bannermen overcame the hardship of initial settlement. As Jing'ebu reported in 1843, 360 of the 598 surviving metropolitan banner households were well off and twenty-two of them were especially affluent.[75] As more metropolitan banner households arrived in Shuangcheng, the quota of metropolitan-origin officials in local government increased. The court organized metropolitan bannermen under a separate wing and appointed individuals from the group as officials. Moreover, the state intentionally created more official posts than the standard quota for one wing unit; this not only facilitated administration but also offered these urban dwellers more opportunities for state stipends. By 1843, besides the one captain and two lieutenants, the court had appointed altogether twenty-eight tax preceptors and soldiers—a total that exceeded the regulated number of precepts and soldiers equipped for one metropolitan banner wing by eleven.[76] In 1844, in order to provide more support to some of the metropolitan bannermen, the court created another forty soldier positions among them.[77] Compared to the 159 rural-origin officials and soldiers, the metropolitan-origin officials and soldiers were still the minority, but given their smaller population size, the metropolitan bannermen were in fact over represented in the local government.

Temple-building by the immigrants continued, and the cult of Guandi—Chinese god of war—thrived. By the Qing, Guandi, an apotheosized hero figure named Guan Yu (162–220), was widely worshiped in North China as a guardian and protector. The Qing state also promoted the worship of this folk deity as an official cult. Some well-known Guandi temples were selected as official temples, and government-sponsored sacrifices were held regularly. The cult of Guandi was so widely accepted that without any government intervention, immigrants brought this cult to Shuangcheng. Among the nine temples recorded in the two gazetteers compiled in the early twentieth century as being built between 1820 and 1850, five worshiped Guandi (SCXZ 1973, 335–42;

SCXXTZ 2006, 640–42). As early as 1821, one or two years after their settlement, rural bannermen in the right and the left *tun* had built a Guandi temple in each.[78] In 1836, the officials, rural and metropolitan bannermen, and civilian commoners residing in the Shuangcheng seat and the central *tun* donated money to build a Guandi temple on the west street.[79] In 1849, a provisional scribe named Taqibu organized immigrants to build another Guandi temple outside of the east gate of the Shuangcheng seat.[80] Apparently, officials and immigrants from all walks participated in the building of Guandi temples.

Compared to the cult of the city god, the cult of Guandi served Shuangcheng better as a popular deity connected to immigrants' spirit world, not only because it is an official cult but also because the cult allowed people to attach different symbolic meanings to one diety according to their own needs, what Prasenjit Duara (1988b) calls a "superscribing symbol." In a period of more than one thousand years, different social and political groups and even the state have interpreted and adapted the Myth of Guan Yu. These interpretations emphasize the different things Guandi represents to different groups: he is a hero who is loyal to authority, a protector of temples and communities, and a provider of health and wealth.[81] These qualities are related to each other and coexisted harmoniously in one deity figure. As a "superscribing symbol," Guandi was especially suited to a newly established immigrant society; immigrants from different social and cultural background were able to take what they needed from the same deity. This also enabled immigrants to re-interpret the image of Guandi in relation to Shuangcheng, thereby coping with the changing social environment.

As immigrants adapted to Shuangcheng, they also gradually increased their family wealth. According to the two capital appeals cited in the beginning of the chapter, in the 1830s and 1840s, officials and immigrants started to clear unassigned land on their own. This development also fits the "potential development" stage in Colson and Scudder's (1982) theoretical framework with respect to the resettlement of involuntary migrants. At this stage, immigrants adapted to the new environment and began to seek new opportunities. Consequently, new social organizations developed, and inequalities widened. This was also the case in Shuangcheng.

Corruption and the Sources of Power

While numerous immigrant households benefited from private land clearing, this process also featured land grabbing by local officials and the rise of some large landholders. In this period, the officials of Shuangcheng were still appointed from the local area and had considerable resources. Prior to 1830, there was no clear evidence that officials used their power for personal gain; beginning in the 1830s, local officials explicitly took advantages of power to line their own pockets. More strikingly, lower-ranked officials, especially, actively profited from their power. For example, while administering the land lots in the streets of the Shuangcheng seat between 1835 and 1843, a scribe named Zhang Jianlong acquired twenty-eight housing lots and collected rent on each lot as his personal income.[82] People gave him the nickname "half-city Zhang" (*Zhang bancheng*). He also privately cultivated eighty-seven *shang* of unassigned land. Another scribe named Taishanbao and a provisional tax preceptor named Delu also privately occupied housing lots in the Shuangcheng seat. These cases represent only the tip of the iceberg.

Some metropolitan bannermen participated in private land cultivation and became rich. For example, the aforementioned woman Wu's household controlled a large amount of land and emerged as a wealthy landlord. In addition to the allocated *jichan* plot, she was able to privately cultivate more land and rented it to a tax preceptor named Wuligunne.[83] In 1837, she also acquired a housing lot in the Shuangcheng seat and rented it to a civilian commoner named Xin Rong to build a shop, collecting an annual rent of 120 strings of cash. Wu also showcased her wealth and status by owning luxury goods. Sometime in the 1830s, her husband Dezhong died. Wu held an elaborate funeral procession for him, using a set of luxurious flags and objects (*zhishi*) that exceeded the scale of what Qing law permitted a regular bannerman to use.[84] This elaborate set of funeral goods was probably very rare in Shuangcheng, so that, later, a village head named Bakesanbu and a captain named Naerhong'a allegedly borrowed it from Wu for the funerals of their fathers.[85]

These cases indicate that while political power associated with official positions was important, capable individuals were able to seek power from other sources to pursue their interests. Woman Wu's power came partially from her wealth. While there is no record of Wu's initial wealth accumulation in Shuangcheng, it very likely began with the state stipends to metropolitan bannermen and Dezhong's position as village head. These would have enabled Wu to buy land and to recruit tenants. Eventually, she was able to use her wealth to manipulate officials of both metropolitan and rural origins and to seize more property. Wu was not only a large landlord but also a money lender. Her debtors came from various backgrounds, ranging from commoners to shopowners to local officials. For example, the shopowners Xilabu and Chenglu borrowed more than four thousand strings of cash from her; a regular bannerman named Zhao Tong borrowed nine hundred strings of cash; and a lieutenant named Ahong'a also borrowed one hundred strings of cash. Taking advantage of a lender-debtor relationship established in the late 1840s, Wu had Ahong'a help her seize 595 *shang* of farmland from a rural-origin soldier named Xilang'a. By 1851, Wu had collected more than one thousand strings of cash from these lands.

Wu also derived power from the imperial state; her litigiousness and the unofficial nature of land clearing in Shuangcheng enabled her to indirectly use the authority of the central government to achieve her goal. Wu's 1829 capital appeal demonstrated her ability to strategically file a lawsuit to attract the attention of the central authority. Building on her success in that appeal, Wu continued to use litigation to manipulate local politics. For example, in 1843, Wu and a metropolitan banner woman surnamed Gao filed another capital appeal, in which they accused six local officials, including Zhang Jianlong, of corrupt conduct. An investigation followed, and the general of Jilin found the officials guilty and punished them. Besides the capital appeals, Wu filed even more lawsuits at the local level.

These examples demonstrate that local people were able to use the state as a source of power to pursue their fortunes, and that they could do so because the officials in the central, provincial, and local governments had different interests. Despite their different interests, they all represented the state and therefore provided local people with multiple channels through which to appeal to the state authority. Thus, state power was present in local society in various forms. At the same time, local people were aware of the different interests of the multitude of state representatives and developed a practice of approaching state representatives until they found the one that could further their interests. This phenomenon existed in many regions of the world across time (Gupta 1995). It was also the case in Shuangcheng. Although the emperor had put into place mechanisms designed to prevent local people from using capital appeals to manipulate him and his subordinates (Ocko 1988), the corruption in Shuangcheng—private land cultivation and the embezzlement of government funds—was exactly what the emperor was wary of. Therefore, Wu was able to achieve her goal by filing capital appeals.[86] For two decades, she was very successful in using this strategy to accumulate wealth. In fact, the culture of local people using capital appeals to access imperial power for their own gain was prevalent in Qing-dynasty China (Ocko 1988; Li 2011).

All the above-mentioned developments—temple building, private land clearing, and corruption—converged in the struggle between woman Wu and some local officials over 595 *shang* of land. These 595 *shang* of land were cultivated by nine households of civilian commoners recruited by a bannerman named Xilang'a. In her 1843 capital appeal, Wu accused these civilian commoners of cultivating state land illegally. The provincial governor sentenced the lead tenant, named Zhou Rong, to prison and ordered the other tenants to stop cultivation, letting the land lie fallow.[87] However, the civilian commoners continued to cultivate the land. Thus, Wu sued these tenants at the local government level. A lieutenant named Qicheng'e investigated Zhou Rong, who had recently completed his sentence. When Zhou begged Qicheng'e to acquiesce and allow the private cultivation, Qicheng'e and Lieutenant Ahong'a, who was surveying the cultivation of *hengchan* land located north of Shuangcheng, asked him to negotiate with Wu, the plaintiff. Zhou therefore begged Wu for help. Wu agreed to settle the case and ensure that Zhou could continue the cultivation, on the condition that Zhou pay Wu a fee amounting to three years' interest of the rent from his land and agree to pay his rent to Wu in the future. In the end, all nine households accepted Wu as their landlord and paid their rent to her.[88] Although extant sources did not provide details on the settlement of the lawsuit, very likely, Wu used her connections in the local government to drop the charge against the civilian commoners. In fact, this lawsuit was within Wu's plan to seize the land. According to a claim by Wu, before she sued these civilian commoners, Ahong'a had made an agreement with her to use the rents paid by the nine households to repay his debt to Wu.[89]

While Wu enjoyed the rents from the 595 *shang* of land as her personal income, a local official named Taqibu saw an opportunity to use these rents for temple-building funds. Taqibu was a rural bannerman from Jinzhou, in Shengjing, who lived in Shuangcheng's central *tun*. In 1848 he advanced to the post of provisional scribe.[90] Probably in the same year, Taqibu investigated Zhou Rong for privately cultivating 595 *shang* of state land and found out that woman Wu was the landlord. He then investigated Wu. Following this investigation, Wu reportedly agreed to use the rent income from the land to fund temple building. In 1849, when the temple was built, Wu donated the land to the temple as a gift, establishing an inscribed board to document this donation.[91] A lieutenant named Yuqing, a scribe named Saerhang'a, two provisional scribes named Chenglu and Aerhang'a, a tax preceptor named Hechun, and a rural bannerman named Daxiu put their names down as witnesses and guarantors of the donation.[92] Taqibu was considered the owner of the temple. Consequently, Wu suffered a loss in her personal income.

The tension between woman Wu and Taqibu over the control of the rents led to a series of conflicts. Even after Wu's donation, Taqibu still did not trust her, suspecting that she continued to take the rents as her personal income. To find out the truth, Taqibu even investigated the Daoists in the temple and the civilian cultivators, which resulted in the suicide of a civilian cultivator named Zhou Zhongyuan.[93] In 1851, Taqibu's superior, Captain Fulehong'a, dismissed him from his official post for neglecting of duty. Considering the dismissal unjust, Taqibu filed a capital appeal, suing Fulehong'a and other local officials for allowing private land cultivation and making profit out of the unassigned state land.[94] When investigating this capital appeal, the general of Jilin paid attention to the 595 *shang* of land and questioned Wu. In response, Wu and Chenggui filed another capital appeal in 1852. The central government carried out the large-scale investigation of local officials and private land cultivation in Shuangcheng, as mentioned in the beginning of the chapter, and decided to reorganize the Shuangcheng banner government.

REFORMS

The Reform of Local Government

The central and provincial governments finally acted to tighten the control of Shuangcheng through institutional reform. In 1851, after adjudicating the capital appeal filed by Taqibu, Guqing submitted a memorial proposing an upgrade of the rank of the Shuangcheng banner government and a reform of the official appointment process.[95] Guqing pointed out that it had been more than thirty years since the initial settlement, and the population in Shuangcheng had significantly increased. An assistant commandant alone could no longer administer the area. He therefore proposed upgrading the title of the principal official of the local banner government from assistant commandant to area commander-in-chief (*zongguan*), with a rank equivalent to vice commander-in-chief.[96] Guqing also proposed that all the higher-ranked officials in Shuangcheng—assistant commandant, captain, and lieutenant—should be appointed from among qualified candidates from the banner garrisons throughout Jilin.[97] Similarly, officials in Shuangcheng also had opportunities to be promoted to banner posts all over Jilin. The court approved Guqing's proposal and, in 1852, the office of the area commander-in-chief was established in the Shuangcheng seat.

This reform first marked the centralization of the administration in Shuangcheng. The office of the area commander-in-chief had independent adjudication within its administrative area. Two departments were established: the Left Department, in charge of military-related affairs, including public security, criminal cases, personnel, and the military itself; and the Right Department, in charge of civil affairs, including finance, taxation, education, and population. The government also consolidated the three banner offices of the central, the right, and the left *tun* into a single office in the Shuangcheng seat. As the only government authority prior to 1882, the office of the area commander-in-chief administered the entire area, including not only the banner villages but also the civilian sections.[98]

Despite the military titles of its personnel, the structure of the Shuangcheng banner government after 1851 was in many ways analogous to that of a civilian county government. The local banner government was equipped with an area commander-in-chief, analogous to a magistrate, and two assistant commandants, analogous to an assistant magistrate (Figure 4.1). The area commander-in-chief—the primary official of the banner government—acted as magistrate to supervise the running of the government, adjudicate legal cases, make decisions on local affairs, and report to the general of Jilin. Six scribes worked for the area commander-in-chief. The core of the government comprised three departments: the Right Department, the Left Department, and the Seal Office, which was in charge of official seals and important documents. Each of the two assistant commandants supervised one of the Right and Left Departments.[99] The two assistant commandants concurrently acted as the principal of the respective wing divisions to supervise the banner captains (Figure 4.1).[100] As the lowest-level state institution, the captain's office was responsible for rent collection, land allocation, population and land registration, and security maintenance. Each captain's office was staffed by a lieutenant in charge of public security, one or two scribes to process official documents, three tax preceptor to collect rent, and a team of thirty-three to thirty-four soldiers led by two vanguards (*qianfeng*).

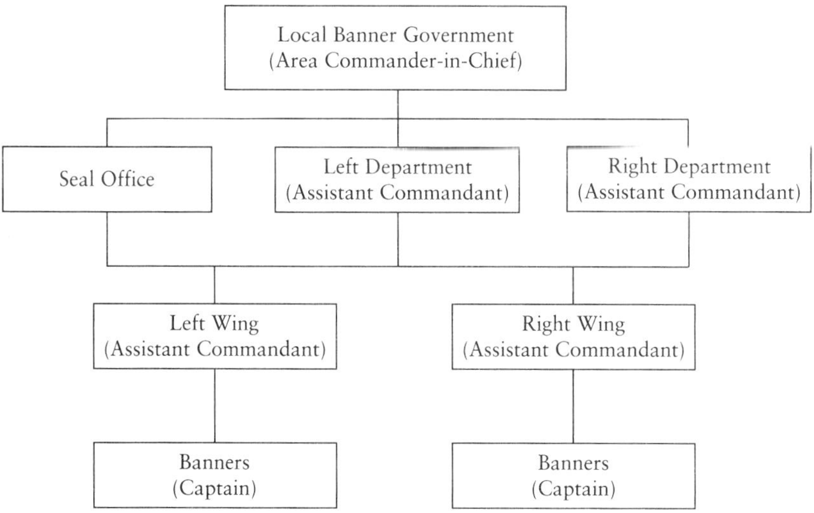

Figure 4.1. The structure of Shuangcheng banner government, 1852–1881.

SOURCES: The regulations regarding the adjustment of the Shuangcheng banner administration in 1855.5 (SCPZGYMDA, 1: 3: 34–54); in 1856.2 (SCPZGYMDA, 1: 1: 34–47); and on 1870.2.5 (SCPXLYMDA, no. 4506).

The restructuring enabled the court to better control official appointments in Shuangcheng. From the 1750s on, all generals, commanders-in-chief, and vice commanders-in-chief of banner garrisons had to be nominated to the Grand Council by the Board of War, so that the emperor could conduct an audience interview (*yinjian*) with each nominee (Ding 2003, 146). The Grand Council would then record the names of those who did sufficiently well in the audience interview on the "noted names" (*jiming*) lists, reserved for those who waited for job openings. When a vacancy appeared, the Grand Council would then consult the "noted names" lists to choose an appropriate candidate and wait for the emperor's special approval (Bartlett 1991, 196–99). This was also the practice in Shuangcheng after 1851. For example, Qingrui, the area commander-in-chief of Shuangcheng (1879–1882; SCXZ 1973, 107), was a Manchu bannerman from the Bordered Yellow Banner in Beijing.[101] He started his career as a scribe, and after fourteen years had ascended to the position of assistant commandant of the Guards' Division, in 1872. In the same year, the captain-general of the Guards' Division nominated him for promotion. In 1877, Qingrui was recommended to the emperor by the Board of War and was approved for the nomination of vice commander-in-chief. Then, in 1879, the emperor appointed him to the post of area commander-in-chief of Shuangcheng. This procedure significantly weakened the ties between the officials and the local society.

The opening up of higher-ranked posts to banner officials from all over Jilin helped to separate the local government from society. As Guqing's comment at the beginning of the chapter shows, Guqing believed that the exclusively local composition of the banner government was the root of the corruption. Although it still could not compare with the rule of avoidance implemented in the civilian government, Guqing's reform did significantly reduce the proportion of officials appointed from the local area. Table 4.2 shows that this policy significantly affected the composition of captains and lieutenants. In 1874, the "foreign" composition of the captains was especially prominent; five of the eight banner captains did not have a home in the 120 banner villages, which means they were probably not one of the original banner immigrants to Shuangcheng. A larger proportion of the lieutenants were from the local area; only two of the seven lieutenants were from elsewhere in Jilin. However, no single captain or lieutenant served the banners under which

TABLE 4.2
The location of the villages of residence of government personnel relative to the banners in which they worked, 1874

	RELATIONSHIP OF HOME TO THE BANNER THEY WORKED		
	INSIDE	OUTSIDE	
Count by title		*In the banner villages*	*Not in the banner villages*
Number of captains	0	3	5
Number of lieutenants	0	5	2
Number of scribes	4	4	4

SOURCES: The salary book of the officials and soldiers in Shuangcheng in 1874 (SCPZGYMDA, 184: 759: 21–39) and the 1874 household registration records (CMGPD-SC).

their residential villages were located, which indicated a rule of avoidance at the village level. Even the scribes, which Guqing did not include in his reform, were not exclusively from the local area; four of the twelve scribes were from somewhere else in Jilin. The composition of banner captains in 1880 reveals a similar pattern.[102] These examples indicate that after 1852 the Shuangcheng banner government became a state institution separate from the society it governed.

The Registration of Nazu Land

Following the institutional reform, the central and provincial governments registered all the land Shuangcheng immigrants privately cultivated, thereby creating a new category of *nazu*, or "rent-paying," land. The process took about three years to complete. In 1854, in his final report on the adjudication of the 1852 capital appeal, Jingchun proposed registering and collecting rents on more than forty-four thousand *shang* of privately cultivated land and another 7,800 *shang* of unassigned waste land, which the officials discovered in Shuangcheng during the land survey.[103] For Jingchun, the state controlling these lands was the only solution to the problem of private cultivation. The court approved the proposal, and began registering privately cultivated land under the names of the immigrants who had land entitlements and claimed ownership of the plot.[104] In the land register, the privately cultivated land was titled *ziken* (additionally cultivated) land. Under the landowners' names, the state recorded the number of plots and their sizes to indicate ownership. In return, the head of each household would pay an annual rent of 660 in cash for each *shang* of land, a standard rate that had applied to all *nazu* land in Jilin since 1852.

Besides the issue of control, the central government also registered these lands to increase revenue. This is in keeping with a national trend toward state recognition of private ownership on banner land that had begun in the early 1850s. In the second half of the nineteenth century, the increasing military expenditure necessary to quell foreign invasions and internal rebellions had aggravated the state's fiscal crisis, and the state turned to banner land as a new source of revenue. In 1852, the state started to collect rent on banner land in Beijing and North China.[105] In a related move, the state accepted land sales between bannermen and civilian commoners and recognized civilian commoners' ownership of banner land in other regions of China proper. In Shuangcheng, although the state still strictly prohibited land transfers between bannermen and civilian commoners, the recognition of private cultivators' ownership of *ziken* land generated rent income.[106] Of the rent of 660 copper coins that the owners paid for each *shang* of land, 600 were allocated to government revenue, and 60 were used to cover expenses incurred in rent collection, including office supplies and the stipends paid to government personnel.

From then on, the local banner government played the role of state representative, registering unassigned land in Shuangcheng under the category of *nazu* land, assigning these lands different titles. In 1856, the government classified the 7,817.9 *shang* of unassigned waste land that Jingchun had reported as *maohuang*, or "raw and uncultivated land," and opened it to legal residents in return for rent.[107] By then, all the farmland in Shuangcheng had been assigned. In 1879, again driven by an urgent demand for revenue, the state conducted another large-scale survey of land in Shuangcheng,[108] measuring the size of each plot and comparing it to the registered size. If the actual size exceeded the registered size as a result of the farmers' encroachment on the plot boundaries, the officials registered the additional land under the title of *fuduo*, or "extra land." From inception to completion, the survey took two years. In 1881, the government registered a total of 19,528.82 *shang* of *fuduo* land.[109] In 1883, an additional 1495.2 *shang* of *fuduo* land was registered. By 1904, the Shuangcheng banner government maintained a total of 70,289.5 *shang* of *nazu* land.[110]

This move also marked the centralization of fiscal management. The rent from *nazu* land became an important source of provincial revenue. In 1867, in addition to covering the local government's regular administrative expenses, the rent also paid 30 percent of the salaries of local officials.[111] In 1882, the percentage of officials' and soldiers' salaries paid from the rent increased to sixty.[112] Moreover, as a portion of provincial revenue, Shuangcheng also regularly provided ten thousand *taels* of silver from its rental income to Sanxing, a banner garrison in Jilin, to pay the officials' and soldiers' salaries.[113]

THE DIALECTIC OF IMPERIAL POWER

The Qing eventually strengthened its control in Shuangcheng. Along with the above-mentioned reforms, the court enlisted the help of existing social organizations and networks to disseminate the imperial ideology. The court kept the Guandi temple built by Taqibu and transformed it into an official temple. By 1868, at the latest, the government had started sponsoring the sacrifice of Guandi.[114] In 1874, two memorial temples were added to the Guandi temple, one dedicated to Fujun and the other to Woshine, the general of Jilin (1848–1850; SCXZ 1973, 86). The images of both generals represented the emperor and the state. These efforts tended to firmly establish the dominance of the imperial state, and the first-generation local officials faded from the historical memory of Shuangcheng people. In 1865, immigrants built another city-god temple in the Shuangcheng seat (SCXZ 1973, 339). The local gazetteer records nothing about the city god figure. Very likely, it was just an anonymous statue representing an official in the other world who was sent by a central authority. Similarly, the editors of the local gazetteer began the history of local banner government in 1852. Given the fact that this period also saw devolution of political power in China proper, the victory of the central state in Shuangcheng is especially noteworthy.

The Qing consolidation of power in Shuangcheng illuminates the hegemonic nature of imperial power: the state exerted undue influence in society not only because it established a top-down government system but also because it constituted the major source of power people drew on to pursue their interests. In other words, state domination did not deprive the local people of power; rather, the power local people had derived from the state. Scholars of state-society relations emphasize the existence of social groups opposing the state interests (Scott 1998). As Migdal (2001, 85) points out, even when local groups formed coalitions with the state's representatives, state institutions still had to compete with non-state institutions to establish "rules of daily behaviors." This was also true in Qing-dynasty Shuangcheng. Yet, the state succeeded in Shuangcheng because even people who did not share the state's interests found it convenient to use state power when it suited their interests. Not only did local officials use state power to seize land, but also commoners, such as woman Wu and others, frequently appealed to the state to intervene in their struggles over privately cultivated land, which the state prohibited.

Finally, the hegemonic nature of imperial power ensured that the state was eventually able to take power back from local people. When the Qing court consolidated its power, woman Wu met her downfall. In a memorial reporting on the adjudication of Wu's 1852 capital appeal, Jingchun called her "a female scoundrel" (*nüzhong guntu*) and condemned her land-grabbing activities and attempts to manipulate local politics.[115] As part of her sentence, Jingchun canceled her banner registration, expelling her from Shuangcheng.[116] In the end, Wu lost all her property and banner privileges. Wu's fate best illustrates the hegemony of the state: although individuals could try to manipulate state power for their own gain, they had no control of this power. In practice, competing individuals enlisted state power through levying charges against each other with officials. However, this was a risky practice, as the state representatives shifted administrative priorities according to changing circumstances. Once the state decided to tackle the problem of manipulation of power, the powerful could, like Wu, lose everything. State privileges could both create and destroy the powerful.

Along with the state efforts in building institutions and consolidating power in Shuangcheng, immigrants also started their own process of constructing the boundaries between different social groups and developing communities. Although the Qing institutionalized the banner villages and households in the process of settling immigrants, these social organizations soon gained a life of their own. The development of these organizations went hand in hand with local practices of land accumulation, transfer, and inheritance. During this process, the immigrants still relied on the state's power to achieve their goals. Immigrants negotiated with the state-designated structural inequality to build village communities, expand household wealth, and create their own upward and downward wealth mobility. The interplay of state rules and the development of these local organizations affected every aspect of the society and ultimately shaped the social hierarchy and identities.

PART II

SOCIAL DEVELOPMENT AND STRATIFICATION

CHAPTER FIVE

Community and Hierarchy

Banner Villages

As an institution that organizes agrarian communities, the village is an important place for examining the social and political structure of rural society. By tying peasant households to a fixed location, the village makes an agrarian community easy for outsiders to locate. This feature provides convenience for the state to map these communities and supervise them directly or indirectly. Yet, the social and political structure of agrarian communities is shaped by more intricate factors as well; other networks—such as kinship, religion, and market—interact with the village community to form the "cultural nexus of power."[1] This "cultural nexus of power" may overlap with or cut across the village communities, thereby creating varying power relations in different communities. For example, G. William Skinner (1964, 1971) emphasizes the importance of market, instead of the village community, in the economic and social life of peasants living on the Chengdu plain in Southwest China. This situation is correlated with the scattered residential pattern of households and a relatively high degree of commercialization in this region. By contrast, villages in the North China Plain were more insular entities in that households were clustered together and there was a low degree of commercialization (Huang 1985, 220–22). Thus, when studying the ways peasant households were embedded in the broader social and political structure of the region, scholars often start by examining the degree of solidarity of village communities: to what extent is a village cohesive, insular entity (ibid.; Duara 1988a; Chang 1991). This question is especially important for understanding the state control of local society: whether the formal and informal administrations at the village level were effective in penetrating the local society.

The history of the Shuangcheng banner villages shed light on this intellectual inquiry by asking the question the other way: to what extent and how these state-designed administrative units grow into cohesive communities. Unlike most villages, which are formed on natural settlements, the banner villages in Shuangcheng were state-planned settlements. When Fujun designed each banner village to accommodate equally twenty-four or twenty-eight rural banner households plus the same number of metropolitan banner households, he also planned the residential arrangement and wealth distribution in the villages. Because the state scattered immigrants from the same place of origin, administrative unit, descent group, and ethnicity into different villages, banner villages in Shuangcheng were extremely heterogeneous. At the same time, because the state allocated *jichan* land to the households equally by population category, the initial distribution of landed wealth was rather uniform in each category. In the early years, these two measures not only undercut the power of any existing social organization, but also prevented any individual household from rising to power based on higher wealth status. Consequently, in the beginning of settlement, the banner villages were communities consisting of households without close connections to each other. Moreover, in villages with both metropolitan and rural bannermen, a two-tier hierarchy based on the unequal distribution of land entitlements between the two categories became the basic social structure.

At the same time, the government's dispersion of descent groups also created an extended social arena for banner immigrants, as their kinship networks had a wide geographical coverage. Most immigrants had relatives in other villages, and they also maintained connections with families back in their places of origin. From time to time, the descendants of rural bannermen escorted their father's coffin back to their places of origin, and some metropolitan bannermen even returned to Beijing to inherit their deceased relative's banner posts.[2] Moreover, the connection between rural bannermen and their families in the place of origin also played an important role in the chain migration of floating bannermen from elsewhere in Manchuria to Shuangcheng. The majority of floating bannermen moved to Shuangcheng because they had relatives living there as rural bannermen. Upon arriving, they usually sojourned with their relatives, looking for employment. They even moved from one village to the other, seeking help from different relatives.[3] Thus, the fragmented kinship ties within villages and extended connections between villagers and outsiders make the Shuangcheng banner villages interesting sites for studying community formation.

To examine the process of community formation in these banner villages, it is important to look into both the structural settings and immigrants' activities. The structural settings of a village include the residential pattern of households, the degree of commercialization in the region, and the administrative structure. In terms of the residential pattern and the degree of commercialization, Shuangcheng banner villages shared many features with villages in North China. As noted earlier, the households in each banner village were clustered together, and commercial activities in the region did not significantly affect people's life style and agricultural production. Nevertheless, the banner villages differed from villages in North China in the degree of direct state control. In these settings, immigrants' activities are indicative of how the process of community formation grew out of their daily interactions. Among all the daily activities, those concerning religious life and the land are especially important, for they reflected how villagers conceived their community in their spiritual world and how they regulated their economic life. In constructing their social relations, immigrants necessarily interacted and negotiated with the state-sponsored structural inequality. This is especially true for the forty villages in the central *tun*. Because both metropolitan and rural banner households resided in the same community, these villages were the locales where the social construction of categorical boundaries took place.

FORMAL STRUCTURE: VILLAGE HEADS

As products of state social engineering, in the Shuangcheng banner villages, a hierarchy of state-appointed agents supervised the villagers. In each banner that consisted of five villages, the government appointed one chief village head (*zong tunda*). Then, in each village, there was one village head (*tunda*) for each population category, along with two appointed precinct heads, or *shijia zhang*, each of whom was in charge of about ten households.[4] Government-appointed headmen were common in banner villages in Manchuria,[5] and this feature distinguished the banner villages from the civilian villages of the time. As has been noted, in late imperial China, the state did not establish formal government institutions at the village level. Instead, it largely relied on the lineage head and other local elites (or gentry), consisting of degree holders and wealthy families, to manage village affairs and maintain social order.[6] Yet local elites in this traditional sense were absent in Shuangcheng in the early years. Thus, government appointed headmen were the only authorities in the banner villages. The duties of the head and chief head included maintaining order in the villages: timely updating of the population registers; checking the progress of production; and, at the end of each year, collecting rent for the government. In sum, the work of a village head and chief head entailed considerable drudgery.[7]

The appointment of village heads and chief village heads followed a set of official procedures. Village heads were selected through a process that took into account villagers' recommendations. For example, in 1822, when the head of the fourth village of the Plain Red Banner in the right *tun* resigned because of illness, his fellow villagers collectively recommended another villager named Yan Jinbang to be the new head. The government approved the recommendation and appointed Yan to the position of village head.[8] In contrast, the selection of the chief village head was exclusively carried out by the government. When the post of chief village head became available, the village and precinct heads in the banner automatically became candidates for the position.[9] The banner captain then would send their resumes, written in Manchu, to the area commander-in-chief, who would review them and appoint one of these candidates to be the new chief village head.[10] Each chief village head earned a monthly stipend of one *tael* of silver and, as a sign of respect for his position, wore a hat with a golden tip, an honor equivalent to that given to *jinshi* and *juren* degree holders.[11] In other words, the chief village head in Shuangcheng acquired a kind of semi-official status, though they were not on the level of a government official.

A central figure, the chief village head connected the banner government and the villagers. As has been true of many typical state-appointed village heads in Chinese history, he had to travel to the captain's offices routinely to report about village activities. Thus, a chief village head had to have tremendous energy and organizational ability. As early as the settlement stage, the government had applied the criteria of "strong, sensible, and at the prime age" (*zhuang sheng dongshi*) to the selection of chief village heads.[12] The responsibilities of this position were so demanding that it was quite common for a chief village head to resign due to physical injuries caused by strain that limited his physical mobility such that he could no longer perform his duties.[13] Moreover, captain's offices had the authority to remove a chief village head from his post if they grew dissatisfied with his performance. Most commonly, this would happen if the chief village head had resisted government directives or acted irresponsibly in fulfilling their duties. For example, in 1822, the government removed Xilabu, the chief village head of the Bordered Yellow Banner, because the bannermen under his supervision did not clear the land in a timely fashion.[14]

Analysis of the profiles of village heads and chief village heads recorded in the banner household registers between 1866 and 1912 shows that these village heads were usually adult males in the prime of life and that the duration of their terms was not long.[15] Over 68 percent of the village heads were aged between 36 and 55. About 21 percent of the village heads first served this role in their thirties while 37 percent first became village heads in their forties. However, more than half of all village heads served in this role for only five years or less. About 20 percent of the village heads served this role for ten years or more. Moreover, having a father who was a village head did not improve the chances a son would become a village head. These results also indicate that in the banner villages, it was rare for one family to monopolize the position of village head.

Having superior organizational ability, village heads soon became intermediaries between the government and villagers. This role was especially prominent when conflicts arose between the two. In 1816, one year after the first one thousand bannermen from Jilin settled in the forty villages in the central *tun*, some of the village heads tried to petition the General of Jilin to reduce the rent quota.[16] This was the first year these rural bannermen had started to clear their lands. Government policy required each rural bannerman to cultivate twenty of the thirty *shang* of land assigned to them. Moreover, in the fourth year of cultivation, each rural bannerman had to pay twenty imperial *shi* of grain to the banner authorities, at a rate of one imperial *shi* for each *shang* of land.[17] Despite the low rent, some rural bannermen found the goal of clearing twenty *shang* of land in four years daunting. In the first month of 1816, Zhang Mao, a precinct head of the second village of the Plain Red Banner, and two other rural bannermen approached Lingde, the chief village head of their banner, and proposed going to the Office of the General of Jilin to request a rent reduction. Lingde agreed to their proposal and wrote to the village heads in all forty villages, inviting them to a banquet and meeting to discuss the petition.

As intermediaries between the government and the immigrants, some village heads tried their best to cooperate with the government even in the event of conflicts, preferring not to go against the government. The heads in the twenty villages in the Left Wing refused to attend the meeting and continued farming. Only the heads of the twenty villages in the Right Wing gathered at the banquet. After some deliberation, they decided to report their plan to Mingbao, the assistant commandant, before leaving for the provincial capital to file the petition. Mingbao instructed the village heads to not to go forward with their plan, pointing out the generosity of the current policy. Mingbao did, however, promise to report the villagers' concerns to the banner general after the fall harvest, when the general would be in town to review the progress of the settlement. In the meantime, he asked Lingde to instruct the villagers to continue farming. Mingbao also ordered the villages to share the cost—9,040 in cash—of the banquet Lingde held to gather the village heads.[18]

Lingde's mediation, however, failed. When Lingde passed on Mingbao's order, the other village heads immediately pressured him to adhere to their original agreement, saying that they would share the cost of the banquet only if they went forward with the plan to petition at the provincial capital.[19] So, despite the assistant commandant's instructions, Lingde decided to organize the petition trip surreptitiously. He wrote a notice asking the villagers to gather at the Jinqian village eight days later. In an attempt to keep the size of the group manageable, Lingde also requested that only two of every four rural bannermen sharing a thatched house go. However, a rural bannerman named Liushiyi spread a rumor that the villagers in the Left Wing had already left for the provincial capital. When they got wind of the rumor, the villagers in the Right Wing headed for the provincial capital on their own, leaving before the designated date. Mingbao sent soldiers to intercept them and eventually caught sixty-five of the group, who came from three different villages. The Revenue and Punishment Departments of the Office of the General of Jilin investigated the case and decided to punish all the villagers involved in this collective action. Lingde and Zhang Mao, the two leading figures, received an especially severe sentence of exile to Urumqi, in today's Xinjiang, more than three thousand kilometers away from Shuangcheng.[20]

This story demonstrates the power of a shared location in community building. Indeed, for immigrants living in the banner villages in the early period, a shared location was the only thing they had in common. Despite the heterogeneity of the village, living and working in the same space soon created ties among villagers. Moreover, in organizing the petition, the village heads had acted as intermediaries between their own villagers and the government, and between their own and other villages. The village heads not only represented the common interests of the villagers but also were responsible for controlling the villagers on behalf of the government. These are indications that the banner villages were gradually developing into cohesive units, and that the villagers recognized the government-appointed authority as their representative. This pattern of community formation based on a shared location also existed in many villages in North China. In some of the village communities in North China, although the households lacked strong kinship ties, villages developed into insular communities through shared everyday production and collective religious activities (Duara 1988a; Chang 1991). Thus in villages in which the households were clustered together and the degree of commercialization was low, the village became the main arena for villagers' social and economic activities. Participating in these activities helped villagers to develop a sense of community. Over time, Shuangcheng banner village saw more and more activities of community building.

SYMBOLS OF COMMUNITIES: VILLAGE TEMPLES AND COMMUNAL LANDS

In pre-1949 China, the village temples and communal lands were considered important indicators of the degree of cohesion of village communities (Fukutake 1951; Hatada 1966, 95–99; Duara 1988a, 125–28). As "public" properties, the village temple and the communal lands marked each village as a public space and a territorial community. By sharing these public properties, villagers also developed a sense of collectivity and an identity that differentiated them from outsiders. This was important in Shuangcheng villages as well. The banner villages were never closed communities. By the 1830s and 1840s, they had become complex settlements that included immigrants from various places of origin, representing the full range of socioeconomic statuses. In the central *tun*, each of the forty villages had an average of seventeen metropolitan-banner households and twenty-four or twenty-eight rural-banner households, together with a number of floating-banner households. In addition, there were some natural settlements called *wopeng* scattered around the banner villages. Some of these *wopeng* were established by floating bannermen, and some by rural bannermen who had moved out of the village to take care of their land. With all the movement within and outside the banner villages, villagers also actively constructed their territorial communities.

Village Temples

As the banner villages grew in population size and composition, villagers built temples to mark these collective entities. Depositions from a protracted land dispute filed by villagers of the fifth village of the Bordered Blue Banner in the central *tun* shows that they had built a temple before 1845.[21] Moreover, three maps drawn by local officials, in 1898 and 1902, following field investigations of seven villages in the central *tun* also show that at least five of the seven banner villages had temples.[22] Figure 5.1 illustrates the map showing the cluster of the five villages of the Bordered Yellow Banner in the central *tun*. As the figure shows, in all four villages that were of interest to the government—the second to the fifth—there was a temple located southwest of the village. South of each temple was an open area called *huichang*, or "meeting place," which very likely was where the villagers gathered during sacrifices (Figure 5.1). The villages illustrated on the other two maps also had a temple and meeting place at the same relative locations to the village. Although the archival documents did not provide information on the date these temples were built, very likely, they were built in the 1840s

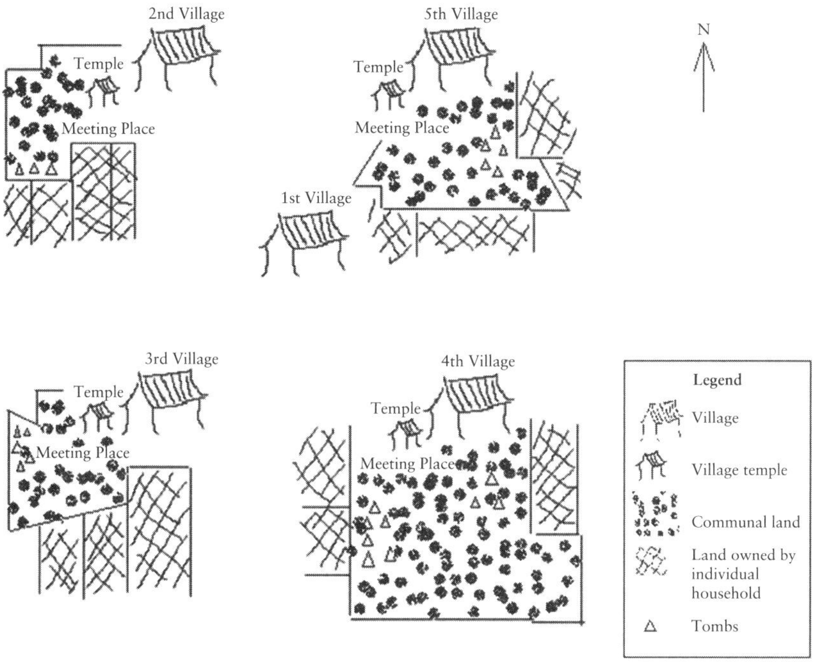

Figure 5.1. The relative location of the village temple and communal land to the village, the second to fifth villages of the Bordered Yellow Banner in the central *tun*, 1898.

SOURCE: The map attached to the government report in 1898 (SCPXLYMDA, no. 30369).

or earlier—the same period the temple in the fifth village of the Bordered Blue Banner was built. The present-day descendants of the banner immigrants interviewed for this study recalled that village temples were prevalent; almost every village had one.[23]

Village temples endowed banner villages with symbolic meaning as territorial and ascriptive communities. As the descendants of banner immigrants reported, a village temple belonged exclusively to the residents of that village; people would not go to the temple of another village.[24] This territorial connection between village residents and their temple is also seen in North China. As Duara (1988a, 124–28) points out, this type of religious association surrounding the village temple is only villagewide, and membership in it was identical to village membership. In other words, the village temple offered a spiritual dimension to the tie based on a shared location. For banner immigrants from different places of origin, ethnicity, and descent group, the village temple was particularly helpful in connecting their spiritual worlds together.

Villagers worshiped a variety of deities in the temples. Tudi (Soil-Ground) was the most common tutelary deity worshiped. Guandi and Guanyin were also worshiped. Moreover, according to the local gazetteer, some of the larger village temples worshiped a set of nine deities called "nine gods" (*jiu sheng*), including the General of the Five Paths (*wudao*), the King of Insects (*chongwang*), the King of Crop Seedlings (*miaowang*), the King of Medicines (*yaowang*), the King of Horses (*mawang*), the Dragon King (*longwang*), the God of Mountain (*shanshen*), Tudi, and the God of Fire (*huoshen*) (SCXZ 1973, 199), who were drawn from popular religion and shamanism. For example, the General of the Five Paths was an underworld deity in charge of all the dead. The cult of the General of the Five Paths became popular in the Tang dynasty (618–907), and this deity was widely worshiped in China proper (Guo 2003, 34–36). The Kings of Insects, Crop Seedlings, Medicines, Horses, and the Dragon King were deities in charge of particular aspects of village life that were closely related to agricultural production. The worship of the Gods of Mountain and Fire had strong Shamanist flavor.

The worship of the nine gods in one place indicates that these temples provided a common space for villagers to create a comprehensive and inclusive territorial community. The historical memory of the descendants of banner immigrants also shows this. Although many of today's senior villagers interviewed for this study had clear memories of the role of the village temple in the early twentieth century, most of them were not able to remember all the deities that were worshiped. One informant in the former first village of the Plain White Banner in the central *tun* replied: "There were a lot." A ninety-three-year-old informant living in the former third village of the Plain Yellow Banner in the central *tun* said: "It had everything you could think of" (*shenme dou you*).[25] Clearly, for the villagers, it was not the specific deities they worshiped that mattered but having a space in which they were able to express their understandings of the world they lived in. As such, the selection of deities was a reflection of village life. Tudi and the General of Five Paths were the tutelary deities in charge of miscellaneous things; the other deities represented various supernatural powers related to particular aspects of agricultural production. Despite their various origins, the nine deities coexisted harmoniously in the temples. As the gazetteer puts it, "where the [nine gods] temple lies was exactly [the place] in charge of the misfortune and fortune of the area" (SCXZ 1973, 199).

In the spiritual world of the villagers, the village temple was like an underworld local office connected to a central authority. Evidence from both the gazetteer and oral history confirms that the villagers had practiced the death ritual of "reporting to the temple" (*baomiao*) for a long time. When a villager died, the family would walk out of the house, point in the southwest direction with a shoulder pole, and give directions to the ghost of their deceased family member by shouting "the southwest road" (*xinan dalu*; SCXZ 1973, 171). Then, the family would report the death by going to the village temple to burn incense and offer sacrifices. One informant explained that all the village temples in Shuangcheng were situated southwest, outside the village, because that was the direction to Fengdu, Sichuan province, the location of hell in Chinese popular religion.[26] Villagers believed that the ghosts of all the deceased went to Fengdu to be examined by the King of Hell and then waited to be given an assignment for their next life. The ritual of "reporting to the temple" was to formally "register" the deceased in the system of the other world.

However, despite the symbolic meaning of village temples, the banner villages in Shuangcheng seldom functioned as ritual communities. With the exception of rainmaking, villagers performed sacrifices at the village temples as individual families, not as an entire village. The descendants of banner immigrants in Shuangcheng recounted that most of the time, sacrificing at the village temple was a family matter. These sacrifices were usually performed during the lunar New Year and on some other special holidays. Usually individuals representing the entire family would go to the village temple to burn incense and say prayers. This situation contrasts with practices in villages in South China and some parts of North China, where collective ceremonies were common and participation in the territorially defined ceremonies was mandatory (Faure 1986, 3–4; Duara 1988a, 124–28). Still, this lack of collectively performed public ceremony was also seen in some villages in North China. For example, Thomas Dubois (2005, 44–47) found that, in Cang County, Heibei province, there was virtually no village ceremony that required the participation of all members.[27]

Thus, in Shuangcheng, rainmaking was the only territorially defined ritual that involved all villagers. In times of drought, each household sent a male member to participate in the ceremony. Each village held its own ceremony, but the procedures were more or less the same. Participants knelt in front of the village temple, each wearing a hat made of willow branches. The leaders said prayers to the Dragon King. Some senior villagers recounted that the ceremony would continue until it rained. If after a few days of kneeling in front of the temple the rain did not come, the villagers then formed a procession and paraded through the village. Everyone in the village was involved in this part of ceremony. All the men were in the procession, and the women, who were not allowed to join the procession, poured water onto the street. When the rain came, villagers would have a banquet and performances to thank the gods.[28]

The development of village temples reveals that, even though the banner people were an institutionalized population, their practices of folk religion had many commonalities with those practiced in the villages on the North China Plain. Admittedly, as planned communities consisting of households of various geographic and social origins, the scarcity of collective religious ceremony reflects the absence of a strong social tie among the households. Yet, the space of the village temple did mark the emergence of the notion of common welfare among villagers. The temple and the meeting place outside it helped to validate villagers' sense of belonging to their shared location. As Nakamura Tetsuo (1984) points out in his research on village communities in North China, village temples and ritual sacrifices to the gods served as indispensable nexus to connect the villagers. Dubois (2005, 48–54) further shows that, even when participation in public ceremonies was not mandatory, village religious activities still promoted the notion of common welfare through villagers sharing religious resources, such as the temples. Village temples in Shuangcheng can also be viewed in this light. Villagers who shared neither a common ancestor nor a place of origin nevertheless had the village temple and meeting place in common. Moreover, the village temple also helped to ease the tensions that resulted from villagers' unequal entitlements to land; despite their fundamental economic inequality, they were equal in their spiritual life, praying and sacrificing to the same gods. In this way, by the mid-nineteenth century, banner villages in Shuangcheng were no longer merely shared locations but also communities where people lived and owned property.

Communal Lands

Along with the erection of village temples, some unassigned land next to the villages also became communal property as pasture land and burial grounds. As Figure 5.1 illustrates, all the communal lands of the second to fifth villages of the Bordered Yellow Banner in the central *tun* were located south of the village, next to the village temple and meeting place. The sizes of the communal lands preserved in the archives varied from 7.37 *shang* to 68 *shang*.[29] As pasture land, villagers' livestock grazed on it. As a burial ground, it mainly accommodated the tombs of floating bannermen who had lived or sojourned in the banner villages. Moreover, such communal pasture lands and burial grounds also existed in other villages, including those in the left and the right *tun*. For example, the report of an investigation of the unassigned lands that located in the borders of the second and fifth villages of the Bordered Blue Banner in the left *tun* in 1879 also revealed that the two villages shared the pasture land and burial ground.[30] Given the fact that, by 1856, the government had registered the majority of farmland in Shuangcheng, very likely, these communal lands had come into being before this time.

The use of communal land as burial ground also demarcated the village community by virtue of villagers' land entitlements. Unlike metropolitan and rural bannermen who could also be buried in the *jichan* land they owned, floating bannermen had no place to rest after death because they did not have any entitlement to land. Consequently, the communal land became the only resting place for deceased floating bannermen. Depositions from two disputes over land and tombs, filed in 1868 and 1869, demonstrated this fundamental difference in bannermen's afterlives. In 1868, a bannerman named Zhu Wanliang sued a rural bannerman named Zhao Gui for destroying his brother's tomb.[31] Zhu Wanliang had come to Shuangcheng from Jilin in 1833 and had lived in the home of his grandfather, Xingtai, in the first village of Plain Yellow Banner in the right *tun*. In the same year, Zhu's blood brother became sick and died; Zhu had no choice but to bury him in the communal land located northwest of the village. Thereafter, Zhu returned to his place of origin. More than thirty years later, when Zhu came back to visit his brother's tomb, he discovered that the land where his brother was buried had been turned into farmland, owned by Zhao Gui. Since Zhu's family was not on either the rural banner or the floating banner registers, it belonged to the unregistered floating bannermen category and did not stay in Shuangcheng very long. Consequently, the tomb of Zhu's brother was not well tended. In the end, a local official accompanied Zhu to investigate the site and found a flattened tomb-shaped plot next to Zhao Gui's land, which Zhu recognized as his brother's tomb. Zhu therefore acknowledged that the tomb was not flattened by Zhao Gui but by "the trampling of livestock."[32] By contrast, in 1869 a rural bannerman named Foningbu filed a case over the land of his deceased brother, whose entire family—the brother himself, his wife, son, and daughter-in-law—were buried in the household's *jichan* plot.[33]

The communal land thus functioned as a public burial ground for floating bannermen. In 1898, the metropolitan and rural bannermen of eight villages—of which six were original banner villages and two were satellite villages[34]—petitioned the government to protect their communal lands. Bannermen in all six original banner villages stated that the communal lands were used mainly as pasture land and "public burial grounds" (*yizhong*) for "bannermen who came from Fengtian after the relocation and who either worked as hired laborers or farmed the land for us" (SCPXLYMDA, no. 30369). The rural bannermen from the two satellite villages stated that, in addition to the tombs of floating bannermen, some of their own ancestors were buried in the communal burial grounds.[35] By 1898, some burial grounds held more than three hundred tombs.

The use of communal land as burial grounds for floating bannermen had symbolic meaning; by giving access to land to those to whom the government had denied entitlement rights, the village was in effect admitting these people as part of the village community. In other words, the public burial ground completed the village's function as a community that the government failed to recognize or accommodate. The tombs of the floating bannermen in the public burial grounds were in theory protected by law. For example, when Zhu Wanliang filed the lawsuit about his brother's tomb in 1868, the government soon sent officials to the village to investigate the location of the tomb (SCPZGYMDA, 164:

657: 90–95). It did not dismiss Zhu's lawsuit simply because his family had no entitlement rights to land.

Due to its importance to the common welfare, not only did the villagers defend their communal ownership of the pasture land and burial ground, but the government also respected and protected this communal ownership. Beginning in the second half of the nineteenth century, communal lands were frequently targeted by some well-to-do families looking to increase their wealth, as they were probably the only lands not yet cleared and registered. In 1869, Zhang Yuxiang, a wealthy metropolitan bannerman living in the fourth village of the Bordered Red Banner in the central *tun*,[36] had encroached on the pasture land shared by the metropolitan and rural bannermen of the fifth village of the Plain Yellow Banner in the central *tun*.[37] A rural bannerman Zhang Dingzhu living in the village reported the encroachment to the banner government. After a field investigation, the banner government ordered Yuxiang to abandon all the extra land other than the area that he had registered; in addition, officials built tamped mounds around the plot to define the boundaries of the pasture land. Similarly, when a bannerman named Shengde attempted to claim the pasture land and burial ground shared by the residents of the second and fifth villages of the Bordered Yellow Banner in the left *tun*, the villagers jointly petitioned the government to turn down the request. Again, the government enclosed the land to prevent encroachment by individual farmers. Later, it also turned down similar requests from two bannermen named Qihang'a and Wulintai.[38]

Toward the end of the nineteenth century, as the Qing government increasingly opened up state land to private owners in exchange for funds, the villagers continued trying to protect their communal lands. In 1898, several civilian commoners offered to pay the government to claim the communal lands of nine banner villages in the central *tun*. Hearing the news, the metropolitan and rural bannermen of each of the villages jointly signed petitions to prevent these civilian commoners from claiming the lands (SCPXLYMDA, no. 30369). In the petitions, they cited their banner privileges—civilian commoners were not allowed to live in the banner territories—to deny the civilian commoners from claiming entitlement to the lands. Then, they took the additional step of offering to register these lands as *nazu* land and pay the government an annual rent to secure their ownership. In fact, the communal ownership of these lands was so secure that even the Chinese Communist Party preserved them during the land reforms in 1946 and 1947. It was not until the agricultural reform beginning in the end of the 1970s that these lands were divided among villagers.[39]

In this way, along with village temples, communal land as a shared resource helped to define the banner villages as territorial communities. The use of communal land encouraged villagers to develop a common understanding of village membership and to construct a boundary between villagers and outsiders. Only people living within the village place could share the rights to the communal land. The sense of village as a cohesive community was enforced when outsiders attempted to trespass on the communal land. As villagers united to defend the communal property rights to the land, they also manifested their identity attached to the shared village location. The collective ownership of communal land became a custom which the government also respected and protected.

ACTIVITIES SURROUNDING LAND

Since land was the major form of property and the means of production for farm families, activities surrounding land not only affected the wealth status of individual households but also shaped the social relations in agrarian communities. Studies on the social and political structure of rural communities show that how people organized agricultural production and the customs regulating land transfers were closely associated with the degree of solidarity of the village communities (Fukutake 1951; Hatada 1966). For example, villages in which residents collectively organized irrigation and watching over crops were more likely to be cohesive, whereas villages in which residents did not engage in such collective activities were less cohesive. Moreover, in many regions of pre-1949 China, land transfer was often an important event for the entire village. Not only did the landowner's fellow villagers act as witnesses to the transfer, but also the rules of land transfer worked to maintain the stability and integrity of the village community. For example, both official law and customs gave priority to buy first to the relatives of the landowner and then his neighbors in the village,[40] in order to avoid the plot being purchased by outsiders without relatives' and neighbors' consent (Zhang 2002a, 95–109; Yang 2009).

In Shuangcheng, the activities of land clearing and land transfer, especially, contributed to the process of community formation. Although the state forbade private land clearing and regulated land transfers, villagers still had considerable leeway to carry out these activities. Before the government registered the *ziken* land, the land privately cultivated by immigrants, in 1854, the acquisition and transfer of these lands were exclusively handled by villagers. Moreover, throughout the entire period, the government did not intervene in the land rental market except to forbid civilian commoners from residing in the banner section. These facts indicate that the banner villages have become autonomous entities to organize the economic and social life of immigrants.[41] Through land clearing and land transfer, villagers developed their own ways to organize labor and to define the relations among themselves and between them and outsiders. Yet, during this process, villagers also had to negotiate the state-designated social hierarchy and the corresponding state policies. This is especially true for the forty villages in the central *tun*. On the one hand, the structural setting of the state-designated social hierarchy provided a reference for local people. Villagers tried to fit their practices into state policies. On the other hand, because the abilities of individual households varied, the upward and downward social mobility at the household level tended to alter the inequality based on population categories. Consequently, immigrants were constantly reshaping the social order in the banner villages, resulting in a full range of diversity across villages.

Land Clearing

Private land clearing in Shuangcheng opened up opportunities for villagers to not only increase their landholdings but also to construct their own hierarchy through collectively organized labor. As chapter 4 shows, shortly after the initial settlement, immigrants, in various ways, started to clear additional land. Yet the experiences of bannermen on their allocated *jichan* land has demonstrated that land clearing was not an easy task. While some bannermen were capable of clearing land as individual households, others chose to organize villagers to clear land to benefit from the collectively organized labor. Similar to what happened with public works, such as irrigation and watching over crops in some other regions in China, collective land clearing marked the villages as cohesive entities.[42] The organization of collective land clearing efforts and the subsequent allocation of the cleared land provided arenas for villagers to negotiate their power and wealth.

Two cases in the archives provide a glimpse at villagers' collective land clearing efforts. In 1882, a metropolitan bannerman named De'an described the collective land clearing effort by the villagers in the first village of the Plain White Banner in the central *tun*.[43] In the early years, De'an's grandfather, Wulibu, and another metropolitan bannerman named Zhuerxing'a had organized their fellow villagers to clear about four hundred *shang* of unassigned land northwest of their village. The villagers agreed to give each metropolitan household 13.1 *shang* of the cleared land, and each rural household 8.4 *shang*. They gave the sixteen *shang* of land left over from the allocation to Wulibu and Zhuerxing'a, eight *shang* each, to thank them for organizing the land clearing.

The second case offers a slightly different picture of collective land clearing efforts. In 1845, eight households of metropolitan bannermen in the fifth village of the Bordered Blue Banner in the central *tun* worked together with the rural bannermen in this village to clear eighty *shang* of unassigned land outside the east gate of the Shuangcheng seat.[44] Then, they divided the land equally between the two population categories, giving forty *shang* each to the metropolitan and rural bannermen. In turn, the eight metropolitan households equally divided the forty *shang* of land among themselves, each receiving five *shang*. Since the distance of the land from their village, more than fifteen *li*, made it difficult to manage, seven of the metropolitan households agreed to delegate their plots to Mulong'a, a Mongol bannerman originally from the Bordered White Banner in Beijing.[45] At the same time, they also collectively donated the forty *shang* of land to the village temple; all the rents collected from these lands were to be used to maintain the temple.

The above two examples reveal the active roles metropolitan bannermen played in collective land clearing and community building. In the first case, two metropolitan bannermen—Wulibu and Zhuerxing'a—were the initiators and organizers of a collective effort to cultivate four hundred *shang* of land. Given the size of the land and the number of households in the village, Wulibu and Zhuerxing'a needed exceptional organizational ability to coordinate the effort. In the second case, it is unclear whether the metropolitan bannermen played a leading role in land clearing; however, the eight metropolitan households' action of donating their lands to the village temple is an indication of their ambition to act as elites in village affairs. Given the importance of the village temple as a symbol of the territorial community, their donation unarguably qualified them as elites who contributed to the public good. Thus, in both cases, metropolitan bannermen played an elite role in organizing public works.

At the same time, villagers' patterns of land allocation suggest a variation in the power dynamics between metropolitan and rural bannermen in these two villages. In the first case, the metropolitan and rural bannermen adopted without modification the method promoted by the state, allocating land by household and giving more land to metropolitan households. In other words, the villagers fully embraced the state-mandated hierarchy to organize the community. This was very likely because the metropolitan bannermen, represented by Wulibu and Zhuerxing'a, occupied a leading position in the village and were able to group households of different categories together. By contrast, in the second case, the metropolitan and rural bannermen divided land by category instead of household; each population category received one equal share. Of course, given the relatively smaller number of metropolitan households in the village, equal division by category still gave each metropolitan banner household more land. However, the fact that the villagers emphasized category instead of household indicates that metropolitan and rural bannermen in this village were socially segregated. The difference in the ways of land allocation between the two villages indicates that banner villages have developed into independent communities with distinctive social relations. Nevertheless, despite the subtle difference, both cases show that villagers treated metropolitan and rural bannermen as two distinct groups.

Moreover, while the banner villages showed many signs of cohesion, they were still not unitary communities with a high degree of solidarity. Besides collective efforts at land clearing, many households also cleared land on their own. This was especially the case for rural bannermen. The banner land registers reveal that in the aforementioned two villages, the amount of *nazu* land owned by the metropolitan bannermen was equal to what they acquired from the collective land clearing effort; whereas many rural bannermen had more land. In fact, because in almost every banner village in Shuangcheng, rural bannermen usually had larger households with many adult males, they were more likely to own *nazu* land than were the metropolitan bannermen. Metropolitan bannermen were also interested in organized land clearance because of their lack of available labor and expertise. With smaller households and less knowledge of farming, metropolitan bannermen were unable to clear land on their own. Thus, they needed the support of a village community, and the labor of rural bannermen, in particular, to do so.

Land Transfer

Because of the state's ownership of the land, land transfers in Shuangcheng had similarities to and differences from practices in regions where private land ownership was the norm. In most regions of late imperial China, local communities handled land transfers free of government intervention, using contracts to define and secure property rights. Although in theory all land transfers were supposed to be registered by the local government, and the contracts were supposed to bear a magistrate's seal, in reality many people chose not to report land sales to the government to avoid a sales tax.[46] When land disputes were brought to court, local people nonetheless presented contracts without a magistrate's seal as evidence of landownership (Osborne 2004).[47] In contrast to the local autonomy elsewhere, the Shuangcheng banner government regulated land transfer with a set of official procedures that seemingly diminished the role of local communities. However, in reality villagers managed to carry out and even legalize land transfers in accordance with state regulations. In this process, village communities still played a central role in validating land transfers. Thus, land transfers can tell us a great deal about local officials and communities adjusted their positions in civil affairs under a state-dominated system and how the interactions between state policies and local practices shaped the social hierarchy.

Official land transfer. State regulations in Shuangcheng prohibited private land transfers not only between bannermen and civilian commoners but also among bannermen. The government established the rules when it made the initial allocation of *jichan* land in 1820: although a *jichan* plot was considered the property of a household, the household could not sell it. When the government discovered that a *jichan* plot had been sold, it would seize the plot, require the seller to forfeit the land and the money from the sale, and punish the parties involved in the transaction.[48] In 1868, the government decreed that the ownership rules regarding *jichan* land would now also apply to *nazu* land.[49]

Any changes in landownership therefore had to go through the official procedures of "returning land" (*tuidi*) and "selecting a replacement" (*jianbu*). According to the official report on landownership changes, these procedures consisted of four steps. First, when a bannerman decided to give up ownership of a plot, he and the chief village head went to the captain's office to report the decision and file a petition requesting permission. The petition followed a standard format, summarizing the type and amount of land and the owner's reasons for wanting to relinquish it. For example, in 1880, in the report of a landownership change between two rural bannermen, Wulibu and Yongcheng, the captain's office of the Bordered Blue Banner first cited Wulibu's petition as follows:

> A *zhengding* Wulibu, who resides in the fifth village of the first *jiala* of my banner, sincerely petitioned [at the office]: "I originally farmed thirty *shang* of *dingque* land,[50] thirty *shang* of *ziken* land, and thirteen *shang* and seven *mu* of *maohuang* land. Now, I am suffering from diseases on my waist and legs. Although I sought to cure these illness[es] for a long time, there has been no improvement at all and I have become disabled. None in my household can help me farm [the land]. Moreover, I have exceeded the age range of [a principal adult male] and indeed have no ability to farm the land. Fearing that the government rent could be delayed, I would like to give up my *dingque* plot as well as my *ziken* and *maohuang* plots and allow the government to select a capable adult male to replace me. Thereby, the land will not be wasted and the government rent will not be delayed."[51]

In the second step, the captain's office selected the replacement and allocated the returned plot to him. In Wulibu's case, the captain's office selected a bannerman from another village:

> According to this petition, [the office] verified that Wulibu is willing to give up his *dingque*, *ziken*, and *maohuang* plots, a total of seventy-three *shang* and seven *mu* of land and allow the government to select an

> adult male to replace him, because he is disabled and exceeds the age of a principle adult male, without an assistant adult male in his household. [Wulibu's proposal] seems reasonable. These plots concern both the *dingque* and rated *nazu* land, and thus, it is not appropriate to let [the ownership] remain unassigned. Therefore, [the office] has followed the rules to select the *bangding* Yongcheng, who is registered under the household of the *zhengding* Chengxi in the second village of the second *jiala*, to replace [Wulibu]. [We] verify that the selected adult male Yongcheng is really strong and capable of farming. Therefore, [we] handed over all the farming tools Wulibu originally acquired from [the government] to Yongcheng.[52]

The third step was to document the change. First, the original owner of the plot and his kin would sign a statement confirming that they had given up the plot. Next, the village head and the precinct head from the replacement bannerman's residential village would sign a written guarantee, attesting to the takeover of the plot and the ability of the replacement bannerman to farm it. If the ownership change involved *nazu* land, the replacement bannerman also needed to state his willingness to pay the rent on time. Finally, in the fourth step the captain's office completed the paperwork and submitted a report of the transfer to the area commander-in-chief:

> In addition to obtaining a written guarantee from Wulibu's relatives, stating that there is no dispute regarding this change in landownership, and a guarantee from the *zong tunda, tunda,* and *jiazhang*, stating that the replacement adult male Yongcheng will not waste the land and delay the rent, [we] also attach a sealed verification. Here we submit all the paperwork and report to your office.[53]

The process as well as the language used in the official report highlighted the state's ownership. They conveyed the impression that the captain's office controlled the selection of the replacement bannerman and thus made the land transfer an official act. In the typical sequence of events in a land transfer, in which the plot first was returned to the captain's office before the selection of a replacement bannerman was made, the captain's office acted as both authority and an intermediary. The standard language used in the official report also signaled the government's firm control over the land. Almost every petition from an original owner contained the phrase, "allow the government to select a replacement" (*ren guan ling jian* or *jiao guan ling ding buchong*).

Similarly, every captain's office reported that the office had "followed the rules to select" (*zhaozhang jian de*) the replacement bannerman. Nor did the official document mention any payment involved in the land transfer. It thus appeared from the official report that the replacement bannerman selected by the captain's office acquired the land for free.

The official language also indicated that as the ultimate owner of the land, the state evaluated the replacement bannerman's physiological and economic conditions in order to maintain equity in land distribution. The state would first verify that the replacement bannerman was of prime age and capable of farming (*nianli jingzhuang kanneng wunong*). This ensured that the land was assigned to a capable farmer who could sustain its cultivation. Moreover, in the transfer of a *jichan* or *dingque* plot, the state would make sure that the replacement bannerman was an assistant adult male (*bangding*) who was neither the household head nor had registered *jichan* land. With the stipulation, the state prevented a principal adult male (*zhengding*) from having multiple *jichan* plots, a sign of land concentration.

The inclusion of the original landowner's relatives and the village and precinct heads in the official selection procedure is a clear indication of the importance of their positions in land transfers—even in a system of state landownership. The requirement of obtaining written guarantees from the relatives of the landowner and the village and precinct heads reveals that the state respected the partial rights of the landowner's extended family and the village community. In theory, after the transfer of a *jichan* or *dingque* plot, the new owner took the land and the house attached to it. If the new owner was from another village, which was quite common in Shuangcheng, the captain's office would move his and his immediate family's registration to the village in which the *jichan* plot was located to formally show that he had joined the village community. The guarantee from the village heads not only indicated that the village community accepted the new owner but also specified the obligations of the village and of the individual landowner to the state: to farm the land and pay rent. The village heads also acted as supervisors of the individual owner. Thus, the official language of the land transfer presented the state's view of landownership in Shuangcheng; the state dominated landownership and its transfer; an individual owner, embedded in his extended family and village community, worked as a bonded laborer for the state.

Private Transfer and Official Records. Despite the seemingly rigorous procedures governing official land transfers, in reality, villagers who wished to give up land had considerable influence over the selection of replacement bannermen. The limited number of government personnel and the geographical distance between the captain's office and the villages made it impossible for the office to do all the research needed to identify a potential replacement bannerman. Instead, the original plot owner, along with his fellow villagers and the village head, played a major role in selecting a replacement. As a practical matter, once the original plot owner had identified a replacement bannerman and had acquired the village and precinct heads' consent for the land transfer, the captain's office usually accepted the replacement and legitimized the transfer. This situation therefore left space for de facto land sales.

A lawsuit filed in 1879 between two rural bannermen, Ren Shicheng and Li Sheng, reveals that some land transfers were, in fact, sales.[54] In that year, Ren sued Li for surreptitiously taking ownership of his land. Ren claimed that, in the 1860s, he had conditionally sold (*dian*) thirty *shang* of land to Li Sheng for sixty strings of cash. Since conditional sale was only a customary practice and, by receiving only a partial price of the plot's market value, the seller reserved the right to redeem the plot within an agreed period of time, Ren thought that he was still the registered owner of this plot. However, Ren later found out that Li had changed the landownership status at the captain's office. Yet, Li described this land transfer as an outright sale (*juemai*) by which the seller transferred all rights and interests to the buyer. According to Li, Ren had relinquished his landownership at the captain's office in 1867, and the captain had reassigned the plot to Li's younger brother Li Ming. Li Sheng had privately paid Ren 120 strings of cash in this land transfer, as "plow and spade money" (*li hua qian*; this is the monetary compensation paid to the original owner for his efforts in clearing the plot). Despite their different accounts of the nature of this land transfer, the original captain's office report of the transfer resolved the dispute. The official record showed that, in 1868, Ren had gone to the captain's office to report that he had decided to give up his position as principal adult male and the associated land plot, citing disability as the reason.[55] The captain's office had then selected Li Sheng's younger brother, Li Ming, as the replacement. At the same time, both the village head and the precinct head, as witnesses, verified that the official land transfer between Ren and Li had taken place. Ren finally lost this lawsuit when official proof of the ownership transfer was produced.[56]

As we see in Ren and Li's case, behind the scenes of an official land transfer, the original owner and the replacement bannerman were often engaged in more complicated negotiations and transactions. The official process of land transfer only served as the final step in legitimizing private land transfers between bannermen. In this case, Ren had agreed to sell his land to Li before they completed the official land transfer. The "plow and spade money" functioned as the land price.[57] The government was also aware of the private land transfer behind the official procedures. In 1867, the Shuangcheng area commander-in-chief ordered the captain's office to place a hold on all land transfer cases during the spring plowing period to make sure farmers focused on farming (SCPZGYMDA, 163: 647: 158–62). In this order, the area commander-in-chief clearly pointed out that, among the various land-transfer cases, "some must be farmers selling off their plots to pay their debt." Therefore, "it is hard to avoid the situation that [some people] set up others to extort the land. I assume all [captains] have discerned this situation." This statement indicates that officials were aware that bannermen used land transfers as sources of income.

In the late nineteenth century, when the state gradually lifted the ban on sales of banner land in other parts of Jilin, even some local officials misinterpreted the state policy and used the words "sell" and "buy" in official reports of land transfers in Shuangcheng. In the second month of 1882, Tinghe, a lieutenant of the Bordered Yellow Banner who had temporarily taken over the duties of the captain, processed two land-transfer cases: one between two metropolitan bannermen, Qinglin and Chengshun, and the other between three metropolitan bannermen, Qingxiang and Qingde as the original owners and Shuangquan as the replacement.[58] In both cases, after summarizing the types and amounts of land they intended to relinquish, the original owners stated that they had sold the plots to the replacement bannermen. Interestingly, Tinghe approved these land transfers according to the official instructions on the land certificates, which stated that "in the future, if the owner had no ability to farm [this plot] and would like to sell it to others, [he] must report it to the local government and acquire a new land certificate."[59] Tinghe was therefore under the impression that the land transfers between these metropolitan bannermen were in accordance with the official rules. He therefore sent personnel to the villages to verify the capabilities of the two replacement bannermen and completed the paperwork.

However, the area commander-in-chief returned Tinghe's report and admonished him for deviating from the rules of land transfer and writing the terms "sell" and "buy" into the official report.[60] The area commander-in-chief explained that the official instructions on land certificates in fact only allowed for sales of *nazu* land among civilian commoners. Since civilian commoners constituted the majority of *nazu* landowners in other parts of Jilin, the Office of the General of Jilin used a uniform land certificate to accommodate their needs. Thus, the official instructions in the certificate only applied to civilian commoners. While pointing this out, the area commander-in-chief re-emphasized the prohibition on land sales between Shuangcheng bannermen.

After receiving the admonishment, Tinghe, in the fourth month of 1882, submitted a revised report (SCPZGYMDA, 208: 870: 97–103). In it, the parties involved remained the same. Following the standard format, the original owners, Qinglin, Qingxiang, and Qingde petitioned to relinquish their ownership over those plots and allowed the government to select replacements. The report then stated that the captain's office had followed the rules in selecting Chengshun and Shuangquan as replacements. Obviously, Tinghe still accepted the fact of the land sales between these metropolitan bannermen and only changed the language in the report to bring them into accordance with the state regulation. The above case reveals that, although the state was aware of the persistence of private land sales, it was only willing to formalize them using the instrument of the official land transfer.

The government and residents' use of official land transfers to formalize private land sales reveals that official rules and local practices, in fact, had a reciprocal relationship in local governance. This kind of reciprocal relationship was typical in regions in which private ownership was the norm (Scogin 1994 and 2001; Huang 2001). In these regions, local officials relied on customary practices to regulate a large society, and contracts drawn in local communities delineated people's rights and obligations. Macauley (2001) points out that this way of governance reflects the Qing's intentional simplification of local society in order to make taxation easier. Yet, this local autonomy does not mean that local practices were outside the government's control. Since official registration and tax records were the most important proofs of landownership, some people preferred to validate their land transfers by obtaining magistrate's seal on the contracts. To do so, local people followed official regulations for drawing up contracts. Thus, by validating land transfers, officials "communicated contractual norms and regulatory requirements to the people" (Scogin 2001, xv).

In Shuangcheng, this reciprocal relationship between official rules and local practices also helped to regulate land transfers among bannermen. Despite the state-dominated system, local banner officials still followed the logic and practices used elsewhere to simplify the local society. In terms of administration, it was simply more convenient for local banner government to accept the results of the negotiations between villagers and legalize them. Thus, Shuangcheng bannermen had considerable room to buy and sell lands privately among themselves, following customary practices, and then to complete the official procedures of land transfer to validate and protect their rights. At the same time, sellers also had to consider the official requirements when identifying a potential buyer. Among these requirements, the most important ones were aimed at securing bannermen's landownership and the privileges of metropolitan bannermen. In order to legalize their private land sales, Shuangcheng bannermen had to ensure that the buyer was a bannerman of the same category as the seller. Such a reciprocal relationship between local practice and official policy enabled the state to regulate the flow of landed wealth in Shuangcheng.

Of course, the land-transfer cases recorded in the government registers only provide a partial view of the complex property regimes in Shuangcheng. These cases were the equivalent of an outright land sale. Besides the outright land sales that followed government regulations, other forms of land transfer widely existed. For example, Shuangcheng bannermen might not report land sales between different population categories to the government. Moreover, conditional land sale was also a common form of land transfer. Isett (2004) shows that, in banner villages in southern Manchuria, some bannermen conditionally sold their land to civilian commoners. To avoid being discovered by the government, villagers even disguised the conditional land sale as a leasehold, substituting the character *zu*, or rent, for the character *dian*, or conditional sale (Isett 2004, 140). Similar practices not only existed in Qing-dynasty Shuangcheng but also were condoned by the banner government. Only in 1902, when the government started to transfer landownership from the state to private owners, did officials make an effort to identify the owners in conditional sales to ensure tax collection.[61] Again, the government tolerance of customary practices indicates that, under both the civilian and banner systems, the Qing followed the same logic of local governance. At the same time, despite the various forms of land transfers in customary practices, official land transfer was an effective channel for communicating government regulations to local people.

Over time, the official procedures of land transfer did help regulate bannermen's behaviors. Before the late 1860s, the government did not centralize the transfer of *nazu* land, and the captains simply selected the replacement without updating the register with the area commander-in-chief.[62] Therefore, metropolitan and rural bannermen could transfer *nazu* land across the categorical boundaries. For example, in the aforementioned collective-land-clearing case by bannermen in the first village of the Plain White Banner in the central *tun*, although the metropolitan bannerman Wulinbu acquired an additional eight-*shang* plot as a reward for his efforts to organize the land clearing, he rented this plot to a rural bannermen and fellow villager named Qingchun because of his own "inability to farm the plot." In 1851, Wulibu's son Quansheng finally sold the plot to Qingchun for forty strings of cash (SCPZGYMDA, 209: 871–2: 135–41). In a lawsuit filed in 1883, the plaintiff, a metropolitan bannerman named Fugui, reported that, in the 1860s, a rural bannerman named Han Changfa bought two plots of land from two metropolitan bannermen (SCLSFMFDA, no. 97). In 1868, dissatisfied with the uncontrolled situation of the registration of the *nazu* landownership, the area commander-in-chief ordered the banner captains to follow the regulations for selecting a replacement for *jichan* land when they processed the transfer of the *nazu* land.[63] Thereafter, the mentioning of land transfers across different population categories became rare in government documents. These examples indicate that bannermen consciously altered their behaviors to accommodate the government policies. In fact, the state regulations were so influential that, even after the fall of the Qing when free land transfer was allowed, the council of Xiping Township in Shuangcheng reported that "many bannermen still followed the old regulation and did not dare to sell their land."[64]

OUTCOMES OF COMMUNITY FORMATION

The development of banner villages in Shuangcheng sheds light on the processes by which immigrants built communities on the frontier. The growth of these villages exhibited characteristics of the "potential development" stage in Colson and Scudder's theoretical framework of resettlement studies (Colson 1971; Scudder and Colson 1982). In this stage, migrants adapt to the new environment and seek new options. Consequently, new social organizations gradually develop. In Shuangcheng, immigrants transformed state-designed villages into communities through everyday activities. Based on a commonly shared territory, religious practices and communal land marked their shared resources and common welfare. Along with other activities, land clearing and land transfer shaped the power relations among villagers. During the process, people living in different villages created their own histories. According to the index of village names compiled by the county government in 1980, 32 of the 120 banner villages had nicknames.[65] Besides the official names associated with their administrative units under the Eight Banners, seventeen of the thirty-two villages were also named after a specific individual or business, reflecting their own distinctive identities.

During the process of community building, the state-designated social hierarchy gradually played out on the ground in the forty villages of the central *tun*. In collective activities of land clearing, capable metropolitan bannermen managed to play a leading role in organizing labor and community affairs. In practices of land transfer, villagers also followed government regulations to select buyers and legalize the transaction. Thus, through policies of land allocation and land transfer, the state communicated the structural inequality to banner immigrants. To gain government protection of their property rights, bannermen also consciously observed the state-defined categorical boundaries and made them social boundaries regulating their everyday life.

At the same time, however, practices of land clearing and transfers eventually created a more stratified distribution of landed wealth in the village communities. On the one hand, these practices enabled some capable rural bannermen to acquire wealth comparable to that of metropolitan bannermen. On the other hand, within the same population category, some households became wealthier than others. All these processes impacted the clear-cut two-tier hierarchy between metropolitan and rural bannermen. In 1876, among the metropolitan and rural bannermen residing in 80 of the 120 villages, 24 percent of rural banner households had landholdings comparable to those of metropolitan bannermen and 14 percent of the rural banner households even rose to the wealthiest group: the top 10 percent of households in landholding.[66] In other words, these rural bannermen crossed the state-defined boundary of wealth status.

The clearing and transfer of *nazu* land was the major cause of the trend of boundary crossing in wealth status. Before the government began regulating the transfer of *nazu* land in 1868, land transfers had reduced the *nazu* landholdings of many metropolitan banner households. The majority of the metropolitan banner households in the two villages for which accounts of collective land clearing efforts have been presereved followed this trajectory. For example, although each metropolitan household in Wulibu's village—the first village of the Plain White Banner in the central *tun*—initially acquired 13.1 *shang* of *ziken* land from their collective land clearing efforts, by 1870, five of the eight metropolitan households had less than thirteen *shang* of *ziken* land, and only three had more than thirteen *shang*.[67] Similarly, in the fifth village of the Plain Blue Banner in the central *tun*, each of the eight metropolitan banner households acquired five *shang* of *ziken* land following their collective land clearing efforts; however, by 1870, five of those had no registered *ziken* land at all, and one other household had less than five *shang* of registered *ziken* land.[68] The only exception was a metropolitan bannerman named Mulong'a, who had 87.8 *shang* of registered *ziken* land. In 1854, when the government began registering *ziken* land, Mulong'a acquired the other metropolitan banner households' consent to register all the forty *shang* of land they had collectively cleared under his own name; in exchange, he promised to use the rental income to maintain the village temple (SCLSFMFDA, no. 52). Apparently, as households incapable of farming gradually transferred their land to the capable ones, gaps in wealth status also arose among households within the same population category.

Results from the analysis of the banner land registers also show that, by 1870, rural bannermen living in the forty villages of the central *tun* had achieved an advantageous status in their *nazu* landholding. As Table 5.1 shows, of the metropolitan and rural bannermen living in the central *tun*, nearly a half (45.7 percent) of the rural banner households owned *nazu* land (e.g., among the top 40 percent of households in *nazu* landholding). Yet, only 30.6 percent of metropolitan banner households owned it. Consequently, in every stratum of households that had *nazu* landholding, the percentage of rural banner households exceeded that of metropolitan banner households. The only exceptions were the wealthiest groups, the top centile and the next 4 percent of households in *nazu* landholdings; metropolitan and rural bannermen had comparable percentages of households belonging to these groups. Together with the aforementioned accounts of land transfers in the early years, these results indicate that, a half-century after the settlement, some rural bannermen successfully enhanced their wealth status by clearing and buying land. At the same time, the clearing and transfer of *nazu* land also created inequality in the wealth status of metropolitan bannermen; while some metropolitan households were able to accumulate a large amount of *nazu* land, the majority of metropolitan households did not have this category of land. These developments also challenged the two-tier hierarchy the state established through the allocation of *jichan* land.

After the local government centralized the process for transferring *nazu* land in 1868, the *nazu* landholdings of metropolitan bannermen remained relatively stable, while rural bannermen's *nazu* landholdings continued to increase. The government regulations stipulated that only land transfers between bannermen of the same population category could be officially recorded. This policy prevented the flow of *nazu* land between different population categories, especially from the metropolitan bannermen to rural bannermen. From 1870 to the end of the 1880s, the number of metropolitan banner households in each *nazu* landholding stratum did not change significantly. By contrast, in 1889, a considerable number of rural banner households rose to the top strata of households in *nazu* landholdings. Moreover, as Table 5.1 shows, in

TABLE 5.1

The nazu *landholding status of the metropolitan and rural banner households living in the forty villages of the central* tun, *1870 and 1889*

Nazu *Landholding status among all registered metropolitan and rural banner households*	1870				1889			
	METROPOLITAN		RURAL		METROPOLITAN		RURAL	
	Number	*Percent*	*Number*	*Percent*	*Number*	*Percent*	*Number*	*Percent*
Top 1 percent	9	1.3	9	0.9	8	0.8	17	1.6
Next 4 percent	24	3.4	36	3.5	24	2.4	49	4.8
Next 5 percent	29	4.1	63	6.2	28	2.8	71	6.9
Next 10 percent	49	7.0	126	12.3	53	5.3	135	13.1
Next 20 percent	104	14.8	233	22.8	104	10.3	274	26.6
No *nazu* land (bottom 60 percent)	487	69.4	556	54.3	790	78.5	485	47.0
Total	702	100.0	1,023	100.0	1,007	100.0	1,031	100.0

SOURCE: CMGPD-SC.

NOTE: The *nazu* landholding status is based on all the registered metropolitan and rural banner households living in the 120 banner villages. Only about 40 percent of these households owned *nazu* land, and the bottom 60 percent had nearly no *nazu* land. The fact that the number of households in the central *tun* slightly exceeded the quota of 698 for metropolitan bannermen and 1,000 for rural bannermen reflects the discrepancy between the state rules and registration practice.

1889, the percentage of rural banner households owning *nazu* land in the forty central-*tun* villages increased to 53 percent. The significant increase resulted from villagers' continuous efforts to exploit uncultivated land. By either encroaching on the empty lands previously used as boundaries between plots or clearing lands that were previously waterlogged, many rural bannermen increased their landholdings, registering the land as extra land (*fuduo di*). Some rural bannermen also purchased land from others. These results indicate that the rural bannermen in the central *tun* were more active than metropolitan bannermen in exploring opportunities to enhance their *nazu* landholding. Thus, although rural bannermen's disadvantage in entitlement to *jichan* land persisted, their increasing *nazu* landholdings helped to close the wealth gap between the two population categories.

Throughout the Qing dynasty, banner villages in Shuangcheng functioned as loosely bound territorial communities, each village having some collective activities and identities; nonetheless, the heterogeneity of residents resulted in a relatively weak bond among villagers. Compared to villages in south and east China, which emphasized closed membership, villages in Shuangcheng are much more open. Land transfers between bannermen living in different villages were common. Moreover, to facilitate the management of land located outside their villages, some bannermen also moved to the satellite villages surrounding the banner villages. This meant that families played especially important roles in organizing everyday life and managing wealth. In addition to village communities, families also strategically utilized other available resources to pursue their fortune.

CHAPTER SIX

Reinventing Hierarchy

Metropolitan Bannermen Family Strategies

KINSHIP AND HOUSEHOLD IN SHUANGCHENG

One prominent social change in late imperial China was that the importance of family and kinship organizations in local society grew over time. As Neo-Confucianism became increasingly influential, lineage—kinship organizations based on the principle of patrilineal descent—flourished in many parts of China (Twitchett 1959; Xu 1980; Chow 1994). The late imperial state enlisted these kinship organizations to organize and manage local society for purposes such as taxation.[1] While empowering lineage at the local level, this process also helped the state to create a social order that reached down to the household and individual. Thus, lineages existed throughout China in a variety of forms. In the south and southeast, lineages became highly corporate and localized; lineages controlled a predominant number of estates and directed the economic and social lives of their members (Freedman 1965, 1966; Baker 1979; Watson 1982; Watson 1985; Szonyi 2002; Faure 2007; Zheng 2009). Elaborate ancestral halls and activities of ancestral sacrifice marked their solidarity. Although lineage organizations in other parts of China did not necessarily control estates to the extent that they did in the south, they still played an important role in their members' socioeconomic lives (Beattie 1979; Ebrey and Watson 1986; Cohen 1990; Xu 2010). Moreover, activities such as genealogy compilation tracing the common descent along the male line, burial in a common graveyard, and holding regular ancestral sacrifices were typical symbols expressing cultural unity among lineage members. This trend also influenced the banner people, and the Qing government sponsored the compilation of Manchu genealogies (Li 1992; Elliott 2001, 326–69; Li 2011).

Families in Shuangcheng, however, were located on the other end of the spectrum; although kinship networks widely existed among the immigrants and facilitated chain migration, these networks lacked representation as social and cultural unities.[2] Not only did the descent groups of bannermen not have ancestral halls or elaborate family burial grounds,[3] they also did not actively document the histories of, and membership in, their families until the late nineteenth century. The genealogies and ancestral scrolls researchers have found in present-day Shuangcheng show that most of the banner immigrants only started to record their ancestors in the 1880s or later.[4] The foreword of the ancestral scroll of a Fu family, which was commissioned between 1885 and 1895, provides evidence of the insignificance of descent to banner immigrants in the early period. It states that before the ancestral scroll was commissioned, "the fathers [of the Fu family] did not [have the habit] to recollect the names of ancestors for offspring at their death beds."[5] Thus, out of concern for family history, the descendants felt the need to record their ancestors. This challenges the conventional understanding that banner people had a long history of compiling and maintaining genealogies, both under official sponsorship and in the families' interests (Li 1992; Elliott 2001, 326–69; Li 2011, 143–47). At least, the banner immigrants in Shuangcheng did not maintain this tradition.

For many families, the ancestral scroll was the only documentation of their family history and ancestors.[6] These scrolls had the same function as the ones Myron Cohen (1990, 515–16) found in rural North China; they replicated ancestral tablets to illustrate genealogical relationships. At the top of the scroll, some families described their histories in a brief foreword, usually in two or three sentences. Then, the family members of each generation were listed on a separate horizontal line, beginning with the founder of the descent group. All the names were also boxed, each box resembling a tablet for an ancestor on the scroll. Unlike genealogies, which also include living family members, these ancestral scrolls included only the names of the deceased. Descendants added new names as family members died. Thus, the ancestral scroll served as a symbol of the roots and history of the descent group. The ancestral scroll was usually owned by the eldest son of the most senior line, who wrapped it in fabric, placed it in a box, and hung the box on the southern or western wall of his house, just below the ceiling of the living room.[7] Only during the lunar New Year did the owner take it out; he organized a sacrifice, in which all the male members of the descent group made a sacrifice to it as if worshiping their ancestors.[8]

Moreover, compared to those in North China, the ancestral scrolls in Shuangcheng paid even less attention to clarifying conjugal relations and differentiating the descendants of different lines. While in the ancestral scrolls in North China the names of wives were placed next to those of their husbands (Cohen 1990, 515–16), the ancestral scrolls in Shuangcheng separated wives from their husbands. The scrolls were divided into two vertical columns. All male members were listed on the right side, and their wives were listed on the left. Although in theory the wives were opposite their husbands, the symmetry was thrown off when a man had more than one wife. Similarly, most ancestral scrolls made no effort to illustrate the descent between father and son. Thus, rather than documents delineating family descent, these ancestral scrolls mainly served as a symbolic representation of the family.

The underdevelopment of kinship organization in Shuangcheng was the result of a combination of three factors: the settlement pattern, the highly institutionalized nature of the Eight Banner population, and the state land-allocation policy. As we have seen, the state dispersed households from the same descent group into different villages. However, this alone does not explain the underdevelopment of kinship organization. If we leave aside the component of urban-to-rural migration, the heterogeneity of the settler population in Shuangcheng was not unique for a frontier settlement. In fact, as Burton Pasternak (1969, 557) points out, the settler populations in the frontier regions of China consisted of "heterogeneous kinship fragments." Different types of social organizations developed on these other frontiers because of their specific institutional, social, and historical contexts.[9] Thus, the history and nature of the Eight Banners are also important for understanding the lack of cultural expression of descent groups as unitary associations.

As the Qing institutionalized the structure of descent groups among the banner people, it simultaneously undermined the importance of the descent group as an independent social organization.[10] The activities of genealogy compilation among banner people illustrate this paradoxical situation, and show the top-down efforts by the state. The Qing court not only kept genealogical records on males as evidence of their inheritance rights to noble titles and official positions, but also sponsored the compilation of genealogies by individual families as a means to preserve Manchu identity (Elliott 2001, 326–29; Li 2011, 143–76).[11] In the mid-eighteenth century, the court also compiled *The Complete Genealogies of the Manchu Clans and Families of the Eight Banners* (*Baqi Manzhou shizu tongpu*). The official effort stimulated genealogy compilation among the banner families. Some families relied on the government and simply copied the official genealogical records. For example, part of the genealogy of a metropolitan banner family with the surname Fu was an official copy of the 1911 Eight Banner household register.[12] Similar situations also existed among banner populations in other parts of Manchuria. Ding et al. (2004, 174–94) found that many of the descent groups among the banner peasants organized under the Shengjing Imperial Household Agency in the Liaodong region did not compile their own genealogies until the early twentieth century. Moreover, among the 286 genealogies of banner families in Manchuria collected by Li Lin (1992, 11–23), only twenty were compiled before 1800, and another twenty were compiled between 1800 and 1850.[13] These studies suggest that it was only after the Qing dynasty started to decline that banner people in Manchuria began to recognize the importance of the descent group as a unitary cultural and social organization.

In Shuangcheng, the state also institutionalized households, the most basic social unit. Different from banner registers elsewhere, which organized households under descent groups, the banner registers in Shuangcheng organized households directly under villages. This shows that the state omitted the descent group as an institution to organize immigrants, putting households under closer control. To facilitate land allocation, the state not only assigned such state positions as principal adult male and assistant adult male to the male members in the household but also divided existing households. To prevent land concentration, the state's land-allocation policy stipulated that one household could only own one plot of *jichan* land, which means one plot of *jichan* land corresponded to one household on the register. Thus, whenever an assistant adult male acquired one plot of *jichan* land through inheriting the land from an extinct household or from a household that had relinquished its ownership, he had to establish a separate household.[14] If the land plot was located outside the new owner's original residential village, this new household would move to the new village location.

As the state created and relocated new households in Shuangcheng throughout the nineteenth century, the already fragmented kinship nexus became even more disconnected, and the sizes of the banner households also became relatively small. In both 1866 and 1904, the majority of metropolitan banner households had only one to eight members (Table 6.1). This "stagnation" in the size of metropolitan banner households was a result of two waves of large-scale household division that were responses to land reallocation; in 1870 and 1878, 225 and 302 households, respectively, were created to meet the designated number of *jichan* plots allocated to metropolitan bannermen. The same table also shows that, in 1866, the rural banner households also did not have a large number of members; households having four to eight members was the largest group, which accounted for 40.4 percent of all rural banner households. Only in 1904, because rural bannermen did not have as many chances as metropolitan bannermen to replace extinct

TABLE 6.1
Household size of metropolitan and rural bannermen in 1866 and 1904

	METROPOLITAN HOUSEHOLDS				RURAL HOUSEHOLDS			
	1866		1904		1866		1904	
Number of living persons	*N.*	*Percent*	*N.*	*Percent*	*N.*	*Percent*	*N.*	*Percent*
0	30	6.0	63	6.3	43	1.7	37	1.4
1–3	221	44.4	392	39.2	385	14.8	268	10.1
4–8	196	39.4	474	47.4	1,047	40.4	884	33.2
9–15	44	8.8	65	6.5	746	28.8	728	27.4
16–20	4	0.8	5	0.5	230	8.9	297	11.2
21–30	3	0.6	1	0.1	115	4.4	268	10.1
31–40					23	0.9	111	4.2
41–50					2	0.07	43	1.6
50 and above					1	0.03	22	0.8
Total	498	100.0	1,000	100.0	2,592	100.0	2,658	100.0

SOURCE: CMGPD-SC.
NOTE: The series of rural banner population registers is missing one register in 1866 and one in 1904. Therefore, the total number of household in both years was less than 3,000.

households, did the number of households with sixteen or more members significantly increase.

This weak kinship organization had far-reaching implications for the process of social formation in Shuangcheng. The absence of powerful lineage organizations made individual families especially vulnerable to the temporal hardship of seasons and harvests. Yet this situation also led families to actively seek resources to support themselves and to ally with other families in various forms to open new fields. Consequently, the absence of lineage organization left space for other forms of social organization to grow. Existing studies on frontier settlement in south and southeast China show that, while the conditions on the frontiers could give rise to highly corporate, localized lineage organizations (Freedman 1966), in some other places, the heterogeneous settler population formed non-kin associations (Pasternak 1972). The rapid development of village communities described in chapter 5 is also an example of this. Thus, the process of social formation in Shuangcheng was marked by the interaction between the agency of individual families and the structural context.

The microhistory of metropolitan banner families is particularly informative about how the strategies used by individual families to survive shaped the social hierarchy in Shuangcheng. Metropolitan bannermen had both advantages and disadvantages in Shuangcheng. On the one hand, they were the top elite in the state-mandated social hierarchy and were privileged. On the other hand, their small household size and inexperience in rural life made them vulnerable to the hardships of frontier life, as is evident in the persistent mortality deficit among metropolitan banner males (Chen, Campbell, and Lee 2005). Compared to rural bannermen, metropolitan families lacked support from extended kin. Therefore, forming non-kin associations that could provide support was an important strategy for metropolitan banner households. Over time, demographic outcomes and the capability to utilize various sources to maintain their wealth status determined the chances that a metropolitan banner family would survive and prosper on the frontier. The interplay of the two factors resulted in divergent destinies for this urban-origin population. The unsuccessful ones simply vanished from the Shuangcheng history, as 225 metropolitan banner households had become extinct by 1869. The successful ones took advantage of the state-mandated social hierarchy of Shuangcheng and transformed metropolitan bannermen from a registration category into a wealthy and powerful social group.

The family founded by a metropolitan bannerman named Hualiantai was one of the successful ones that achieved affluence and prosperity. The records on the government registers for this family show that it started as a household of six in 1826; by 1911, it had developed into a descent group of seven households consisting of twenty-nine people.[15] Two households of this family had once been among the top 1 percent of households in *nazu* landholding, although they later sold off the land. Their history of household development and wealth expansion was highly intertwined with state policies, localized events, and the trajectories of other metropolitan banner families. Thus, the history of Hualiantai's family traces the transformation of the metropolitan bannermen along with the strategies families employed to cope with social and political changes and to accumulate and maintain their wealth.

ARRIVAL AND SURVIVAL

In the spring of 1826, a *xiansan* bannerman named Hualiantai moved to Shuangcheng with five members of his family.[16] Originally administered by the Manchu Bordered Yellow Banner in Beijing, Hualiantai had a Sinicized surname, Guo. His five family members included his wife and three sons: the eldest son Jiertahun, thirteen years old; the second son Jiertuhun, eight years old; and the youngest son Jiertukan, one year old (Figure 6.1).[17] They had traveled with another 147 households of Manchu and Mongol bannermen from Beijing to Shuangcheng.[18] Upon their arrival, the family settled in the fifth village of the Plain White Banner in the central *tun* and received one plot of *jichan* land.

Compared to his peers, Hualiantai had a relatively large and complete household. Throughout the Qing dynasty, the average banner household in Beijing had less than four members (Han 1987, 52). Moreover, ever since the initiation of the recruitment of metropolitan bannermen to Shuangcheng, the government had constantly adjusted its definition of a household in order to recruit poor metropolitan bannermen. Although prior to 1825, the government had always tried to have at least one conjugal unit per household, in 1825 Fujun further loosened the definition

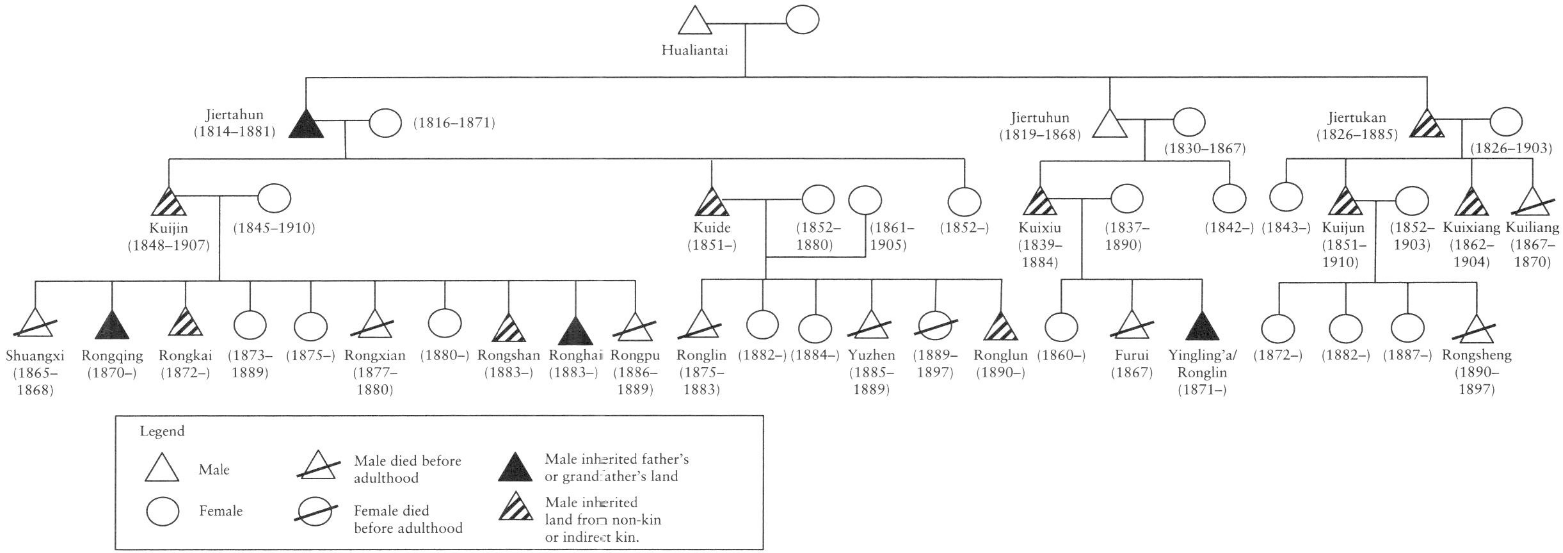

Figure 6.1. Hualiantai's family, the first to fourth generations.

SOURCES: The household registers compiled by the Bordered Yellow Banner between 1866 and 1912 (SCPGBTDHKDM 1834663–1834723).

NOTE: Some family members do not have the year of death specified because their deaths are not observed in the household registers.

of household to allow a single bannerman to be counted as a household by himself. Therefore, the 189 households that moved to Shuangcheng in 1826 and 1827 included a considerable number of households headed by unmarried bannermen, and 119 of them consisted of three or fewer members. Thus, although Hualiantai did not hold any banner post, the relatively large size of his household was an advantage in Shuangcheng; it is what enabled Hualiantai's family to survive the hardship of rustication and even to prosper.

By 1866, the earliest year from which we have surviving register data, Hualiantai's household had expanded to eighteen members, spanning three generations.[19] Hualiantai and his wife disappeared from the household register of that year, which indicates that they had died quite some time before. Hualiantai's eldest son Jiertahun, then fifty-three years old, now headed the household. Jiertahun had been able to acquire an official position as a tax preceptor and had earned the honor of wearing a peacock's tail of the fifth rank (*wupin hualing*). He was retired in 1866 and lived with his immediate family and the families of his two brothers. Jiertahun and his wife, woman Luo, had two sons, who were nineteen and sixteen years old, and a fifteen-year-old daughter. His elder son, Kuijin, married woman Wu and they had a two-year-old son named Shuangxi.[20] Jiertahun's second younger brother Jiertuhun, then forty-eight years of age, had once served in the post of lieutenant, a relatively high official position, and earned a military honor (*jungong*). However, by 1866, he had been removed from his post and lived with his wife, woman Ge, and their children. Jiertuhun and woman Ge's son, Kuixiu, was twenty-eight years of age and was married to a woman with the surname Bai, with whom he had an eight-year-old daughter. Jiertuhun's twenty-five-year-old daughter also lived in the household. The third son of Hualiantai, Jiertukan, was then forty-one years old. He had a wife, two sons, aged sixteen and five, and a twenty-four-year-old daughter. This big family is one of the seven metropolitan banner households in 1866 that had more than sixteen members (Table 6.1).

The household and land registers indicate that this family was able to achieve a high socioeconomic status. Jiertahun and Jiertuhun served the state as banner soldiers and earned state stipends. Compared to Jiertahun, Jiertuhun was more successful, having advanced to the higher-ranking position of lieutenant. The Eight Banners in Manchuria had supplied a large number of soldiers and officers to quell the Nian rebellion in North China and the Muslim rebellion in the northwest during the 1850s and 1860s, and it is very likely that Jiertuhun achieved his official position based on military merit. The official positions of both brothers brought the family to prominence. Although neither brother still held an active banner post, they maintained a large amount of *nazu* land. In 1866, Jiertahun registered a total of 122.2 *shang* of *nazu* land.[21] Clearly, Hualiantai and his sons had been very successful in acquiring unassigned land during the first four decades of settlement and became large land holders. The power and financial resources that came with their former official positions must have contributed to their success in acquiring *nazu* land. At the same time, as one household, this large family owned only one plot of *jichan* land.

In contrast with the success of Hualiantai's family, 225 metropolitan banner households became extinct. These families were annotated as extinct because they had not been able to secure an heir after the death of all the members. The majority of the households that became extinct had arrived in Shuangcheng with relatively small households, which undermined their chances of surviving the hardships of adjusting to a rural life. Prior to 1869, when a metropolitan banner household became extinct, the local government simply retained the *jichan* land that had been allocated to it, collecting rent from the rural banner household that was originally assigned to farm the land for the metropolitan household.

Hualiantai's family, however, soon also experienced hardship. Between 1866 and 1869, five members of the family died. All the three brothers' families had losses. Jiertuhun's wife died between 1866 and 1867, followed by Jiertuhun himself, who was marked in the register compiled in 1868 as "died." The following two years saw the death of three young children: Jiertahun's grandson Shuangxi disappeared after the 1868 register was compiled, at age four; Jiertuhun's grandson Furui was registered as a newborn in the 1867 register and disappeared afterward; Jiertukan's youngest son, Kuiliang, registered in 1868, died between 1869 and 1870, at age three.[22]

The deaths of the three young children were very likely related to a flood in 1868 and the consequent harvest failure. In the sixth month of 1868, after more than twenty days of continuous heavy rain, a flood ravaged sixty banner villages east of the Shuangcheng seat and the civilian settlements in the same area.[23] The flood not only submerged a total of 2,872.25 *shang* of land but also killed people and destroyed houses. The accompanying hailstorm damaged crops throughout Shuangcheng, resulting in harvest failure in 1868 and also affecting production in 1869. In the household-level survey on the amount of *nazu* land affected by the disaster, local officials reported that a total of 30,862.29 *shang* of land had experienced harvest failures, about 60 percent of the total amount of registered *nazu* land.[24] A total of thirty-two *shang* of *nazu* land owned by Hualiantai's family was affected by the flood. The aftermath of this natural disaster—malnutrition resulting from the food shortages and diseases caused by the flooding—was likely the cause of the abnormally high death rate in this family.

The experience of Hualiantai's family provides an example of a rural family's demographic response to disaster. The deaths of the three young children in this family show that wealth, prominence, and high socioeconomic status could not protect the family from such disasters. Research on the demographic responses to economic hardship among the banner populations living in Liaodong and among peasants in northeastern Japan reveals the same result (Campbell, Lee, and Bengtsson 2004, 78). At times of economic stress, people of different socioeconomic statuses in these rural communities all faced the same mortal hazards.

Hualiantai's descendants used strategic marriages to survive the hardship. They married off the two daughters who had reached their late twenties. At the age of twenty-six, Jiertuhun's eldest daughter married and moved out of the household in 1868, the year her father died.[25] In the following year, Jiertukan's eldest daughter also got married and moved out at the age of twenty-six.[26] In fact, compared to women in other historical Chinese populations, twenty-six was a very late age for a first marriage; in pre-twentieth-century China, the mean age of first marriage for women living in Zhejiang, Beijing, and Liaoning ranged from 17.8 to 20.7 (Lee and Wang 1999, 67, table 5.1), and in Shuangcheng 80 percent of daughters were married by age twenty (Chen, Campbell, and Lee 2014, 414, figure 11.1). The late marriage age of the daughters in Hualiantai's family was in accordance with the finding that women from families with a higher socioeconomic status married later than those from families of lower socioeconomic status. As existing studies reveal, marriage in late imperial China was characterized by female hypergamy; families with higher socioeconomic status tended to wait until they found a worthy husband for their daughters (Lee and Wang 1999, 81–82; Chen, Campbell, and Lee 2014). Since the marriages of the two daughters in Hualiantai's family occurred during a period of economic hardship, it is very likely that these economic circumstances forced the family to marry off their daughters. Eventually, large household size was the factor that enabled the family to endure the aftermath of the natural disaster. Despite all the misfortunes, in 1870, this household still had fourteen living members on the household register. In addition to the thirteen existing members who survived the disaster, Jiertukan's eldest son, Kuijun, married woman Liu in 1869. With the formation of new conjugal units, this household still showed signs of prosperity.

MANAGING HOUSEHOLDS AND WEALTH, 1870–1878

Household Division and Wealth Accumulation

In 1870, Hualiantai's descendants welcomed the opportunity to expand their landholdings by receiving additional *jichan* plots that had originally belonged to extinct households. In that year, Fuming'a, the general of Jilin (1866–1870), submitted a memorial recommending the allocatation of the *jichan* plots of 225 extinct households to the existing large metropolitan households that did not have enough land to support all the members. Importantly, Fuming'a only took the *jichan* landholdings of these households into consideration and totally neglected their *nazu* landholdings. Thus, Fuming'a's memorial noted that, of the 473 remaining metropolitan banner households, 158 were quite large. Moreover, "90 households indeed had no support (*yangshan*), and 62 households had barely sufficient support."[27] Given this, the government laid out the rule as follows:

> [We should] differentiate those who had support from those who had not. For those households who had no support, every four people, men or women, could receive a plot. For those who had a little support with a large household, every six or seven people, men or women, could receive one plot.[28]

Although this quote indicates that the government tried to maintain an equitable distribution of land based on household size, the officials did not take the *nazu* landholdings into consideration, and therefore the allocation of the 225 plots of *jichan* land was essentially a reward to those families that had not only survived the hardship of the first forty years of settlement but had also achieved a relatively large household size.

With a household of fourteen members but only one plot of *jichan* land, Hualiantai's family benefited from this land reallocation; in 1870, this family received two more *jichan* plots and thus was divided into three households. Each of the three brothers' families became one independent household. Jiertahun continued to head the original household, which now only consisted of his wife and children. Kuixiu, the son of the deceased Jiertuhun, acquired the *jichan* plot originally allocated to Bahabu, a Beijing Manchu bannerman who had moved to Shuangcheng with his wife in 1824.[29] By 1869, Bahabu and his wife had died, and without a male heir, the household was considered extinct. Living in the same village, Kuixiu conveniently inherited Bahabu's land and established his own household, residing on it with his wife, Bai, and their daughter. Jiertahun's third younger brother, Jiertukan, also inherited a *jichan* plot that had originally been allocated to a metropolitan bannerman named Wenying, and became the head of his own household,[30] living with his wife and two sons.

Following this land allocation, the landholdings of Hualiantai's descendants reached its peak. The 1870 land register shows that in addition to three plots of *jichan* land, the three households had a total of 226.9 *shang* of registered *nazu* land,[31] 104.7 *shang* more than their *nazu* landholdings in 1866. This indicates that, between 1866 and 1870, despite the excessive mortality the family experienced, the three brothers managed to acquire more land. The 226.9 *shang* of *nazu* land was not equally distributed among the three households: Jiertahun only received 10.4 *shang*, Kuixiu 108.8 *shang*, and Jiertukan 107.7 *shang*. The *nazu* landholdings of Kuixiu's and Jiertukan's households placed both in the top 1 percent of all the metropolitan and rural banner households.[32]

The uneven distribution of *nazu* land among the three households also indicates that, although the land register began recording Hualiantai's family as three households in 1870, this family had very likely divided into three separate economic units much earlier than that. This reveals that over time, the meaning of Shuangcheng banner household as an economic unit had separated from its meaning as an administrative unit. While the government register continued to take the original banner household as a unit of administration, land allocation, and rent collection, banner immigrants had developed diverse arrangements to define the basic unit of consumption, residence, and production. In some households, adult sons equally divided their family property on the death of their parents, following the customary practice of partible inheritance.[33] For the sake of convenience, officials continued to record these sons under the original household and the landholding of the entire family under the household head's name. Despite the formalities that were maintained on the government registers, the households established upon partible inheritance acquired independent property rights, which was recognized not only by the local community but also by local officials; any property acquired after the household division belonged not to the extended household named in the register but to the household that acquired it.

Thus, the uneven *nazu* landholdings of the three households probably resulted from their different efforts to acquire land after the original household was divided. Hualiantai's three sons probably divided their family property upon the death of their parents and established independent households. After this early household division, Jiertuhun and Jiertukan were able to acquire a considerable amount of *nazu* land and significantly increase the wealth of their individual families. To accommodate the official rules of household and land registration, they registered all the land under the name of the official household head, Jiertahun; nevertheless, the property rights of each family were clearly defined. Therefore, once Jiertuhun and Jiertukan's households also became administrative units, they were able to officially register their household property separately, leaving Jiertahun only 10.4 *shang* of *nazu* land.

In 1870, although the families of Hualiantai's descendants were affluent, they faced different opportunities and challenges. Jiertahun, as the eldest brother, lived with his wife, Luo; his eldest son, Kuijin; Kuijin's wife, Wu; his second son, Kuide; and a daughter.[34] Although the household had the least *nazu* land among the three brothers, the thirty-five *shang* of *jichan* and 10.4 *shang* of *nazu* land provided them with a decent life. Although the nuclear family of Jiertuhun and woman Ge's son, Kuixiu, was the wealthiest of the three households, this family had not yet successfully produced a male heir. Having only one daughter,

Kuixiu's landholding, amounting to 143.8 *shang*, was massive for a family of three. Aged thirty-two and thirty-four respectively, Kuixiu and his wife were still in their prime and able to manage these landed properties. However, the lack of a male heir would eventually jeopardize the family's fortune. At the same time, Jiertukan's household seemed to have achieved the best balance of land and family size of the three. With a total of 142.7 *shang* of land, Jiertukan and his wife, woman Fu; his two sons, Kuijun and Kuixiang; and Kuijun's wife, Liu, had much to look forward to.[35]

Selling Off Nazu Land

From 1870 on, the three households had dramatically different luck in marriage and reproduction, which significantly affected their sizes and prospects of further development. The size of Jiertahun's family expanded significantly; whereas Kuixiu's and Jiertukan's household sizes remained small. Following in their father's footsteps, Jiertahun's sons, Kuijin and Kuide, both became soldiers. At the same time, this branch was successful in reproduction; between 1870 and 1878, Kuijin's wife Wu gave birth to five children, three sons and two daughters. Kuide also got married and had a son.[36] By contrast, Kuixiu and his wife were only able to have one son during this period. As mentioned earlier, the only other surviving child in this family was a daughter who was born around 1860; she married and moved out of the household in 1876, leaving Kuixiu's household as a nuclear family with three members. Jiertukan's two sons were also unsuccessful in expanding their families. Kuijun, Jiertukan's eldest son, and his wife only had one daughter during this period, and Kuixiang, who was seventeen years old in 1878, was single.[37]

In this period, the *nazu* landholdings of all the three households significantly declined. The 1876 land register shows that Jiertahun's household did not own any *nazu* land.[38] The *nazu* land registered under Kuixiu's name had been reduced to 83.7 *shang*.[39] Similarly, the *nazu* landholding of Jiertukan's household had also shrunk to 66.8 *shang*, a reduction of 40.9 *shang* from his 1870 possessions. Moreover, even the ownership of the 66.8 *shang* of remaining land was in question. Under Jiertukan's name, two new names—those of a metropolitan bannerman Mingshan and his son Changling—appeared, indicating that they shared the ownership of these plots. Jiertukan officially transferred his *nazu* landownership to Changling in 1879, and an official ownership-transfer document was issued (SCPZGYMDA, 202: 839: 353–57). According to this document, Jiertukan reported to the captain's office that, due to the geographic distance between two plots of land and his residence, he no longer had the ability to manage them. Therefore, he hoped to return these two plots, one 20.6 *shang* and the other 14.1 *shang* in size, and let the government reassign them to farmers who could manage them. The captain's office selected Changling, who resided in a village ten *li* from Jiertukan's village, as the replacement farmer. As a result, in that year, the *nazu* land registered under Jiertukan's name was further reduced to 32.1 *shang*. The landownership transfer between Jiertukan and Changling was an obvious case of land sale, because Changling was only three years old in 1879. Evidently, Changling's father Mingshan, a thirty-eight-year provisional granary official (*wei cangguan*), was the de facto owner and manager.

The land transfer between Jiertukan's and Mingshan's families also sheds light on the story of wealth accumulation by Mingshan, a second-generation immigrant and the son of a high official. Mingshan's father, Fuqing'e, a bannerman who had originally belonged to the Manchu Plain Red Banner in Beijing, settled in the second village of the Plain Red Banner in the central *tun* and became a banner captain.[40] After Fuqing'e's death, Mingshan's eldest brother, Ming'an, succeeded him as the head of the household and divided the household property with Mingshan. As household head, Ming'an had all the *jichan* land, leaving Ming'shan only twenty-one *shang* of *nazu* land.[41] In 1866, Mingshan began his official career as a scribe in the banner government.[42] Between 1869 and 1870, Mingshan acquired one of the 225 *jichan* plots re-allocated from the extinct metropolitan households and officially established his household in the third village of the Plain White Banner in the central *tun*, a village outside of his previous banner administration.[43] Then, Mingshan started to expand his landholdings by purchasing land from others.[44] On establishing his own household, Mingshan registered 114.2 *shang* of *nazu* land under his previous residential village.[45] In 1876, his *nazu* landholdings increased to a total of 211 *shang*, 139.4 *shang* in his previous residential village and 71.6 *shang* in Jiertukan's village.[46] The rise of Mingshan's family illustrates the flow of landed wealth among the immigrants.

Although Hualiantai's descendants sold off their *nazu* land, they still enjoyed considerable wealth. Not only did they still have *jichan* plots, but the *nazu* land they sold also generated cash income. Archival sources show that the land price in the 1850s was around twelve strings of cash per *shang*.[47] Since the price would not have been lower in the 1870s, by selling off their *nazu* land, Jiertukan and Kuixiu each acquired more than 1,600 strings of cash. Very likely, Jiertukan and Kuixiu sold their *nazu* land to cope with labor shortages resulting from their failure to expand the sizes of their families. In a frontier society like Shuangcheng, where the labor-land ratio was low, labor was an important asset. Even wealthy families were not able to manage their land if they did not have enough adult males.

THE EXPANSION OF WEALTH IN 1878

Exchanging Money for Land

At the same time that they sold off their *nazu* land, Hualiantai's descendants welcomed another opportunity to acquire more *jichan* land and exhibited their power and wealth. Since ultimately only 698 metropolitan households arrived in Shuangcheng, 302 of the one thousand plots of land that had been designated to them remained; the government left these with the rural households that had originally cleared them. These rural households continued to farm the plots, paying an annual rent of 660 in cash per *shang*. In 1876, the government finally decided to distribute the 302 remaining *jichan* plots. However, rather than allocate them to the metropolitan banner households already in Shuangcheng, the court planned to relocate more metropolitan bannermen from Beijing.[48] Thus, the court ordered Ming'an, the general of Jilin (1877–1883), to investigate the reserved plots in Shuangcheng.

The metropolitan bannermen in Shuangcheng got wind of these plans and protested that they themselves needed the plots. In the second month of 1878, when the general of Jilin sent personnel to investigate these plots, the metropolitan adult males who did not yet have *jichan* plots filed a petition to the general of Jilin requesting the 302 remaining *jichan* plots:

> Our grandfathers and fathers are all banner servants from the capital. Starting from the fourth year of Daoguang (1824), [they] were relocated

> to Shuangcheng in groups. Each household received a plot of thirty-five *shang*. Other than this [land grant], [we] had no additional property. To date, fifty years have passed and our households grow larger and larger. In each village, there are more than five hundred households of assistant adult males who work as wage labors to make a living. Many of the elderly and young children are suffering from cold and hunger. Since there are still 10,570 *shang* of land which was designated to the metropolitan bannermen, [we] sincerely supplicate [you] to allocate the land to us assistant adult males as private property without rent and thus to support [our living].[49]

To help secure government approval, these metropolitan bannermen relieved the government of its economic obligations to *jichan* landowners. As we have seen, in previous land allocations, the government not only granted land to the metropolitan bannermen, but also provided them with all of their living and farming essentials—including housing, farm tools, and livestock. The metropolitan bannermen's petition stated that this time the government need not provide them with living and farming support. Moreover, they even offered the government economic benefits in exchange for allocating these plots:

> Having received the heavenly kindness that fed us for years, [we] all have consciences. [Since] it is currently the time of putting down the bandits, we are happy to contribute three strings of cash for each *shang* of land to subsidize military expenses. This monetary contribution adds up to more than thirty thousand strings of cash. [We do this] with the intention of rendering service to repay the heavenly kindness.[50]

In addition to the military subsidy, these metropolitan bannermen also agreed as a group to contribute a total of one thousand *taels* of silver as reward funds to the armies.[51] The 302 *jichan* plots altogether would generate 31,710 strings of cash—equivalent to ten thousand *taels* of silver—plus one thousand *taels* of silver.

The general of Jilin found the offer attractive. In the second half of the nineteenth century, Jilin, like many other provincial-level governments in China, also faced serious financial challenges. To fight various rebellions throughout the country, the government had to support a large number of armies. The salaries of officials and soldiers alone came to 400,000 *taels* of silver a year.[52] In the third month of 1878, Ming'an sent a memorial to the emperor, pointing out that relocating more metropolitan bannermen to Manchuria would be a difficult and costly task, and requesting that the emperor allocate the reserved plots to the present metropolitan bannermen and collect the money the bannermen would contribute to support military expenditures.[53]

Moreover, Ming'an carried his plan out despite the central government's reservations. The emperor agreed to Ming'an's general proposal. However, the Board of Revenue had reservations about giving the plots to the existing metropolitan bannermen, and thus ordered Ming'an to hold off on this action until the board had deliberation on it further.[54] But Ming'an began allocating the plots as soon as he received the emperor's edict of approval, also in the third month. By the fifth month of 1878, the local government had collected 21,710 strings of cash and had started to transport the collected revenue to the general's office.[55] In the ninth month of 1878, when the Board of Revenue turned down Ming'an's request, Ming'an claimed that he was not aware of the board's earlier order. By that time, the bannermen had already taken the plots, and it was impossible to retrieve them. In the seventh month of 1879, the local government finished the allocation and transported the remaining one thousand *taels* of silver to the provincial government.[56]

Once more, Hualiantai's descendants greatly benefited from the allocation of these *jichan* plots. By contributing money to the government, eventually, every adult male in this family acquired one plot of *jichan* land. Jiertahun's two sons, Kuijin and Kuide, and Jiertukan's two sons, Kuijun and Kuixiang, each had one plot (Figure 6.1). Only Kuixiu's household did not acquire an additional *jichan* plot, perhaps due to the young age of his son. Thus, in 1878, Hualiantai's descendants acquired four plots of *jichan* land altogether. This is how, despite having sold their *nazu* land, Jiertahun's and Jiertukan's families remained wealthy. The metropolitan banner families had to pay 105 thousand in cash (a rate of three thousand in cash per *shang*) as the military subsidy and 3.3 *taels* of silver as reward funds to the armies to acquire one plot of *jichan* land. Thus, Jiertahun's and Jiertukan's families each paid 210 thousand in cash and 6.6 *taels* of silver.

The Transformation of Metropolitan Bannermen

These events marked the transformation of metropolitan bannermen from a state-defined population category into a wealthy and powerful social group in the local community. In the Qing banner registers, *jingqi*, or metropolitan bannerman, was a general term that referred to any bannerman administered by the banner institution in Beijing. This institutional distinction put them in a higher position in the banner hierarchy and increased their entitlements to wealth. Thus, in the late 1870s, when the court planned to relocate more metropolitan bannermen to the northeast, it still considered those to be relocated from Beijing the same as those already settled in Shuangcheng. However, after a half-century in Shuangcheng, the metropolitan bannermen there owned considerable land and were deeply embedded in the local social structure. Their privileges in land entitlements generated shared interests and a distinctive identity. Their wealth and social status had given them the power to act collectively to prevent their counterparts in Beijing from joining them and sharing their privileges and wealth. Through this collective action, metropolitan bannermen in Shuangcheng bestowed a new identity on this population category.

This transformation happened within a national context of the devolution of political power and the development of local society. In the second half of the nineteenth century, continuous foreign invasions and internal rebellions had drained the central government's coffers and significantly weakened the Qing court's control of the provinces. Provincial governors had greater autonomy to resist the orders of the central government and carry out plans of their own. At the same time, various local organizations, independent of state sponsorship—which some scholars have characterized as "pre-capitalist enterprise"—rose to become main actors in managing local affairs (Tsou 1981a). Shuangcheng society, originally a state creation, also developed on its own. In offering a substantial monetary contribution to the government, the metropolitan bannermen as a collectivity had actively negotiated with state authority and enlisted the help of the general of Jilin to pursue their own interests.

Metropolitan bannermen became a powerful group through long-term wealth accumulation. Over a half-century, a significant number of metropolitan banner households expanded their wealth and became affluent, as Hualiantai's descendants had done. In the first round of land allocation in 1878, 206 metropolitan banner households acquired 246 plots of land. Of the 206 households, 159 acquired one plot each, 39 acquired two plots each, and 8 acquired three plots each. Jiertahun's and Jiertukan's families were among this elite group, as was the aforementioned Mingshan's household. Mingshan was the principal clerk who took charge of the allocation of the 302 *jichan* plots.[57] As a result, he not only acquired a plot of *jichan* land for his son, Changling—who was only two years old and had just appeared on the population register—but also reserved a plot for his cousin's son.[58] The existence of a significant proportion of wealthy households made the category of metropolitan bannermen a powerful social group.

Moreover, metropolitan bannermen became a meaningful social group also because of their strategy to act collectively in pursuit of their interests. Without the support of extended kin networks, metropolitan families especially needed allies based on non-kin connections. While village community was such a connection, the state category of metropolitan bannermen also provided a ready-to-use structure. Metropolitan banner families more or less shared a place of origin. Most importantly, they shared privileges in terms of government aid, which constituted an important source of power. This commonality provided the ground for individual metropolitan banner families to ally with one another. In so doing, metropolitan bannermen capitalized on their privileges and enforced the boundaries of this social category.

RETAINING FAMILY WEALTH, 1879–1906

As the metropolitan bannermen established themselves as a wealthy and powerful group in Shuangcheng, the future wealth status of a metropolitan banner family was dependent on their ability to have an heir who could carry on the family line and wealth. This was especially true for metropolitan bannermen whose wealth mainly consisted of *jichan* land, because the inheritance and registration of this land was subject to state intervention. To uphold the principle of equitable distribution, the government forbade the holding of more than one plot of *jichan* land by any person (*yiren buzhun chengling liangfen dingque*). At times, this rule even prevented the biological kin of household heads from inheriting land.[59] Although metropolitan bannermen used various strategies to negotiate the implementation of state policies and to expand their wealth, they complied with this one-plot-per-person rule. For example, in the 1878 allocation of *jichan* land, the number of *jichan* plots some metropolitan banner households acquired exceeded the number of adult males in the household. The heads of those households then registered the additional plots under the names of their male children, establishing them as the heads of separate households. Consequently, 192 new households were headed by males below the age of twenty, the official age of adulthood in Shuangcheng. Moreover, 88 of the 192 child household heads were below the age of ten. Clearly, having a male heir was a necessity to maintain the ownership of a *jichan* plot.[60]

Hualiantai's descendants also faced the issue of transmitting the family wealth to later generations. After the 1878 land allocation, Hualiantai's descents had a total of seven *jichan* plots. Accordingly, this descent group had seven registered households, each of which was a nuclear family. Each surviving male member of the second and third generations had a plot of *jichan* land and was a household head. Because of the state's one-plot-per-person rule, none of the males of the third generation was eligible to inherit the lands of the second generation. Thus, having heirs in the fourth generation was crucial to retaining their family wealth.

In the thirty years following the 1878 allocation of *jichan* plots, the third generation of this descent group had dramatically different luck in reproduction. Jiertahun's elder son, Kuijin, and his wife were extremely successful in producing heirs. Already having produced four sons and two daughters by 1878, the couple registered four more children between 1880 and 1886: a daughter born between 1880 and 1881, twin boys born between 1883 and 1884, and another son born between 1886 and 1887. In total, this couple had ten registered children.[61] Although their first, fourth, and seventh sons and first daughter died early, four of their sons and two daughters survived into adulthood (Figure 6.1). By contrast, Kuijin's younger brother, Kuide, and their cousins all struggled to produce a male heir. Although Kuide and his wife had a son in 1875, mother and son died in 1880 and 1883, respectively. Kuide immediately remarried. Between 1882 and 1891, the couple gave birth to three daughters and two sons. Yet only the first two daughters and the younger son survived into adulthood. Kuixiu, Jiertuhun's only surviving son, also had just one son during this period. Moreover, Jiertukan's two sons, Kuijun and Kuixiang, were not able to produce a surviving son at all. This difference in reproductive success soon determined the fortunes of these families when inheritance was involved.

The first *jichan* plot available for inheritance was Jiertahun's. By 1879, Jiertahun had become a widower at the age of sixty-six. After his two sons established their separate households, he was the only member remaining in the household. Jiertahun died sometime between 1879 and 1881. Although in theory Jiertahun's sons had the first right to inherit his land, the state's regulation superseded this right, and so Kuijin and Kuide, who each already had one plot of *jichan* land, were not eligible to inherit their father's land. The family then passed the rights of inheritance to Jiertahun's eldest grandson Rongqing, who was Kuijin's eldest son. In 1883, Rongqing, at the age of fourteen, was registered as the head of an independent household, of which he was the only member, although he very likely still lived with his parents. As in the case of Changling, the registration of Rongqing as an independent household head was only done to conform to the state rule. Therefore, Kuijin's family in fact had two plots of *jichan* land.

While Jiertahun's descendants were able to keep the land within this branch, Jiertukan's descendants faced difficulty in producing a male heir and retaining his *jichan* plot. After their two sons each had a *jichan* plot and headed their own households in 1879, Jiertukan and his wife were the only two members remaining in the household; both were fifty-four years old. Jiertukan died sometime between 1884 and 1885, at the age of fifty-nine, and his wife remained in the household as a widow. At the time, Jiertukan had no grandson. Jiertukan's elder son, Kuijun, and his wife only had a thirteen-year-old daughter registered, and the second son, Kuixiang, at the age of twenty-three, was still single. Because Kuijun and Kuixiang could not inherit the plot left by their father, if neither of the brothers produced a son, their branch would lose the ownership of Jiertukan's *jichan* plot after the death of their mother.

Since Kuixiang remained single throughout the period under study, the task of producing an heir became Kuijun and his wife's responsibility. The couple made at least three attempts. In 1885, Kuijun registered his second daughter, who was born sometime between 1882 and 1883. Between 1887 and 1888, the couple gave birth to another daughter. Yet they did not register her until they finally gave birth to a son, named Rongsheng, between 1890 and 1891. Here was the male heir the family had been longing for. Thus, Kuijun registered Rongsheng immediately in 1891. Unfortunately, Rongsheng died between 1896 and 1897, while his grandmother was still alive.[62] When Jiertukan's wife died sometime between 1901 and 1903, this family had no heir to inherit the *jichan* plot.

Eventually, Jiertahun's grandson inherited Jiertukan's *jichan* plot. In the 1904 household register, Jiertahun's second grandson Rongkai took Jiertukan's *jichan* plot and became an independent household head (SCPGBTDHKDM, 1834666: 75). Rongkai inherited his great uncle's *jichan* plot under a rule stipulating that if the landowner had no eligible heir, the inheritance rights belonged to existing relatives of the owner (*enque*).[63] Compared to the selection of heirs for lands left behind by extinct households, which required the area commander-in-chief to review the profiles of the candidate households and sanction the selection, the selection of heirs for *enque* was simpler; the captain's office and the village head took full responsibility for handling the inheritance of *enque*, and the closeness of blood and birth order decided the precedence of inheritance rights. In practice, it was typically the descent group itself that selected the heir from among the close kin of the landowner. The captain's office and the village head simply sanctioned their decision. Therefore, in the inheritance of *enque*, the descent group had great power and authority to decide the heir. In this case, Rongkai acquired the inheritance rights as the second grandson of Jiertukan's eldest brother. Rongkai's elder brother Rongqing had inherited his grandfather's land, and so Rongkai had first precedence among the close kin to inherit Jiertukan's plot.

At the same time that the fourth generation was inheriting land left behind by the second generation, some deceased members in the third generation were also passing down their lands to the fourth generation. When Kuixiu died between 1883 and 1884, at the age of forty-five, his only son, Ronglin, inherited his land and the household headship, at the age of fifteen.[64] It was a straightforward process. The inheritance of the unmarried and childless Kuixiang's *jichan* plot, however, was more complicated. Kuixiang died between 1903 and 1904, without an heir. His brother Kuijun also did not have a surviving heir. Therefore, Kuixiang's plot was open to Jiertahun's and Jiertuhun's descendants.

The records in the household and land registers reflect the competition between the descendants of Jiertahun's and Jiertuhun's branches of the family over the inheritance rights of Kuixiang's *jichan* plot. Unlike the other inheritance cases in this family, in which the heir replaced the deceased household head immediately after his or her death, Kuixiang's name remained on the registers as the head of an empty household for at least three years after his death. Accordingly, in the 1906 land register of the Bordered Yellow Banner he was still recorded as the owner of the plot; this indicates that descendants of Jiertahun' and Jiertuhun's branches still had not settled on the heir of this plot (SCPGBTDHKDM 1834667: 82). Only in the 1907 household register, did Ronglin, Jiertuhun's only grandson, appear as the head of Kuixiang's extinct household. Three years later, the headship of Kuixiang's extinct household changed again. The 1911 household register states that Rongshan, one of the twin boys born to Kuijin, had replaced Ronglin as the household head (SCPGBTDHKDM 1834667: 81); this is a clear indication that he finally acquired the ownership of Kuixiang's *jichan* plot from Ronglin. The same register also shows that Ronghai, Rongshan's twin brother, inherited the household headship and the land left over by his father, Kuijin, who was recorded as deceased in 1907.

The competition over the inheritance rights to Kuixiang's plot happened at a time the state landownership in Shuangcheng was undergoing a structural change. In 1902, the state began gradually privatizing the land in Jilin. In 1906, the government announced the decision to collect rents from all the *jichan* lands.[65] Following this move, the government also allowed land transfers between bannermen and civilian commoners in Shuangcheng.[66] Consequently, the state policy prohibiting a person to own more than one *jichan* plot loosened up. After Ronglin inherited this *jichan* plot in 1907, he became the owner of two plots of *jichan* land, one from his father and the other from Kuixiang.[67] This victory in the competition over the inheritance rights of Kuixiang's plot shows that even though Ronglin was the only descendant in his branch, he still was positioned to acquire the plot of land. Yet, Ronglin's ownership of Kuixiang's *jichan* plot faced further challenges from Jiertahun's branch. In 1911, Ronglin and his wife had reached the ages of thirty-eight and thirty-seven, respectively. Yet the couple still did not have a registered child. Thus, although Ronglin controlled two plots of *jichan* land, because he was without an heir, the inheritance rights to both two plots were challenged by kin who had heirs.

The story of Hualiantai's family sheds light on the causal relationship between demographic performance and socioeconomic status.

Quantitative studies of the influence of demographic performance on the patterns of inequality over the long term reveal that, in historical China and England, families of higher socioeconomic status were more likely to have more children (Harrell 1985; Wolf 2001; Clark and Hamilton 2006; Shiue 2008; Tsuya et al. 2010). This positive association between socio-economic status and fertility also existed in Shuangcheng; compared to those with fewer landholdings and without members who were officials, families with more landholdings or with members who were officials were more likely to have registered children (Chen, Lee, and Campbell 2010). Most scholars have assumed that having higher socioeconomic status enabled families to have more children. By contrast, the story of Hualiantai's family highlights the importance of reproductive success as a determinant of wealth status: those who had more male children became rich. Hualiantai's three sons had similar social and economic backgrounds, and this descent group only had four generations in the period under study. Even in this relatively homogeneous descent group, difference in the ability to have surviving sons was the major cause of differentiated wealth status. In fact, because of the state land-allocation policy that maintained an equitable distribution of *jichan* land, male children became a form of capital with which metropolitan banner families could expand their *jichan* landholdings.

By the end of the Qing, land distribution among Hualiantai's descendants was marked by the triumph of Jiertahun's branch. By 1911, Jiertukan's line had become extinct.[68] Kuijun died sometime between 1908 and 1911, and Ronglun, Jiertahun's grandson and Kuide's eldest son, inherited this plot. Thus, six of the seven *jichan* plots were registered under the names of Jiertahun's descendants; four belonged to Kuijin's sons and two belonged to Kuide and his son. By contrast, Jiertuhun's branch only had one plot of *jichan* land.

WEALTH, DEMOGRAPHIC PERFORMANCE, AND SOCIAL FORMATION

Walking through time with Hualiantai's family, we find that, by the late Qing, the interaction between state policies, the wealth status of individual families, and the demographic performance of those families has transformed metropolitan bannermen into a powerful and wealthy group. At first glance, this seems to be because state land allocation turned metropolitan bannermen into landlords on the rural frontier and gave them privileges in future land accumulation. Yet, metropolitan bannermen became a wealthy and powerful social group not simply because the state imposed this hierarchy from the top down; rather, successful metropolitan banner families actively capitalized on their privileges to expand their landholdings and strengthen their power.

The long-term interaction between wealth status and demographic performance changed the composition of metropolitan bannermen. As a privileged group, the most serious threat to the wealth status of a metropolitan banner family was household extinction. Therefore, having surviving heirs was crucial to their success. Those without at least one heir became extinct and vanished from the history of Shuangcheng; those that survived became wealthy. The demographic history of Hualiantai's family shows that, in a rural frontier society, even wealthy families experienced high mortality during times of hardship. The demographic performance of particular families was therefore distinguished by how successful they were in marriage and reproduction. In the first four decades after the settlement, ability to continue the family line created dramatic differences in the fates of metropolitan bannermen. This finding is in line with results from quantitative analysis of other populations in historical China. In their study on the development of descent lines in two other historical populations, Song, Campbell, and Lee (2015) found that males with high social status were more successful in sustaining their descent lines. Moreover, having a lower probability of extinction at each point of time contributes more to this success than having a large number of sons. Thus, in the late Qing, metropolitan bannermen in Shuangcheng were no longer a simple aggregation of official immigrants from Beijing and Rehe. They were families capable of expanding the size of their families and using various sources of power to pursue their interests.

Finally, strategies used by these successful metropolitan banner families to enhance their socioeconomic status generated forces of social change. Although the family history drawn from government archives only captures part of the experiences of metropolitan bannermen, when situating this in the broader context of the development of this immigrant society, we see that Shuangcheng provided banner families a wide range of settings in which to exercise agency. By expanding their family size, successful metropolitan banner families were able to develop into descent groups consisting of multiple households. Although these descent groups were not as elaborate as those in other parts of China, they were a sign of prosperity. Moreover, these successful families also worked together as a group to pursue their collective interests. Their membership in the category of metropolitan bannermen—the top elite—was the basis for their alliance. Well aware of their privileges and the different interests of the state representatives, metropolitan banner families were able to appeal to officials and utilize state power in the process of pursuing their benefits. By actively using these resources, they successfully maintained their privileges and sustained the state-mandated social hierarchy.

CHAPTER SEVEN

Sustaining Hierarchy

Wealth Stratification

When talking about wealth stratification in historical China, people usually reference two influential sayings: "the rich have large fields connected by crisscross paths, and the poor do not even have enough land to stick an awl into" (*fuzhe tian lian qianmo, pin zhe wu lizhui zhidi*) and "from rags to riches and back in three generations."[1] The first saying depicts an extreme situation of land concentration. In the second century BC, an official named Dong Zhongshu (179–104 BC) used this rhetoric to illustrate the consequences of the privatization and the free transaction of land (HS, book 4, 1137). His purpose was to persuade the emperor of the Western Han (202 BC–AD 8) to enforce state control of land and maintain equal land distribution among commoners, because maintaining equal land distribution and ensuring a large base population that paid taxes and provided labor services was crucial to the dynasty's rule. The second saying illustrates a society with dramatically fluctuating wealth mobility. Together, these sayings summarize two assumptions about the outcomes of a totally free land market—volatility and inequality: the distribution of landed wealth was highly unequal at both the national and community levels, and the wealth statuses of individual families was unstable.

For centuries, these two sayings have influenced people's understanding of political economy and wealth stratification in premodern and early modern China. The central government's power always faced competition from wealthy landowners, who tended to accumulate large amounts of land and to control the population working on it (He 1956,

1958). The transition from a system of relatively egalitarian land distribution to one in which landownership was highly concentrated has thus been a central component of the canonical theory of the "dynastic cycle" (Li and Jiang 2005, 12). At the beginning of almost every Chinese dynasty, the new state redistributed land relatively equally among the populations who paid taxes to the state and provided it with labor, to break up the land concentrations that had formed during the previous dynasty. In spite of these efforts, elite families constantly sought to expand their wealth and power through land sales and seizure, and wealth was eventually re-concentrated. Consequently, the country saw growing inequality, increasing social and political unrest, and declining state control over the population, which eventually led to the fall of the dynasty. During the periods of land concentration, contemporaries repeatedly invoked the first saying to describe the dramatic inequality in wealth status between the rich and the poor, to the point where it became a standard idiomatic expression. By the mid-twentieth century, this traditional conception, together with writings by Marxist theoreticians,[2] became framed in communist class terms and led to a widely accepted and rarely questioned understanding that landlords and rich peasants, who accounted for less than 10 percent of the rural population, occupied 70 to 80 percent of the land.[3]

However, recent studies have challenged this view of increasing land concentration in Chinese history. Using survey data collected in the early twentieth century, some scholars have argued that, although land distribution in China was highly unequal, there is no evidence to show that distribution became increasingly concentrated over the long term.[4] In other words, the pattern of land distribution in historical China was stable. Based on government tax registers compiled between the fifteenth and early twentieth centuries, some scholars have even asserted that, during most periods in late imperial China, land distribution was not concentrated (Chao and Chen 1982; Chao 1986; Qin and Su 1996; Chao 2003).[5] The fact that tenants' land-use rights became the equivalent of partial ownership offset the inequality in land distribution (Chao 2003, 296–302). However, because the data used in existing studies are scattered and sometimes incomplete, the debate over wealth inequality in historical China continues.[6]

Land distribution in Shuangcheng contributes to this debate by illuminating a long-term pattern of wealth stratification in an age of drastic social and political change. The period under study falls at the end of the "dynastic cycle" of the Qing, as the country saw an increasing devolution of political power and the rise of local elites. At the national level, from the 1850s to the early twentieth century, various local organizations that were independent of state sponsorship rose to provide essential services in local society (Jones 1979; Tsou 1981b; Rankin 1986; Li 2005). This trend resulted not only from the decline of the central government's power but also from the long-term growth in wealth among the local elites, which enabled them to develop some forms of "precapitalist enterprise" (Tsou 1981a). In Manchuria, an indication of these changes was the privatization of state land beginning in the 1860s, as the state gradually opened up land to free migration and eventually allowed free land transfers. In Shuangcheng, the privatization of banner land began in 1902 and was finally completed in 1906, marked by the government's collecting rent on *jichan* land.[7] Five years later, the Qing dynasty fell, and a republican government assumed authority. Whether land distribution in Shuangcheng became increasingly concentrated during this period provides a reference to studies of wealth stratification in pre-revolutionary China.

Moreover, by providing a panoramic view of the socioeconomic hierarchy based on landownership, the patterns of land distribution in Shuangcheng furthers our understanding of social formation in this region. As previous chapters have shown, ever since the initial settlement of the immigrants, capable households have made efforts to expand their landholdings through land clearing and transfers. The metropolitan bannermen used state policies and capitalized on their privileges to maintain and promote their elite status. Rural bannermen gradually gained advantages in *nazu* landholding (Table 5.1). As people from all walks of life used strategies to survive and prosper on the frontier, the pattern of land distribution and its change over time shed light on the consequences of the agency of local people in the social hierarchy.

THE OVERALL PATTERN OF LAND DISTRIBUTION, 1876

Since we have relatively complete land records in 1876, the pattern of land distribution in this year serves as a point of departure for examining the level of land concentration and the underlying social hierarchy in Shuangcheng.[8] For the whole area, except the forty banner villages of the left *tun*, the government registers this year record a total of 4,021 households, of which 698 are metropolitan bannermen, 2,076 belong to rural bannermen, 579 belong to floating bannermen,[9] and 668 are civilian commoners.[10] In addition, there is an estimate of 3,500 unregistered household living in this area (see Appendix B). How the official landownership was distributed among the 7,521 households sheds light on the social hierarchy a half-century after the settlement of Shuangcheng.

Including the unregistered households in the denominator results in an unequal distribution of land.[11] As Figure 7.1 shows, the top decile of households owned 48 percent of registered land in Shuangcheng. The top centile of households alone owned 15 percent of land, and the top 5 percent of households owned 34 percent of the land. Moreover, the bottom 55 percent of households owned nothing. The Gini coefficient of the land distribution is 0.72. While the level of inequality presented in this

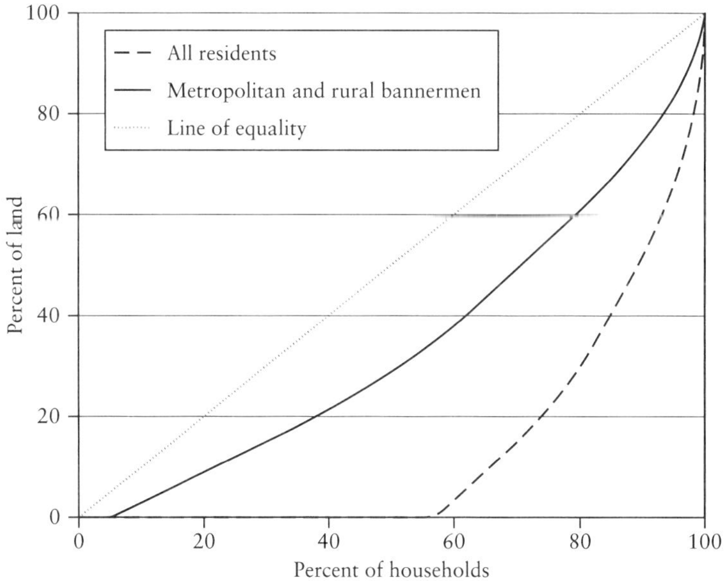

Figure 7.1. The distributions of all land (Lorenz curves) among Shuangcheng residents and among the metropolitan and rural bannermen, 1876.

SOURCE: CMGPD-SC.

NOTE: The residents of the forty banner villages in the left *tun* are excluded from the calculation because the *jichan* land registers for these villages did not survive.

figure is high, it is still not comparable to the national estimate made by the Chinese Communist Party in 1947 that the top decile of households owned 70 percent of the land (Zhongyang dang'an guan 1992, 547). Interestingly, similar patterns of land distribution were found in Jilin and Heilongjiang in the 1930s. Based on survey data compiled in the Manchukuo period, Reardon-Anderson (2005, 220, table 4, regions 2 and 3) estimates that the top 5 percent of households owned from 29 to 39 percent of land, and around 60 percent of the households had no land.

The unequal land distribution in Shuangcheng has its origin in the structural inequality sponsored by the state. Floating bannermen and the unregistered population accounted for 86 percent of the households in the landless group (Figure 7.1). These people were structural have-nots, as the state assignment of differentiated land entitlements prevented them from officially owing land. In this sense, the estimated size of unregistered population has significant impact in the pattern of land distribution, as it determined the size of the landless group. If the number of unregistered households is more than the estimated number, the land distribution could be more unequal, and vice versa.

While land entitlement is a major source differentiating the landed and landless groups, the contrast between the wealth status of the two was enlarged by the fact that the low population density enabled all the landed households to own an amount of land that would have been considered large elsewhere in China. As a recently settled frontier, Shuangcheng's population in the 1870s was still small. Thus, even the smallest landholder in Shuangcheng might have been regarded as a rich peasant in more densely populated areas. For example, in late nineteenth century, in two villages in Suian, Zhejiang province, the largest landholding for a household was between seventy and a hundred *mu*, which was equivalent to seven to ten *shang* (Chao and Chen 1982, 156).[12] The majority of households in these two villages had less than seven *mu* of land. In nine Hebei and Shandong villages in 1890, a household owning one hundred *mu*, or ten *shang*, of land was considered "rich," and the richest household owned seven hundred *mu*, or seventy *shang*, of land (Huang 1985, 76–77, table 4.2). By contrast, an average rural banner household in Shuangcheng had 18.33 *shang* of land, and all except four of the landed households owned one or more *shang* of land. The relatively large size of these landholdings is common in elsewhere in Manchuria.

In 1909, in northern Manchuria, farmers owning less than ten *shang* of land were classified as small farmers, and those whose landholding was between ten and fifty *shang* were middle famers. Only those with more than fifty *shang* of land were referred to as large landholders (MMTKK 1909, 16). Therefore, in a frontier region, the most prominent inequality was that between the haves and have-nots.

Although the landed households were in general well off, the top decile of households distinguished themselves from the rest of the landed households in having significantly larger amounts of land. While the top decile of households had 48 percent of land, the second decile of households owned 22 percent of land, and the third and fourth deciles of households owned only 28 percent of land. In the 1876 land register, a household in the top centile had a minimum of 123.3 *shang* of land, and the largest landowner had 776.17 *shang* of land. To be classified in the top 5 percent of households in landholding, a household needed a minimum of 53.46 *shang* of land.

Moreover, these large landholders consisted of households from diverse population categories. Figure 7.2 illustrates the composition of each population category measured by the landholding status of its members. While 27.6 percent of metropolitan banner households and 13.6 percent of rural banner households were in the top decile of households, a considerable number of civilian commoners—accounting for 42.5 percent of those registered as civilian tenants—were also in this wealthy group. In addition, some households classified as tenants or banner tenants were also in the top decile of households. Most noticeably, forty-three civilian tenant households were in the top centile of households, and the two largest landowners, who owned 776.17 and 702.88 *shang* of land, were civilian commoners.[13] At the same time, only ten metropolitan bannermen and eighteen rural bannermen households were in the top centile in landholding. These results indicate that the privileged metropolitan and rural banner households did not dominate the wealthiest group. Instead, some civilian commoners—who in theory had no land entitlement—owned a large amount of land.

A closer examination of the civilian commoners shows that the large landholdings recorded in the land registers were likely products of the early settlement stage. As chapter 3 has shown, most of these civilian commoners were residentially segregated from their banner counterparts.

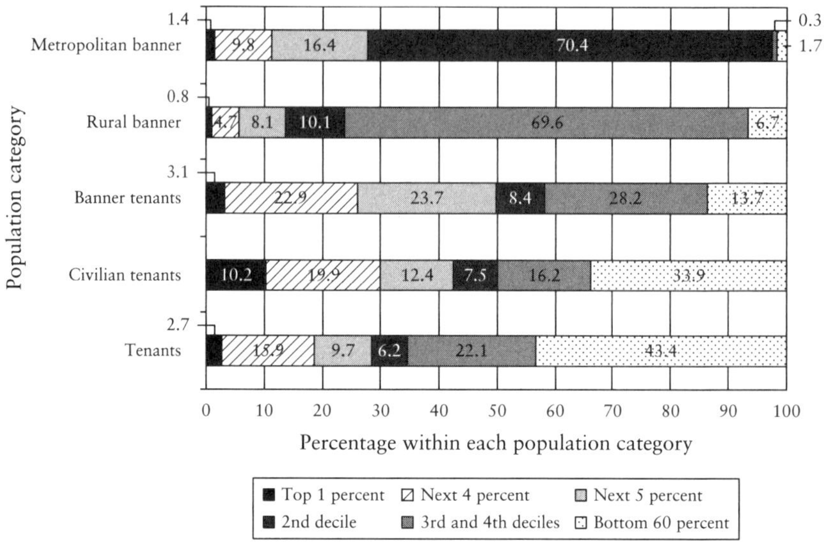

Figure 7.2. The composition of each population category, by landholding status, 1876.

SOURCE: CMGPD-SC.

NOTE: The residents of the forty banner villages in the left *tun* are excluded from the calculation.

All but one of the forty-three civilian tenants from the top centile of households lived and owned land in the civilian sections. Similarly, 165 out of 175 of the civilian tenant households from the top decile did so. A few examples of the early civilian settlers indicate that some names of the landowners on the civilian land registers remained unchanged from the time of initial registration. For example, in the 1876 land registers, a civilian commoner named Zhou Rong owned a total of 471 *shang* of land (SCPGBTDHKDM 1834731: 658). In the 1840s, he organized nine households of civilian commoners to privately cultivate 595 *shang* of land, and this land became the target of the struggle between woman Wu and Taqibu described in chapter 4. Thirty years later, although the amount of land changed, Zhou Rong still appeared on the land registers as the owner. Thus, the large landholdings of civilian tenant households were very likely the legacy of contractors who organized settlement and land clearing in the civilian sections prior to the 1850s.

The composition of the civilian commoners' landholdings also illustrates the trajectories of their land accumulation. The land they owned mainly consisted of four types: *gongzu*, the land civilian commoners had cultivated prior to the official settlement of Shuangcheng; *suique*, the land allocated to individual banner officers and soldiers with active positions;[14] *hengchan*, the land north of Shuangcheng that the government rented to civilian commoners to fund the stipends paid to the metropolitan bannermen and to cover office expenditures; and *ziken*, the land Shuangcheng immigrants privately cultivated following the official settlement and registered with the government in 1854. Except for *ziken* land, all the other three categories of land were located outside the banner sections. As the histories of these lands indicate, these civilian commoners had cleared land in Shuangcheng prior to the arrival of the banner settlers. Some of the settlers were able to register their households and lands with the government. Moreover, because the government needed laborers after the settlement of bannermen, these civilian commoners had the opportunity to act as contractors to further claim large amounts of land. For example, a civilian commoner named Yu Yuanxun had settled and cultivated land in Shuangcheng before the arrival of bannermen.[15] In 1820, he was able to register 15 *shang* of *gongzu* land. Then, in the 1820s, he claimed 105 *shang* of *suique* land from the government. At the same time, he privately cleared 50 *shang* of land, which was registered as *ziken* land in 1854. His landed wealth added up to 170 *shang*. Thus, as contractors, these large landholders in the civilian sections had government sponsorship.

Unlike the large civilian landholders, whose lands consisted of a variety of types, metropolitan and rural bannermen from the top decile of households mainly owned *jichan* and *nazu* land. After the settlement, some of the capable banner settlers were able to recruit tenants and privately cleared sizeable areas of land. Moreover, as chapter 3 discusses, when the government started to register privately cultivated land in 1854, some banner households took advantage of their land entitlements and seized lands from the civilian commoners and floating bannermen whose names were not on the government registers. Through this maneuvering, some capable metropolitan and rural bannermen became the wealthy group.

Above all, the unequal pattern of land distribution in Shuangcheng was the product of the interaction between the frontier settlement and the assignment of differentiated land entitlements by the state. The large landholdings mainly came into being in the first thirty years of the settlement. In the late nineteenth century, despite the deterioration of the state's fiscal situation and the development of social organizations in Shuangcheng, there is no evidence that land distribution became more concentrated than it had been in the early period. While the analysis in the following section will prove this among the metropolitan and rural banner households, the story of Zhou Rong sheds some light on the changes in the size of civilian commoners' landholdings. In the 1840s the government found that he cultivated 595 *shang* of land;[16] in 1876 the landholdings registered under his name shrank to 471 *shang*. The pattern of land distribution illustrates a frontier society full of opportunities for entitled and capable people in the early years of settlement.

At the same time, if tenants' land-use rights were taken into consideration, land distribution in Shuangcheng will be less unequal. Archival sources and notes from fieldwork indicate that, in Shuangcheng, managerial landlords who hired a large number of laborers to farm the land were uncommon. Instead, landlords usually rented their lands to individual tenants and collected rents from them. This is especially true for the banner lands (MMTKK 1911, 12). Thus, given the unequal assignment of land entitlements and the large amounts of land the entitled households had, tenancy was prevalent. As in China proper, these tenants usually enjoyed stable use rights for the land they farmed, and some of them even rented out their lands to other tenants—an indication that tenants in fact had gained partial ownership of their lands. Because of this, Kang Chao (2003, 296–302) maintains that, after tenants' partial landownership is taken into consideration, land distribution in China was equal, even in an area that had a concentrated distribution of registered landownership. This is also the case for land tenure in Shuangcheng. Having no registered land did not necessarily lead to poverty. In fact, some tenants rented sizeable amounts of land and were well-to-do. For example, a lawsuit filed in 1897 reveals that, in the 1860s, a floating bannerman named Wu Chengkui rented twenty-seven *shang* of *jichan* land from a metropolitan bannerman named Li Baocheng.[17] Wu farmed the land for more than thirty years and built a thatched house with sixteen rooms. Then, Wu rented the land and house to another floating bannerman, named Zhao Qinglin. In the transaction, Wu not only collected a deposit of two hundred strings of cash but also specified that Zhao pay him an annual rent of fifteen *dou* of grains for each *shang* of land he rented. The phenomenon of tenants becoming wealthy persisted into the mid-twentieth century. In 1946, before the communist Land Reform, the economic circumstances of tenant households in Shuangcheng were so stratified that the communist register classified their class status into three categories: the rich, the middle, and the poor tenants.[18] The rich tenants were those who either hired laborers to work on their lands or rented their land to someone else.

LAND DISTRIBUTION AND WEALTH MOBILITY AMONG METROPOLITAN AND RURAL BANNERMEN

Given the highly unequal pattern of land distribution and dynamic composition of the large landholders in Shuangcheng, it is necessary to examine the implications for the state-designed social hierarchy. In other words, with some civilian commoners being large landholders, to what extent and by what measures were the metropolitan and rural bannermen still the elite? Figure 7.2 illustrates the advantages metropolitan bannermen had over other population categories in terms of wealth status; an overwhelming majority of metropolitan banner households belonged to the top two deciles of households; whereas households of other population categories are distributed across the landholding strata. The wealth status of rural banner households was diversified. Although a considerable number of rural banner households belonged to the top decile, about 70 percent of them fell into the third and fourth deciles, which means these households only kept their *jichan* land and perhaps a moderate amount of *nazu* land. This overview shows that, in 1876, metropolitan bannermen were able to maintain their status as an elite group because they were endowed with a relatively homogeneous wealth status, ensured by the *jichan* plot. From this preliminary observation, the pattern of land distribution among the metropolitan and rural bannermen and their wealth mobility help answer the question of whether their elite status endured in the last few decades of the dynasty.

Distribution

The overall distribution of land among the metropolitan and rural banner households exhibits a pattern of stratification without concentration. As Figure 7.1 shows, the shares of land by the top centil and top decile of households were 6 percent and 26 percent, respectively. The bottom decile of households owned 2 percent of land. While the disproportionate share of land among the wealthiest groups indicates some level of inequality, the pattern of land distribution among metropolitan and rural bannermen was still relatively equal. This relative equality is especially indicated by the low percentage, only about 5 percent, of households without any land. The Gini coefficient of the land distribution is 0.31. Thus, compared with the highly unequal land distribution among the entire population in Shuangcheng, the level of inequality in land distribution among metropolitan and rural bannermen was low.

This moderate inequality in land distribution existed in many agrarian communities in East Asia at different points in time. For example, in two villages in the late nineteenth-century Japan, the top decile of households owned 22 percent of land, and the bottom decile of households shared 3.4 percent of land (Kurosu 2010). In 1941, in four villages in Hebei and Shandong, the top decile of households owned between 22 percent and 38 percent of land, and the bottom decile of households owned between 1 percent and 4 percent of land (Myers 1970, 44, figure 2). In 2002, the top decile of the population in rural China had 30.5 percent of the wealth, and the bottom decile possessed 2 percent (Li and Zhao 2007).[19] While these statistics of land distribution vary in terms of the scale of society and time period, they all suggest that in East Asia, land distribution among the population entitled to own it was not concentrated.

The respective distributions of *jichan* and *nazu* lands indicate that the above pattern of land distribution was a product of an equal distribution of *jichan* land and an unequal distribution of *nazu* land. As Figure 7.3 shows, in 1876, the majority of metropolitan and rural banner households had one plot of *jichan* land. Only 2 percent of metropolitan banner households and 6 percent of rural banner households had no *jichan* land. Moreover, in each population category, less than 1 percent of households had more than one plot of *jichan* land. This pattern of distri-

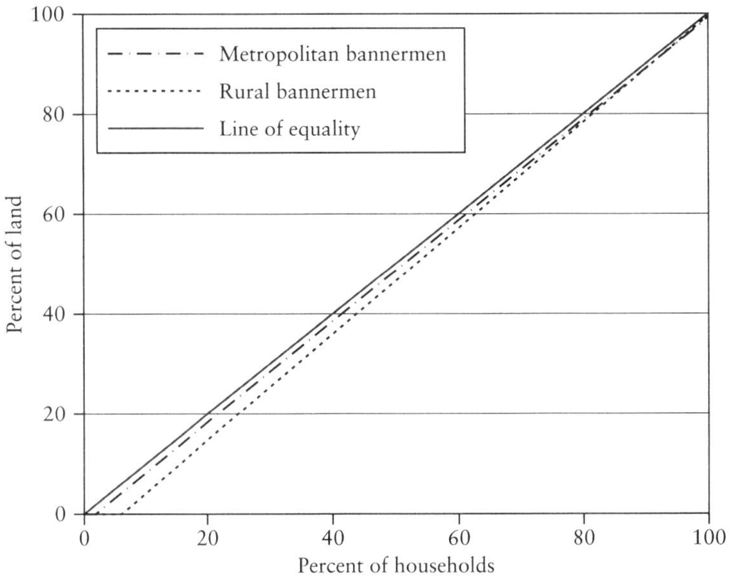

Figure 7.3. The distributions of *jichan* land (Lorenz curves) among metropolitan and rural bannermen, 1876.

SOURCE: CMGPD-SC.

NOTE: The base population consists of metropolitan and rural bannermen living in the eighty villages of the central and the right *tun*.

bution shows that in registration most of the landed households followed the regulation that each household could have only one plot of *jichan* land. Overall, the state land-allocation policy was effective in maintaining an equal distribution of *jichan* land within each population category.

Even thirty years later, the distribution of *jichan* land remained relatively equal. Figure 7.4 compares the distributions of *jichan* land among the metropolitan bannermen in all forty villages and the rural bannermen in twenty villages in the central *tun* in 1875–1876 and 1906–1907. In both periods, the metropolitan and rural bannermen were in two segments in the land distribution. Rural bannermen occupied the lower segment, and metropolitan bannermen occupied the upper segment. Land distribution in each segment was equal. Inequality did grow slightly over time because of an increase in the percentage of households without *jichan* plots, from 2 percent in the 1870s to 7 percent in the 1900s (Figure 7.4).[20] Moreover, in 1906–1907, 3 percent of metropolitan banner

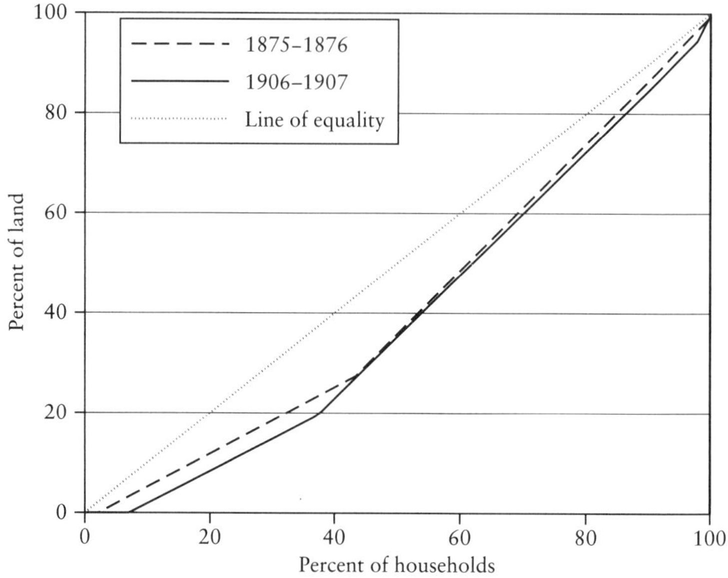

Figure 7.4. Comparison of the distributions of *jichan* land (Lorenz curves), 1875–1876 and 1906–1907.

SOURCE: CMGPD-SC.
NOTE: The *jichan* land distributions are based on data on rural bannermen living in twenty villages of the central *tun* and all metropolitan bannermen. These households belong to three banner administrations: Plain Yellow, Bordered Yellow, and Plain Red. See Wang et al. (2016) for the village locations. Only these banners are included in the analysis because they had complete *jichan* records for both periods.

households and 6 percent of rural banner households had more land than was originally assigned to them. For example, twenty-nine metropolitan banner households had two plots of *jichan*.[21] Yet, despite the greater stratification of *jichan* landholdings among bannermen in 1906–1907, the majority of households still had one plot of *jichan* land, which ensured a relatively equal land distribution. This situation indicates that, although the economic and social changes over the thirty-year period caused some households to lose their lands, the overall pattern of *jichan* land distribution persisted. Given the fact that in 1906 the government made an effort to identify the de facto landowners to reflect the results of free land transfers and to facilitate rent collection, the persistence of the pattern of land distribution indicates that banner house-

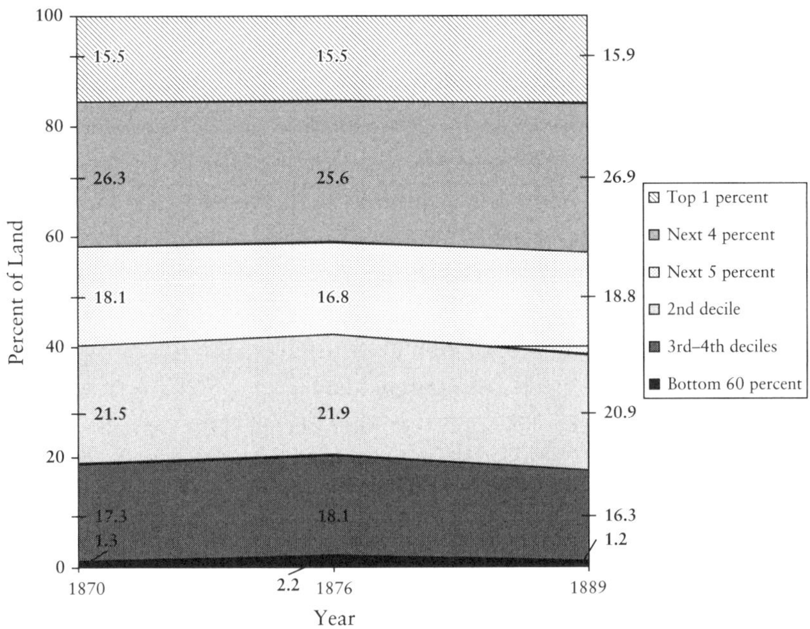

Figure 7.5. The distribution of *nazu* land among metropolitan and rural banner households, illustrated by percentage share of land by each *nazu* landholding stratum, 1870–1889.

SOURCE: CMGPD-SC.

NOTE: The base population consists of all metropolitan and rural bannermen living in the 120 banner villages.

holds were still able to maintain their *jichan* land and thus their elite status.

While the distribution of *jichan* land within each population category was equal, the distribution of *nazu* land was concentrated. As Figure 7.5 shows, in 1870, the bottom 60 percent of the metropolitan and rural banner households virtually had no *nazu* land. At the same time, the top decile had 59.9 percent of *nazu* land. The share of land for the top centile of households was 15.5 percent; the next four percent of households shared 26.3 percent, and the next five percent had 18.1 percent of land. This level of concentration is even greater than that of the distribution of land among the entire population in Shuangcheng. Since the *nazu* lands were privately cleared by settlers, the government did not make an effort to intervene in its distribution. Thus, the concentrated distribution illustrates the inequality in the bannermen's abilities in acquiring more land on their own; only about 40 percent of the metropolitan and rural banner households were able to own *nazu* land.

Moreover, the overall pattern of the *nazu* land distribution remained stable in the twenty-year period between 1870 and 1889. As Figure 7.5 shows, the percentage share of land held by each landholding stratum did not change significantly. This is especially true for the top centile of households. The distribution of *nazu* land tended to be slightly equalized in 1876, marked by a reduction in the percentages of land owned by the second to tenth centiles of households and increases in percentages of land held by households from the other deciles. However, this trend seemed to reverse in 1889, which saw increases in the percentages of land held by the top decile of households and a decrease in the percentage of land shared by the second to fourth decile groups. Thus, compared to that of the 1870s, the level of *nazu* land concentration in 1889 slightly increased.

At the same time, although the pattern of *nazu* land distribution was stable, the landholdings of the top decile of households increased over time. As chapter 4 shows, throughout the Qing, the government constantly registered land that had been privately cleared by immigrants under the *nazu* category. These activities increased the size of *nazu* land owned by individual households. The increase in *nazu* size is most significant for households located in the top decile. In 1870, a household owning 24.7 *shang* or more of *nazu* land could be placed in the top decile group, whereas the bar for this group was raised to 26 *shang* in 1876 and 29.6 *shang* in 1889. The increase in the landholdings of the top centile group is most significant. The bar for the top centile group was 91.7 *shang* in 1870, and it was raised to 101.1 *shang* in 1876. Further, in 1889, the top centile of households in *nazu* landholding had 112.8 *shang* or more of this land.

The above patterns of land distribution among metropolitan and rural bannermen illustrate how state policies of land allocation and immigrants' activities of land accumulation functioned differently to influence the level of equality and inequality in this agrarian society. State policy maintained equal distribution of *jichan* land within each population category and, at the same time, maintained inequality between the population categories. As the within-category equality created homogeneity among the households in each population category, the between-category inequality drove a wedge between the wealth statuses of metropolitan and rural bannermen, thus maintaining a hierarchy between the two. By contrast, *nazu* landholding as the result of immigrants' private activities of land cultivation and land transfer was the main factor that explains the variations in wealth statuses of households within and across the categories. For metropolitan bannermen, *nazu* landholding enabled them to become the wealthiest households in Shuangcheng. Since the allocated *jichan* land was by itself sufficient to place a metropolitan banner household in the second decile of households (Figure 7.2), any additional *nazu* land helped a household move up to the highest decile. For rural bannermen, because one plot of *jichan* land only guaranteed the household's status in the fourth decile in landholding (Figure 7.2), the *nazu* landholding was especially important because it allowed them to compete with metropolitan bannermen in terms of wealth status and challenge the state-mandated social hierarchy.

Thus, while state policies were still effective in maintaining the between-category inequality among the majority of the metropolitan banner and rural banner households, private land accumulation also produced a large number of rural bannermen who were able to compete with metropolitan bannermen in terms of wealth status. Throughout this period, rural bannermen were active in acquiring *nazu* land. As Figure 7.2 illustrates, in 1876, 23.7 percent of rural banner households were able to acquire additional land and rise to the top two deciles of households in landholding. Moreover, compared to metropolitan bannermen, a much larger proportion of rural banner households had *nazu* land, and this percentage constantly increased over time (Table 5.1).

The land distribution among metropolitan and rural bannermen also tells a story enriched by both persistence of the overall pattern and mobility at the individual household level. Despite the social and political changes in the last few decades of the Qing dynasty, land distribution in the Shuangcheng area did not become more concentrated. This finding is similar to what other scholars have found in Manchuria and other parts of rural China (Myers 1970, 217–25; and 1976; Huang 1985; Li and Jiang 2005). At the same time, land sales were still widespread. Through land transfers, people like Hualiantai's descendants sold off their *nazu* land (chapter 6) and people like Mingshan acquired a large amount of *nazu* land. If we only look at changes in *nazu* landholdings, these stories perfectly reflect the aphorism "from rags to riches and back again in three generations." Thus, the juxtaposition of stability in land distribution and dramatic stories of wealth mobility is an important feature of the property regimes of rural China. To better understand wealth mobility in agrarian communities and its impact on wealth distribution in historical China, it is important to examine changes in the wealth statuses of individual households over time.

Mobility

The mobility in households' *nazu* landholdings among the metropolitan and rural bannermen between 1870 and 1889 sheds some light on the wealth mobility of agrarian households in the region. The banner land registers provide complete *nazu* land records for residents in all 120 banner villages in 1870, 1876, and 1889. *Nazu* land records are suitable for analyzing wealth mobility because, compared to *jichan* land, *nazu* land was less subject to state control; in effect, the acquisition of *nazu* land allowed for greater individual agency. Moreover, among all land categories, *nazu* land also proves to have been the major factor in wealth stratification and the creation of households with massive amounts of land. Therefore, changes in the wealth status of those considered as rich households in 1870, defined as the top 5 percent of households in *nazu* landholdings, and that of households without *nazu* land in the same year, which was the bottom 60 percent of households, are informative in the upward and downward wealth mobility in this agrarian society. In other words, we observe how many households rose from rags to riches and whether and how rich households were reduced to rags.[22]

The rich households in 1870, those in the top 5 percent in *nazu* landholding, experienced considerable downward mobility in this twenty-year period. As Table 7.1 shows, 14.1 percent of these households moved to the bottom 60 percent in 1889, which indicates that they lost almost all their *nazu* lands. The downward wealth mobility for metropolitan banner households is especially prominent; 27.3 percent of the rich metropolitan households became nearly landless in *nazu* in 1889, which was 16 percentage points more than in the rural banner households. If adding the households that disappeared from the registers before 1889—a result of a household becoming extinct or elderly household members joining a relative's household due to aging—about one-third of the rich metropolitan banner households in 1870 lost their *nazu* land. Finally, only 36.4 percent of the metropolitan banner households that were among the top 5 percent of households in *nazu* landholding in 1870 still had this status in 1889. Compared to their metropolitan counterparts, the rich rural banner households were more successful at maintaining their *nazu* landholding status. As Table 7.1 shows, 56.6 percent of rural banner households in the top 5 percent in *nazu* landholding in 1870 were able to remain in the same stratum in 1889. About 13.2 percent of the rural banner households in the top 5 percent in *nazu* landholding in 1870 moved downward to the bottom 60 percent in 1889 or disappeared, indicating they lost almost all their *nazu* lands. In both the metropolitan and the rural bannermen, another 30 percent of the households in the top 5 percent in *nazu* landholding in 1870 moved downward to lower strata in 1889, but most of them were able to stay in the top sixth to tenth centiles or the second decile. Overall, only a little over a half of the households that were in the top 5 percent in *nazu* landholding in 1870 still had that status twenty years later.

At the same time, the results for the bottom 60 percent of households in 1870 illustrate the two sides of the story of wealth mobility in rural China: on the one hand, there is considerable upward mobility since quite a few households did rise into higher strata of *nazu* landholding;

TABLE 7.1
The 1889 nazu *landholding status of the households that had been in the top 5 percent in* nazu *landholding in 1870*

	METROPOLITAN		RURAL		TOTAL	
Household groups in nazu *landholding*	*Number*	*Percent*	*Number*	*Percent*	*Number*	*Percent*
Top 5 percent	12	36.4	90	56.6	102	53.1
Next 5 percent	7	21.2	34	21.4	41	21.4
2nd decile	2	6.1	7	4.4	9	4.7
3rd to 4th deciles	1	3.0	7	4.4	8	4.2
Bottom 60 percent	9	27.3	18	11.3	27	14.1
Disappeared	2	6.1	3	1.9	5	2.6
Total	33	100.0	159	100.0	192	100.0

SOURCE: CMGPD-SC.

TABLE 7.2
The 1889 nazu *landholding status of the households that had been in the bottom 60 percent in* nazu *landholding in 1870*

	METROPOLITAN		RURAL		TOTAL	
Household groups in nazu *landholding*	*Number*	*Percent*	*Number*	*Percent*	*Number*	*Percent*
Top 5 percent	8	1.6	38	2.1	46	2.0
Next 5 percent	12	2.4	56	3.1	68	3.0
2nd decile	18	3.6	92	5.1	110	4.8
3rd to 4th deciles	29	5.7	245	13.7	274	11.9
Bottom 60 percent	351	69.2	1,246	69.7	1,597	69.6
Disappeared	89	17.6	111	6.2	200	8.7
Total	507	100.0	1,788	100.0	2,295	100.0

SOURCE: CMGPD-SC.

on the other hand, the rate of persistence of the wealth status of these bannermen between 1870 and 1889 was high. As Table 7.2 shows, eight metropolitan banner households (1.6 percent) and thirty-eight rural banner households (2.1 percent) rose from the bottom 60 percent in 1870 to the top 5 percent in 1889 in the *nazu* landholding status. Besides these cases of dramatic upward mobility, another fifty-nine metropolitan banner households (11.7 percent) and 393 rural banner households (21.9 percent) rose from the bottom 60 percent in 1870 to the top four deciles in 1889 through the acquisition of *nazu* land. At the same time, however, the majority of households that had no *nazu* land in 1870 still did not own any in 1889; about 69.6 percent of the bottom 60 percent of metropolitan and rural banner households in 1870 remained in the same stratum in 1889. This rate of persistence is the same for both metropolitan and rural bannermen.

The foregoing results further confirm both the mobility and the persistence of the property regime in rural China. In particular, the experience of downward mobility deserves a close look. The considerable wealth mobility indicates that bannermen actively transferred their landownership according to the household's demographic and economic conditions. In just twenty years, a significant number of households experienced reductions in *nazu* landholdings. While these reductions could have been caused by a household division that divided family property among all the sons, a household might also have sold its land when confronted with a shortage of labor or financial difficulties. These cases of downward wealth mobility also opened up space for households from lower landholding strata to move up.

At the same time, the persistence of the wealth statuses among the majority of households should not be overlooked. Despite a high level of downward mobility experienced by the top 5 percent of households, there is considerable persistence in the *nazu* landholding status of the top 1 percent of households. For both metropolitan and rural banner households, about 60 percent of those located in the top centile in *nazu* landholding in 1870 were able to maintain their status in 1889, and another 20 percent of this group were located in the top second to fifth centiles in *nazu* landholding in 1889.[23] As discussed, there is a similarly high persistence rate in the *nazu* landholding status of those located in the bottom 60 percent.

Moreover, it is also important to keep in mind that, while upward mobility in *nazu* landholding status indicates upward wealth mobility, downward mobility in *nazu* landholding is not necessarily a sign of overall downward wealth mobility. Because metropolitan banner households took advantage of two opportunities, in 1870 and again in 1878, to acquire more *jichan* land, it is important to realize that the considerable downward mobility in *nazu* landholding among metropolitan bannermen perhaps indicates a change in the composition of their landed wealth during this period. Like Hualiantai's descendants, who sold their *nazu* land but gained more *jichan* plots, some metropolitan bannermen strategically exchanged their *nazu* land for cash and acquired more rent-free *jichan* land. These households were still affluent.

PATHS OF WEALTH ACCUMULATION

As it does in every society, the pattern of wealth distribution in Shuangcheng resulted from the interactions between a series of institutional processes—state intervention, inheritance, and market—and the characteristics of individual households. The form and consequences of these interactions were deeply embedded in the specific social and political systems. The story of Hualiantai's family sheds light on the influence of family size, gender composition, and the government positions of family members on the wealth mobility of banner families in Shuangcheng. Hualiantai's descendants maintained and expanded their *jichan* landholdings through inheritance; they inherited *jichan* plots not only from their fathers but also from extinct households. At the same time, the state policy stipulating that one household could have only one plot of *jichan* land prevented the concentration of land at the household level. Moreover, being metropolitan bannermen and having members who were officials and soldiers was also important to their success in achieving affluence. Finally, Hualiantai's descendants sold off their *nazu* land, which indicates that there was an active land market in Shuangcheng and that families were able to use it to adjust their landholdings. While the story of Hualiantai's descendants provides an anecdotal example, an analysis of the CMGPD-SC dataset offers an overview of the relation of metropolitan and rural bannermen's wealth status to family size and gender composition, and to family members' achievement in government positions.

Family Size and Gender Composition

Family size and gender composition influenced households' wealth status in Shuangcheng in terms of both the number of family laborers and qualification for official landownership. In agrarian societies, family size and gender composition are important determinants of a family's consumption needs and production capacity. While consumption influences a family's need for land, production capacity shapes its ability to farm or manage their land. Existing studies of both European and East Asian societies reveal a positive association between family size and wealth status; higher-status families were more likely to have more children (Harrell 1985; Clark and Hamilton 2006; Shiue 2008; Tsuya et al. 2010). Moreover, in Shuangcheng, the state also ensured that the allocation of *jichan* land was commensurate with household size. As previous chapters show, as early as the time of initial settlement, the government regulated the household sizes of qualified metropolitan bannermen. It also divided the rural banner households with large numbers of members and allocated additional plots to the resulting new households. In addition, when re-allocating land from extinct households, the government prioritized households with more members.

Results from the analysis of the household and land registers in Shuangcheng confirm the positive association between household size and wealth status: the numbers for both the metropolitan and rural bannermen show that the higher the wealth status, the larger the mean household size. As Table 7.3 shows, in 1876, the households belonging to the landholding stratum of the bottom 60 percent of all Shuangcheng residents had the smallest family size, which was three for metropolitan bannermen and six for rural bannermen. Since the allocated *jichan* plot easily placed any metropolitan or rural banner household into the landholding stratum of the third to fourth deciles or above, being in the bottom 60 percent stratum indicates that these households had lost their *jichan* plot. Moreover, metropolitan banner households belonging to the top decile had a mean household size of five or six and those in the second decile had a mean size of four. The association between household size and wealth status is especially strong among the rural bannermen. The households belonging to the top centile of all Shuangcheng residents in landholding had a mean size of seventeen. For the landed rural banner households below the top centile, the mean household size started from fifteen and, respectively, declined to eleven, nine, and nine. These results underline how demographic success and economic prosperity in Shuangcheng typically went hand in hand.

Besides family size, the age-sex composition of households also influenced wealth status; the majority of wealthy households had capable adult males. Moreover, as the age-sex composition of a household changed over time, families used various strategies to balance their production and consumption needs (Bengtsson 2004). The story of Hual-

TABLE 7.3
Mean household size (number of living persons) and number of adult males (ages 20–50) by jichan *and* nazu *landholding status, 1876*

	METROPOLITAN BANNER		RURAL BANNER	
Household groups in jichan *and* nazu *landholding*	*Household size*	*N. of Adult males*	*Household size*	*N. of Adult males*
Top 1 percent	5	2	17	8
Next 4 percent	6	2	15	7
Next 5 percent	5	2	11	5
2nd decile	4	2	9	4
3rd to 4th deciles	—	—	9	4
Bottom 60 percent	3	1	6	3

SOURCE: CMGPD-SC.
NOTE: There are too few metropolitan banner households located in the 3rd to 4th deciles to calculate the mean.

iantai's descendants best illustrates the wax and wane of landholdings in conjunction with a household's demographic cycle. When Hualiantai's sons Jiertuhun and Jiertukan expanded their *nazu* landholdings, they were both in their prime. Yet after the death of Jiertuhun and his wife, in 1866 and 1867, respectively, this household became a nuclear family consisting of Jiertuhun's son, his wife, and their daughter. Although Jiertuhun's thirty-two-year-old son was an adult male, the small family size perhaps made the management of their massive amount of *nazu* land difficult. Similarly, by the time Jiertukan established his own household in 1870, he was already forty-five years old. Yet this age fell within the range that the government defined as adult male (*ding*), and Jiertukan's family continued to enjoy several years of prosperity. In 1876, when Jiertukan turned fifty-one and exceeded the age limit of government-defined adult male by one year, he gradually sold his land to Mingshan.

The statistical results also reveal a positive association between the number of adult males in a household and its landholding status. As Table 7.3 shows, for rural bannermen, the mean number of adult males in the top centile landholding stratum was eight, which is the highest among all strata. In progressively lower wealth strata, the mean number of adult males gradually declined from seven to three. For metropolitan bannermen, those belonging to the top two deciles in landholding status on average had two adult males, while those located in the bottom 60 percent stratum only had an average of one adult male. This overview indicates that although metropolitan and rural banner households did not necessarily rely on family labor to farm the land, having male members of working age was still important, since they still needed capable personnel to manage their land.

While the number of adult males is important, in Shuangcheng, it was the presence of male members—regardless of age—that determined whether a household could officially own land. Although the state stipulated that only the principal adult male between the ages of twenty and fifty could register *jichan* land, in practice, the state allowed household heads to be older or younger, as long as there were males in the family. This was especially true for metropolitan bannermen, who in the state land allocation in 1878 established eighty-eight households headed by children who were under ten years old. Yet, even under the loosened state policy, a male heir was required for the household to continue.

A household headed by a widow would lose all its land if the family failed to secure a male heir before her death. In the story of Hualiantai's descendants, the land registered under the three households headed by Jiertukan, Kuijun, and Kuixiang were transferred to other households for this reason.

Therefore, family size and age-sex composition in Shuangcheng not only accounted for a household's upward mobility in wealth accumulation but also explained most of the dramatic downward mobility; the decline of family wealth usually started with the aging of the household head, the disability of male members, or, most crucially, the absence of a surviving heir. For example, as discussed in chapter 5, aging and disability were the primary factors that forced Shuangcheng households to give up land. Since families could not completely control their demographic outcome, even the wealthiest families could not escape decline.

Political Achievement

If demographic outcomes reflect the unpredictable nature of life, political achievement signals individual merit and agency. In China, political power is highly associated with wealth. The autocratic nature of the Chinese state legitimated the intervention of political power in economic activities. This tradition not only enabled the state to redistribute wealth but also endowed political elites with privileges that allowed them to use power to accumulate land.[24] Therefore, two forms of political power interacted with one another to influence land distribution in China: state power and individual power derived from a connection to the state. Compared to other population categories in Shuangcheng, metropolitan and rural bannermen were privileged in their access to state power in that households in both categories were entitled to have land. While the basic entitlement associated with population categories ensured that the majority of metropolitan and rural banner households would have a *jichan* plot (Figure 7.4), the capability of household members to derive power from their connection to the state was especially important in explaining variations in households' *nazu* landholdings.

The major path to political power for males was to become an official. Beginning in the tenth century, the merit-based civil service examination became a major means for people to achieve official positions. An average man could achieve wealth and social status through an official career earned by the civil service exam. Because the examination was highly competitive, achieving an official career required tremendous aspirations and talent. Although the banner system provided bannermen with more opportunity for political achievement than the civil service examination system did for civilians, advancement still required that a bannerman have individual ability and talent. In the Qing, bannermen not only enjoyed special quotas in the standard civil service exam but also could become officials through the special translation examination, or could even bypass the exam system through the banner hierarchy (Elliott 2001, 133–74). In Shuangcheng, a bannerman could start his career in government either by holding a *shengyuan* title (the licentiate degree in the civil service exam) or as a soldier (*pijia*).[25] Both paths could lead to the same career. A *shengyuan* title holder would start as a scribe; a soldier could also be promoted to a scribe position if he was capable of handling paperwork. Then a scribe might be promoted to tax preceptor, from tax preceptor up a level to lieutenant, and up another level to banner captain, and so on. Any of the above paths, however, required successful performance as an indicator of the candidate's talent.[26] When assigning official positions, the local government had to send the candidate's resume to the banner general for review. Previous experience and performance were the major criteria for obtaining a position.

The stories of wealth accumulation by Hualiantai's descendants and Mingshan that we saw in chapter 6 also show the connection between individual political achievements and family wealth status. Two of Hualiantai's sons—Jiertahun and Jiertuhun—were officials, and Mingshan's father was a captain, a high-ranking official in Shuangcheng. While their being local officials in the early years helped the families to accumulate *nazu* land, Mingshan's personal story most clearly demonstrates the role of political achievement and individual ability in wealth accumulation in the later years. As the second son in the family, Mingshan could not inherit his father's *jichan* plot.[27] Yet he was able to overcome his birth-order disadvantage, becoming a scribe and achieving occupational mobility outside his family.[28] The job provided him two resources: a stable salary and power. Mingshan earned an annual salary of twenty-four *taels* of silver as a scribe, and thirty-six *taels* of silver when he later became a granary official.[29] This stable income was indispensable for his land acquisition. Moreover, although Mingshan's scribe position did not make him a high official, he was assigned the task of processing the paperwork related to *jichan* land allocation and thus directly controlled the assignment of *jichan* plots. This convenience enabled Mingshan to acquire land for both his and his elder brother's families. In 1870, his brother's eldest son was able to acquire a *jichan* plot at age six.[30] In 1878, when Mingshan was in charge of the allocation of 302 *jichan* plots, he managed to reserve one plot for his brother's second son, who was so young that he had not yet been registered.[31]

Political achievement also commonly facilitated the attainment of higher wealth status by bannermen. Throughout the entire period under analysis, official families—families with at least one member who either had served or was currently serving the government as officials or soldiers—were concentrated at the top decile of households in the hierarchy of *nazu* land possession. As Table 7.4 shows, the proportion of official families in the top centile of households was especially high. In 1870, 31.6 percent of the top centile of households had members serving as officials or soldiers in the government, which is more than six times the proportion of official families (4.8 percent) in the entire population in the same year. Moreover, this concentration of official families in the top centile of households was prominent for both metropolitan and rural bannermen; 33.3 percent of the metropolitan and 31 percent of the rural households had members who were officials. In 1889, the concentration of official families in the top centile of households remained at the same level; 33.3 percent of these households had members working for the

TABLE 7.4
Percentages of households with officials in each stratum of nazu *landholding, 1870 and 1889*

	1870			1889		
Household groups in nazu *landholding*	*Metropolitan*	*Rural*	*Total*	*Metropolitan*	*Rural*	*Total*
Top 1 percent	33.3	31.0	31.6	25.0	35.3	33.3
Next 4 percent	20.8	7.7	9.7	29.2	16.1	18.0
Next 5 percent	10.3	3.7	4.7	25.0	13.3	14.8
2nd decile	14.3	4.1	5.4	13.2	8.1	8.8
3rd to 4th deciles	7.7	3.2	3.8	16.4	7.7	8.7
Bottom 60 percent	6.2	3.7	4.2	10.4	5.5	7.0
All	8.0	4.1	4.8	12.1	7.6	8.7

government, which was four times the proportion of official families (8.7 percent) in the entire population. At the same time, households in the higher strata universally had a higher proportion of official families.

In fact, in the later period, political achievement became increasingly associated with a higher status in *nazu* landholding. Over time, the percentage of official families increased across all strata of the *nazu* landholding status.[32] Yet this increase was especially prominent among the households located in the top second to tenth centiles in *nazu* landholding and among rural bannermen. As Table 7.4 shows, in 1870, official families accounted for 7.7 percent of the rural banner households in the top second to fifth centiles in *nazu* landholding, this percentage increased more than twofold, to 16.1 in 1889. For the households located in the top sixth to tenth centiles, the percentage of official families among rural bannermen increased from 3.7 in 1870 to 13.3 in 1889; that among metropolitan bannermen increased from 10.3 in 1870 to 25 in 1889. This indicates that, faced with the structural disadvantage of unequal entitlement to *jichan* land, rural banner families actively used the political status of individual members to either maintain or enhance their *nazu* landholding status. Moreover, the significant increase in the proportion of official families in the top *nazu* landholding strata also suggests that relationship between land and political achievement could work the other way around; landed wealth also enabled family members to succeed in their careers as officials and soldiers.

At the same time, although the use of bureaucratic power to accumulate wealth was common, not all families with power were able to translate it into material gain. Despite the opportunities provided by political achievement to accumulate land, there was still tremendous stratification in landed wealth among official families. As Table 7.4 reveals, some official families were still located at a lower stratum in *nazu* land possession. In 1870, official families accounted for 4.2 percent of the bottom 60 percent of households, and in 1889, the percentage of official families in the bottom 60 percent was 7. In addition, in 1870 and 1889, 3.8 percent and 8.7 percent, respectively, of the households in the third to fourth deciles were official families. This phenomenon indicates that some official families were either not interested in accumulating land or not very good at it. Moreover, there was no positive association between official rank and wealth status. For example, the majority of the households who sustained a top 1 percent status in *nazu* landholding were not high-ranking official families but middle- and lower-level official and soldier families. Mingshan's case also reveals that despite his low rank as a scribe, his duties in the land-allocation process gave him more opportunities for wealth accumulation. In private land accumulation, what mattered was not official rank per se, but whether the individual in the household was associated with bureaucratic power and wanted to use that power for material gain.

Economic Development and Market

The development of a market economy is also an important factor to consider when discussing land distribution. Existing studies on land distribution have focused on the role of two components of the market economy: the *factor markets*, or the markets for land, labor, capital, and other raw materials of agricultural production, and *commercialization*. Economists studying rural economies in pre-revolutionary China have agreed that the factor markets were imperfect as political institutions and powerful families could detain labor and lands, hindering the free transfer of these essential factors (Myers 1970; Chao 1986; Benjamin and Brandt 1997). Moreover, recent studies also indicate that freer factor markets help to reduce the level of inequality in land distribution (Chao 1986, 104; Benjamin and Brandt 1997). At the same time, during the Qing and the early twentieth century, the commercialization of agriculture and other goods happened in the Yangtze River region, Pearl River Delta, and some regions in North China (Jing and Luo 1978; Watson 1985; Brandt 1989; Faure 1989). This trend in general brought Chinese farmers higher incomes, and the high return from commercial activities then gave farm families the funds they needed to purchase more land through the market (Myers 1970, 166–92; Chao 1986, 105; Brandt 1989; Faure 1989).

The land market—one important factor market—in Shuangcheng was confined. The state forbade land sales, especially between bannermen and civilian commoners. Although bannermen still bought and sold land through the market, only the transfers that met all the requirements of an official land transfer, or *dingbu*, could be registered with the government. In other words, only buyers in the same population category as that of the seller could secure their rights to the purchased land through the government. Although various forms of land transfer took place in Shuangcheng, the state regulation and security of landownership was an important consideration when the immigrants evaluated potential sellers or buyers. Thus state restrictions on land transfer did inhibit immigrants' activities in the land market, so that some bannermen did not dare to sell their land, even after the government lifted the ban on land transfers.[33]

As noted earlier, commercial activities surrounding agricultural products flourished in Shuangcheng. As a major grain distribution center, Shuangcheng saw the establishment of businesses that collected grain products grown in the area and transported them to such port cities as Yingkou in Fengtian (MMTKK 1909, 49–56). Some entrepreneurs produced wine, oil, and flour, and these businesses also acted like banks, providing loans to people (MMTKK 1911, 18–25). In 1867, the number of businesses in Shuangcheng had reached 156,[34] and, by 1911, there were 573 businesses in the greater Shuangcheng area (ibid., 17). Yet merchants from North China dominated commerce in the area. In 1867, of the 139 businesses for which the owner's place of origin was recorded, seventy-eight were owned by merchants from Zhili, twenty were owned by Shandong merchants, thirteen were run by merchants from Shanxi, and twenty were owned by people from elsewhere in Manchuria.[35] Local merchants from Shuangcheng, where their households were registered, only owned eight businesses. Moreover, compared to some of the large businesses, those owned by local people were relatively small.[36] In 1911, the survey report by the Southern Manchuria Railway Company listed the eleven most important businesses in Shuangcheng (ibid., 18–19). Nine were owned by merchants from Zhili or Shanxi, and only one was owned by a merchant with a Shuangcheng registration.

While few bannermen and civilian commoners with a Shuangcheng registration started their own businesses, the development of commerce in this area still created disparities in immigrants' wealth statuses. Results from a separate statistical analysis reveal a positive correlation between the distance from a family's residential village to the nearest market center and the amount of *nazu* land the family had; the easier a family's access to the market center, the more *nazu* land it owned (Chen, Lee, and Campbell 2012). This indicates that commercial activities did improve Shuangcheng families' fortunes in terms of land accumulation. The Southern Manchuria Railway Company survey report compiled in 1911 noted that the largest landlord family in Shuangcheng was surnamed Li, and that it owned 2,500 *shang* of land. Residing in a banner village forty *li* away, this Li family also owned a business in the Shuangcheng seat (MMTKK 1911, 12).

The following story of commercial activities and land accumulation by a rural bannerman named Wang Guifeng and his family, which is based on oral history and archival records, sheds some light on the reciprocal relationship between the two activities.[37] Guifeng was the second son in a rural banner family living in a banner village in the right *tun*.[38] Toward the end of the nineteenth century, Guifeng accumulated more than a hundred *shang* of land and became a large landholder. The entire family then moved to an area two *li* south of their village and built a large brick house with a courtyard. Consisting of this large landlord family and several tenant households, their new residence became a natural settlement (*wopeng*) named after Wang Guifeng.[39] According to Guifeng's grandson, Guifeng became a large landholder after he failed at running a business in the Shuangcheng seat. When Guifeng was young, he had owned a pawn shop in the Shuangcheng seat. The business failed because the goods did not sell. He then returned to the village and started to buy land from others and recruited tenants to clear uncultivated land. This story shows that returns from commercial activities provided farm families economic power in land accumulation. Even though Guifeng failed in business, he still had sufficient funds to purchase land and organize land clearing.

While the historical memory of Guifeng's grandson emphasizes how commercial activities made land accumulation possible, the archival records reveal the opposite. The household and land registers show that this family's land accumulation activities were started by Guifeng's grandfather, Haicheng. Sometime between 1870 and 1876, Haicheng started acquiring *nazu* land.[40] By 1876, in addition to his *jichan* land, Haicheng owned 44.4 *shang* of *nazu* land.[41] This placed the Wang family in the top 5 percent of households in *nazu* landholding among the metropolitan and rural bannermen. The family's *jichan* and *nazu* landholdings combined placed it among the top 5 percent of all the households in Shuangcheng in 1876. In 1889, the family still owned this land and had even slightly expanded its *nazu* landholdings by encroaching on the waste land along the border, bringing its *nazu* landholdings to 46.5

shang.[42] Very likely, it was the income from the land that provided family members like Wang Guifeng the initial funds to start his business.[43] Therefore, land accumulation and commercial activities were mutually beneficial.

The evidence of commercial activities in Shuangcheng shows that, although the market economy explained some disparities in households' landholdings, it did not have significant impact on the way of agricultural production and thus the overall pattern of land distribution. The differential land entitlements assigned by the state restricted the development of a free land market. This restricted land market also prevented land from flowing between different population categories, which made it possible for the majority of privileged metropolitan and rural bannermen to preserve their *jichan* land. As we can see from the results discussed in this chapter, the equal distribution of *jichan* land within both the metropolitan and rural bannermen categories laid the foundation for the overall pattern of land distribution. At the same time, some households did become large landlords by clearing uncultivated land or purchasing land from others, and commercial activities played a positive role in the activities of land accumulation by individual families. Yet, because few Shuangcheng residents engaged in a high level of commercial activities, the impact on the pattern of land distribution was limited. Thus, under the state-dominated system, the most important factors influencing the wealth statuses of agrarian households were family demography and the political achievement of family members.

THE MAKING OF A LANDED CLASS

The patterns of land distribution in Shuangcheng explain why the state-designated social hierarchy eventually played out on the ground: throughout the Qing dynasty, the majority of metropolitan and rural bannermen were able to preserve their wealth status, which sustained them as a powerful landed class. This was the consequence of the long-term interactions between state policies and immigrants' efforts to accumulate land. The state's assignment of differential land entitlements laid the foundation of the social hierarchy. At the same time, Shuangcheng residents also employed various strategies to acquire land. These activities interacted with family demography and the market economy to create upward and downward wealth mobility. Moreover, the interactions took place alongside a series of social and political changes, including the devolution of political power and the privatization of state land in Manchuria. These changes made it possible for some members of the disadvantaged groups to rise into the wealthiest group in Shuangcheng. Yet their rise did not threaten the status of metropolitan and rural bannermen. Not only did state policies regulate the flow of wealth; the privileged groups also used the state structure to empower themselves and to strengthen their wealth status. Although a few metropolitan and rural bannermen households lost their land, the majority of them still had an elite status in terms of wealth.

The relatively equal and stable pattern of land distribution among metropolitan and rural bannermen is also noteworthy, because it sheds light on the key factors influencing wealth stratification in agrarian communities in early modern China. That there was relative equality in land distribution among metropolitan and rural bannermen is consistent with findings by studies of land distribution in rural communities in Hebei, Shandong, Shaanxi, and Zhejiang. These findings show that among the people with land entitlements, the pattern of land distribution was characterized by stratification without concentration. Moreover, with household being the basic unit of agricultural production, demographic and economic differentials at the household level were the major causes of upward and downward wealth mobility. Yet the wealth mobility of individual households did not have a significant impact on the overall pattern of land distribution. Thus, although there were numerous stories about families going "from rags to riches and back in three generations," the social hierarchy in rural society was stable. Rather, it was the differential land entitlements that constituted the most distinctive source of inequality. In Shuangcheng, the highly unequal pattern of land distribution among all residents (Figure 7.1) was a consequence of the unequal distribution of land entitlements between different population categories. Exclusion from land allocation and even from the state registration system explained the existence of a large number of have-nots.

These findings call for a reappraisal of bannermen's status and the social structure in Manchuria in the last decades of the Qing. Our previous understanding of this issue is based on two widely accepted theses: the decline of bannermen's status and the transformation of Manchuria by Han Chinese immigrants. In the nineteenth century, the deterioration in the quantity and quality of government support to bannermen was a trend all over the country. At the same time, a large number of civilian commoners settled in Manchuria and cultivated banner lands as tenants. By working on banner lands, many civilian commoners gained de facto ownership of the land. Because numerous complaints by contemporaries and records of court cases involving illegal land transfers between bannermen and civilian commoners have been preserved, many scholars believe that bannermen in Manchuria lost control of their banner land to civilian commoners (Diao 1993; Diao and Yi 1994; Isett 2004; Reardon-Anderson 2005; Isett 2007). The administrative shift from the banner system to a civilian system reinforced this view. However, recent studies of the manor lands of the Qing nobles show that, despite all the social and political changes, the bannermen who worked as the heads of the manor lands (*zhuangtou*) in Fengtian acquired large amounts of land as their own property and even became political elites in the end of the dynasty (Enatsu 2004).

The Shuangcheng story offers a more comprehensive view. When landownership is divisible, both trends—civilian tenants gaining partial landownership and bannermen continuing to be landlords—can happen at the same time. In Shuangcheng, many floating bannermen and civilian commoners enjoyed a decent income by working as tenants, and some of them also secured their use rights over the land. Yet as the officially registered landowners, bannermen still had control over their lands and occupied the top strata of the social hierarchy. Of course, regional variations also existed in Manchuria. In places such as Bodune, where the settlers mainly consisted of civilian commoners, such banner privileges were not prominent. Nonetheless, in those places where bannermen had already become landlords, the persistence of the social hierarchy should be recognized.

The pattern of land distribution and the underlying social hierarchy in Shuangcheng generated far-reaching consequences when institutional reform at the end of Qing removed the banner privilege. At first glance, the loss of institutional support undercut bannermen's power and privilege, and the government's new policy allowing free land transfers between bannermen and civilian commoners challenged bannermen's socioeconomic status. In practice, because the majority of bannermen had successfully preserved their wealth status over time, the privatization of banner lands beginning in 1902 created an opportunity for them. Enatsu (2004, 40–49) shows that, when it privatized the banner lands in Fengtian, the government simply sold the land to the existing owners. Thus, bannermen who worked as the heads of the manor lands in Fengtian, who already managed a massive amount of land, became large private landowners. Similarly, metropolitan and rural bannermen in Shuangcheng also benefited from the privatization of banner lands; by paying a rent to the government for the *jichan* and *nazu* plots they had already owned, metropolitan and rural bannermen enjoyed greater ownership, including the right to freely transfer their plots. These bannermen then became private owners of these lands. Consequently, despite the loss of their banner privileges and the fall of the Qing dynasty a few years later, metropolitan and rural bannermen converted their entitlements into socioeconomic status and sustained their wealth and power in local society.

Moreover, the institutional reforms further boosted the wealth status of the landed class because rising land prices significantly increased the market value of their land. In a frontier society, land prices are usually low during the initial settlement period, when there is abundant uncultivated land. As the population increases over time, rising demand for land leads to higher prices. In Manchuria, the price of the banner land was also kept low by the government restriction on free land transfers that limited the size of the land market and thus the market value of the land. In Shuangcheng, although the quality of the land owned by bannermen was better than that owned by the civilian commoners, the price of bannermen's land was lower (MMTKK 1911, 5). After the government eliminated the institutional restrictions on land transfers and allowed a freer land market, the value of the banner land increased. Archival data show that, during the 1840s and 1860s, the price of one *shang* of land fluctuated between ten and twenty strings of cash.[44] By the 1910s, the price of one *shang* of land in Shuangcheng had increased to a range of between 85 and 350 strings of cash.[45] The Japanese field survey report compiled in 1909 shows the average price of one *shang* of land in Shuangcheng to be 250 strings of cash (MMTKK 1909, 36).[46] Even after considering the factor of inflation, the increase in land price is still dramatic.[47] The price of banner land in elsewhere in Manchuria followed a trajectory similar to that in Shuangcheng.[48] Therefore, despite the dramatic changes in administrative institutions, the structural inequality in Shuangcheng persisted. This structural inequality was so durable that, even after the fall of the dynasty, the social construction of the categorical boundaries defined by the Qing continued into the Republic of China.

CHAPTER EIGHT

Social Formation in the Early Republic

In December 1912, one year after the fall of the Qing dynasty, a rent-resistance movement swept through the 120 banner villages of Shuangcheng. It divided the villagers into two groups: the rural bannermen in the eighty villages of the right and the left *tun*, and the metropolitan and rural bannermen in the forty villages of the central *tun*. The conflict arose when the rural bannermen of the right and the left *tun*, who farmed some of the *jichan* land owned by the metropolitan and rural bannermen of the central *tun*, refused to continue paying rent on these plots. The ensuing struggle between the two groups involved actions at both the local village and the provincial-government levels. The central *tun* residents rode their wagons into the villages in the right and the left *tun*, one after another, and pressed their tenants for rent; when the central-*tun* residents were refused, they sometimes initiated fights. Simultaneously, at the seat of the provincial government, the representatives of the central-*tun* residents accused the representatives of the right and the left *tun* for organizing this collective action.[1]

The bannermen of the right and the left *tun* filed a rebuttal, accusing the central-*tun* residents of bringing false charges against them. In their plaint, these rural bannermen singled out the metropolitan bannermen and expressed their chronic grievances:

> The residents in the new *tun* (the right and the left *tun*) were restricted by the residents of the old *tun* (the central *tun*) for no reason. Metropolitan bannermen enjoyed the profits of the *sula* (a reference to rural bannermen in the context of Shuangcheng). We were not willing to have this special

> suffering. Yet in the Qing [the court] gave the metropolitan bannermen special treatment. Although we *sula* in the new *tun* suffered from [this inequality] like ulcers deeply rooted in our bones, nobody had sympathy for us. We thus had to let them manipulate us.[2]

As the lawsuits unfolded, the representatives of rural bannermen of the right and the left *tun* further attacked the unequal assignment of entitlements by the Qing. They especially pointed out the contrast between the political system under the Qing and that of the Republic, using the rhetoric of "citizenship" and equal entitlements to argue for their property rights.

> [In the Qing,] not only was the Shuangcheng government the government for metropolitan bannermen, but everything under heaven (*tianxia*) was also for metropolitan bannermen. How can [we] little people fight against the powerful? We were overshadowed by the power of the metropolitan bannermen; they ride roughshod over us and control us like masters over servants. We have hidden our grievances for more than ninety years. Now the Republic has been established, and the five ethnic groups (the five ethnic groups officially recognized by the Republic of China, including Han, Manchu, Mongol, Hui, and Tibetan) have become one family. We are all citizens (*gongmin*) [of the Republic] and therefore should have equal entitlements.[3]

This conflict reveals two pairs of competitive social groups: the first pair is metropolitan bannermen versus rural bannermen; the second pair is bannermen residing in the central *tun* versus those residing in the right and the left *tun*. Both pairs were products of the Qing land-allocation policy. The state created the first pair intentionally; whereas the subordination of bannermen in the right and the left *tun* to the central *tun* bannermen was a consequence of the spatial patterns of settlement and land allocation. The residents in the right and the left *tun* became tenant farmers for those in the central *tun* because part of the land the state allocated to the residents of the central *tun* was located in the right and the left *tun*, and the right- and the left-*tun* residents had originally cleared this land. This arrangement therefore resulted in a hierarchical landlord-tenant relationship between the central-*tun* residents and the right- and the left-*tun* residents. Moreover, the fact that all metropolitan bannermen had settled in the central *tun* blended the categorical inequality with the spatial inequality, thereby producing a strong animosity against metropolitan bannermen among the right- and the left-*tun* residents. After the collapse of the Qing, the previously suppressed tensions between these groups found vehement expression in the rent-resistance movement.

The conflict and the associated political struggle marked the continuation of the social construction of categorical boundaries defined by the Qing. Following the regime change the process of social construction that had begun in the early years of settlement entered a new stage. The late Qing and early republican periods saw a national trend toward elite activism. Local self-governance, a movement initiated during the late Qing reform that began in 1902, developed rapidly in this period (Kuhn 1975; Min 1989). By actively participating in the political reforms, local elites, who already controlled plenty of resources in social and economic arenas, ushered in the political transformation of local society (Rankin 1986; Zhang 2000; Li 2005). This trend also developed in Manchuria; for example, in Fengtian, the banner landlords of the Qing manor lands also actively participated in the election of a provincial assembly (Enatsu 2004). The social groups in Shuangcheng not only began organizing themselves for collective action but also articulated their distinctive identities using weapons made available by the new republican regime. In this sense, the social construction of categorical boundaries in Shuangcheng was finally completed in the early years of the Republic of China.

The rent-resistance movement, when viewed from a long-term perspective, illuminates the processes that made the social hierarchy durable. The unequal distribution of land entitlements shaped the identities of immigrant groups, and the particular spatial inequality intensified the tension among immigrants. These processes also accompanied immigrants' efforts to improve their wealth status. Finally, by using the categorical boundaries to organize collective actions and direct local politics, elite activism at the time of regime change strengthened these boundaries, sustaining the social structure founded by the Qing.

CATEGORICAL INEQUALITY REVISITED

By the end of the Qing, the land entitlements assigned by the state were no longer what differentiated the population categories in Shuangcheng;

instead differentiation derived from wealth status and the identities immigrants had developed based on their previous entitlements. In 1906, when the privatization of the banner lands in Shuangcheng concluded, all immigrants in theory had equal entitlements. Yet metropolitan and rural bannermen had converted their entitlements into wealth and become a landed class. At the same time, there were differences in socioeconomic status within each category. Some members of the lower-status groups—rural bannermen, floating bannermen, and civilian commoners—had achieved a wealth status comparable to that of metropolitan bannermen, which tended to blur distinctions between the population categories. This meant that, besides wealth status, the identities of immigrants also became important in defining social groups.

The structural inequality defined by the state had played a crucial role in the development of identities. Social identity theories hold that the formation of social groups has several important components: social categorization, comparison, and competition (Tajfel and Turner 1986; Abrams and Hogg 2006; Brown and Ross 2010). The state-designated categories provided the basis for all three components. Upon the immigrants' arrival in Shuangcheng, the state-designated social hierarchy informed immigrants about their social relations; immigrants learned that they received differential land entitlements because they belonged to different categories. In the century following the initial settlement, categorical inequality became embedded in immigrants' life experiences. As immigrants actively tried to advance in socioeconomic status, they were in constant competition with members of other social groups. Capable metropolitan and rural bannermen used their land entitlements as capital to accumulate more land. At the same time, civilian commoners, floating bannermen, and rural bannermen were persistent in their efforts to cross the barriers the state placed on their wealth and social status. During these interactions, immigrants in a certain category compared themselves with those in other categories, developing a perceptual understanding of their own social status. This understanding then reinforced their group-based identities, which persisted even after the removal of the institution that supported the categorical inequality. This process of identity formation was especially prominent among metropolitan, rural, and floating bannermen.[4]

Floating Bannermen versus Metropolitan and Rural Bannermen

Since floating bannermen in Shuangcheng occupied an awkward social position—they were both national elites because of their membership in the Eight Banners and local non-elites because they had no land entitlement—their interests often conflicted with those of metropolitan and rural bannermen, who were the haves. As was seen in chapter 3, although the state made floating bannermen the structural have-nots, it still considered them members of the banner community. This meant that the state not only made an effort to maintain their registration, but also explored employment opportunities for them to ensure their livelihood, granting them local government posts and government student titles and directing them to newly developed settlements. In other words, banner membership gave floating bannermen opportunities to improve their underprivileged wealth status and compete with metropolitan and rural bannermen.

During the process of land acquisition, whenever floating bannermen contested the privileges of metropolitan and rural bannermen, the haves cited official regulations to defend their interests, in particular the one prohibiting floating bannermen from registering land (*fuding buzhun lingdi*). For example, in a land inheritance case that resulted in a lawsuit in 1878, an unregistered floating bannerman named Chenghe claimed that he had been adopted by his father's deceased cousin, a rural bannerman named Jichengbu, as the heir. When Jichengbu died in 1874, Chenghe rented Jichengbu's land to the village head, Zhao Shiyu. Chenghe later discovered that, in 1877, Zhao Shiyu reported the plot as extinct-household land and had it officially assigned to his brother, Changlin. Chenghe then sued Zhao Shiyu. Zhao cited the regulation prohibiting floating bannerman from owning land to deny Chenghe's inheritance rights. After checking the registers and interrogating villagers, the captain's office found that Chenghe was an unregistered floating bannerman and determined that his adoption by Jichengbu had not been authentic. Chenghe's inheritance was therefore not legitimate.[5] Interestingly, as more land disputes erupted between floating bannermen and metropolitan and rural bannermen, it was not the government but the metropolitan and rural bannermen who most frequently cited the official regulations to prevent the floating bannermen from owning land.

The case of Wulintai (see chapter 3) illustrates an official conflict between metropolitan and rural bannermen as haves and floating bannermen as have-nots.[6] In 1879, Wulintai's petition for the state's permission to open and register two unused plots located outside the banner villages was indicative of the historical momentum of floating bannermen's efforts to officially obtain land in Shuangcheng. Perhaps because of the occupational achievements of Wulintai and his family members, the banner government did not simply reject Wulintai's request by pointing out that as a floating bannerman he could not own land. Instead, the area commander-in-chief sent personnel out to look at the two plots and determine whether they were indeed arable and unclaimed. For a time, it seemed that Wulintai had a good chance to increase both his own wealth status and that of floating bannermen in general.

The on-site investigation revealed that both plots were being used as communal land by metropolitan and rural bannermen.[7] One of the plots, more than fifty *shang* in size, was located on the north border of the central *tun*; the other, 120 *shang* in size, was located in the east border of the left *tun*. Bannermen in the adjacent villages were using both plots as grazing land and burial grounds. The metropolitan and rural bannermen of the three villages closest to the two plots, one in the central *tun* and two in the left *tun*, thus filed a joint petition to defend their public land, stating that opening the two plots would interfere with their livelihoods. Therefore, Wulintai's request conflicted with the interests of the haves. After reviewing all the reports, the government finally denied Wulintai's request. Obviously, metropolitan and rural bannermen used their privileges to block a floating bannerman's access to land, and in doing so protected their socioeconomic status as haves.

The social and institutional boundaries surrounding these population categories shaped Shuangcheng immigrants' identities and created long-lasting historical memories. In 2013, Mr. Fu, who lived in a former banner village in Shuangcheng, described his understanding of the classification of immigrants.[8] Fu's great grandfather had moved to Shangcheng from Jinzhou and worked there as a laborer throughout his life. Thus, Fu's household had been an unregistered floating bannermen. When we asked Fu about his ethnicity, he said that he was Manchu, or *manzu* in contemporary Chinese terms. However, he soon clarified his ethnic background: "Among Manchu people, there were regular Manchu people (*zhengshi man ren*) and people attached to Manchu (*sui man*). [The latter] were not authentic Manchu." Then, we asked, "Who were the regular Manchu people?" He said, "The regular Manchu people were those from Beijing. They were authentic metropolitan bannermen and Manchu." With this explanation, Fu implied that he belonged to the group that was only "attached to Manchu."

In fact, Fu's understanding of who was authentic Manchu confused ethnic background with population categories. Fu's wording "attached to Manchu" probably comes from the term "attached to the Eight Banners (*suiqi*),"[9] a description widely used on the Liaodong Peninsula to refer to the Han people who migrated to this region and joined the Shengjing Imperial Household Agency as laborers (Ding et al. 2004, 196–309; Ding and Qiu 2011). If we apply this concept, Manchu bannermen from Shengjing should belong to regular bannerman. Having originated in the garrison in Jinzhou and carrying the surname Fu, Fu's family very likely belonged to the regular Manchu banner and therefore was authentic Manchu.[10] This very confusion tells us of the far-reaching influence of the differentiated land entitlements on people's identity. The fact that Fu's ancestors were not official banner immigrants to Shuangcheng and had no land entitlement eventually led them to differentiate themselves from metropolitan bannermen in ethnic terms.

Metropolitan Bannermen versus Rural Bannermen

Although metropolitan and rural bannermen worked together to defend their collective interests against challenges from the have-nots, chronic tensions existed between the two categories. This tension resulted from the two-tier hierarchy established by the state land-allocation policy, in which rural bannermen were subordinate to metropolitan bannermen. As chapter 3 documents, the state's unequal treatment of metropolitan and rural bannermen began at the time of settlement and penetrated every aspect of their lives. A metropolitan banner household not only owned almost twice as much *jichan* land as a rural banner household but was also exempted from labor service in Shuangcheng. As chapter 4 shows, rural bannermen were discontent over their unequal treatment and resisted the dominance of metropolitan bannermen from very early on.

At times, rural bannermen joined together to assert their collective interests and contest the two-tier hierarchy. In 1874, during the construction of the city wall (see chapter 3), some rural bannermen protested against the metropolitan bannermen being exempted from this labor service. Guan Shengde, a rural bannerman and the head of one of the forty villages in central *tun*, filed a petition with the general of Jilin, asking to be exempted from working on the wall.[11] In the petition, Guan had allied himself with several other rural bannermen to represent all the rural bannermen in the 120 villages and express their grievances:

> While [we] had already finished building the city wall, it was not expected that [parts of the city wall] would collapse every year and have to be repaired annually. Except the adult males in the Plain Yellow and the Bordered Yellow Banners (metropolitan bannermen) who had never been asked for service, we, the adult males in the other six banners (rural bannermen), had to repair the city wall at our own costs. [Moreover], it was set up as the rule in perpetuity.[12]

The government's unequal treatment of rural bannermen was a constant reminder of their inferior status. Expressing these grievances, however, reinforced the boundaries between the two groups.

At the same time, metropolitan bannermen acted to strengthen their position as the top elite. Although the state policy helped to maintain metropolitan bannermen's superiority, as we have seen, the relationship between metropolitan and rural bannermen was never one of simple domination and subordination. As second-class elites, rural bannermen had power to accumulate land and to challenge metropolitan bannermen. Rural bannermen's ability to farm became their advantage. Their success in expanding their *nazu* landholdings indicated their power and ability. The metropolitan bannermen perceived this success as a challenge to their dominance. Social identity theory suggests that social groups attempt to differentiate themselves from other groups when facing challenges from those groups. This is especially true when the group's aim is to "maintain and achieve superiority over an out-group on some dimensions" (Tajfel and Turner 1986, 156–57; Brown and Ross 2010). Metropolitan bannermen sought to uphold their dominant status in various ways. As was seen in chapter 5, they acted as elites in the village and donated land to the village temple. Some metropolitan bannermen also treated rural bannermen like slaves in everyday life (see chapter 3), a behavior meant to assert their superiority.

Above all, the interactions between immigrants of various origins constituted a process of social categorization during which social boundaries based on unequal land entitlements gained symbolic meaning and gave rise to collective identities. Both the elite categories and the lower-status groups participated in social differentiation. Concerned about losing their dominant status, the elite groups tried to block the lower-status groups' access to resources and to continually remind these groups of the structural inequality. Social identity theory also suggests that lower-status groups are more likely to develop a collective identity when they perceive group boundaries as impermeable (Abrams and Hogg 2006, 199). This was true in Shuangcheng. As the lower-status groups—rural and floating bannermen—contested the boundaries, they simultaneously reinforced the understanding that the categorical boundaries were obstacles to a higher socioeconomic status.

Still, during the processes of boundary-crossing and social categorization, an elite group of rural bannermen emerged, as we have seen, primarily through land accumulation. As chapters 5 and 7 show, a large number of rural banner households steadily increased their *nazu* landholdings in the last three decades of the nineteenth century. By 1876, in the eighty villages of the central and the right *tun*, 505 households of rural bannermen were in the top two deciles of all Shuangcheng households in landholding status.[13] Their wealth status was comparable to that of metropolitan bannermen. If we take the rural bannermen living in the left *tun* into consideration, the number could be higher. Although these rural-banner elites did not account for the majority of rural banner households, the size of this group was comparable to that of the entire metropolitan bannermen category, which in 1876 was 698 households. These rural-banner elites not only owned a large amount of land but also had access to political power through family members who held official positions. Thus, by the end of the nineteenth century, the rural-banner elites had become powerful rivals of metropolitan bannermen in Shuangcheng. When the institutional changes finally came, the elite rural bannermen would be the first ones to rise up and overturn the structural disadvantages imposed on them by the Qing land entitlement policies.

SPATIAL INEQUALITY

In addition to the categorical inequality, a spatial inequality created by the state's reduction of the quota of metropolitan banner households in

1829 and the subsequent adjustment in the size of *jichan* land allocated to each banner household generated a major conflict among the metropolitan and rural bannermen living in the 120 villages. Along with the categorical inequality, the chronic tension triggered the rent-resistance movement. Moreover, the spatial inequality was significant in identity formation in Shuangcheng because it gave rise to an exploitative relationship between the central-*tun* and the right- and the left-*tun* residents. Rural bannermen living in the right and the left *tun*, who rarely had a chance to interact with metropolitan bannermen in everyday life, developed a perceptual understanding of the group-based social hierarchy informed by this exploitative relationship. Therefore, residents living in the right and the left *tun* also joined the process of constructing a distinctive identity for rural bannermen.

Policy Adjustment in 1829

In 1829, when the state reduced the quota of designated metropolitan banner households from three thousand to one thousand, it made plans to allocate the *jichan* land that had been prepared for the expected additional two thousand metropolitan households to the existing official banner immigrants in Shuangcheng. This process entailed adding 15 *shang* to each metropolitan banner household and 8.33 *shang* to each rural banner household.[14] However, officials soon encountered a spatial constraint, because all the additional lands were located in the right and the left *tun* and had been cleared by the rural bannermen living in the eighty villages of the two *tun*. The government therefore decreed that each rural banner household in the right and the left *tun* could take 18.33 *shang* of the 30-*shang* plot it had farmed as *jichan*.[15] It would then have to distribute the remaining 11.67 *shang* to metropolitan and rural bannermen in the central *tun*, of which 7.5 *shang* was given to the metropolitan household and 4.17 *shang* was given to the rural household. Then, the land from two rural banner households of the right and the left *tun* made the designated amount of 15 *shang* for one metropolitan household and 8.33 *shang* for one rural household in the central *tun*.[16] In other words, each central-*tun* banner household now had "enclaves" in the right or left *tun*.

The policy adjustment differentiated banner immigrants by residential space: the residents of the central *tun* versus those of the right and the left *tun*. Rural bannermen living in the right and the left *tun* faced another inequality because a new state policy arbitrarily turned them into tenants on the additional land allocated to the central-*tun* metropolitan and rural bannermen. The distance between the central *tun* and the right and the left *tun* made it impossible for the central-*tun* residents to manage their right- and left-*tun* enclaves. The state therefore stipulated that the original farmers of those plots should continue to farm the land and pay rent in kind to the central-*tun* residents. The rent was originally set to 0.5 *shi* per *shang*, payable in a mix of millet, sorghum, and beans. In 1853, when the residents of the central *tun* complained that this income was insufficient to support their families, the government increased the rent to 0.8 *shi* of grain per *shang*. In addition, the residents of the right and the left *tun* were responsible for transporting the grain to their landlords' homes in the central *tun*. If they chose not to do this, they would have to pay an additional 0.2 *shi* of grain for each *shang* to subsidize the cost of transportation.[17] Thus the rural bannermen of the right and the left *tun* were institutionally subordinate to the metropolitan and rural bannermen of the central *tun*.

The property regime created by the policy adjustment was even more complicated than the tenant-landlord relationship. By farming these lands, or even by renting them out, rural bannermen in the right and the left *tun* could produce more earned income than their landlords. In 1912, when investigating the rent-resistance movement, local officials estimated the income the enclaves generated based on informants' reports. If a rural bannerman of the right or the left *tun* rented out the enclave of a central-*tun* resident to private tenants, he could collect a rent of 2.2 or 2.3 *shi* of grain for each *shang*.[18] Since he only had to hand over 0.8 *shi* of grain per *shang* of land to his landlords in the central *tun*, he could keep 64 percent of the rent income for himself. In this scenario, the income of rural bannermen of the right and the left *tun* could even compete with that of the metropolitan bannermen (Table 8.1). A metropolitan household controlled twenty *shang* of *jichan* land in the central *tun* plus the twelve *shi* of grain collected as rent on its enclaves in the right or the left *tun*. Each rural banner household in the right and the left *tun* not only controlled 18.33 *shang* of *jichan* land, but also had a potential rent income of 16.34 *shi* of grain from the enclave of the central-*tun* residents. The rural bannermen of the central *tun*, however, were the most

TABLE 8.1
Comparison of household landed property and estimated incomes from jichan *land after the 1829 policy adjustment*

	CENTRAL *TUN*		RIGHT AND LEFT *TUN*
Landed property and estimated incomes	*Metropolitan bannermen*	*Rural bannermen*	*Rural bannermen*
Size of *jichan* land under control (*shang*)	20	10	18.33
Rent income from the enclaves of the central-*tun* residents (*shi*)	12	6.66	16.34
Size of the enclave (*shang*)	15	8.33	11.67
Shares of rent per *shang* (*shi*)	0.8	0.8	1.4

SOURCE: Case summary of the land dispute between the central-*tun* and the right- and the left-*tun* residents in 1913 (MGSCXGSDA, no. 270).

disadvantaged; their households controlled only ten *shang* of *jichan* land plus 6.66 *shi* of grain collected from their 8.33-*shang* enclaves.

More importantly, this arrangement granted the rural bannermen of the right and the left *tun* partial ownership of these *jichan* plots. As the original farmers who had cleared the land and managed it since the initial settlement, rural bannermen of the right and the left *tun* had gained stable use rights to those lands. State policy ensured their permanent use rights. When making the policy adjustment in 1829, the state stipulated that the arrangement would be effective forever, that the tenants in the right and the left *tun* should not delay or short the rent, and that landlords in the central *tun* should not deprive the tenants of the land.[19] Moreover, when allocating the lands to the central-*tun* residents, the government did not measure the plot and specify the boundaries. In other words, the landlords in the central *tun* did not even know the physical location of their enclaves. The arrangement resembled a permanent tenancy and subsequent two-tiered form of landownership that was common in China proper (Huang 1990, 70–105; 2001; Yang 2009). In this sytem, tenants owned the "topsoil," and landlords owned the "subsoil." In highly commercialized areas, absentee landlords sold their ownership of "subsoil" like stocks, without knowing the physical location of the land. The 1829 allocation of the additional *jichan* plots also resulted in a separation of the ownership of the enclaves of the central *tun* residents; the rural bannermen in the right and the left *tun* as the de facto cultivators had considerable control over these lands.

The arrangement produced grievances on both sides. Because the rent set by the government was lower than the market rate, the metropolitan and rural bannermen living in the central *tun* were discontent with their financial losses. Rural bannermen of the central *tun* especially suffered because they earned much less from the *jichan* land than did their counterparts in the right and the left *tun*. Although the rural bannermen in the right and the left *tun* had gained economically, they were disaffected by the central-*tun* residents' exploitation of their labor. As the rural bannermen in the right and the left *tun* wrote in their 1912 accusation:

> If the land in the new *tun* (the right and the left *tun*) was indeed cleared by metropolitan bannermen, we could still negotiate [the ownership transfer]. Yet [the land] was exclusively cleared by [the residents of] the new *tun*. [We] worked painstakingly with our labor, but they just seized our product without any effort and held it for years (MGSCXGSDA, no. 270).

In other words, since the rural bannermen in the right and the left *tun* had significantly contributed to the value of these lands as the original cultivators, they considered themselves the owners. These grievances resulted in chronic tension between the two groups. Conflicts over the control of these lands arose from time to time throughout the course of the Qing.

This spatial inequality was crucial for the identity formation of the rural bannermen living in the right and the left *tun*, because it provided them with a perceptual understanding of the structural inequality. Social identity forms from the interactions among members of different groups. The interactions constantly remind members of one group of the differences between themselves and members of other groups, who then develop a sense of belonging to their own group. Living in the same villages as metropolitan bannermen, rural bannermen in the central *tun* developed and articulated their identity very early on as they interacted with metropolitan bannermen in everyday life. By observing the privileges of metropolitan bannermen, these rural bannermen consciously drew a boundary between themselves and the metropolitan bannermen. In the early years, almost all complaints against metropolitan bannermen were filed by rural bannermen living in the central *tun*. Moreover, when these central-*tun* rural bannermen filed complaints, they tended to establish themselves as representatives of all rural bannermen, including those living in the right and the left *tun*. In contrast with their counterparts in the central *tun*, the rural bannermen in the right and the left *tun* only had an abstract knowledge of the structural inequality because they seldom interacted with metropolitan bannermen. This spatial inequality, however, made the structural inequality obvious to rural bannermen in the right and the left *tun*. It divided the rural bannermen, but more importantly, it made the privileges of metropolitan bannermen something the rural bannermen in the right and the left *tun* could feel every day.

Conflicts in the Qing

With the passage of time, the enclaves became the site of power struggles between the central-*tun* and the right- and the lef-*tun* residents. In the early years, a purely spatial term represented these conflicts. In 1853, to accommodate the increasing size of their population, the central-*tun* residents petitioned the government to withdraw their enclaves from the right- and the left-*tun* residents and allow the central-*tun* residents to manage the plots themselves.[20] As for the rural bannermen of the right and the left *tun*, who shared an exploited victim mentality, they often used rent resistance to fight against the central-*tun* residents and exhibit their own power. In 1881, the residents of the central *tun* reported that the residents of the "new *tun*" (the right and the left *tun*) refused to transport the rent to the central *tun*. Moreover, even when the central-*tun* residents went to the right and the left *tun* to collect their rent, the residents gave them only chaff and blighted grain.[21]

Beginning in the late nineteenth century, the conflicts between the two groups became more and more organized. In 1881, the residents of the central *tun* and those of the right and the left *tun* confronted each other as distinct groups. In that year, Zhao Fuxing, a rural bannerman in the central *tun* filed a lawsuit with the local banner government, suing the rural bannermen of the right and the left *tun* for not paying sufficient rent to their landlords.[22] Zhao intended to withdraw his land from the residents of the "new" *tun* and manage it himself. The local banner government investigated the chief village heads from the eighty villages of the right and the left *tun*. These chief village heads defended their villagers' interests and denied Zhao's charge. They also pointed out that since only Zhao had requested to withdraw land, they would not give up their plots. The government therefore denied Zhao's request. Dissatisfied with the adjudication of the local government, Zhao submitted his petition to the general of Jilin in 1882.[23] This time, Zhao stated clearly that he was representing all metropolitan and rural bannermen of the central *tun*. Zhao had found five cosigners—three metropolitan bannermen and two rural bannermen—from the forty villages of the central *tun*. The right- and the left-*tun* representatives consisted of four chief village heads. All these representatives attended the hearing at the seat of the general of Jilin.

The banner government, however, preferred to maintain the status quo. In 1853, when the residents of the central *tun* first requested permission to withdraw their land, the government mitigated the conflict by increasing the rent by 60 percent, from 0.5 *shi* to 0.8 *shi*.[24] Although records of the outcome of the 1882 case are not preserved in the archives, the ongoing spatial tension indicates that the state did not change its policy; the central-*tun* residents remained landlords, and the right- and the left-*tun* residents remained sharecroppers. When rent disputes arose between the two parties, the government always tried to treat them as individual cases. The government's rationale can be illustrated by the adjudication of a 1902 lawsuit in which a group of rural bannermen of the right and the left *tun* tried to have the government deny the central-*tun* residents' ownership of their enclaves. The government refused this petition, stating, "[You] are extreme examples of those who act in ways that are neither humane nor righteous. Those who pay rent are tenants, and those who live on rent are landlords."[25]

The decision by the state to privatize *jichan* land intensified the struggle over the ownership of the enclaves. In 1902, to increase revenue, the state decided to collect rent on all banner land in Manchuria, including the allocated *jichan* land.[26] To collect this rent, the state first issued a deed to every landowner, noting the size of his plot and its boundaries. In the deeds issued to the residents in the central *tun*, the government indicated the total amount of land to be 35 *shang* for each metropolitan banner household and 18.33 *shang* for each rural banner household. The deed issued to each rural banner household in the right and the left *tun* stated the total amount of land to be 30 *shang*, with an annotation that 11.67 of the 30 *shang* belonged to residents in the central *tun*. In addition, for each central-*tun* household, the government also indicated the size of the enclaves in the right and the left *tun*.[27] The rural bannermen in the right and the left *tun* considered the state's move a threat to their partial ownership of the enclaves; once the residents of the central *tun* acquired private ownership, they could deprive the rural bannermen of the right and the left *tun* of these lands. At the same time, these rural bannermen also saw this institutional change as an opportunity to overturn their landlords. Thus, in 1902, the rural bannermen of the new *tun* petitioned the general of Jilin to eliminate the requirement that they pay rent to the central-*tun* residents and to have the deeds to those plots issued to the actual rural banner farmers of the right and the left *tun*.[28]

This struggle continued until the end of the Qing. In 1906, when the banner government updated the de facto ownership of land plots to facilitate rent collection, a rural bannerman named Huachun again petitioned the general of Jilin to issue a deed of thirty *shang* of land to each rural banner household of the right and the left *tun*.[29] As usual, the general turned down his request, citing the evidence that the ownership assignments were clearly specified on the land deeds and that they conformed to the state land-allocation policy. Yet, the government's decision did not stop the efforts of the rural bannermen. In 1909, Guangzhi, a scribe who resided in a village in the right *tun*,[30] and several other representatives of the right- and the left-*tun* bannermen, offered a donation of two hundred thousand strings of cash if the state would agree to Huachun's request.[31] Before the provincial government could issue its decision,[32] Zhao Rongchun, a lieutenant administering twenty villages of the left *tun*,[33] colluded with the officials administering the other sixty villages in the new *tun* to not record the boundaries of the enclaves in the land registers. As a local of the left *tun*, Zhao used his political power to defend the economic interests of his own social group. This resistance significantly hindered the issuing of land deeds to the central-*tun* residents; by 1912, the central-*tun* residents still had not received the deeds to their plots in the right and the left *tun*.[34]

ELITE ACTIVISM AND IDENTITY FORMATION IN THE EARLY REPUBLIC

The political transition after the fall of the Qing provided more momentum for the right- and the left-*tun* residents to alter the unequal relationship between themselves and the central-*tun* residents. As the Qing dynasty fell, a republican government was established in 1912. This transitional stage featured the coexistence of multiple institutions and the rise of elite activism. On the one hand, the republican government preserved the banner administration, including it in the county government and renaming it the Office of Banner Affairs. However, the county government was far from consolidated in the early republican period, so the banner administration continued to administer the banner villages and had considerable autonomy. On the other hand, following the trend of local self-governance, the provincial assembly (*ziyi ju*) and local councils provided elites with new arenas in which to exercise their agency. The Jilin provincial assembly was founded in 1909. In Shuangcheng, local councils were established in the county seat and in important towns between 1909 and 1913 (SCXZ 1973, 139–40). Local elites actively used the new institutions to pursue their interests. In this way, chronic tensions created by the spatial and categorical inequalities under the Qing received new representation.

In 1912, the election for the national assembly (*guohui*) of republican China brought elite activism in Shuangcheng to a new level. Although the first national election was largely confined to the upper classes, competitive elections brought about a tide of liberalism.[35] The election consisted of a series of indirect polls at the local and provincial levels that began in December 1912 and concluded in January 1913 (Young 1977, 113–14). The national assembly consisted of two houses: the House of Representatives and the Senate. The qualified voters cast ballots for electors, who then chose a total of 596 members for the House of Representatives. The provincial assemblies selected 274 members for the Senate. Shuangcheng local elites actively participated in this election. To enhance their chances of being elected, they took the advantage of living on the border of Jilin and Heilongjiang provinces and participated in the elections in both provinces. In the end, eight Shuangcheng locals were elected to the national assembly; four were elected from Jilin, and the other four from Heilongjiang (Wang 1968, 205). Given the fact the elites in more than 1,600 counties all over the country competed for the 870 seats in the national assembly, the achievement of Shuangcheng local elites was remarkable.

At this point, some Shuangcheng elites were not only influential at the local level but also had the power and resources to participate in higher-level politics. Among the eight Shuangcheng locals elected to the national assembly was Mo Dehui, a metropolitan bannerman and later a prominent political figure in republican China. Although the family settled in Shuangcheng in the early years, Mo Dehui's father Minghai had served as a scribe in the Eight Banner troops in Xinjiang for nineteen years (Mo 1968, 1–2). Upon returning to Shuangcheng, Minghai continued to serve the banner government (ibid., 6). Mo Dehui lived with his family in the Shuangcheng seat and received good education. In 1906, Mo Dehui entered the Northern Police Academy (*Beiyang gaodeng xunjing xuetang*), and in 1910, he was appointed the chief of the police department in Binjiang County (today's Harbin) in Heilongjiang province (ibid., 20). In 1912, he was elected to the House of Representatives by the electors in Jilin. Thereafter, Mo Dehui was active in some high official positions, such as the governor of Fengtian (1926–1927), and minister of agriculture and commerce (1927–1928).[36] The high level of political participation by Shuangcheng elites also influenced local politics.

Some rural bannermen also had the power and prestige to participate in politics. Two representatives of the right- and the left-*tun* residents—Zhao Rongchun and Wu Chengzhu—were especially active. Zhao Rongchun's family was prominent in the village. The 1889 land register recorded a total of 29.4 *shang* of land for Zhao Rongchun's household.[37] By 1911, not only did Zhao Rongchun hold the post of lieutenant but both he and his son also held the title of government student (*wentong*),[38] indicating their prestige. Wu Chengzhu served as a tax preceptor under the same banner administration as Zhao. Wu was registered under the household headed by his father. In 1889, Wu Chengzhu's father had a total of 41.4 *shang* of *nazu* land.[39] Although the two households did not own a large amount of *nazu* land in 1889, their landholding was comparable to that of an average metropolitan banner household. Both men actively participated in local self-governance. In 1912, Wu Chengzhu was in charge of the Office of Election Affairs of Dong'an Township, the seat of the left *tun*, and had been elected a member of the township council.[40]

Catalyzed by the tide of political participation, the repressed grievances of the residents in the central *tun* and the right and the left *tun* finally led to the collective rent-resistance movement described at the beginning of the chapter. In the autumn of 1912, as the time for rent collection approached, Zhao Rongchun went to the provincial government to follow up on the petition filed by Guangzhi back in 1909. In a related move, Zhao Rongchun and Wu Chengzhu also requested the county government's permission to delay collecting the rents for the central *tun* residents. When the request was denied, the two men took advantage of their banner posts and wrote a notice on official paper. Then they went door to door, circulating it among the residents of the eighty villages of the right and the left *tun*, asking them not to pay rent to the central-*tun* residents.[41] Zhao Rongchun assured these bannermen that he would successfully negotiate their landownership at the provincial government. Zhao and Wu's positions in the banner government and on the township council assured the rural bannermen in the right and the left *tun* of the organizers' ability to negotiate, and convinced them to refuse to pay rent to the bannermen from the central *tun*.

This event soon resulted in a factional struggle in the Office of the Banner Affairs between officials from the central *tun* and those from the right and the left *tun*. The central-*tun* faction accused Zhao Rongchun and Wu Chengzhu of cheating the rural bannermen of the right and the left *tun* in order to pursue their own personal material and political interests.[42] This charge was based on the fact that Wu Chengzhu had collected a monetary donation of one thousand strings of cash in the left *tun*, and used this money to travel to the provincial capital to file a lawsuit regarding the landownership of the enclaves. In addition, Wu canvassed the left-*tun* residents during his election campaign for the township council, promising that if they elected him, he would act as a representative to negotiate the landownership for them.[43] Facing this threat, the central-*tun* banner officials banded together and succeeded in expelling all personnel from the right and the left *tun* from the Office of the Banner Affairs. All active officials who originated in the right or the left *tun* were removed from their posts and permanently denied the right to serve the banner administration. Following this success, the banner administration forwarded a letter to the county government, urging it to order the right- and the left-*tun* residents to turn in their rents to the central-*tun* landlords (MGSCXGSDA, no. 398). The county government followed this recommendation.

Having failed at the level of county government, the right- and the left-*tun* representatives tried to find a way to succeed at the provincial government level. They used the new concept of equality, an ideology introduced and supported by the republican government, and placed their hope on the provincial assembly. In March 1913, they wrote a petition to the county government, emphasizing the importance of equal rights and entitlements in the new social order: "Since now [the polity] has changed to the Republic, [all people], whether Manchu or Han, are citizens. Thus we should have equal rights."[44] They requested that the county government wait for the provincial assembly to discuss this case before making a decision.

After investigating this case, the provincial assembly tried to mediate the conflict by asking the bannermen in the central *tun* to sell their ownership of the enclaves to the residents of the right and the left *tun*. The provincial government ordered Shuangcheng's local officials to report on the origins of the conflict. Once it realized that both the rural bannermen in the right and the left *tun* and the bannermen in the central *tun* had partial ownership of these lands, the provincial assembly suggested a price of 135 strings of cash for each *shang*, which was half of the market value. The rural banner elites in the right and the left *tun* supported the proposal. Obviously, this is the solution they were aiming for. Given their active participation in self-government, they very likely made this suggestion at the provincial assembly. The residents in the central *tun*, however, rejected it, dissatisfied with the price the provincial assembly decided and not willing to give up their ownership of the enclaves.[45] Since the price of the banner land increased dramatically after the privatization of banner land, landownership itself became a kind of capital. The central-*tun* residents had no incentive to easily give up their ownership—even if they were suffering financial losses; even as the right- and the left-*tun* residents refused to pay rent, the central-*tun* residents continued to pay rent to the government for their enclaves.

In the end, the new republican institution failed to find a quick solution to this chronic conflict. The representatives of both sides, consisting of members from elite families, engaged in a prolonged debate at the county government.[46] Zhao Rongchun and Wu Chengzhu were among the representatives from the right and the left *tun*, and Mo Dehui's cousin, Mo Desheng, was among the representatives of the central *tun*.[47] The provincial assembly found it difficult to persuade either party in this conflict, as both had compelling reasons to back up their requests.

The rural bannermen of the right and the left *tun* used the rhetoric of "citizenship" and "equal entitlements" as weapons vehemently attacking the unequal distribution of land entitlements under the Qing. For them, the landlord-tenant relationship between the residents in the central *tun* and those in the right and the left *tun* was a product of the categorical inequality of the past. Therefore, the new republican regime should rectify this inequality. However, the central-*tun* residents also could find institutional and legal support under the republican regime; they emphasized the fact that they had held these enclaves for more than ninety years to demonstrate their property rights to these lands. The emphasis on property rights was in line with the legal reform launched in the first decade of the twentieth century. During the late Qing, reformers imported property-rights theory, which considered property rights to be unitary and exclusive. Both the revised Qing civil code and republican civil codes accepted this concept (Huang 2001, 108). According to this concept, the central-*tun* residents had exclusive, impartible rights to their enclaves. Thus, the negotiation reached a deadlock; although the new ideology advocated equal entitlements, the new republican regime was also committed to protecting property rights.

By the eleventh month of 1913, as the time of rent collection approached, the conflict remained unresolved. The provincial government thus decided to maintain the status quo, stipulating that, for the year of 1913, the right- and the left-*tun* residents should still send rent to the central-*tun* residents.[48] The landlord-tenant relationship between the central-*tun* residents and the right- and the left-*tun* bannermen persisted until the late 1930s. In 1938, the local government under the Manchukuo regime issued an order, stating that, provided there was agreement between the two parties, the landlords in the central *tun* should sell their rights of rent collection to their tenants in the right and the left *tun* (SCXZ 1990, 145).

Although the rural bannermen in the right and the left *tun* did not immediately succeed in altering the unequal landlord-tenant relationship imposed in the Qing, these events marked their emergence as a social and political group in Shuangcheng. Like the metropolitan bannermen in the 1870s, the rural bannermen developed a group identity and became powerful through a long-term process of boundary making and enforcing. This process involved a set of cultural, social, and institutional factors, including immigrants' places of origin and lifestyles and the state's assignment of differentiated land entitlements. Because they were from the garrisons in Manchuria, rural bannermen always kept a distinct identity from the metropolitan bannermen. At the same time, they were a diverse group consisting of members from seventeen garrisons. They eventually developed a group identity not only because they lived in the same village communities but also because they received the same land entitlements from the state. The differentiated government treatment of them relative to the metropolitan bannermen generated a sense of repression and grievances among them, which eventually informed their group identification.

Wealth accumulation played an important role in making the rural bannermen into a prominent social group. Although the rural bannermen vehemently attacked the differentiated land entitlements, they themselves also enjoyed some privileges in this system. Their land entitlements gave them the power to accumulate more land on their own. Moreover, as capable farmers, they also enjoyed more income at the household level than did many metropolitan bannermen. As chapter 7 shows, the long-term wealth accumulation gave rise to a considerable number of wealthy rural banner households. The fact that they were willing to pay a price of 135 strings of cash *per shang* to buy the enclaves from the central-*tun* residents reflects their affluence. These elite rural bannermen not only owned as much land as the metropolitan bannermen but also served the local government as officials or earned titles through the government-sponsored exam system.

Eventually, elite activism enabled the rural-banner elites in the right and the left *tun* to articulate the identity of rural bannermen. Studies on collective identity have demonstrated the important role social movements can play in creating group consciousness (Taylor and Whittier 1992). The rural-banner elites of the right and the left *tun* expressed their collective identity in two ways: when interacting with the county and provincial governments, they used the rhetoric of equal entitlement and citizenship, a set of new concepts the republican government had just adopted, to attack the origins of inequality in Shuangcheng; in the villages, they mobilized rural bannermen to participate in the rent-resistance movement. They used good tactics to approach rural bannermen as a group. Despite the fact that the conflict regarding the ownership of the enclaves resulted from spatial inequality and that there were one thousand households of rural bannermen living in the central *tun*, the rural-banner elites in the right and the left *tun* focused their grievances on the categorical inequality between metropolitan and rural bannermen. Through this strategy, the rural-banner elites in the right and the left *tun* not only tried to win sympathy from the republican government but also intended to remind the rural bannermen in the central *tun* of their commonalities. Moreover, the mobilization of villagers of the right and the left *tun* also helped to enforce their group consciousness. Activities such as circulating the rent-resistance notice door to door and promising to represent the rural bannermen at the provincial government highlighted the common interests of this group. Therefore, the rent-resistance movement contributed to the development of rural bannermen into a collectivity.[49]

LAND ENTITLEMENT AND THE PERSISTENCE OF HIERARCHY

The rent-resistance movement in the early Republic marked the completion of the social construction of categorical boundaries in Shuangcheng. By organizing the rent resistance and engaging in the subsequent political struggles, rural bannermen articulated a collective identity. In this sense, it also reveals a paradox: the movement that aimed to overturn the structural inequality reinforced the boundaries between the social categories. This consequence indicates that, in the century following the founding of Shuangcheng society, these boundaries have deeply embedded in the society. The state's unequal assignment of land entitlements defined these boundaries, and immigrants' activities in maintaining or promoting their socioeconomic statuses strengthened them. As these boundaries demarcated people's interests and shaped their identities, they also determined the way people organized themselves in collective actions. The social hierarchy founded by the Qing land-allocation policy therefore became durable.

The process of social formation in Shuangcheng demonstrates the power of wealth in transmitting social hierarchy across political regimes. The stable pattern of land distribution helped sustain the structural inequality. In the early Republic, despite wealth mobility at the individual household levels, the majority of metropolitan and rural bannermen succeeded in maintaining their status, and the wealth gap between the haves and have-nots persisted. Thus, despite the change of polity from an imperial to a republican system, the landed wealth helped to transmit metropolitan and rural bannermen's privileges into the new regime. More than thirty years later, on the eve of the Communist Land Reform in 1947, the pattern of land distribution in Shuangcheng remained unequal (Noellert 2014, figures 6 and 7).[50] In fact, the persistence of the pattern of wealth distribution was a worldwide phenomenon. As Piketty (2014, 336–76) shows, despite all the revolutions and reforms and the development of capitalism, wealth distribution in European countries was highly concentrated throughout the eighteenth and nineteenth centuries. The persistence of the pattern of wealth distribution indicates that social hierarchy and boundaries defined by wealth status have been durable.

By documenting the detailed process of social formation, the Shuangcheng story also illuminates the mechanism that made the structural inequality durable: the duality of landownership as both entitlements and property rights makes possible the conversion of political privileges into economic advantages. While both entitlements and property rights denote landownership, the importance of each varied under different political systems. In an ideal modern society that grants everyone equal entitlement, property rights determine people's wealth status. Yet, under a state-dominated system, the state could organize the society by assigning differentiated entitlements to people. In this regard, property rights are not clearly defined, and land entitlement plays a more important role in determining wealth status. At the same time, since land entitlement is associated with a specific political regime, it was mutable. New regimes could reorganize the society through the redistribution of wealth. Only when the concept of property rights developed and took precedence over entitlement, could the social hierarchy built on the distribution of landownership become stable. Many societies, in both China and western Europe, saw the role landownership played in converting the political privileges of the old elite class into stable socioeconomic status, thereby carrying the social structure of the past into the modern times (Enatsu 2004; Piketty 2014, 336–76).

The story of Shuangcheng illustrates that process. In the Qing-dynasty Shuangcheng, landownership was first determined by the state's assignment of land entitlements, and this entitlement per se was mutable. Once the state allocated the land to bannermen, both the state and local communities developed mechanisms to define and secure the use rights of the land. The concept of property rights gradually came into being in this region, although its definition was still not clear under the Qing. Finally, the privatization of banner land in the early twentieth century reinforced the property rights of the landowners. Landowners actively participated in this process. They used various strategies, especially privileges associated with their land entitlements, to accumulate wealth under the Qing. During the institutional and political changes in the end of the Qing, these landowners also embraced the new ideas of property rights and successfully secured their socioeconomic status. Unless the state used coercion to redistribute land among the population, the previous landowners would continue to enjoy their property rights. In Shuangcheng, only when the Communist Party carried out land reform and redistributed land among the entire rural population, did the pattern of land distribution become equal (Noellert 2014, 87–89).

Epilogue

While the Shuangcheng case tells a story of social formation under state domination in one county in the Qing, China saw more large-scale projects of social engineering in the twentieth century. In the 1950s, the People's Republic of China launched a series of projects to organize and control the population and wealth throughout the country. The goal of these projects was multifold: they marked the effort at state-building by the CCP, a socialist revolution, and a modernization movement to develop the economy. To achieve these goals, the PRC directed resources to the most desirable sectors for socialist construction. Thus, the state created various categories and classified people according to their birthplace, household registration, and employment status. These categories were associated with differential state entitlements (Wang 2005; Wang 2008). Of all the categorical inequalities in the PRC, the most fundamental ones were the rural-urban divide and the spatial inequality created by the *hukou* household registration system. Although the *hukou* system differed from the Eight Banners system in Shuangcheng in many aspects, parallels between the two can be seen in the logic of creating a social hierarchy through resource allocation and in the subsequent stratification system.

The rural-urban divide under the *hukou* system was produced by a state policy that aimed at concentrating resources in the urban area to develop heavy industry. In the early 1950s, the PRC developed a household registration system for collecting and managing information on the personal identity, kinship, and legal residence of Chinese citizens.

The original purpose was to administer local society and manage the population. Yet, the *hukou* system soon became a tool to facilitate resource allocation. In the same period, the state collectivized agricultural production and established a socialist planned economy. This planned economy was characterized by a system of unified procurement and unified sale of grain (*tonggou tongxiao*) and a food-rationing system in the urban area (Oi 1989, 29–65). The state set a quota of grain procurement each year, and peasants were required to deliver the quota to procurement agencies at prices set by the government. In the cities, all residents were guaranteed a supply of certain amount of grain at a fixed price. These measures were aimed at extracting as much agricultural surplus as possible to facilitate the heavy-industry-oriented development strategy. With this move, the *hukou* system became rigid and produced "institutional exclusion" (Wang 2005, 1–31). As the state restricted and even eliminated migration, the *hukou* system functioned to define and maintain the boundary between the two segments of population. In addition to grain rationing, urban residents also enjoyed state employment, a pension, public housing, and health care provided by their work unit (*danwei*). The peasants, however, were denied access to these benefits because they had an agricultural household registration. Thus, even as it attempted to maintain an egalitarian distribution of wealth within each population category, the PRC also created inequality between the urban and rural *hukou* holders.

During the socialist era, the inequality between the rural and urban household categories affected many aspects of people's lives (Davis and Wang 2009). One immediate repercussion could be seen in the different fates of the rural and urban populations during the Great Leap Forward (1958–1961). As this economic and social campaign to industrialize the country led to famine, the urban residents survived because of the grain-rationing system (Brown 2012, 53–76). The peasants, however, suffered from severe food shortages, and almost all of the famine-related deaths occurred in the countryside (Wang 2005, 45). Urban Chinese were also privileged in education and political life. People with a rural *hukou* origin had only limited chances of gaining higher-level education and party membership (Wu and Treiman 2004). Moreover, despite the fact that the size of urban population was much smaller than that of the rural population, people with an urban *hukou* origin occupied the majority of seats in the National People's Congress (Wang 2005, 116). In other words, the *hukou* system established the urban *hukou* holders as elites in both political and economic terms.[1]

As China's market economy has developed in the post-socialist era, the structural inequality of the *hukou* system generated more profound consequences. Since the system concentrated resources and capital in urban areas, it greatly contributed to economic growth in the cities (Wang 2005, 117–23).[2] Rapid economic development and industrialization enlarged the income gap between the cities and the countryside (Li and Luo 2010; Sicular et al. 2010). Regional inequalities have also widened the income and wealth gap; compared to people living in the coastal regions, people living in the inland rural areas in particular lagged behind (Wang 2010). Moreover, the demand for labor and the rural-to-urban migration threw the rural *hukou* holders to the bottom of the social hierarchy. Beginning in the 1990s, in response to the increasing demand for labor in the coastal areas and the lure of higher incomes, rural residents in the less developed areas flocked to the city to find employment as migrant workers. Although these migrant workers contributed greatly to economic development, for a long period they did not receive entitlements and had no access to such resources as education and health care in the cities, because they did not have a *hukou* in the city in which they worked. Some scholars have described this phenomenon as "differential citizenship" (Solinger 1999; Wu 2010). The persisting inequality in the entitlements for urban residents, rural residents, and rural-to-urban migrants has led the three groups to develop distinctive perceptions of distributive justice and the ways to organize themselves (Wang 2010).

Moreover, in the transitional economy in post-socialist China, political capital—connections to government and the party—has become a prominent determinant of socioeconomic status. In recent years, the widening gaps in income and wealth within the urban population have blurred the clear-cut rural-urban divide. With further development of market economy and the persistence of the party state, individuals with close connections to government and the party were able to capitalize on their political power to pursue economic interests (Liu 2009). This is especially true in the process of privatization of the state-owned or collectively-owned properties. Rent-seeking and opportunity hoarding were common mechanisms through which the elites could become wealthy. This is the case not only in the urban areas but also in the countryside; as the state directed agricultural land for nonagricultural use, rural cadres were able to seize significantly larger shares of profits than their fellow villagers (Zhou 2009).

Above all, the stratification system in contemporary China has many parallels with that of the Qing-dynasty Shuangcheng. Then as now the state created structural inequality by assigning differential entitlements to people based on their membership to a certain category defined by state registration. The purpose of creating this structural inequality was to direct resources to the state-designated elite population. This unequal distribution of entitlements between population categories was accompanied by a relatively equal distribution of wealth within each category (Wang 2008). Moreover, at times of institutional or economic reform, the elite groups, especially those with close connections to state power, were able to convert their privileges into property, thereby making the inequality durable.

The parallels between the two stratification systems illuminate state-sponsored inequality and the associated pattern of social formation in Chinese history from a long-term perspective. Of course, recognizing these parallels does not mean that there is a causal relationship between the Shuangcheng case and the PRC system. Rather, the Shuangcheng settlement and the *hukou* system were two independent projects of state-initiated social engineering. Yet the very coincidences indicate that the statecraft performed by the PRC and the subsequent process of social stratification have existed in the past. At the same time, comparing the two systems sheds light on a modern aspect of the PRC state. Whereas the Qing only carried out the social-engineering project in one county, the PRC had the ability to create structural inequality on a massive scale. Moreover, the goals of state-building during the Qing differed from those of the PRC; even under the state-dominated system, the Qing still intentionally left considerable room for local people to organize their everyday life. By contrast, the statecraft of PRC represented a significant expansion of the modern state; it invested great effort to penetrate down into the local communities and reorganize the society.

REFERENCE MATTER

APPENDIX A: NAMES AND TERMS OF OFFICE OF THE GENERALS OF JILIN

The following is a list of the generals who are mentioned in the book. Names are listed in alphabetical order.

Boqitu	1827.7–1829.2
Fujun	1814.2–1817.2; 1818.9–1822.6; 1824.2–1827.7
Fukejing'e	1830.3–1831.9
Fuming'a	1866.2–1870.9
Guqing	1850.5–1853.1
Husong'e	1829.2–1830.2
Jing'ebu	1840.4–1848.12
Jingchun	1853.1–1864.12
Ming'an	1877.4–1883.2
Songlin	1817.2–1818.9; 1822.6–1823.9
Songyun	1823.9–1824.2
Woshine	1848.12–1850.5
Xiangkang	1835.6–1835.12; 1836.4–1840.4

APPENDIX B: AN ESTIMATION OF THE NUMBER OF UNREGISTERED HOUSEHOLDS IN SHUANGCHENG IN 1876

To analyze the patterns of land distribution among all residents in Shuangcheng, it is necessary to estimate the population sizes. As chapter 3 discusses, in addition to the registered populations, there was a large unregistered population. The size of the unregistered population is important in analyzing land-distribution patterns because members of this group did not receive any state entitlements and were therefore considered landless. At the same time, it is also a challenge to estimate the size of the unregistered population in a single county, because these migrants were geographically mobile. Without registered properties, they came to seek their fortune in this frontier society and left for other regions if they saw better opportunities. Thus, the size and composition of the unregistered population was in constant flux.

Given this challenge, I estimate the number of unregistered households based on the size of registered land in 1876 and the number of laborers required to farm the land. The 1876 land registers recorded a total of 174,384 *shang* of land (SCPGBTDHKDM, 1834731). After deducting the amount of land registered under the rural bannermen living in the forty villages of the left *tun*, who were excluded from the calculation of the land distributions in Figure 7.1, the total amount of land was 137, 871 *shang*. If we adopt the farming capacity we estimate for an adult male in chapter 3, which is ten *shang*, cultivating the 137,871 *shang* of land requires a minimum of 13,787 adult males.

To get the number of unregistered adult males, I deduct the number of registered adult males from the estimated 13,787 laborers needed for farming. The 1876 banner household registers recorded a total of 6,646 adult males among the metropolitan, rural, and floating bannermen in the central and the right *tun*. In addition, the 1876 land registers also recorded 734 civilian commoners as landowners. As chapter 3 has discussed, some of the 734 civilian commoners were contractors who recruited a large number of tenants to farm the land and collected rents from the tenants. These contractors themselves would not farm the land. Therefore, I estimate that on average, the registered civilian commoners had one adult male in each household that participated in farming. Thus, the registered banner and civilian adult males add up to 7,380.

After deducting this number from the 13,787 laborers required to farm the land in Shuangcheng, we see that in 1876, there were probably 6,407 unregistered adult males.

The next step is to estimate the household size of these unregistered adult males and then to get the number of unregistered households. Since the unregistered adult males mainly worked as tenants and hired laborers, their household size could be quite small and even single. If we still take two as the estimated number of adult males in each unregistered household, the 6,407 adult males will make about 3,200 households. If we estimate the average number of adult males in each unregistered household to be 1.5, there will be 4,270 households. Given this range, it is reasonable to use 3,500 as the number of unregistered households in the calculation of land distribution in 1876. Of course, due to the lack of accurate data, this estimate is by no means perfect. Yet it helps to provide an overall sense of the pattern of land distribution in Shuangcheng. Since all the unregistered households belong to the landless category, an increase in their number elevates the level of inequality in land distribution, and a decrease, in turn, reduces the level of wealth inequality.

NOTES

Chapter One

1. The term "Manchuria" used to be controversial because it is associated with the colonial interests of Russia and Japan in this region in the nineteenth and twentieth centuries. However, Mark Elliot (2000) reveals that beginning in the seventeenth century, the term "Manchuria" gradually developed into a typonym referring to the area in Northeast Asia that the Manchu rulers of the Qing claimed as their place of origin, into which they invested a unique identity. Therefore, in this book, I use "Manchuria" as a historical term to refer to the region that in the twentieth century has become Northeast China.

2. About the itinerary of the first group of metropolitan bannermen, see Jiang Jixian's memorial on 1824.1.28 (JJCLFZZ 03-3387-38), and Rongzhao and Qiying's memorial on 1824.2.22 (JJCLFZZ 03-2846-34). On many occasions, Shuangcheng is also called Shuangchengbao or Shuangchengpu.

3. The name list of the first group of metropolitan banner immigrants archived in the Ningguta vice commander-in-chief's office in 1824 (NGTFDTYMDA, 52: 289).

4. The total number of households is summarized from China Multi-Generational Panel Data: Shuangcheng (CMGPD-SC) and the report of the Shuangcheng banner government regarding the *baojia* system in 1866 (SCPZGYMDA 160: 636-1: 354–60).

5. Compared to the 1860s, the number of registered households and size of the population in 1910 significantly increased as a result of immigration and the expansion of administrative area and government registration.

6. Wang (2005) and Von Glahn (2012) pay attention to the historical precedents of *hukou* household registration in PRC and trace the history of household registration in China back to its origins in the sixth century BC. Both studies consider the *hukou* system a continuation of the civil registration practices in imperial China. While this point is well taken, the *hukou* system shares more features with the banner registration in Shuangcheng than it does with civil registration in the past.

7. Since the 1970s, numerous studies have examined this trend, including the two edited volumes by the Center for East Asian Studies at the University of Chicago (Jones 1979; Tsou 1981b); Kuhn (1980); Rowe (1984, 1992); Rankin (1986); and Esherick and Rankin (1990).

8. For example, Davies et al. (2011) estimate that in 2000, 71 percent of the global wealth was concentrated in the hands of 10 percent of adults, and that about half of the adult population had nearly nothing.

9. "Liaodong" refers to the geographical area east of the Liao River in today's Liaoning province. In the early seventeenth century, Nurhachi and Hong Taiji established the Manchu State in this area.

10. In the Qing bureaucracy, at almost every level of government, the court stipulated that some posts could only be filled by Manchu and Mongol bannermen. Moreover, the state also arranged special examinations for Manchu and Mongol bannermen (Rhoads 2000; Elliott 2001).

11. The three ethnicities—Manchu, Mongol, and Han—refer to institutionalized population categories. The ethnic composition of bannermen was actually more complicated than this. There were also Xibe, Korean, and some other small ethnic groups.

12. A metropolitan bannerman with the lowest soldier's rank received two *taels* of silver as monthly salary; whereas a garrison bannerman of the same rank only received one tael of silver (Ding 2003, 220). Bannermen in the garrisons received both silver and grain salaries, with the exception of those in Shengjing, who did not receive a grain salary. Instead, they worked on state-allocated land to supplement their livelihoods.

13. Before the nineteenth century, bannermen in the garrisons were not allowed to take exams in the provinces where the garrisons were located. To take exams, they had to travel to Beijing, and this inconvenience prevented many from entering the government (Ding 2003, 219–21).

14. For example, in 1771, the court identified more than six thousand widowers, widows, and orphans in the metropolitan banner population who could barely make a living. Some of them had even become paupers (Liu 2008, 719).

15. See the articles collected in HCJSWB, book 18, juan 35, "baqi shengji," 1–45.

16. Ding (1985) and Wei Y. (2010) studied in detail the 1742 relocation of metropolitan bannermen to Lalin.

17. Shuangcheng is about 75 kilometers from Acheng, where the capital of the Jin dynasty was located.

18. The Willow Palisade (*liutiaobian*) was a barrier the Qing government erected in 1681 to prevent Han Chinese from moving farther into Manchuria and encroaching on banner land. It was constructed of two parallel one-meter-high earthen levees, spaced three-and-a-half meters apart, and crowned with a fence of willow fronds (Edmonds 1979).

19. The only exception was in what is present day Liaoning, where the government of the Fengtian prefect administered all the civilian affairs.

20. The state had established a civilian local government in Jilin in the 1730s to govern a handful of settlements of Han-Chinese immigrants who had entered Jilin surreptitiously and were registered by the government (Lee 1970; Fan 2007, 222–23).

21. Under the equal-field system, the state owned the land and allocated a plot to each adult man and woman. By farming their plots, households paid taxes and provided labor services to the state (Han 1984). On military farms during the Ming dynasty, the state also owned the land and assigned one plot to each household (Wang 1965).

22. The population figure in 1850 is from Ho (1959, 283, appendix 2). The population figure in 1907 is from Fan (2007, 70). Liang (1980) provides similar results.

23. See the memorials by Ming'an on 1878.9.9 and in 1881 (QDJLDASLXB, 58–62, 7).

24. See Ming'an's memorial on 1882.3.22, which is enclosed in the correspondence between the Office of the General of Jilin and the Shuangcheng banner government (SCPXLYMDA, no. 14936).

25. See the twenty-eight rules made by the General Bureau of Tax Counting and Land Opening (*qingfu fanghuang zongju*) on 1902.7.15 (SCPZGYMDA, 268: 1195: 1–18). Although the decision was made in 1902, it took the government three years to prepare for the transition. Also see the order from the Office of the General of Jilin to the banner government in 1906.2 (SCPZGYMDA, 275: 1237: 35–39)

26. See the order of the provincial government on 1906.3.27 (SCPZGYMDA, 276: 1238: 225–26).

27. Shuangcheng still occupies a leading position in grain production today. In 2005, the grain yield of Shuangcheng ranked tenth among all counties in China (GJTJJ 2005).

28. Some scholars have considered the high agricultural productivity and the commercialization of agricultural products in Manchuria as signs of economic development and advancement in agricultural production (Yi 1990, 163–65). Recent studies of Chinese economic history emphasize the growing output per capita and structural change in the economy—such as specialization of agricultural production and investment in capital and technology—as the indicators of economic development (Huang 1985, 1990; Myers 1991). In this sense, the agricultural economy in northern Manchuria in the early twentieth century did not develop (Zhao 1972; Reardon-Anderson 2005, 196–98).

29. Upon its establishment in 1882, the civilian government acquired the rights to manage the banner land. But in 1885, the banner government was able to get these rights back (Ren 2013). Thus the civilian government only managed the land in Shuangcheng for a very brief period.

30. The continuation of the banner administration in Shuangcheng was provided for in the abdication agreement between the Qing and the Republic of China. The emperor's abdication was made contingent upon the Republican government's agreement to maintain the Eight Banner system to administer the affairs of bannermen (Tong 1994).

31. In his study of the *hukou* system of contemporary China, Fei-ling Wang (2005, 4–9) synthesizes a theory of institutional exclusion as the framework. I borrow this concept to show the parallels between the Eight Banners in Shuangcheng and the *hukou* system.

32. This incomplete landownership in China has given rise to scholarly debate regarding the nature of landownership in early China over whether the land was state-owned or privately owned. The articles collected in *Lishi yanjiu bianjibu* (1957) best represent the various positions in this debate. Yang Guozhen (2009) reconciles this debate by pointing out the incomplete form of landownership that persisted throughout the imperial time.

33. Before the eighth century, state landownership was the dominant form, although the state allowed private land transactions very early on. The state did not collect taxes on land, but levied a poll tax and required that commoners provide labor services to the state, which it justified by considering these as repayment to the state for having authorized land use rights. In 780, a tax reform by the Tang state introduced the principle of tax collection based on household land and property; this reform marked the state's recognition of private landownership. This transition continued in the following dynasties and was finally completed in the mid-eighteenth century, when the Qing state began to collect taxes exclusively on land.

34. There is a rich body of scholarship on the two-tiered form of landownership in traditional China. The earliest studies date back to the 1930s. Some recent scholarship includes Chao and Chen (1982); Huang (1985; 2001, 99–118); and Yang (2009, 70–105). For a complete review of the scholarship, see Cao (2012).

35. Because this practice was widespread in China, regional variations existed.

36. In recent years, economic historians worldwide have paid attention to differences between wealth and income, especially the implications for social inequality. In general, scholars point out that wealth inequality is more persistent than income inequality because of the inheritance practices that transmit wealth from one generation to the next. See Lindert (2000); Keister (2000); and Piketty (2000, 2014).

37. Sewell (1992, 20–21) discusses the different agency of social actors based on social position and the social system under which they live.

38. Primogeniture in property inheritance was practiced not only by bannermen in Shuangcheng but also by those working on the manor lands in the surrounding areas of Beijing (Qiu 2014, 258–60).

39. See Wang et al. (2016, appendix B) for a more detailed discussion of the archival sources.

40. Chao and Chen (1982); Chao (1986, 2003); Qin and Su (1996); Hu (2012) have used government land registers to study land distribution. However, because of the issues of preservation, the land registers used by previous studies are scattered and only available for a few villages. Another source for studying land distribution is survey data collected in the early twentieth century. These data provide more contextual information, but they also are conducted at the village level. See Myers (1970) and Huang (1985).

Chapter Two

1. For frontier settlement in southwest China, see Li (2012). For the northwestern frontier, see Millward (1998); Perdue (2005). For the settlement history of Taiwan, see Shepherd (1993).

2. For example, from 225 BC to AD 725, the state directly or indirectly moved at least sixteen million people. See Lee (1978).

3. For earlier examples, see Lee (1978, 1982).

4. Scholarship on migration to this region began during the 1930s, a time when the Chinese state was indeed weak and fragmented. The two pioneering scholars, Ho (1931) and Lattimore (1932) may have dismissed state contributions to the early development of Manchuria. Lee (1970) attributes the development of the northeast frontier to Han Chinese migrants, and describes this process as the Sinicization of the northeast frontier. Later scholarship has followed this general narrative and mainly focused on the practices of Han Chinese migrants. See Diao and Yi (1994); Reardon-Anderson (2005); Isett (2004, 2007).

5. Japanese and Chinese scholars have paid attention to Shuangcheng settlement since the 1940s but have differing evaluations of its later development. Komekura Jirou (1941) conducted a field study and recounted the founding history of Shuangcheng. He holds the opinion that Han Chinese commoners entered the banner villages after the settlement and transformed the banner society into a Han Chinese society (ibid., 146), though some of his findings contradict this conclusion. Eshima Hisao (1999) was the first scholar to state that, after the fall of the Qing, it was likely that many metropolitan bannermen kept their upper-class status. The two major studies of Shuangcheng settlement by Ding Yizhuang (1985, 1987) and Wei Ying (2010) also examine the state's planning and settlement of banner migrants. Although both studies note the positive impact of the Shuangcheng relocation project, they consider the settlement a failure, drawing on evidence that it did not find an effective solution for the livelihood problem of the banner population in general and that the state's recruitment efforts failed to meet the original quota of metropolitan banner households.

6. Most of these policy discussions were collected in HCJSWB, book 18, juan 35; and HCDXTGZY, juan 31.

7. Songyun was experienced in planning settlements. Before working as the minister of the Board of Civil Office, he had held the post of general of Yili (1802–1808, 1813–1815), in present day Xinjiang (QSG, book 37, 11115–17). Songyun's major achievement as general of Yili was the successful settlement of several rustication sites in Xinjiang.

8. In these three years, officials investigated the pasture land in western Liaoning, Shengjing, and Shuangcheng and Lalin in northern Jilin. See the court memorials by Saichong'a, Cheng'an, Songyun, and Fujun et al. on 1812.5.6, 1812.7.6, 1812.7.12, 1812.8.12, 1812.8.25 (JJCLFZZ 03-1875-10; 03-1875-41; 03-1875-43; 03-1875-52; 03-1875-56).

9. See Fujun's biography in QSG, book 37, 11119.

10. A *jinshi* degree is the highest degree a male can earn through the civil service examination. The translation exam is easier than the regular civil service exam, and the Qing court offered it to bannermen to enhance their chances of acquiring a degree.

11. About the opening of pasture land in western Liaoning, see the court memorials by Songyun, Hening, and Fujun on 1812.8.12, 1812.8.25, 1813.9.26, 1814.9.8 (JJCLFZZ 03-1875-52, 03-1875-56, 03-1875-86, 03-1876-74, 03-1878-20), and the court memorial by the Grand Council on 1814.11.22 (JJCLFZZ 03-1878-51). As their punishment, Songyun and Hening had their salary ranks downgraded by two grades.

12. See the memorial submitted by Fujun and Songning on 1815.4.29 (SCPTTJL, 17–18) and the Jiaqing emperor's reply to the memorial on 1815.5.14 (SCPTTJL, 3).

13. The memorial of Fujun and Songning on 1815.4.29 (SCPTTJL, 17–18). In this document, Fujun stated that the area extended 75 *li* between the north and south ends and 130 *li* between the east and west ends.

14. See the court memorial by the Grand Council on 1814.11.22 (JJCLFZZ 03-1878-51).

15. See Fujun's order about checking unregistered civilians on 1815.5.10 (SCPTTJL, 190).

16. See the edict of Jiaqing Emperor on 1817.7.19 (SCPTTJL, 2). The officials rejected some other unpopulated locations in Jilin because they were too far away from the banner garrisons. Even Shuangcheng, at first glance, did not meet the emperor's expectations. Voicing this concern in 1813, the court waited another two years before approving Shuangcheng as the relocation site (JJCLFZZ, Saichong'a, 1813.5.8, 03-1896-14).

17. Alchuka and Lalin are two banner garrisons that were established in response to the 1742 relocation of metropolitan bannermen to this region (Ding 2003, 81).

18. See Fujun's memorial recounting the planning of Shuangcheng settlement on 1822.7.4 (ZPZZ 04-01-22-0045-046). In the Qing dynasty, the state often used tamped mounds as border markers on the unpopulated northeast frontier.

19. The Qing emperors arranged the banner locations according to the Chinese philosophy of the Five Elements, *wuxing*. See BQTZ, book 1, 17.

20. See Fujun's memorial on 1818.8.27 (SCPTTJL, 21).

21. See Fujun's report to the Jiaqing emperor on 1822.7.4 (ZPZZ 04-01-22-0045-046).

22. Fujun's purpose in doing this was to prevent a repeat of the failure of an earlier attempt to relocate three thousand metropolitan bannermen from Beijing to Lalin, an area southeast of Shuangcheng, in 1748. The bannermen relocated there ended up escaping from the farm because of their lack of knowledge and ability to farm the land.

23. The four banner garrisons in Jilin are Ningguta, Alchuka, Jilin, and Bodune.

24. See the memorial by Fujun on 1816.9.6 (ZPZZ 04-01-23-0168-35).

25. See Fujun's memorial on 1818.8.27 (SCPTTJL, 23).

26. See Fujun's memorial on 1821.1.6 (SCPTTJL, 44).

27. Among these three thousand households, the Shengjing bannermen outnumbered Jilin bannermen because the Jilin bannermen did not participate actively in farming activities and some eventually abandoned the settlement. See Songlin's memorial on 1822.5.15 (ZPZZ 04-01-22-0044-018).

28. Ibid.

29. Most of the bannermen who were relocated from Shengjing to Shuangcheng were banner soldiers stationed in banner garrisons that were of strategic military importance.

30. See the memorial by Songlin on 1822.5.15 (ZPZZ 04-01-22-0045-046). In this memorial, Songlin included a description of the bannermen from Fuzhou and Gaiping, two banner garrisons close to the coastal area.

31. See Fujun's memorial on 1820.5.17 (JJCLFZZ 03-1883-15).

32. See the memorial of Fujun on 1821.1.6 (SCPTTJL, 42–47).

33. See HCJSWB, book 18, juan 35, 33–39. Yinghe proposed explaining the benefits of moving to Shuangcheng as follows: first, these bannermen could have free state land and change their property status from have-nots to haves; second, the move would be easy because the government would provide migrants with stipends and accommodations; finally, by farming the land in Shuangcheng, these bannermen would eventually live a good life.

34. For the number of volunteer banner households relocated in 1826 and 1827, see the memorials by the Board of Revenue on 1825.10.27 (JJCLFZZ 03-3388-24 and 03-3388-25), the memorial by Fujun on 1825.11.26 (JJCLFZZ 03-3388-27), the memorial by Nayancheng on 1826.3.27 (JJCLFZZ 03-3388-35), and the report of the

Office of the Vice Commander-in-Chief of Ningguta in 1827 (NGTFDTYMDA, 54: 649–660). Given the fact that the number of households for the Manchu and Mongol banners in Beijing reached about 116,000 (Han 1987), the number of households that volunteered to move to Shuangcheng was indeed small.

35. QSL (Daoguang reign, 1821–1850), book 34, 1037a.

36. QSL (Daoguang reign), book 34, 1178b.

37. See Fujun's memorial on 1828.10.19 (JJCLFZZ 03-3388-47).

38. See Hengqing's memorial on 1831.12.19 (JJCLFZZ 03-4078-031).

39. See Fujun's memorial on 1828.10.19 (JJCLFZZ 03-3388-47).

40. See QSL (Daoguang reign), book 35, 587b, and book 35, 629b. In 1829, Chengge, the minister of the Grand Council, mentioned the difficult living situation of the bannermen in Rehe, saying that a banner soldier had to use his stipend to support eight to nine household members (QSL, Daoguang reign, book 35, 508a).

41. See Yu'en's memorial on 1830. *run* 4. 23 (ZPZZ 04-01-35-0956-008).

42. See Yu'en's memorial on 1831.2.23 (ZPZZ 04-01-35-1206-001); Baochang's memorial on 1832.2.24 (ZPZZ 04-01-01-0735-007); and Baoxing's memorial on 1832.4.5 (NGDKDA 203000-001).

43. See the report of Shuangcheng banner government in 1868.5 (SCPZGYMDA, 163: 653: 191–95), which recounted that the total number of metropolitan bannermen settled in Shuangcheng was 698. So, no metropolitan banner household moved to Shuangcheng after 1838.

44. Ding 1985.

45. QSL (Jiaqing reign, 1796–1820), book 31, 519a.

46. Relocating bannermen with lower economic status was a common practice. Fujun found that some of the migrants sent to Shuangcheng were indeed too young or too old to farm. Moreover, some migrants were people without a stable occupation and likely to become troublemakers. For example, in 1820, the banner government in Shuangcheng sent Yichong'e, a bannerman from Fuzhou, and his families back because he had a bad reputation as a trouble-maker in his place of origin and was insubordinate in Shuangcheng (SCPTTJL, 113).

47. See the order from the office of the general of Jilin on 1820.5.13 (SCPTTJL, 146).

48. There are a number of different translations of the term *zu* or *zongzu* in previous scholarship. The most common translations are "clan" and "lineage." In his research on imperial control in rural China, Hsiao Kung-chuan (1960, 323) uses Hu Hsien Chin's definition of *zu* as "a group descended from one ancestor who settled in a certain locality or neighborhood." James Watson (1982) maintains that a lineage should have four characteristics: "corporate base, group consciousness, ritual unity, and demonstrated descent." Watson also provides a similar definition for clans, which were organized as corporations, with collectively owned property and joint activities. Because of these

varied meanings assigned to *lineage* and *clan*, I use the term *descent group* for *zu*, to include a larger variety of kinship structures.

49. See Songlin's memorial on 1822.5.15 (ZPZZ 04-01-22-0044-068).

50. This is also a worldwide phenomenon in migration; migrants are usually people with relatively higher socioeconomic status in the local society.

51. Bannermen with a banner post usually had two forms of salary, silver and grain. The silver was distributed monthly, and the grain salary was distributed twice every year. A vanguard (*qianfeng*), tax preceptor, military protector *(hujun)*, and horse-soldier (*mabing*) each had a monthly stipend of four *taels* of silver and an annual grain salary of forty-six *hu* (about 2,461 liters) of rice. A foot soldier had a monthly stipend of three *taels* of silver and an annual grain salary of twenty-two *hu* (about 1,177 liters) of rice (BQTZ, book 1, 550–51).

52. The post of supported soldiers was created in the mid-eighteenth century to accommodate the increasing population of unemployed bannermen (QDBQTZ, book 2, 643–47). Although some supported soldiers also received a grain salary, it is not guaranteed by the court.

53. See Fujun and Fudeng'a's memorial on 1822.2.11 (SCPTTJL, 51).

54. See Yinghe's memorial on 1825.7.11 (JJCLFZZ 03-3388-21).

55. See HCJSWB, book 18, juan 35, 39.

56. This calculation is based on the food rationing standard of the Qing granary system. According to Pierre-Etienne Will and R. Bin Wong (1991, 525), the Qing food ration followed a rate of 0.3 *shi*/month for adults and 0.15 *shi*/month for children. Therefore, the twenty-two *hu* (eleven *shi*) grain salary for a foot soldier could feed three adults for a whole year. The forty-six *hu* (twenty-three *shi*) grain salary for a tax preceptor or military protector could feed about six adults and one child for a whole year.

57. DQHDSL, juan 843, 1–11. Also see Liu (1998c).

58. Previous studies on the livelihood issues of the Eight Banners have identified the pauperization of the banner soldiers, but it is still not clear when their financial struggles became particularly acute. The poverty of bannermen was reflected in four major developments: government cuts and restrictions on their financial support, the increase of the banner population, the loss of landed property for some bannermen, and the corruption of some banner officials. These developments caused some banner soldiers not only to sell their grain salaries in exchange for immediate cash but also to mortgage their future salary for loans (Elliott 2001; Wei 1995). Some bannermen also sold their allocated banner lands and houses. Although such phenomena reflected the deterioration of the financial status and living conditions of some bannermen, this did not necessarily mean they were poorer than most of the population of Beijing. As the Qing emperors and officials described it, most of these bannermen fell into poverty through extravagant spending and the pursuit of a luxurious life. In Liu Xiaomeng's (2008, 717–36) recent study on

the impoverishment of the banner population, most evidence of the hardship of banner soldiers' life emerges only after the mid-nineteenth century. Thus, in the 1820s, most banner soldiers were still probably better off than the average people in Beijing.

59. Data for grain prices come from Li (2007, 117, fig. 4.2). In 1822, the price for wheat was 2.25 *taels* of silver per *shi* and the price for millet was 1.9 *taels* of silver per *shi*.

60. The wealth stratification among metropolitan bannermen had intensified since the mid-eighteenth century. While some banner officials and soldiers sold their land and housing, other bannermen managed to accumulate more landed wealth and become major landlords (Liu 1998a).

61. See Fujun's memorial on 1818.12.6 (ZPZZ 04-01-22-0041-27).

62. According to Zelin (1984, 158–59), the provincial civil budget of Anhui in 1729 was 179,244 *taels* of silver, about a hundred thousand *taels* less than the budget for relocating bannermen to Shuangcheng. Even after considering the possibility of rising costs in the nineteenth century, the cost of the relocation project is extraordinary.

63. See Fujun's memorials on 1814.11.14 (SCPTTJL, 13) and on 1818.12.6 (ZPZZ 04-01-22-0041-27).

64. In the Qing, the Imperial Household Agency controlled the collection and sale of ginseng. To subsidize the relocation expense, Fujun used *shenyu yin*, a special tax collected from merchants who bought ginseng from the collectors. Depending on the quality of the ginseng, merchants had to pay up to twenty *taels* (760 grams) of silver for each *tael* of ginseng. The estimated income from *shenyu yin* in Jilin province was thirty to forty thousand *taels* of silver (Song and Wang 1991, 23).

65. See Songning's summation of an earlier memorial of Fujun on 1818.10.20 (ZPZZ 04-01-30-0486-011).

66. The only comparable migration is the relocation of three thousand metropolitan banner households to Lalin from 1742 to 1758, which I mentioned in the introduction (Ding 1985; Wei, Y. 2010).

67. All the metropolitan bannermen and most of the rural bannermen moved to Shuangcheng in groups under government supervision. Each metropolitan banner household was provided with a wagon. Several officials accompanied the wagon trains and provided accommodation along the way. See Jiang Jixian's memorial on 1824.2.2 (JJCLFZZ 03-3387-38), and Lucheng's memorial on 1825.3.7 (JJCLFZZ 03-3388-4 and 03-3388-6).

68. See Songlin's memorial on 1822.7.12 (SCPTTJL, 58). The wage for a hired laborer was three thousand copper coins each year. In 1825, the Office of the General of Jilin changed the thirty *taels* of silver into copper coins and used the money to hire labor for metropolitan bannermen. See Fujun and Wolengtai's memorial on 1825.3.8 (JJCLFZZ 03-3388-8).

69. See the map drawn by Komekura (1941, 142, fig. 5). The layout of the streets remains the same today.

70. Fujun had planned to mix the residences of rural and metropolitan bannermen in the right and the left *tun* as well. Yet due to the topographical constraints, the villages in the right *tun* and the left *tun* were not as regularly shaped as those in the central *tun*. The pairing of the residences of the rural and metropolitan bannermen was not carried out. In the end, because the quota of metropolitan bannermen was cut to one thousand, none of the metropolitan banner households settled in either the right or the left *tun*.

71. See Songlin's memorial reporting the initial arrangement of the lots on 1822.7.20 (SCPTTJL, 61).

72. See Fujun and Songning's memorial on 1814.11.14 (SCPTTJL, 13).

73. See Fujun's communication with the general of Shengjing on 1819.5.28 (SCPTTJL, 98–99), and his memorial on 1821.1.6 (SCPTTJL, 44).

74. According to Scudder and Colson's framework, resettled communities develop in four stages: recruitment, transition, potential development, and handing over/incorporation. In the "recruitment" stage, the government makes decisions on where to move the migrants and associated logistics. In the "transition" stage, which refers to the first several years after the initial settlement, the dislocated individuals are still adjusting themselves to the new environment and show tremendous dependence to existing authorities. In the "potential development" stage, the individuals begin to adapt to the new environment, seeking new options, and new social organizations gradually develop. Consequently, the authority of old institutions declines, and inequality in the community widens. The "handing over / incorporation" stage deals with the long-term success of resettlement, demonstrated by the incorporation of the community into a larger territorial framework and the community playing a role in production and commerce (Scudder and Colson 1982; Scudder 1985).

75. Fujun's memorial on 1825.3.9 (ZPZZ 04-01-35-1386).

76. See the memorials by Boqitu and Wolengtai on 1828.4.8 (ZPZZ 04-01-16-0132-078), on 1829.3.26 (ZPZZ 04-01-01-0704-034), Baoxing and Wolengtai's memorial on 1833.4.15 (ZPZZ 04-01-22-0054-101), and Xiangkang and Xianling's memorial on 1838. *run* 4.14 (NGDKDA 154023-001).

77. See the memorial of Songlin on 1822.7.20 (SCPTTJL, 60).

78. This is based on the descriptive statistics of the distribution of metropolitan banner households in the 1866 household register. The detailed results are not presented here.

79. Baerhu was a Mongol ethnic group originating in the area of today's Mongolia. In 1692, five thousand Baerhu people were moved to Shengjing and resided in the banner garrisons (Du 1994). The origin of Taimanzi is less clear, as very few official sources mentioned this group of people. According to Ren

Yuxue and Xie Xiaohui, Taimanzi was likely Han people who served as slaves for Mongols.

80. Yet Komekura did not describe in detail what kind of sacrifice the villagers participated in.

81. QSG, book 37, 11122. Also see Fujun's memorials on 1819.8.1 and 1822.1.11, in which Fujun described the history of Dou's career (SCPTTJL, 38 and 46).

82. See Fujun's memorials on 1819.8.1 and 1822.1.11 (SCPTTJL, 38 and 46). In 1818, Dou was dismissed from his position because he failed to maintain the roads in good condition for the emperor's tour.

83. See the investigation report by Rongzhao and Qiying on 1824.3.25 (JJCLFZZ 03-3387-41).

84. Ibid.

85. See the report of survey of the Shuangcheng area on 1864.6.28 (SCPZGYMDA, 158: 628:155).

86. See the memorial of Jing'ebu in 1844 (HCDXTGZY, book 14, juan 31, 6b).

87. Previous studies have characterized the Shuangcheng settlement as a failure because it did not meet the recruitment quota for metropolitan bannermen; my study reveals that this did not prevent the settlement from succeeding. That the number of metropolitan households was smaller than anticipated in fact reduced the government's burden in settling households, which was obviously the most difficult task in the settlement process and long-term development.

88. Ding et al. (2004, 174–94) examines the descent groups among the Han-martial bannermen living in Liaodong during the Qing. Haihong Li (2011) studies the kinship organization among the bannermen living in China proper. Both studies reveal that the Qing emperors institutionalized *zu* and turned it into a layer of administration among the banner people. Also see Lee, Campbell, and Chen (2010).

Chapter Three

1. Scholarship on the Qing expansion in Taiwan best documents the strategies the state employed to contain the aborigine people (Shepherd 1993; Ke 2001). The state empowering certain social groups to carry out its administrative goal is best documented by Faure (2007).

2. When measuring the land in Shuangcheng, the government used the standard of 720 *bu* as one *mu* and five *chi* (one *chi* in the Qing equals 0.32 meter) as one *bu*. See the order from the local banner government to the banner immigrants on 1822.10.10 (SCPTTJL, 201). Therefore, in Shuangcheng, one *shang* equals about 1.84 hectares.

3. In Qing-dynasty Shuangcheng, there were three major categories of land for bannermen: *jichan di*, or private-property land, *nazu di*, or rent-

paying land, and *suique di*, or position-dependent land. In 1870, there were 90,000 *shang* of *jichan* land, 65,638.9 shang of *nazu* land, and 9,220 *shang* of *suique* land. Throughout Shuangcheng's history, *jichan* remained the largest land category. See the 1891 government report on the land types and amounts in Shuangcheng (SCPGBTDHKDM, 1834732: 676).

4. See QDBQTZ, book 1, 538–39. In the registers, the captain recorded every adult male as one household and wrote down his name, age, and occupation, and then noted the names and occupations of his father and brothers. The captain then recorded the name and age of the adult male's sons and younger brothers separately, with the note "*linghu*, another household."

5. See the register of banner migrants from the garrison of Xiuyan in Shengjing (LNGBHK, 1932015: 2882).

6. See the land certificate included in a lawsuit that resulted from a land dispute on 1912.6.23 (MGSCXGSDA, no. 328). This land certificate was issued to Huxitai, who settled in Shuangcheng in 1815. In 1912, Huxitai's grandson presented this certificate as proof of ownership.

7. In Shuangcheng, two measurements of the volume of grain existed, market *shi* and imperial *shi*. One market *shi* was the equivalent of two and a half imperial *shi* (HCZDLZ, book 3, 14b; SCPZGYMDA, 335: 1488: 9). The weight of one *shi* of grain was the average of three kinds of grains: millet, sorghum, and soybean (SCPZGYMDA, 209: 873: 113). The grain rent in Shuangcheng usually consisted of a mix of the three kinds. According to Yi (1990, 450), one imperial *shi* of millet weighs 126.9 kilograms, one imperial *shi* of sorghum weighs 127.9 kilograms, and one imperial *shi* of soybean weighs 130.1 kilograms. The average weight of one imperial *shi* of the three grains is 128.3 kilograms. One market *shi* of grain in Shuangcheng therefore equals 320.8 kilograms. Of the two measurements, the market *shi* was more commonly used in local society. As for the beginning date of rent collection, the government postponed it to the seventh year, because of the rural bannermen's failure to clear enough land.

8. See the order from Fujun to the Shuangcheng banner government on 1819.9.23 (SCPTTJL, 104).

9. Ibid.

10. In the land registers preserved in the local banner government archives, the 1876 and 1889 registers recorded the four boundaries of each plot.

11. See the adjudication of the land disputes between Meng Yonggui and Yi Yongfa on 1912.9.18 (MGSCXGSDA, no. 328).

12. See Songlin's memorial on 1822.5.15 (SCPTTJL, 54).

13. See Jing'ebu's memorial on 1844.5.7 (HCDXTGZY, book 14, juan 31, 7a).

14. See the report regarding the history of the construction from the area commander-in-chief to the general of Jilin in 1874.7 (SCPZGYMDA, 184: 759: 235–42).

15. See Jing'ebu's memorial on 1844.5.7 (HCDXTGZY, book 14, juan 31, 6b).

16. See Qiying's memorial on 1829.5.13 (JJCLFZZ 03-3743-046).

17. The annual growth rate of the rural banner population was calculated from the population data of 1824 and 1910, since by 1824, the majority of rural bannermen had settled in Shuangcheng.

18. See the memorial of Binliang, Jing'ebu, and Woshine on 1843.12.14 (ZPZZ 04-01-12-458-0074).

19. See the local government order in 1868.5 (SCPZGYMDA, 163: 653: 191–95) and the government's recount of this land allocation in 1879.5 (SCPZGYMDA, 201: 835: 70–85).

20. See the order from the general of Jilin to Shuangcheng banner government on 1879.4.5 (SCPZGYMDA, 201: 833-1: 53–66).

21. Since the population increase between 1824 and 1866 was the result of a combination of immigration and natural increase, to measure the rate of natural increase, the annual growth rate of the metropolitan banner population was calculated from the population data of 1866 and 1910.

22. See the memorial of Songlin on 1822.7.20 (SCPTTJL, 58).

23. Ibid

24. After the rural bannermen from Shengjing settled in Shuangcheng, Fujun divided some of the relatively large rural banner households into smaller households. Therefore, the estimated number of adult males per household could be two or even only one. In addition, this estimate does not count women.

25. See Fujun's communication with the Shuangcheng banner government on 1815.5.10 (SCPTTJL, 190).

26. See Fujun's public admonishment to Shuangcheng bannermen on 1816.6.28 (SCPTTJL, 194).

27. See Songlin's estimate in his memorial on 1822.7.20 (SCPTTJL, 58).

28. See the Daoguang emperor's edict on 1822.6.16 (DGCSYD, book 2, 340a–b). Also see Fujun's memorial on 1822.7.4 that replied to the Daoguang emperor's edict (ZPZZ 04-01-22-0045-046).

29. See Fujun's summation of the Daoguang emperor's edict on 1824.3.25 in his memorial filed on 1824.4.27 (ZPZZ 04-01-22-0047-014).

30. See the survey report of registered farmland in Shuangcheng and Bodune in 1841 (JJCLFZZ 03-58-3391).

31. See the 1891 government report on the land types and amounts in Shuangcheng (SCPGBTDHKDM, 1834732: 676).

32. See a detailed discussion on Fujun's rationale in keeping civilian commoners in the areas surrounding the *tun* seat in Ren, Li, and Kang (2012).

33. The civilian section in the northern border of Shuangcheng developed in 1820 (ZPZZ 04-01-22-0045-046).

34. See the Regulation of Shuangcheng Relocation (*Shuangcheng tunwu zhangcheng*) compiled by Songlin on 1823.6.5 (ZPZZ 04-01-22-007-2391). Although these lands were intended to subsidize officials' and soldiers' busi-

ness expenditures, because the lands were allocated to individual officials and soldiers, the income generated from the land provided them another type of personal stipend.

35. See the Daoguang emperor's edict on 1836.4.15 (DGCSYD, book 16, 153b–154a).

36. See Xiangkang and Xianling's memorial on 1836.7.1 (ZPZZ 04-01-22-0056-036).

37. See Jing'ebu's memorial in 1844 (HCDXTGZY, book 14, juan 31, 6b).

38. This information was collected from interviews of local residents in 2007 and 2013.

39. This percentage is calculated based on the land registers.

40. See the 1876 land registers of the civilian section (SCPGBTDHKDM, 1834731: 658). The sources of these large land holdings were mainly *suique* and *gongzu* land, of which civilian commoners accounted for the majority of tenants.

41. See Fujun's order to officials in Shuangcheng on 1819.11.7 (SCPTTJL, 136). In this order, Fujun cited the report of Tumin, the captain of the left *tun*, on this matter.

42. See the local government report to the general of Jilin on the *baojia* organization in Shuangcheng in 1866 (SCPZGYMDA, 160: 636: 354–60). Also see Zhao (2000). In the Qing, the *baojia* system was an administrative system for watching and checking the number, movements, and activities of civilian commoners (Hsiao 1960, 26–31). In theory, every ten households constituted one *jia*, and every ten *jia* constituted one *bao*. In practice, however, the number of households in each *jia* and *bao* varied according to context.

43. According to the scattered records of civilian commoners, I estimate their average household size to be seven.

44. See Jing'ebu's memorial in 1844 (HCDXTGZY, book 14, *juan* 31, 6b). These 565 civilian households, located in the area outside the banner villages, contained 1,500 adult males and a total of three thousand to four thousand people.

45. See the local government report on the *baojia* organization in Shuangcheng in 1866 (SCPZGYMDA, 160: 636: 354–60).

46. The civilian commoners, however, made up the majority of the merchant population in Shuangcheng. In 1867, of the 156 major shop owners in Shuangcheng, 109 were civilian commoners from Zhili (today's Hebei province), Shandong, and Shanxi (SCPZGYMDA, 163: 647: 8–36).

47. In 1882, when the civilian government was established, the administrative area was expanded accordingly. The civilian government administered not only Shuangcheng, but also the area previously belonging to Lalin (SCXZ 1990, 19).

48. SCXZ (1990, 829). These 1,831 households included 26,237 civilian commoners.

49. The size of the metropolitan and rural population was calculated based on data from the banner population registers of 1889 and 1890 (CMGPD-SC).

50. The information on floating bannermen was drawn from extant register data of 1888 and 1894 (CMGPD-SC), whenever the date was closest to 1890.

51. In the floating-banner population registers, households originated from Shengjing accounted for 99.94 percent of the total number of households, and those from Jilin only accounted for 0.06 percent (CMGPD-SC).

52. See the reply from the general of Jilin to the general of Shengjing on 1820.2.18 regarding some rural bannermen moving to Shuangcheng without the government's organization (SCPTTJL, 139–42). The general of Shengjing had reprimanded the officials of Jinzhou, a garrison in Shengjing, for letting the banner migrants move to Shuangcheng individually, resulting in the move of those not listed on the official roster.

53. According to the grain price data analyzed by James Lee and Cameron Campbell (1997, 32–34), between 1822 and 1829, the monthly low grain price significantly increased, which pointed to a harvest failure during this period. The peak of the crisis occurred around 1825 and 1826. Moreover, in 1870, the local banner government investigated twelve floating bannermen to determine the authenticity of their banner affiliation. The deposition of those floating bannermen who came to Shuangcheng in the 1820s also indicated that a drought in that period had caused these bannermen to migrate (SCPZGYMDA, 312: 1400: 1–8).

54. See Yijing's memorial on 1835. 11.12 (ZPZZ 04-01-22-0055-002).

55. See local government's retrospective summary of floating banner registration in 1879 (SCPZGYMDA, 202: 838-3: 337–41).

56. See the investigation report in 1870 (SCPZGYMDA, 312: 1400: 1–8).

57. See Table 3.3 and Wang et al. (2016) for a list of reasons floating bannermen used to justify their stay.

58. The government exclusively used the registers compiled by the banner administrations in the migrants' places of origin to identify official migrants. In his communication with the general of Shengjing on 1819.11.24, Fujun mentioned that some relatives of the rural bannermen who accompanied the official migrants to Shuangcheng petitioned him to become rural bannermen (SCPTTJL, 111). Fujun, however, rejected their request because they were not on the rosters of official migrants sent by the banner administrations in Shengjing.

59. See Fuming'a's memorial on 1866.5.22 (JJCLFZZ 03-4721-047). Also see the local banner government's notice to the banner captains in 1881.11 (SCPZGYMDA, 208: 865: 9–17).

60. See the local banner government's notice to the banner captains in 1881.11 (SCPZGYMDA, 208: 865: 9–17).

61. See the petition filed by Wulintai in 1879.12 (SCPZGYMDA, 203: 841: 294).

62. Ibid.

63. The general of Jilin's communication with the general of Shengjing on 1819.9.15 (SCPTTJL, 101). However, in the settlement stage, whether a floating bannerman could become a rural bannerman was often determined by the specific official on a case-by-case basis. In the same year, Fujun had rejected the same request by another group of floating bannermen (SCPTTJL, 111).

64. See Yijing's memorial on 1835.11.12 (ZPZZ 04-01-22-0055-002).

65. CMGPD-SC.

66. See the memorial of Fuming'a on 1866.5.22 for the official regulation (JJCLFZZ 03-4721-047). Also see a case reported by the Shuangcheng banner government in 1880.2 for a real example (SCPZGYMDA, 205: 851: 2–6). In this case, the widow of a rural bannerman named Mu Hong petitioned to the government to allow her husband's nephew Mu Guozhen to inherit the household's land. Mu Guozhen moved from Jinzhou to Shuangcheng in 1878. The government approved this inheritance case.

67. Beginning in the 1850s, the court decided to open state land in Jilin and Heilongjiang, and used the rent collected from this land to subsidize military expenditures. In the floating-banner population registers, Bodune, Wuchang, Hulan, and Bayansusu were the most common destinations of those who migrated away from Shuangcheng.

68. The government intentionally recruited floating bannermen to the newly opened regions of Jilin. For example, in 1867, the officials proposed to recruit floating bannermen to Wuchang (SCPZGYMDA, 163: 651: 20–27). In 1881, the Shuangcheng banner government also tried to recruit floating bannermen to Sanxing, a garrison in Jilin with newly opened land, as state tenants (SCPZGYMDA, 208: 865: 9–17).

69. See the survey conducted by the civilian government of Shuangcheng on the banner population and their ages and marital status in 1911 (JLJJYMDA J001-37-4224). The discrepancy between the banner population in 1911 and the Manchu population in 1910 survey indicates that, since the two surveys were conducted by different governments, they used different mechanisms and measures to identify Manchu or banner people.

70. See the government report on types and amounts of land (SCPGBTDHKDM, 1834732: 676). The total amount of land here includes 24,766 *shang* of *sanwangshang* land, a type of land located between Shuangcheng and Lalin and was regularly controlled by the banner government in Lalin. This type of land is included in the total amount because the count of registered civilian households in 1890 included those residing in Lalin.

71. According to Songlin, in the 1820s, an adult male alone could farm six to seven *shang* of land (SCPTTJL, 58). Because the farming conditions

could have been poorer in the early stage of settlement, in 1890, an average adult male would probably have farmed more land. So I take ten *shang* as the average amount of land an adult male could farm in 1890.

72. In 1866, when the local government established the *baojia* system, a total of 1,208 households resided in the seat of Shuangcheng. According to my estimation, at least a half of them were civilian commoners (SCPZGYMDA, 160: 636: 354–60). By 1890, the government had begun to permit free migration, so there could have been more civilian commoners residing in the seat of Shuangcheng.

73. According to the 1910 census, the mean household size among the Han was 7.6. Given this household size and the fact that migrant populations usually had younger age structures and lower dependency ratios, the estimated average number of adult males per household was two.

74. See Jing'ebu's description of metropolitan bannermen in his memorial on adjusting policies in Shuangcheng in 1844 (HCDXTGZY, book 14, juan 31, 7a).

75. Since these unregistered residents mainly worked as tenants and hired laborers, they probably had smaller families. Hired laborers, in particular, were likely to be single males. Thus, I estimate that on average each adult male had one or two dependent.

76. According to our fieldwork notes, up until the 1950s, a large amount of land still remained uncultivated. Thus, Shuangcheng had the capacity to accommodate more immigrants.

77. For example, see SCPZGYMDA, 185: 762: 281–83. As noted earlier, the practice of checking civilian commoners started in the 1836, and the practice of checking for floating bannermen began later.

78. A partial reason for the delay also concerned the difficulty involved in determining whether the new migrants would settle in Shuangcheng. For example, many floating bannermen who were not registered claimed to be visiting relatives in Shuangcheng.

79. See the report by the captains of the Plain Yellow and Bordered Yellow Banners, Anxiang and Enrong, on 1891.10.12 (SCLSFMFDA, no. 23390).

80. For example, depositions from a land dispute in 1883 (SCLSFMFDA, no. 97) reveal that a metropolitan bannerman named Fugui seized a plot of land from a civilian commoner named Bei Fukun in this way. Bei had registered the land he cleared under Fugui's name and paid Fugui a rent. However, after the land was cultivated, Fugui rescinded Bei's right to farm and rented the land to someone else. Instead of fighting for his rights as a tenant, Bei handed the plot over to Fugui, getting only seventy-five strings of cash for the house he had built on the plot.

81. The total amount of land in Figure 3.1 includes the amount of *sanwanshang* land, which in a strict sense did not belong to Shuangcheng. The

sanwanshang land was owned by both bannermen from Lalin (banner tenants on the land registers) and civilian commoners. Therefore, if *sanwanshang* land is excluded from the total amount of land, the percentage share of land for the metropolitan and rural bannermen is even larger.

82. These banner tenants probably consisted of bannermen from such adjacent areas as Lalin and some floating bannermen. Floating bannermen were categorically barred from officially owning land in Shuangcheng, but some individuals still managed to register *nazu* land.

83. More comprehensive results on land distribution are presented in chapter 7.

Chapter Four

1. Capital appeals are appeals local people could file with the emperor to challenge perceived injustices in the adjudication of legal cases by magistrates. The Qing emperors established the capital-appeal system to ensure fairness in the judicial process (Ocko 1988; Li 2011).

2. See the memorial by Huashana on 1851.3.24 (JJCLFZZ 03-4534-036).

3. Ibid.

4. See Guqing's memorial on 1851.9.6, reporting the investigation of the capital appeal (JJCLFZZ 03-4536-013).

5. See the memorial by Jingchun and Linrui on 1854.4.5, reporting the reexamination of the capital appeal (JJCLFZZ 03-4539-026).

6. Ibid.

7. See the report of the Shuangcheng banner government in 1853.11, regarding sending the defendants and witnesses involved in this capital appeal to the Office of the General of Jilin (SCPZGYMDA, 1: 1: 18–22).

8. See Guqing's memorial on 1851.9.20 (JJCLFZZ 03-4187-011).

9. For studies on local government in the Qing dynasty, please see Ch'ü (1962); Zelin (1984); and Wei (2010).

10. The rule of avoidance was in effect as early as the second century BC. By the Qing dynasty, the court had established elaborate rules to prevent officials from developing any ties with the local society (Wei Qingyuan 1989; Wei Xiumei 1992).

11. See Guqing's memorial on 1851.9.20 (JJCLFZZ 03-4187-011).

12. See the memorial of Fujun and Songning on 1814.11.14 (JJCLFZZ 03-1878-054).

13. Ibid. Fujun and Songning recommended selecting the provisional assistant commandant from captains; and provisional captains from defenses (*fangyu*) in the banner garrisons in Jilin.

14. See the order from the general of Jilin to the local banner government in 1819.10 (SCPTTJL, 130-31).

15. See Fujun's memorial on 1820.4.17 (ZPZZ 04-01-22-0042-064).

16. See Fujun's memorial on 1822.7.4 (ZPZZ 04-01-22-0045-046).

17. The total number of tax preceptors, scribes, and soldiers of the Shuangcheng banner government was comparable to that of a regular county government, which usually had about seventy scribes and eighty runners (Wei, G. 2010, 145–68).

18. See the plan for the Shuangcheng settlement that Fujun and Songning presented in their memorial on 1814.11.14 (JJCLFZZ 03-1878-054).

19. See Songlin's recounting of the history of the use of civilian assistants in supervising the settlement in his memorial on 1823.4.10 (SCPTTJL, 67–68).

20. See Fujun and Muteng'e's memorial on 1820.5.17 (SCPTTJL, 40–41); and the Jiaqing emperor's edict on 1820.6.13 (SCPTTJL, 5).

21. See the memorial by Fujun and Muteng'e on 1820.5.17 (SCPTTJL, 41).

22. Ibid.

23. Ibid., for Shuyi's service. Shujing'e's age was calculated based on his age at death, as reported by Rongzhao and Qiying in their memorial on 1824.4.20 (ZPZZ 04-01-01-666-017).

24. See Fujun's instruction to Shujing'e on 1820.8.16 (SCPTTJL, 149).

25. Ibid.

26. See Fujun's correspondence with Shujing'e on 1821.8.4 (SCPTTJL, 164–65).

27. See Fujun's memorial on 1821.10.26 (SCPTTJL, 49–50).

28. See Rongzhao, Qiying, and Fujun's memorial on 1824.4.20 (ZPZZ 04-01-01-666-017). Here the rules refer to a set of rules governing officials, which were stipulated in the Great Qing Code.

29. In *Brief History*, Wang Lütai compiled all the government correspondence regarding the Shuangcheng settlement between 1817 and1822, including edicts, memorials, correspondence between the generals of Jilin and Shengjing, orders sent from the general of Jilin, and local government orders and notices circulated among the immigrants. See SCPTTJL.

30. See Fujun's order to the immigrants to restrict the activity of silk production on 1822.5.13 (SCPTTJL, 208).

31. See Shuyi's deposition in Rongzhao and Qiying's memorial on 1824.2.29 regarding Shujing'e's case (ZPZZ 04-01-26-0047-052).

32. See Fujun's order to the local banner government on 1822.5.10 (SCPTTJL, 173) and the order circulated among the immigrants on 1822.5.13 (SCPTTJL, 208).

33. See Fujun's orders on 1822.5.10 and 1822.5.13 (SCPTTJL, 173, 208).

34. See Shuyi's deposition in Rongzhao and Qiying's memorial on 1824.2.29 (ZPZZ 04-01-26-0047-052).

35. See Songlin's memorial on 1822.5.15 (JJCLFZZ 03-3386-056)

36. See Songlin's memorial on 1823.4.10 (SCPTTJL, 67–68).

37. See Wang Lütai's deposition in Rongzhao, Qiying, and Fujun's memorial on 1824.4.20 (ZPZZ 04-01-01-666-017).

38. The memorial was written by Wang Lütai and submitted under Songli's name on 1823.8.14 (ZPZZ 04-01-12-0373-109).

39. See Rongzhao, Qiying, and Fujun's memorial on 1824.4.20 (ZPZZ 04-01-01-666-017).

40. Ren, Li, and Kang (2012) include a more detailed discussion of the different perspectives of Fujun and Songlin on the issue of civilian commoners.

41. See Shuyi's accusation cited in Rongzhao and Qiying's memorial on 1824.2.29 (ZPZZ 04-01-26-0047-052).

42. Ibid.

43. See Daoguang emperor's edict on 1823.9.3 (DGCSYD, book 3, 339a).

44. Shuyi's accusation included in Rongzhao and Qiying's memorial on 1824.2.29 (ZPZZ 04-01-26-0047-052).

45. See Songlin's memorial on 1823.9.17 (ZPZZ 04-01-16-122-031).

46. See the memorial by Rongzhao and Qiying on 1824.2.29 (ZPZZ 04-01-26-0047-052).

47. Ibid. See also the memorial by Songyun on 1824.3.22 that explains the delay in reporting and investigating this case (ZPZZ 04-01-01-670-18).

48. See Rongzhao, Qiying, and Fujun's memorial on 1824.4.20 (ZPZZ 04-01-01-666-017).

49. See Fujun's memorial on 1824.5.28 (ZPZZ 04-01-01-0659-029).

50. See the memorial by the Board of Revenue in 1841 (JJCLFZZ 03-3391-081). The court appointed two lieutenants, two tax preceptors, and fifteen soldiers from among the metropolitan bannermen in 1826. Metropolitan bannermen did not have a captain until 1832.

51. For the entire process, see Shuyi's deposition, cited in Husong'e's memorial on 1829.12.15, regarding the capital appeal filed by woman Wu (ZPZZ 04-01-01-0713-006).

52. See the name list of the fifty-three households of metropolitan bannermen submitted by the Board of Revenue on 1823.12.23 (JJCLFZZ 03-3387-033). *Shengyuan* was a licentiate degree granted to a person who passed the local-level civil service exam.

53. See the name list attached to the official communication of the Board of Revenue on 1821.12.27 (SCPTTJL, 115–16).

54. See Fujun's report on 1824.5.28 on the settlement of the first group of metropolitan bannermen (ZPZZ 04-01-01-0659-029).

55. See Fujun's memorial on 1824.5.3 (ZPZZ 04-01-01-0658-021); and woman Wu's recounting of the accusation she filed in 1829, cited in Qiying's memorial on 1829.5.13 (JJCLFZZ 03-3743-046).

56. See Husong'e's report on the investigation of the 1829 capital appeal on 1829.12.15 (ZPZZ 04-01-01-713-006).

57. Ibid.

58. Ibid.

59. See Qiying's memorial on 1829.5.13, reporting the capital appeal (JJCLFZZ 03-3743-046).

60. Ibid.

61. See Husong'e's memorial on 1829.12.15 (ZPZZ 04-01-01-0713-006).

62. Ibid.

63. Ibid.

64. Ibid.

65. Ibid.

66. Ibid.

67. Although rural bannermen paid rent on the extra *jichan* land they cultivated for incoming metropolitan bannermen, the income from this rent was controlled by the provincial government and was used to pay back the loans from the ginseng tax, which was used on settling the immigrants. See Fujun and Songlin's various reports on 1822.6.27, 1822.12.3, and 1823.5.15 (JJCLFZZ 03-3195-033, 03-3041-063, 03-3289-043).

68. For the land types and the use of rent income, see Fujun's memorial on 1822.5.29 (ZPZZ 04-01-22-0045-046) and a survey done in 1841 of the types, acreage, and usage of registered farmland in Shuangcheng (JJCLFZZ 03-58-3341-127). Ren, Li, and Kang (2012, 516–17) also have a discussion on these two types of land.

69. The budget of the county government was not only tight but the income also went to pay for some fixed items only. These included the salaries of magistrates and other personnel in the county government and some office expenditures. There was no room in the budget for flexible spending (Zelin 1984, 29–42; Wei, G. 2010, 298–331).

70. From the mid-eighteenth century on, Qing officials' salary included both the nominal salary and supplementary salary (*yanglian yin*) that was intended to increase officials' income and thus prevent corruption (Ch'ü 1962, 22–32).

71. Nancy Park (1997) points out that corruption was interpreted differently in written law, official culture, and the popular consciousness. The popular conception of corruption concerned its effect on the population. This perception applies in the Shuangcheng case. The metropolitan bannermen were especially wary of officials taking away their wealth.

72. See Husong'e's memorial on 1829.12.15 (ZPZZ 04-01-01-0713-006).

73. Ibid.

74. In his study on Chen Hongmou, William Rowe (2001) analyzes Chen's view of state-society relations and reveals that some local officials during the Qing consciously restricted the scope of government activities and fostered societies with autonomy.

75. See the memorial by Binliang, Jing'ebu, and Woshine on 1843.12.14 (ZPZZ 04-01-12-458-074), which says that "of the 598 surviving metropoli-

tan banner households, twenty-two were affluent and had abundant food and clothing, 338 had sufficient food and clothes, 180 had enough food but lacked proper clothes, fifty-eight were extremely poor." Although the majority of surviving metropolitan bannermen lived well, this makes it clear that their economic conditions also became stratified.

76. Ibid.

77. Ibid. To create these forty positions, the general of Jilin also decided to eliminate the eleven posts that were previously appointed. Therefore, in the end, the posts in the metropolitan bannermen wing exceeded the standard size of official personnel by twenty-nine.

78. See the banner government's survey report of the temples in Shuangcheng area on 1884. run 5. 8 (SCPXLYMDA, no. 16822).

79. Ibid. The local gazetteer compiled in 1926 also recorded this Guandi temple and traced the date of erection to 1769 (SCXZ 1973, 338). Since the banner government's survey was produced earlier, here I follow the date of construction reported by the local banner government.

80. Ibid.

81. In some areas and among merchant groups, Guandi was also worshiped as the God of Fortune (*Caishen*).

82. See Woshine and Bingliang's memorial on 1843.12.6 (JJCLFZZ 03-3817-023).

83. Ibid.

84. See Jingchun and Linrui's memorial reporting the adjudication of the 1852 capital appeal on 1854.4.5 (ZPZZ 04-01-01-856-017).

85. Ibid.

86. Wu also took advantage of her gender. In the Qing legal system, the fabrication of charges by plaintiffs was a punishable offense. In 1843, although the banner general found that a lot of Wu's charges were fabricated, he let her go without punishment because some of her charges were real, and because she was, after all, just an "ignorant" woman (JJCLFZZ 03-3817-023).

87. See Woshine and Bingliang's memorial on 1843.12.6 (JJCLFZZ 03-3817-023).

88. See Jingchun and Linrui's memorial on 1854.4.5 (ZPZZ 04-01-01-856-017).

89. Ibid.

90. See Huashana's report on 1851.3.24 on the capital appeal filed by Taqibu (JJCLFZZ 03-4534-036).

91. Ibid.

92. See Jingchun and Linrui's memorial on 1854.4.5 (ZPZZ 04-01-01-856-017).

93. Ibid.

94. See Huashana's memorial on 1851.3.24 (JJCLFZZ 03-4534-036) and Guqing and Sabing'a's memorial on 1851.9.6 (JJCLFZZ 03-4536-013). According to Taqibu, the real reason of his dismissal was that he refused to collude with the corrupt officials, especially Fulehong'a, to make profits out the unassigned state land.

95. See Guqing's memorial on 1851.9.6 (JJCLFZZ 03-4187-010). Kato Naoto (1996) also examined this administrative reform and the problems of control the Qing faced.

96. Ibid.

97. Ibid.

98. In 1882, when a civilian government was established in Shuangcheng, the title of the principal official of the local banner government was downgraded from area commander-in-chief to assistant commandant.

99. See the official exchange regarding the institutional reform, which the Shuangcheng banner government received on 1855.5.18 (SCPZGYMDA, 1: 3: 35).

100. All banner organizations in Shuangcheng were divided into two wings, right and left. Each of the assistant commandants supervised one wing.

101. See the resume of Qingrui reported on 1880.6 (SCPZGYMDA, 93: 364: 201–2).

102. See the career record book of the officials and soldiers in 1880 (SCPZGYMDA, 93: 364: 199–220).

103. JJCLFZZ 03-4539-026. SCXZ (1990, 145) claims that the amount of land registered was 42,502 *shang*.

104. As described in chapter 3, in this process, unregistered civilian commoners and floating bannermen had to register their lands under metropolitan and rural bannermen, turning themselves into tenants of the official immigrants.

105. QSL (Xianfeng regin 1851–1861), book 40, 830b–31a. In 1852, the state allowed land transfers between bannermen and civilian commoners in Beijing and Zhili, but the archives in Jilin and Shuangcheng show that land transfers between bannermen and civilian commoners were still prohibited.

106. As noted in chapter 1, the immigrants' ownership of the *nazu* land was incomplete. The fact that the government collected rent rather than tax from the land indicates the state's claim of the ownership. However, in practice, immigrants' rights over their registered land was the equivalent of land ownership.

107. See the government report to the general of Jilin regarding the tracking of *fuduo* land in 1880.6 (SCPZGYMDA, 205: 849-2:195).

108. See the order of the Shuangcheng government regarding checking extra land in the local area in 1879.11 (SCPZGYMDA, 202: 838-1: 39–43).

109. See the government-reported list of land types and amounts in Shuangcheng in 1891.4 (SCPGBTDHKDM, 1834732: 676).

110. See the government list of land types and amounts in 1904 (SCPGBTDHKDM, 1834733: 688).

111. See the official report regarding the distribution of the officials and soldiers' salaries (SCPZGYMDA, 162: 645: 40–43). In 1867, 70 percent of the salaries came from the provincial government, and the other 30 percent, amounting to 2,657.25 strings of cash, came from the rent income preserved in Shuangcheng.

112. See the notice of distributing the soldiers' and clerks' salaries on 1882.8.9 (SCPZGYMDA, 209: 874: 31). The salary of high officials came from the provincial government, while 60 percent of the salaries of soldiers and clerks, amounting to 7,846.2 strings of cash, came from local rent income.

113. See the notice from the provincial government regarding the distribution of salaries in the locations in Jilin (SCPZGYMDA, 204: 846: 220–25).

114. See the financial report of the Shuangcheng government on expenditure on sacrifices in 1868, which included the expenditure on Guandi sacrifice (SCPZZYMDA, 165: 662: 106). Each year the government provided funds to hold three official sacrifices of Guandi on the sixteenth day of the second month, the first day of the seventh month, and the fourth day of the eighth month (SCPZGYMDA, 184: 755: 253–62).

115. See Jingchun and Linrui's memorial on 1854.4.5 (GZZPZZ 04-01-01-856-017).

116. See Jingchun's memorial on 1857.5.14 (JJCLFZZ 03-4243-032).

Chapter Five

1. The notion of "cultural nexus of power" is developed by Duara (1988a, 15–16). Nakamura (1984) explores the religion and market networks among villagers living on the North China Plain.

2. See the exchange between the Left Wing assistant commandant and the area commander-in-chief of Shuangcheng in 1880.6, regarding sending a metropolitan bannerman named Fuzhi back to Beijing to inherit his ancestor's post (SCPZGYMDA, 94: 368: 148–52).

3. This is based on interviews with the descendants of rural bannermen and floating bannermen, conducted by Matthew Neollert and Shuang Chen in June 2013.

4. In the central *tun*, the metropolitan bannermen and the rural bannermen were supervised by separate village heads, who were appointed from the same population category as the supervisees.

5. Beginning around 1725, the Qing government appointed village headmen, giving them the title *shoubao*, in the villages of southern Manchuria (Isett 2007, 63–64).

6. Local elite, or "gentry," was a comprehensive and stratified group. Scholars have been exploring the category "local elite" since the 1950s. Generally speaking, it includes degree holders, wealthy families, lineage heads, and

even families with strong military backgrounds. Social status, landed wealth, and power often worked together to mark a family's gentry status (Chang 1955; Hsiao 1960; Esherick and Rankin 1990).

7. This model of governance has a counterpart in civilian society. For example, the tax head (*liangzhang*) in the Ming dynasty had a similar relationship with the government (Liang 1957).

8. See the order from the Office of the General of Jilin to the Shuangcheng banner government on 1822.8.14 (SCPTTJL, 179).

9. See the biographic information on the candidates for the Plain Red Banner chief village head position in 1866 (SCPZGYMDA, 162: 643: 89–90).

10. Some resumes of the candidates for chief village head were preserved in the local archives. For examples, see SCPZGYMDA, 202: 839: 219–26 and 271–78.

11. See the addendum to the settlement plan Fujun submitted to the Jiaqing emperor on 1820.4.17 (SCPTTJL, 40).

12. See the order from the Office of the General of Jilin to Shuangcheng banner government on 1822.8.14 (SCPTTJL, 179).

13. For example, in 1822, the village head of the fourth village of the Plain Red Banner, Ye Xian, resigned because of an ulcer on his left leg that prevented him from walking (SCPTTJL, 179). In 1866, the chief village head of the Plain Red Banner, Wang Zhili, and the chief village head of the Plain Blue Banner, Zongfu, both resigned their positions because of illnesses that made them physically incapable of performing their duties (SCPZGYMDA, 162: 643: 81–82 and 129–31).

14. See the order from the Office of the General of Jilin to the Shuangcheng banner government on 1822.8.14 (SCPTTJL, 179).

15. Tables associated with the calculation results in this paragraph are not presented here.

16. See the report from the Office of the General of Jilin to the Board of Punishment on 1816.6.23, regarding the petition by the rural bannermen (SCPTTJL, 79–81).

17. See the plans and regulations for the Shuangcheng settlement approved by the emperor, cited by the Office of the General of Jilin on 1815.2.16 (SCPTTJL, 77).

18. See the report from the Office of the General of Jilin to the Board of Punishment on 1816.6.23 (SCPTTJL, 79–81).

19. Ibid.

20. Ibid.

21. See the court records of the land dispute filed on 1882.8.19 between two metropolitan bannermen respectively named Bao Dongrui and Ao Yongshun (SCLSFMFDA, no. 52).

22. See the government report of the investigation of the case (SCPXLYMDA, no. 30369 and no. 33962). Officials drew the maps to illustrate the situation with the communal lands of the concerned villages. The

temples of two of the seven banner villages were not seen on the map because the officials did not draw the areas west of the villages, a typical location for village temples.

23. Interviews with villagers living in the Shuangcheng villages during May 30–June 7, 2013, conducted by Shuang Chen and Matthew Noellert. Almost all the village temples were torn down in the 1950s and 1960s.

24. Ibid.

25. Interviews conducted by Matthew Noellert and Shuang Chen, June 2013.

26. Notes based on author's interview with Liang Yueying, Shuangcheng city, June 1, 2013.

27. According to DuBois, in Cang County, even the rainmaking ceremony did not require the attendance of all villagers.

28. Based on interviews conducted by Matthew Noellert and Shuang Chen, June 2013.

29. The information of the land sizes is from the original maps attached to the government report on 1898.5.2 (SCPLSFMFDA, No. 30369).

30. See the local banner government's report to the General of Jilin in 1880.2, regarding the request of a floating bannerman named Wulintai to claim the unassigned land in that area (SCPZGYMDA, 204: 846: 246–54).

31. See the local banner government's order to the captain of the Bordered Blue Banner in 1868.9, regarding the decision on this lawsuit (SCPZGYMDA, 164: 657: 90–95).

32. Ibid.

33. See the local banner government's order to the Right Wing office in 1869.11, regarding the decision on this lawsuit (SCPZGYMDA 164: 659: 28–39).

34. These satellite villages were formed as a result of these bannermen moving there to tend their assigned or acquired lands.

35. Information collected from fieldwork by Matthew Noellert and Shuang Chen shows that some metropolitan and rural bannermen also buried their ancestors in the communal ground.

36. The 1870 land register of the Plain Yellow Banner (SCPGBTDHKDM, 1834732: 667) recorded that Yuxiang had 130 *shang* of registered *ziken* land and 20.6 *shang* of *baqianshang* land, a total of 150.6 *shang* of *nazu* land.

37. See the General of Jilin's order to local officials regarding the investigation of Yuxiang's case in 1868.9 (SCPZGYMDA, 165: 662: 60–61, 68–70).

38. See the local officials' recount of the various attempts by bannermen to claim communal lands in Shuangcheng's history, which was included in the local government's report to the general of Jilin on 1880.2.25 regarding Wulintai's request to claim communal land (SCPZGYMDA, 204: 846: 246–54).

39. This information is based on a conversation with Matthew Noellert, who in June 2012 interviewed present-day villagers in Shuangcheng regarding the history of the banner villages.

40. This rule has been written in the official law since the Song dynasty. Ever since then, even in times when the law was not enforced, customary practices still followed it (Wang 2004).

41. Isett (2004) reveals that a similar phenomenon could be seen in banner villages in southern Manchuria: bannermen sold their land to civilian commoners despite the state prohibition. Without the state sanction of these land sales, civilian commoners' property rights were exclusively secured by customs developed among villagers.

42. Because most of the land in Manchuria was not irrigated, there are no records in Shuangcheng about public irrigation works. According to R. H. Tawney (1932, 30), in the 1910s only about 2 percent of farmland in Jilin and Liaoning was irrigated.

43. See the final report on the case regarding the land disputes between De'an and Shuanzhu over the ownership of the plot acquired by De'an's grandfather through the collective land clearing effort (SCPZGYMDA, 209: 871-2: 135–41).

44. See the court records of the land dispute filed on 1882.8.19 between two metropolitan bannermen respectively named Bao Dongrui and Ao Yongshun, regarding the ownership of the forty *shang* of land the metropolitan banner households in this village acquired through the collective land clearing effort (SCLSFMFDA, no. 52). The depositions described the history of collective land clearing.

45. The three-generation register of the Plain Yellow Banner, compiled in 1892 (SCPGBTDHKDM 1834697: 306).

46. A land contract carrying the magistrate's seal is called a "red contract"; if there is no magistrate's seal it is called a "white contract." Myron Cohen (2004) notes that a large majority of land-sales contracts in Minong, Taiwan, were white contracts.

47. Of course, as Osborne shows, contracts alone did not serve as proof of landownership. The magistrate would also examine other evidence, such as tax records and the testimony of the parties involved.

48. See the order of the Shuangcheng banner government on 1815.2.16 (SCPTTJL, 75–76)

49. See the government order regulating the transfer of *nazu* land in 1868.8 (SCPZGYMDA, 164: 656: 158–61).

50. *Dingque* land refers to the thirty *shang* of land each rural banner household received from the government on arriving at Shuangcheng. Thus, for the rural bannermen in the right and left *tun*, each plot of *dingque* land consisted of 18.33 *shang* of *jichan* land, which belonged to the rural household, and 11.67 *shang* of land that belonged to the central *tun* residents but was farmed by the right and left *tun* residents.

51. See the local government's report to the general of Jilin regarding the land transfer between Wulibu and Yongcheng on 1880.3.5 (SCPZGYMDA, 204: 847: 54–55).

52. Ibid.

53. Ibid.

54. The local government's final report on the lawsuit regarding the land dispute between Ren Shicheng and Li Sheng, on 1880.12.10 (SCPZGYMDA, 203: 844: 245–51).

55. The government report on the transfer of nine plots of land in 1868.11 (SCPZGYMDA, 164: 659: 8–15).

56. The local government's final report on this case, on 1880.12.10 (SCPZGYMDA, 203: 844: 245–51).

57. Although this is implicit in Ren and Li's case, in another case involving a land transaction between two civilian commoners, "plow and spade money" clearly referred to the land price (SCPZGYMDA, 203: 844: 9–21).

58. See the area commander-in-chief's order on 1882.2.19 (SCPZGYMDA, 208: 869: 151–157).

59. Ibid.

60. Ibid.

61. See the twenty-eight rules made by the General Bureau of Tax Counting and Land Opening on 1902.7.15 (SCPZGYMDA, 268: 1195: 1–18).

62. See the recounting of this situation by the area commander-in-chief in 1868 (SCPZGYMDA, 164: 656: 159–61).

63. See the order by the area commander-in-chief in 1868 (SCPZGYMDA, 164: 656: 159–61).

64. Cited from the order from the Office of Banner Affairs to the banner captains on 1912.8.24 (MGSCXGSDA, no. 366).

65. The index is preserved in the Shuangcheng Municipal Archives. I thank Matthew Noellert for compiling the nicknames and generously sharing them with me.

66. These results are based on analysis of the CMGPD-SC. The table associated with the calculation results is not presented here. More comprehensive analyses and results are presented in chapter 7.

67. See the 1870 banner land register (SCPGBTDHKDM, 1834731: 650).

68. Ibid.

Chapter Six

1. Faure (2007), Zheng, (2009), and Xu (2010) have traced the development of lineages along with the evolution of households and household groups as a unit of taxation in south, southeast, and central China.

2. This is also the situation in present-day Shuangcheng. Yan Yunxiang (2003) analyzes changes in village life in one Shuangcheng village from 1949 to 1999. He identifies a strong individualism and weak patriarchal control during the socialist reform period. He therefore concludes that it was the socialist state in its early stages that destroyed the traditional culture and values

and patriarchal power. This study suggests that the lack of traditional values in Shuangcheng has historical roots.

3. According to interviews conducted during fieldwork in June 2013, families in Shuangcheng did develop their burial grounds. These burial grounds were initially created in a large area outside the village, which was shared by the villagers. As families continued to bury their deceased members together, particular territories gradually developed for specific families. Yet these burial grounds are not comparable to those located on the estates of lineages in other parts of China.

4. This information is based on the twelve genealogies and ancestral scrolls collected by Matthew Noellert and Shuang Chen between 2011 and 2013. In 2007, Eric Li also attempted to collect genealogies in the banner villages.

5. The Fu family ancestral scroll collected by Matthew Noellert and Shuang Chen in June 2013. This Fu family was relocated from the banner garrison in Jilin in 1815.

6. Of the twelve genealogies and ancestral scrolls collected in Shuangcheng, only four appeared in the form of a book. Of these four genealogies, two were compiled and published by members living in the immigrants' places of origin.

7. According to the 1926 edition of the gazetteer, for houses facing south or north, the west wall was considered the highest position, and, for houses facing east or west, the south wall was considered the highest (SCXZ 1973, 174).

8. This is based on various oral histories collected by Matthew Noellert and Shuang Chen between 2005 and 2013. The account of sacrifice among banner people in the 1926 edition of the gazetteer did not explicitly mention the practice of ancestral sacrifice.

9. Freedman (1966, 160–64) cited rice cultivation and the need for irrigation as the catalysts for the formation of highly corporate and localized lineage organizations. Faure (2007) illustrates the development of lineage organizations along with the effort of the imperial state to control the local area. Pasternak (1972) describes the variations in the social organizations in two villages in Taiwan. According to Pasternak, patrilineal affiliation did not play a definitive role.

10. Before the Eight Banners became the basic institution for organizing the Manchu people, the descent group or clan was the most important social organization. Sergei Mikhailovich Shirokogoroff (1924) documents the power and importance of clan organization among the Manchu people living in Aihun, Heilongjiang, in the early twentieth century. Living on the periphery, these people nonetheless retained the original clan organization.

11. The genealogies used for inheritance purposes only included the male members of the descent group, while some of the genealogies compiled by ban-

ner families included both male and female members. Moreover, the banner household registers also served as genealogical records.

12. The Fu family genealogy was collected by Matthew Noellert and Shuang Chen in Shuangcheng city in June 2013. Although the family had a copy of their genealogy compiled around the 1890s, family members stopped updating this version. Later descendants used a copy of the 1911 household register instead. While the version based on the 1911 household register included more branches, it did not specify the relationships between different households.

13. Although Li (1992, 1–10) asserts that the Manchu people paid considerable attention to genealogy compilation, his data do not support this argument.

14. On inheriting the *jichan* plot, the selected adult male became the head of a new household recorded in the registers. The records of his immediate family—wife and children—would also be moved under the new household.

15. The study of this family draws on government archival documents, mainly the various population and land registers. Compared to private materials, the government registers are especially informative about the intersection of the interests of the state and individual families, such as family decisions on when to register their children and whom they chose to inherit a specific land plot. In addition, compared to genealogies which easily omit family members who died early and did not have descendants, household registers recorded family members prospectively and thus provided a more comprehensive view of the entire family (Campbell and Lee 2002).

16. See the list of metropolitan banner immigrants to be moved in 1826 (JJCLFZZ 03-3388-25).

17. The 1826 list of the immigrants did not provide detailed information regarding the household head's family members. Therefore, the family members and their ages are inferred from the 1866 Shuangcheng banner household register (SCGBTDHKDM 1834686: 218), and it is unclear who is the fifth family member of Hualiantai.

18. The list of the metropolitan banner immigrants to be moved in 1826 (JJCLFZZ 03-3388-25, 03-3388-27).

19. See the 1866 Shuangcheng banner household register (SCPGBTDHKDM, 1834686: 218).

20. Kuijin first appeared on the 1866 register as Kuisheng; he changed his name to Kuijin beginning in the 1868 register. Kuijin's wife and son were first recorded in the household register compiled in 1868, when the boy was already four years old, which indicates that he was born around 1865.

21. See the 1866 land register of first *zuoling* of the Left Wing (SCPGBTDHKDM 1834730: 638).

22. See the banner household registers compiled in 1866–1870 (SCPGBTDHKDM 1834663: 23, 26; 1834686: 217, 218; and 1834723: 509).

23. See the report of the local government to the General of Jilin in 1868.8 regarding the statistics on the damages caused by the flood (SCPZGYMDA, 164: 656: 16–99).

24. See the household-level survey of damages caused by the flood and the storm compiled by the local government in 1869.8 (SCPGBTDHKDM 1834730: 646). The government only surveyed the amount of *nazu* land suffered from the flood because of its interest in rent-collection.

25. The 1868 household register of the Bordered White banner of the first Zuoling of the Left Wing (SCPGBTDHKDM 1834723: 509).

26. The 1869 household register of the Bordered White banner of the first Zuoling of the Left Wing (SCPGBTDHKDM 1834663: 23).

27. See the government's recounting of the history of the allocation of extinct household land (SCPZGYMDA 201: 835: 70–85).

28. Ibid.

29. See the records of inheritance of the *jichan* plots of the 225 extinct metropolitan households (SCPGBTDHKDM 1834731: 649: image 3325) and the list of the metropolitan bannermen who moved to Shuangcheng in 1824 (NGTFDTYMDA, 52: 289 ce).

30. See the record of inheritance of the *jichan* plots of the 225 extinct metropolitan households (SCPGBTDHKDM 1834731:649: image 3324).

31. See the 1870 land register of the Bordered Yellow Banner (SCPGBTDHKDM 1834731: 650).

32. In 1870, a household owning 91.7 *shang* or more of *nazu* land belonged to the stratum of top 1 percent among all the metropolitan and rural banner households in *nazu* landholdings.

33. Shuang Chen (2009, 222–61) discusses in detail the practice of partible inheritance in the Qing-dynasty Shuangcheng. At the same time, some families in Shuangcheng also followed state regulations to pass down their land to only one son in the household. Similar practices of primogeniture inheritance also existed on the manor lands in the surrounding areas of Beijing (Qiu 2014, 258–60).

34. See the 1870 banner household registers (SCPGBTDHKDM 1834663: 26).

35. Ibid.

36. See the banner household registers compiled between 1870 and 1878 (SCPGBTDHKDM 1934663: 25, 26, 29, 30, and 31; 1834664, 34, 35, 37, and 40).

37. The banner household registers compiled between 1870 and 1878 (SCPGBTDHKDM 1934663: 25, 26, 29, 30, and 31; 1834664, 34, 35, 37, and 40).

38. See the 1876 banner land register (SCPGBTDHKDM 1834731: 659).

39. Ibid.

40. See the 1903 Three Generation Book of the Bordered Yellow Banner (SCPGBTDHKDM, 1834666: 74). The exact year when Fuqing'e moved to Shuangcheng, however, is unclear.

41. See the complaint of Mingshan's son, Zhao Yanling, regarding a land dispute between himself and Ming'an's son, Zhao Changde, in 1914.10 (SCMGXGSDA no. 1453).

42. The local archives show that Mingshan was responsible for checking and finalizing the salary book of government personnel. See the salary book of 1874.7 (SCPZGYMDA, 184: 759: 9) and 1879.7.10 (SCPZGYMDA, 201: 837-1: 65).

43. See the 1870 population register of the Bordered Yellow Banner (SCPGBTDHKDM, 1834663: 26).

44. According to Zhao Yanling, Mingshan bought all the land after officially registering his own household (SCMGXGSDA, no. 1453).

45. See the 1870 banner land register (SCPGBTDHKDM 1834731: 650).

46. See the 1876 banner land register (SCPGBTDHKDM 1834731: 659).

47. See the recall of land price by Zhao Cunxi, a resident in Shuangcheng, in his deposition regarding a land dispute between himself and his cousin on 1913.3.18 (SCMGXGSDA, no. 1111).

48. See the communication between the general of Jilin and the Ningguta vice commander-in-chief on 1876.11.5 (QDHLJLSDAXB, 123–25). Also see the official documents attached to the note from the general of Jilin regarding allocating the reserved metropolitan *jichan* plots in Shuangcheng and Bodune to the original farmers in return for monetary contributions (SCPZGYMDA, 201: 833-1: 53–66).

49. See the petition filed by the metropolitan bannermen from the Plain Yellow Banner on 1878.2.25 (SCPZGYMDA, 200: 826-3: 360–66). The metropolitan bannermen from the Bordered Yellow banner also filed a petition with similar language (SCPZGYMDA, 200: 826-3: 398–402).

50. See the petitions filed by the metropolitan bannermen from the Plain Yellow and Bordered Yellow Banners in 1878 (SCPZGYMDA, 200: 826-3: 360–66, and SCPZGYMDA, 200: 826-3: 398–402).

51. See the order from the local banner government to banner captains on 1878.4.25 regarding the collection of monetary donations (SCPXLYMDA, no. 10543) and the report from the assistant commandant to the area commander-in-chief on 1878.5.10 regarding the amount of money collected (SCPXLYMDA, no. 10557).

52. See the order from the local banner government to the captains in 1866.12 regarding the collection of taxes and rents (SCPZGYMDA, 161: 639: 155–62).

53. See the two orders from the general of Jilin to the local banner government in 1879.4 (SCPZGYMDA, 201: 833-1: 53–66, 73–83), which enclosed the correspondance between Ming'an and the central government, regarding the allocation of the 302 plots of *jichan* land.

54. See the two orders from the general of Jilin to the local banner government in 1879.4 (SCPZGYMDA, 201: 833-1: 53–66, 73–83).

55. For the amount of money collected, see the metropolitan banner captains' report to the area commander-in-chief on 1879.5.10 (SCPXLYMDA, no. 10557).

56. See the notice from the Right Department to the Left Department in 1878.6 regarding the personnel assignment for sending the collected monetary donations to the Office of the general of Jilin (SCPZGYMDA, 200: 829: 135).

57. See Mingshan's deposition for the land dispute between his brother's and cousin's households on 1880.10.10 (SCPZGYMDA, 204: 845: 96).

58. Ibid. In acquiring the land, Mingshan did all the work and even paid the monetary contribution for his cousin.

59. For example, in 1848, the local government denied a rural bannerman named Shuangzhu the right to inherit his father's *jichan* land, because Shuangzhu had already inherited his elder uncle's *jichan* land in 1838. See the history of land inheritance of Shuangzhu's family, which is included in the local government's report on a lawsuit filed by Shuangzhu's cousin Jiushizi in 1866 (SCPZGYMDA, 162: 643: 270–71, and 164: 657: 6–15).

60. This is based on the analysis of the name lists acquired from the pledges of metropolitan bannermen who obtained land in the 1878 *jichan* land allocation (SCPGBTDHKDM, 1834732: 665, 666), which were linked to CMGPD-SC.

61. Information in this paragraph is drawn from the banner household registers compiled between 1878 and 1891 (SCPGBTDHKDM 1834664: 40, 42, 44; 1834665: 48–51, 53–58).

62. See the 1896 and 1897 banner household registers (SCPGBTDHKDM, 1834666: 65, 69).

63. See the government's recounting of the history of the allocation of extinct household lands (SCPZGYMDA, 201: 835: 70–85).

64. See the 1885 household register of the Bordered Yellow Banner (SCPGBTDHKDM 1834665: 50). Before 1889, Ronglin was registered under the Manchu name Yingling'a. He changed his name to Ronglin in the 1889 household register (SCPGBTDHKDM 1834665: 55).

65. See the order from the Office of the general of Jilin to Shuangcheng banner government in 1906.2 (SCPZGYMDA, 275: 1237: 35–42). According to this order, 70 percent of a household's landholdings were considered taxable. Each household would pay a total of 660 in cash for each *shang* of land.

66. See the order from the Office of the general of Jilin to Shuangcheng banner government in 1906. *run* 4 (SCPZGYMDA, 276: 1238: 223–27).

67. On the 1907 household register, Ronglin appeared as the head of two households (SCPGBTDHKDM 1834666: 76).

68. Information in this paragraph is drawn from the banner household registers compiled between 1908 and 1912 (SCPGBTDHKDM 1834667: 77, 81; 1834699: 341).

Chapter Seven

1. This proverb is also known as "wealth does not sustain beyond three generations" (*fu buguo sandai*).

2. Works by Marxist theoreticians also have established the belief that commercialization of agriculture led to the disintegration and proletarianization of the peasants (Lenin 1964, 172–90; Kautsky 1988).

3. This estimate was first formally presented by the Central Committee of the Chinese Communist Party in "Zhonggong zhongyang guanyu banbu tudifa dagang de jueding" [The decision regarding the promulgation of the Outline Land Law] in October, 1947 (Zhongyang dang'an guan 1992, 547). After the communist victory in China, it was frequently cited by communist leaders and became the basis for the Land Reform. It was also commonly accepted by academics when discussing land distribution in China.

4. For example, Myers (1970, 217–40) reveals that in the few North China villages he studied, land distribution had been very unequal before 1900. Moreover, in the first three decades of the twentieth century, the disappearance of some large landholders and landless households made the land distribution more equal. Myers (1976) also shows that from the Qing to the Republic, land distribution in villages in Manchuria did not become more unequal. Huang (1985, 76–77, table 4.2) shows that the size of land owned by rich households diminished over time during the late nineteenth and early twentieth centuries.

5. Li Wenzhi and Jiang Taixin (2005, 302–32) also maintain that during the Qing dynasty, small peasants rather than landlords owned the majority of land and that there was no land concentration.

6. Joseph Esherick (1981) points out that the lack of longitudinal and comparable landholding data is the main obstacle to achieving a better understanding of land distribution in pre-revolutionary China.

7. See the order issued by the general of Jilin on 1906.3.27 (SCPZGYMDA, 276: 1238: 225–26).

8. The existing land registers compiled in 1876 record *jichan* landholdings for all bannermen living in the central and right *tun*, a total of eighty villages. They also contain complete records for the owners of all *nazu* land, including land in both the banner and the civilian sections. However, the 1876 *jichan* land registers for the two banners administering the forty villages in the left *tun* have not survived. Therefore, these forty villages are excluded from the analysis of the overall pattern of land distribution.

9. The numbers of the floating banner households living in the villages administered by the Plain Red and Bordered Red Banners are from the registers compiled in 1873.

10. While the numbers of banner households are from the CMGPD-SC, the number of civilian households are from the area commander-in-chief's

report on the *baojia* system to the General of Jiln in 1866 (SCPZGYMDA, 160: 636: 354–60). Since the government did not make any additional effort to register civilian commoners until the early twentieth century, the number of civilian households should be stable.

11. To ensure a full coverage of population, one type of *nazu* land, *baqianshang di*, is excluded from the analysis. This is because some bannermen's *baqianshang* land records are not linked to the population data due to the lack of address information. Since the *baqianshang* land only accounted for a small proportion of registered farmland in Shuangcheng and since each plot is equally sized at 20.6 *shang*, excluding this land only has a negligible effect on the patterns of land distribution.

12. The size of one *shang* in Shuangcheng, which equals 7200 *bu*, was much larger than that in Zhejiang, which equals 2400 *bu*. Therefore, the landholdings of households in Shuangcheng were even larger than those of the farmers in Zhejiang. Of course, after taking the crops grown on the land into consideration, the value of lands in Shuangcheng probably was not comparable to that of the lands in Zhejiang. This is because dry-field agriculture is less productive than rice-field agriculture in Zhejiang. Yet the difference in land size per household of these two regions is striking.

13. To save space, results of the calculation of the categorical composition of each landholding stratum are not presented here.

14. Since the *suique* land was allocated only to officials with active position, the officials did not have stable ownership of it. The civilian tenants, who claimed *suique* land in the early period of Shuangcheng settlement, had stable use rights of the land. As tenants, they paid a rent of 660 in cash for each *shang* of land they farm, the same rate of *nazu* land. Thus, when calculating the pattern of land distribution, the *suique* land is considered landed wealth owned by the civilian commoners.

15. See the adjudication of a land dispute between Yu Yuanxun's son and a civilian commoner named Xun Zhiyong in 1880.6 (SCPZGYMDA 203: 844: 9). The deposition described the history of land accumulation of the Yu family.

16. See Woshine and Bingliang's memorial on 1843.12.6 (JJCLFZZ 03-3817-023).

17. See the lawsuit about the land disputes between Zhao Guoyou and Zhao Qinglin, which was filed on 1897.11.28 (SCLSFMFDA, no. 1886).

18. See *Shuangchengxian tudi mianji renkou dengji dengji bu*.

19. Compared to that in 1995 China, the stratification in 2002 had increased; in 1995, the top decile of population shared 26.2 percent of wealth, and the bottom decile shared 3.1 percent.

20. Interestingly, the increase of landless households occurred among both metropolitan and rural bannermen, and in 1906–1907 both categories each had about 7 percent of households without *jichan* land.

21. This result is not illustrated in figure 7.4.

22. These households were not really in "rags" because the majority of them had *jichan* land.

23. The results of this analysis are not presented here. An old version of results can be found in Chen (2009, 282, table 8.4).

24. Chinese historians have agreed that, in historical China, officials' land acquisition via the use of bureaucratic power was a major cause of land concentration (He 1956; Yang 1990; Qin and Su 1996).

25. Sometimes a bannerman can be both *shengyuan* and soldier.

26. The *yin* privilege also existed within the banner system. *Yin* privilege benefited the candidate by giving him an easy start on his official career. Yet the official positions acquired through *yin* privilege were usually low-ranking or were honorific titles without specific duties. The candidate's future career still depended on his ability and performance.

27. Results from the analysis of inheritance practices in Shuangcheng show that, in most families, the eldest son inherited the father's *jichan* plot (Chen 2009, 227, table 7.1). This was also the case in Mingshan's family (SCMGXGSDA no. 1453).

28. See the salary book of Shuangcheng banner officials compiled in 1874.7 (SCPZGYMDA 184: 759: 9).

29. Ibid.

30. The 1869 household register of the Plain Red Banner in the central *tun* (SCPGBTDHKDM 1834663: 23) and the record of non-kin inheritance of the *jichan* plots of the 225 extinct metropolitan households (SCPGBTDHKDM 1834731: 649).

31. See the summary of Ming'an's case on 1880.10.10 (SCPZGYMDA 204: 845: 96).

32. The only exceptions are the percentages of official families in the metropolitan banner households located in the top centile and the second decile of households in *nazu* landholdings, which declined from 33.3 percent in 1870 to 25 percent in 1889 and from 14.3 percent in 1870 to 13.2 percent in 1889, respectively.

33. The order from the Office of Banner Affairs to the banner captains on 1912.8.24 (MGSCXGSDA, no. 366).

34. See the list included in the report from the area commander-in-chief to the general of Jilin regarding the money donated by local businesses in 1867.3 (SCPZGYMDA, 163: 647: 8–36).

35. Ibid.

36. The scale of the business can be derived from the amount of money they donated. The largest businesses donated 150 strings of cash, whereas the donation by local businesses ranged from 3 to 10 strings of cash (ibid.).

37. The oral history is based on two interviews of Mr. Wang, Guifeng's grandson, conducted by Matthew Noellert and Shuang Chen on May 31 and

June 2, 2014. To protect privacy, the residential village of the interviewee is not presented here.

38. This information is acquired by matching information from oral histories with the records in the banner household registers.

39. This *wopeng* has been abandoned as the residents moved out in the second half of the twentieth century. Wang Guifeng died in the late 1940s.

40. The 1870 land register shows that Wang Haicheng did not own any *nazu* land (SCPGBTDHKDM 1834731: 656).

41. The 1876 land register of the Bordered Red Banner (SCPGBTDHKDM 1834696: 285).

42. The 1889 land register of the Bordered Red Banner (SCPGBTDHKDM 1834732: 674).

43. Since Guifeng's grandson did not have any memories about the generations preceding his grandfather's, it is unclear when the family started the pawn shop in the Shuangcheng seat.

44. The price information is collected from various cases involving land sales and conditional sales. There is a wide range of land prices because of the variations in the conditions of each specific plot and any attached value to it.

45. The depositions in a lawsuit between Zhao Cunxi and Zhao Xiaoguan regarding the dispute over a plot of land, which was first filed on 1913.3.18 (SCMGXGSDA, no. 1111).

46. Interestingly, the survey report also revealed that, when the banner land became a transferable merchandise, it helped to lower the land price in the area. Before the government allowed free land transfer, the land price in the area was around 400 strings of cash for each *shang* because of the high demand. The banner land increased the supply of land and therefore lowered the land price to 250 strings of cash.

47. In Shuangcheng, the silver price in 1867 was 2,650 in cash (SCPZGYMDA, 163: 649: 12–13), and in 1906, the silver price was around 3,375 in cash (SCPZGYMDA, 276: 1238: 77–83). The silver price increased by 27 percent, whereas the land price increased tenfold.

48. For example, in Lishu County in Jilin, land prices for a *shang* of land ranged from 10 to 20 strings of cash in 1855; by 1904, prices increased to from 230 to 280 strings of cash per *shang* (Kong 1986, 65).

Chapter Eight

1. See the correspondence between the Provisional Office of Banner Affairs of Shuangcheng and the Shuangcheng civilian government regarding this case, sent on 1912.12.6 (MGSCXGSDA no. 398).

2. See the report of the representatives of the right and the left *tun* to the county government on 1912.12.29 (MGSCXGSDA, no. 270).

3. See the plaint to the Shuangcheng county government by the representatives of the right and the left *tun* on 1913.3.9 (MGSCXGSDA, no. 270).

4. Since the civilian commoners were residentially and institutionally segregated from bannermen, they seldom confronted metropolitan and rural bannermen as a group.

5. See the official report of this case filed in 1878.3 (SCPZGYMDA, 200: 829: 69–74).

6. See the official reports on this case in 1879.12 and the investigation results in 1880.2 (SCPZGYMDA, 203: 841: 294; and 204: 846: 246–54).

7. See the results of the investigation, filed in 1880.2 (SCPZGYMDA 204: 846: 246–54).

8. This is according to an interview conducted by Matthew Noellert and Shuang Chen in June 2013.

9. By the end of the Qing dynasty, banner affiliation was being used interchangeably with Manchu to describe bannermen's ethnic background. In the 1950s, when the People's Republic of China started to register people's self-reported ethnicity, many descendants of Han-martial bannermen reported themselves as Manchu. Therefore, Fu's use of *sui man* is likely a variation of the term *suiqi*.

10. During the Qing, Manchu tribes surnamed Furha, Fulkulu, and Fuca all adopted the Sinicized surname Fu.

11. See the report by the area commander-in-chief to the general of Jilin in 1874.7 (SCPZGYMDA, 184: 759: 235–42).

12. Ibid.

13. This result is calculated using the CMGPD-SC dataset.

14. For details of this policy adjustment, see chapter 3.

15. See the investigation report by the local police office on 1912.4.18 (MGSCXGSDA, no. 270). The report recounted the history of the adjustment of the land allocation policy. Records on the 1876 land register of the Bordered White Banner (SCPGBTDHKDM, 1834731: 659) also illustrate the composition of the *jichan* plots in the right and the left *tun*.

16. Although the land each central-*tun* rural banner household received from the right and the left *tun* added up to 8.34 *shang*, here I follow the official regulation to use the number 8.33.

17. See the reports by the assistant commandant regarding land disputes between the central-*tun* and the right- and the left-*tun* residents, filed in 1882.4 (SCPZGYMDA, 209: 870: 289–98) and on 1882.6.27 (SCPZGYMDA, 209: 873: 113–21), respectively.

18. The investigation report by the local police office on 1912.4.18 (MGSCXGSDA, no. 270).

19. Ibid.

20. See the order from the Shuangcheng banner government in 1881.7, which concerns a lawsuit filed by Zhao Fuxing, a rural bannerman living in

the central *tun*, on withdrawing the land from the right and left *tun* (SCPZGYMDA, 207: 864: 95–99). The order cited the precedent in 1853.

21. See the deposition of the central-*tun* residents in their petition to the provincial government, which was cited in the order from the local banner government in 1882.4 (SCPZGYMDA, 209: 870: 209–15).

22. Ibid and a follow-up of this case in 1882.4 (SCPZGYMDA, 209: 870: 289–98).

23. See the order from the local banner government in 1882.4 that cited the central-*tun* residents' petition (SCPZGYMDA, 209: 870: 209–15).

24. See the recounting of the previous disputes by the area commander-in-chief in 1881.7 (SCPZGYMDA, 207: 864: 95–99).

25. See the rebuttal of the central-*tun* representatives to the proposal of the right- and the left-*tun* residents regarding the purchase of the enclaves from the central-*tun* landlords in 1913.10 (MGSCXGSDA, no. 270). The central-*tun* representatives cited the reply from the local government to the right- and left-*tun* residents in 1902.

26. See the government order on 1902.7.15 (SCPZGYMDA, 268: 1195: 1–18).

27. See the official recounting of the solution offered by the government to the debate on land deeds in the report from the assistant commandant of Shuangcheng in 1907.5, which was enclosed in the government correspondence on 1908.2.6 (JLQSQWC J049-03-0466).

28. See the various recounts of this case in 1912 (MGSCXGSDA, no. 270).

29. See the government correspondence regarding this case on 1908.2.6 (JLQSQWC J049-03-0466).

30. About Guangzhi's background, see the accusation of the central-*tun* residents in 1912 (MGSCXGSDA, no. 270) and the 1909 household register of the Bordered Blue Banner (SCPGBTDHKDM, 1834722: 497).

31. See the petitions submitted by the central-*tun* and the right- and the left-*tun* representatives, on 1813.12.29 (MGSCXGSDA, no. 270). In recounting the case of Guangzhi, the document did not explain the source of the two hundred thousand strings of cash. Yet another account of this case said that Guangzhi offered to contribute all the rent belonging to the central-*tun* residents to the government. Therefore, these cash probably represent the monetary form of the rent the right- and the left-*tun* residents owed to the central-*tun* residents.

32. Ibid. According to the right- and the left-*tun* representatives, the provincial governor Xiliang ordered an investigation of this case and a search for a solution. However, the case was put aside because of the regime change in 1911.

33. See the 1911 household register of the Bordered White banner (SCPGBTDHKDM, 1834684: 196).

34. See the rebuttal of the central-*tun* representatives to the right- and the left-*tun* residents' request on 1913.10 (MGSCXGSDA, no. 270).

35. The voting rights in this election were restricted to literate males over twenty-one years old with either an elementary school education or over Ch$500 immovable property or an annual direct tax bill of over Ch$2. According to Young (1977, 114), only from 1 or 2 percent to 8 percent of the population registered to vote.

36. Mo Dehui continued to be active in national politics in the 1930s and 1940s. Later, he was appointed as the president of the Examination Yuan (1954–1966) of the Republic of China in Taiwan (Mo 1968, 134).

37. See the 1889 land register of the Bordered White Banner (SCPGBTDHKDM, 1834732: 674). In 1896 Zhao Rongchun was registered under a household as the nephew of the head (SCPGBTDHKDM, 1834682: 682).

38. See the 1911 household register of the Bordered White Banner (SCPGBTDHKDM, 1834684: 196).

39. See the 1889 land register of the Bordered White Banner (SCPGBTDHKDM, 1834732: 674).

40. See Su Changhai's accusation of Wu Chengzhu on 1912.12.29 (MGSCXGSDA, no. 270).

41. See the accusation by the central-*tun* representatives on 1912.12.8 (MGSCXGSDA, no. 398).

42. See the accusation by the central-*tun* representatives on 1912.12.8 and 1912.12.29 (MGSCXGSDA, no. 270 and 398).

43. See Su Changhai's accusation of Wu Chengzhu on 1912.12.29 and 1913.1.17 (MGSCXGSDA, no. 270).

44. See the petition filed by the right- and the left-*tun* representatives on 1913.3.9 (MGSCXGSDA, no. 270).

45. See the exchanges and petitions by the representatives of the right and the left *tun* and the central *tun* filed in 1913. 10 (MGSCXGSDA, no. 270).

46. Ibid.

47. Mo Dehui's grandfather had three sons. Mo Desheng's father was the eldest son, and Mo Dehui's father was the youngest son (Mo 1968, 9). Mo Dehui's father moved to the county seat, whereas the extended Mo family remained in the original banner village (SCPGBTDHKDM, 1834684: 198).

48. See the exchanges and petitions by the representatives of the right and the left *tun* and the central *tun* filed in 1913. 10 (MGSCXGSDA, no. 270).

49. Of course, given the complexity of local politics, their collective action also faced challenges. In the last month of 1912, Su Changhai, a rural bannerman and Wu Chengzhu's fellow councilor in the Dong'an Township, accused Wu Chengzhu at the county government of illegally collecting monetary donations and cheating people (MGSCXGSDA, no. 270). An investigation of Su's background shows that he was an absentee landlord who was only registered on the particular banner register in 1911 as a new household (SCPGBTDHKDM, 1834684: 196). This case in fact demonstrates that a common living experience is equally important for the formation of collective identity.

50. Noellert illustrates the pattern of land distribution using the land and population registers maintained by the Chinese Communist Party in 1947. Since these land-reform data are not linked to the Qing dynasty data, it is unclear whether the descendants of metropolitan and rural bannermen still owned the majority of land. Yet, the overall pattern of land distribution in 1947 was similar to that in the Qing dynasty.

Epilogue

1. Although the CCP leaders made several efforts to rectify the structural inequality, this system continued to maintain the rural-urban divide (Wang 2005, 47). The *hukou* system is durable because it is interlocked with other aspects of administration, including local control and public security as well as the educational and social security systems (Wu 2010, 58). Reforming the *hukou* system means reducing the privileges of the urban residents, which presents a challenge to governance.

2. Although in the early stage of economic reform, the countryside also achieved considerable economic growth, the advantage of the rural sector disappeared very soon.

GLOSSARY

Alchuka 阿勒楚喀

Baerhu 巴尔虎
bangding 帮丁
baojia 保甲
baomiao 报庙
Baqi Manzhou shizu tongpu 八旗满洲氏族通谱
baqianshang 八千晌
Bayansusu 巴彦苏苏
Beiyang gaodeng xunjing xuetang 北洋高等巡警学堂
bendi qiren 本地旗人
bitieshi 笔帖式
Bodune 伯都讷
Boqitu 博启图
bu zai ce fuding 不在册浮丁
bu 步
bubing 步兵
buzhi quxiang 不知去向

Caishen 财神
cang shi 仓石
Changlin 长林
Changling 长龄
Chenggui 成桂
Chenghuang 城隍
Chengshun 成顺
chengzhong jingqi di fuding 承种京旗地浮丁
chi 尺
chipin 赤贫
chongwang 虫王

Daoguang 道光
Dezhong 德中
dian 典
dianhu cun 佃户村
dingque 丁缺
Dong Zhongshu 董仲舒
Dou Xinchuan 窦心传
dou 斗
dutong 都统

enque 恩缺

fangyu 防御
Fengdu 丰都
fengdui 封堆
Fenghuangcheng 凤凰城
Fengtian 奉天
Fenxundao 分巡道
fu buguo sandai 富不过三代
fu dutong 副都统
fu tunda 副屯达
fuding buzhun lingdi 浮丁不准领地
fuding 浮丁
fuduo 浮多
fuhu 浮户
Fujun 富俊
Fuming'a 富明阿
Fuqing'e 付清额

Furui 福瑞
fuzhe tian lian qianmo, pinzhe wu lizhui zhidi 富者田连阡陌, 贫者无立锥之地
Fuzhou 复州

Gaizhou 盖州
gongcang 公仓
gongmin 公民
gongzu 公租
Guan Yu 关羽
Guandi 关帝
guandian 官店
Guangning 广宁
Guanyin 观音
Guohui 国会
Guqing 固庆

Han 汉
Hanjun 汉军
Harbin 哈尔滨
Heilongjiang 黑龙江
hengchan 恒产
hu 斛
Hualiantai 花连太
Hubei 湖北
huichang 会场
hukou 户口
Hulan 呼兰
Hunchun 珲春
huoshen 火神
Husong'e 瑚松额

jia wu chanye nian yi cheng ding zhi xiansan 家无产业年已成丁之闲散
jiabing 甲兵
jiala 甲喇
jianbu 拣补
Jiang Jixian 蒋伋铦
jiangjun 将军
jiao guan ling ding buchong 交官另顶补充
Jiaqing 嘉庆
jichan 己产
Jiertahun 吉尔他珲
Jiertuhun 吉尔吐珲
Jiertukan 吉尔吐堪
jikou shoutian 计口授田
Jilin 吉林
jiming 记名
Jing'ebu 经额布
Jingchun 景淳
jingqi yi 京旗翼
jingqi 京旗
Jingshi 京师
*jingshi*经世
jingtian 井田
jinshi 进士
Jinzhou 金州
jiu sheng 九圣
juemai 绝卖
jungong 军功
juntian 均田
juntun 军屯
juren 举人

Kaiyuan 开原
Kuide 魁德
Kuijin 魁锦
Kuiliang 魁亮
Kuishou 魁寿
Kuixiang 魁祥
Kuixiu 魁秀

Lalin 拉林
lantou 揽头
liangzhang 粮长
Liaodong 辽东
Liaoyang 辽阳
lihua qian 犁铧钱
lijia 里甲
lingcui 领催
Lingde 凌德
linghu 另户
liumin 流民
liutiaobian 柳条边

longwang 龙王

mabing 马兵
manzu 满族
maohuang 毛荒
mawang 马王
miaowang 苗王
Ming'an, Mingshan's brother, 明安
Ming'an, the general of Jilin 铭安
Mingbao 明保
Mingshan 明山
minjie 民界
minren 民人
Mulong'a 穆隆阿
Muteng'e 穆腾额
muzhang 牧长

nazu 纳租
Neiwufu 内务府
nianli jingzhuang kanneng wunong 年力精壮, 堪能务农
Ningguta 宁古塔
nüzhong guntu 女中棍徒

pijia 披甲

qianfeng 前锋
Qicheng'e 奇成额
qijie 旗界
Qingde 庆德
qingfu fanghuang zongju 清赋放荒总局
Qinglin 庆林
Qingrui 清瑞
Qingxiang 庆祥
qiwu chengban chu 旗务承办处

Rehe 热河
ren guan ling jian 任官另拣
rendong 认东
Ronghai 荣海
Rongkai 荣凯
Rongqing 荣庆
Rongshan 荣山
Rongsheng 荣升
ruding chenmin 入丁陈民

Saichong'a 赛冲阿
sanwanshang 三万晌
Shaanxi 陕西
shang 晌
shanshen 山神
Shengjing 盛京
shengyuan 生员
shenme dou you 什么都有
shenyu yin 参余银
shi 石
shijia zhang 十家长
shoubao 守保
Shuangcheng 双城
Shuangchengpu tuntian jilue 双城堡屯田纪略
Shuangquan 双全
Shuangxi 双喜
Shujing'e 舒精额
Shuyi 舒义
Sichuan 四川
Songhua 松花
Songlin 松箖, also known as Songning
Songning 松宁
Songyun 松筠
sui man 随满
suiqi 随旗
suique 随缺
sula 苏拉

Taimanzi 胎蛮子
Taqibu 塔奇布
tianxia 天下
Tinghe 廷和
tonggou tongxiao 统购统销
tuidi 退地
tun 屯
tunda 屯达
tunding 屯丁
tuntian 屯田

Tuoyun 托云
Tuqing 图庆

Wang Guifeng 王贵凤
Wang Haicheng 王海成
Wang Lütai 王履泰
wei cangguan 委仓官
wei xiaoqi xiao 委骁骑校
wei xieling 委协领
wei zuoling 委佐领
weiguan 委官
weizhi (violating the edict) 违旨
weizhi (violating the rule) 违制
wentong 文童
wopeng 窝棚
Woshine 倭什讷
Wu Chengzhu 吴成珠
Wuchang 五常
wudao 五道
Wula 乌拉
Wulibu 乌力布
Wulinbu 乌林布
Wulintai 乌林太
Wupin hualing 五品花翎

Xiangkang 祥康
xiansan 闲散
xiaoqixiao 骁骑校
xieling 协领
xinan dalu 西南大路
Xingjing 兴京
Xiongyue 熊岳
Xiuyan 岫岩

yamen 衙门
yanglian yin 养廉银
yangshan 养赡
yangyubing 养育兵
yaowang 药王
yi 翼
yicang 义仓
Yichong'e 依崇额
Yijing 奕经
yin 荫
Yinghe 英和
Yingkou 营口
yinjian 引见
yinzhuang 阴状
yiren buzhun chengling liangfen dingque 一人不准承领两份丁缺
yizhong 义冢
Yizhou 义州
yuan 冤
Yu'en 裕恩

zhang bancheng 张半城
Zhang Jianlong 张见龙
Zhang Mao 张茂
Zhang Yuxiang 张玉祥
Zhao Fuxing 赵富兴
Zhao Qinglin 赵庆林
Zhao Rongchun 赵荣春
zhaozhang jian de 照章拣得
zhengding 正丁
zhengshen qiren 正身旗人
zhengshi man ren 正式满人
zhifu 知府
Zhili 直隶
zhishen buzhun suan hu 只身不准算户
zhishi 执事
Zhou Jin 周金
Zhou Rong 周荣
zhou 州
zhuang sheng dongshi 壮盛懂事
zhuangtou 庄头
Zhuerxing'a 朱尔兴阿
zhushi 主事
ziken 滋垦
ziyi ju 咨议局
zong tunda 总屯达
zongguan 总管
zongzu 宗族
zu 族
zuoling 佐领

REFERENCES

Archival sources are cited according to the form of the document (e.g., microfilm or original file) and the way the archive catalogs them. The original or digitized files are cited by the original cataloged case number. Microfilm materials without a case number are cited by the reel number, packet (*juan*) number in the original collection, and page number appearing on the specific image, if available. For example, an image preserved in *Shuangchengpu zongguan yamen dang'an*, microfilm reel 200, juan 829, with a page number of 135 is cited as SCPZGYMDA 200: 829: 135. The date information for all archival documents is cited by Western calendar year, lunar month, and day. For example, the sixth day of the first month of the first year of the Daoguang reign is cited as 1821.1.6. Abbreviations for frequently cited collections are listed here and are used in the notes

Unpublished Archival Sources

JJCLFZZ. *Junjichu lufu zouzhe* [The memorial file copies by the Grand Council]. Catalogue no. 3. First Historical Archives, Beijing.

JLJJYMDA. *Jilin Jiangjun yamen dang'an* [The archives of the general of Jilin]. Catalogue No. 1. Changchun: Jilin Provincial Archives, Changchun, Jilin.

JLQSQWC. *Jilin quansheng qiwuchu dang'an* [The archives of the Jilin Provincial Office of Banner Affairs]. Catalogue No. 49. Changchun: Jilin Provincial Archives, Changchun, Jilin.

LNGBHK. *Liaoning guanbing hukou* [The Liaoning population registers for officers and soldiers]. Liaoning Provincial Archives, Shenyang, Liaoning; also in the Genealogical Society of Utah, microfilm.

MGSCXGSDA. *Minguo Shuangcheng xian gongshu dang'an* [Archives of the republican government of Shuangcheng County]. Catalogue no. 3, Shuangcheng Municipal Archives, Shuangcheng, Heilongjiang.

NGDKDA. *Neige daku dang'an* [Archives of the Grand Secretariat]. Academia Sinica, Taibei.

NGTFDTYMDA. *Ningguta fudutong yamen dang'an* [Archives of the Ningguta Vice Commander-in-chief's Office]. Catalogue no. 31. First Historical Archives, Beijing.

SCLSFMFDA. *Shuangcheng lishi fumin fu dang'an* [Archives of the Shuangcheng civilian Government]. Catalogue no. 2, Shuangcheng Municipal Archives, Shuangcheng, Heilongjiang.

SCPGBTDHKDM. *Shuangchengpu guanbing tunding hukou dimu* [The Shuangchengpu population and land registers for officers, soldiers, and farmers]. Catalogue no. JB10, Liaoning Provincial Archives, Shenyang, Liaoning; also in the Genealogical Society of Utah, microfilms no. 1834661–1834733.

SCPXLYMDA. *Shuangchengpu xieling yamen dang'an* [Archives of the Shuangchengpu Assistant Commandant's Office]. Catalogue no. 1, Shuangcheng Municipal Archives, Shuangcheng, Heilongjiang.

SCPZGYMDA. *Shuangchengpu zongguan yamen dang'an* [Archives of the Shuangchengpu Area Commander-in-chief's Office]. Catalogue no. JB10, Liaoning Provincial Archives, Shenyang, Liaoning.

Shuangchengxian tudi mianji renkou dengji dengji bu [Registration of land acreage and population class classification of Shuangcheng County]. Compiled by the Communist government in 1948.7. Shuangcheng Municipal Archives, Shuangcheng, Heilongjiang.

ZPZZ. *Gongzhong dang zhupi zouzhe* [Palace memorial archives memorials with emperor's response]. Catalogue no. 4. First Historical Archives, Beijing.

Datasets

CHGIS, China Historical Geographic Information System, Version 4. Cambridge, MA: Harvard Yenching Institute, January 2007, http://www.fas.harvard.edu/~chgis/data/chgis/downloads/v4/.

CMGPD-SC, China Multi-Generational Panel Dataset, Shuangcheng, 1866–1913. Constructed by Lee, James, Shuang Chen, Cameron D. Campbell, and Hongbo Wang. ICPSR35292-v3. Ann Arbor: Inter-university Consortium for Political and Social Research [distributor], 2015–02–09. http://doi.org/10.3886/ICPSR35292.v6.0.

Published Sources

Abrams, Dominic, and Michael A. Hogg. 2006. *Social Identifications: A Social Psychology of Intergroup Relations and Group Processes.* New York: Routledge.

Arrondel, Luc, and Cyril Grange. 2006. "Transmission and Inequality of Wealth: An Empirical Study of Wealth Mobility from 1800 to 1938 in France." *Journal of Economic Inequality* 4 (2): 209–232.

Atsutoshi, Hamashima. 1992. "The City-God Temples (Ch'eng-huang miao) of Chiangnan in the Ming and Ch'ing Dynasties." *Memoirs of the Research Department of the Toyo Bunko* 50: 1–27.

Baker, Hugh D. 1979. *Chinese Family and Kinship*. London: Macmillan, 1979.

Baron, James N., and William T. Bielby. 1980. "Bringing the Firms Back In: Stratification, Segmentation, and the Organization of Work." *American Sociological Review* 45: 737–65.

Barth, Fredrik, ed. 1998. *Ethnic Groups and Boundaries: The Social Organization of Culture Difference*. Long Grove, IL: Waveland Press.

Bartlett, Beatrice S. 1991. *Monarchs and Ministers: The Grand Council in Mid-Ch'ing China, 1723–1820*. Berkeley: University of California Press.

Beattie, Hilary. 1979. *Land and Lineage in China: A Study of T'ung-ch'eng County, Anhwei, in the Ming and Ch'ing Dynasties*. Cambridge: Cambridge University Press.

Bengtsson, Tommy. 2004. *Living Standards and Economic Stress, Life Under Pressure: Mortality and Living Standards in Europe and Asia, 1700–1900*. Cambridge, MA: MIT Press.

———. 2014. "The Influence of Economic Factors on First Marriages in Historical Europe and Asia." In *Similarity in Difference: Marriage in Europe and Asia, 1700–1900*, by Christer Lundh and Satomi Kurosu, et al. (authors), 121–68. Cambridge, MA: MIT Press.

Benjamin, Dwayne, and Loren Brandt. 1997. "Land, Factor Markets, and Inequality in Rural China: Historical Evidence." *Explorations in Economic History* 34 (4): 460–94.

Blau, Peter M. 1994. *Structural Contexts of Opportunities*. Chicago: University of Chicago Press.

BQTZ. 1985. *Baqi tong zhi chu ji* [Comprehensive history of the Eight Banners, first collection], 8 books, 250 juan. Edited by Ertai. Original ed. 1739. Changchun: Dongbei shifan daxue chubanshe.

Brandt, Loren. 1989. *Commercialization and Agricultural Development: Central and Eastern China, 1870–1937*. Cambridge: Cambridge University Press.

Brown, Jeremy. 2012. *City Versus Countryside in Mao's China: Negotiating the Divide*. New York: Cambridge University Press.

Brown, Rupert J., and Gordon F. Ross. 2010. "The Battle for Acceptance: An Investigation into the Dynamics of Intergroup Behavior." In *Social Identity and Intergroup Relations*, edited by Henri Tajfel, 155–78. Cambridge: Cambridge University Press.

Cain, Mead T. 1978. "The Household Life Cycle and Economic Mobility in Rural Bangladesh." *Population and Development Review* 4 (3): 421–38.

Campbell, Cameron, and James Lee. 2002." "State Views and Local Views of Population: Linking and Comparing Genealogies and Household Registers in Liaoning, 1749–1909." *History and Computing* 14 (1–2): 9–29.

Campbell, Cameron, James Lee, and Tommy Bengtsson. 2004. "Economic Stress and Mortality." In *Life under Pressure: Mortality and Living Standards in Europe and Asia, 1700–1900*, by Tommy Bengtsson, Cameron Campbell, and James Lee, 61–84. Cambridge, MA: MIT Press.

Cao, Shuji. 2012. "Chuantong Zhongguo xiangcun diquan biandong de yiban lilun" [A general theory on changes in land tenure in traditional China]. *Xueshu yuekan* 12: 117–25.

Chang, Chung-li. 1955. *The Chinese Gentry: Studies on Their Role in Nineteenth-Century Chinese Society.* Seattle: University of Washington Press.

Chang, Ying-hwa. 1991. "Qing mo Min chu Huabei nongcun de cunluo zuzhi he cunji guanxi" [Village organization and extra-village relations in agrarian villages in North China in late Ch'ing dynasty and early Republican times]. *Bulletin of the Institute of Ethnology, Academia Sinica* 72: 25–62.

Chao, Kang. 1986. *Man and Land in Chinese History: An Economic Analysis.* Stanford, CA: Stanford University Press.

———. 2003. *Lishi shang de tudi zhidu yu diquan fenpei* [Land tenure and land distribution in history]. Beijing: Zhongguo nongye chubanshe.

Chao, Kang, and Chung-i Chen. 1982. *Zhongguo tudi zhidu shi* [Land institutions in Chinese history]. Taibei: Lianjing chubanshe.

Chen, Shuang. 2009. "Where Urban Migrants Met Rural Settlers: State Categories, Social Boundaries, and Wealth Stratification in Northeast China, 1815–1913." PhD diss. University of Michigan.

Chen, Shuang, Cameron Campbell, and James Lee. 2005. "Vulnerability and Resettlement: Mortality Differences in Northeast China by Place of Origin 1870–1912, Comparing Urban and Rural Migrants." *Annales de Démographie Historique* 110 (2): 47–79.

———. 2014. "Categorical Inequality and Gender Difference: Marriage and Remarriage in Northeast China, 1749–1913." In *Similarity in Difference: Marriage in Europe and Asia 1700–1900*, by Christer Lundh and Satomi Kurosu et al. (authors), 393–436. Cambridge, MA: MIT Press.

Chen, Shuang, James Lee, and Cameron Campbell. 2010. "Wealth Stratification and Reproduction in Northeast China, 1866–1907." *History of the Family* 15 (4): 386–412.

———. 2012. "Land Distribution in Northeast China: Demography, State, and Market, 1870–1907." Paper presented at the XVIth World Economic History Congress, Stellenbosch, South Africa, July 9–13.

Chow, Kai-wing. 1994. *The Rise of Confucian Ritualism in Late Imperial China: Ethics, Classics, and Lineage Discourse.* Stanford, CA: Stanford University Press.

Ch'ü, T'ung-tsu. 1962. *Local Government in China under the Ch'ing.* Cambridge, MA: Harvard University Press.

Clark, Gregory, and Gillian Hamilton. 2006. "Survival of the Richest: The Malthusian Mechanism in Pre-industrial England." *Journal of Economic History* 66 (3): 1–30.

Cohen, Myron L. 1990. "Lineage Organization in North China." *Journal of Asian Studies* 49 (3): 509–34.

———. 2004. "Writs of Passage in Late Imperial China." In *Contract and Property in Early Modern China*, edited by Madeleine Zelin, Jonathan K. Ocko, and Robert Gardella, 37–93. Stanford, CA: Stanford University Press.

Colson, Elizabeth. 1971. *The Social Consequence of Resettlement*. Manchester: University of Manchester Press.

Crossley, Pamela Kyle. 1990. *Orphan Warriors: Three Manchu Generations and the End of the Qing World*. Princeton, NJ Princeton University Press.

Davies, James B., Susanna Sandström, Anthony Shorrocks, and Edward N. Wolff. 2011. "The Level and Distribution of Global Household Wealth." *Economic Journal* 121 (551): 223–54.

Davis, Deborah, and Feng Wang. 2009. "Poverty and Wealth in Postsocialist China: An Overview." In *Creating Wealth and Poverty in Post-Socialist China*, edited by Deborah Davis and Feng Wang, 3–19. Stanford, CA: Stanford University Press.

DGCSYD. 2008. *Daoguang chao shangyu dang* [The archives of the edicts of the Daoguang reign]. Edited by the No.1 Historical Archives. Guilin: Guangxi shifan daxue chubanshe.

Diao, Shuren. 1993. *Dongbei qidi yanjiu* [Research on banner land in Northeast China]. Changchun: Jilin wenshi chubanshe.

Diao, Shuren, and Xingguo Yi. 1994. *Jin sanbainian dongbei tudi kaifashi* [The history of land clearing in Northeast China in the last three hundred years]. Changchun: Jilin wenshi chubanshe.

Ding, Yizhuang. 1985. "Qingdai jingqi yizhu Dongbei tunken shimo" [The beginning and ending of the rustication of metropolitan bannermen in Northeast China in the Qing]. Master's thesis, Minzu University of China.

———. 1987. "Shilun Qingdai zhongye jingqi de Shuangchengpu tunken" [A tentative discussion on the rustication of metropolitan bannermen in Shuangcheng in mid-Qing]. *Beifang wenwu* 1: 81–86.

———. 2003. *Qingdai Baqi zhufang yanjiu* [Research on the Eight Banners garrisons in the Qing dynasty]. Shenyang: Liaoning minzu chubanshe.

———. 2009. "Youguan Qingchao Baqi rending hukouce de jige wenti" [Regarding several issues in the Qing Eight Banners population registers]. In *Qingshi luncong*, edited by Jiefu Zhang et al., 43–49. Beijing: Zhongguo guangbo dianshi chubanshe.

Ding, Yizhuang, and Yuanyuan Qiu. 2011. "Qi min yu Man Han zhijian: Qingdai 'suiqiren' chutan" [Between bannermen and civilian commoners and

Manchu and Han: a preliminary investigation on the "suiqiren" in the Qing]. *Qingshi yanjiu* 1: 69–77.

Ding, Yizhuang, Songyi Guo, Zhongqing Li, and Wenlin Kang. 2004. *Liaodong yimin zhong de qiren shehui* [Immigration and the Eight Banner Society in Liaodong]. Shanghai: Shanghai shehui kexue chubanshe.

Diprete, Thomas A., Paul M. de Graaf, Rudd Luijkx, Michael Tahlin, and Hans-Peter Blossfeld. 1997. "Collectivist vs. Individualist Mobility Regimes? How Structural Change and Individual Resources Affect Men's Job Mobility in Four Countries." *American Journal of Sociology* 103 (2): 318–58.

DQHDSL. 1991. *Daqing huidian shili* [Supplementary regulations and substatutes of the collected statutes of the great Qing dynasty]. 920 juan. Edited by Tuojin, 1818. Taibei Wenhai chubanshe. Reprint.

DQLL. 1995. *Daqing lüli* [The Great Qing code with substatute]. 47 juan. Tianjin: Tianjin guji chubanshe.

Du, Xingzhi. 1994. "Baerhu menggu yuanliu kao" [Examination of the origin of Baerhu-mongols]. *Neimenggu shida xuebao* 3: 28–34.

Duara, Prasenjit. 1988a. *Culture, Power, and the State*. Stanford, CA: Stanford University Press.

———. 1988b. "Superscribing Symbols: The Myth of Guandi, Chinese God of War." *Journal of Asian Studies* 47 (4): 778–95.

DuBois, Thomas David. 2005. *The Sacred Village: Social Change and Religious Life in Rural North China*. Honolulu: University of Hawai'i Press.

Ebrey, Patricia, and James Watson, eds. 1986. *Kinship Organization in Late Imperial China, 1000–1940*. Berkeley: University of California Press.

Edmonds, Richard. 1979. "The Willow Palisade." *Annals of the Association of American Geographers* 69 (4): 599–621.

Elliott, Mark. 2000. "The Limits of Tartary: Manchuria in Imperial and National Geographies." *Journal of Asian Studies* 59 (3): 603–46.

———2001. *The Manchu Way: The Eight Banners and Ethnic Identity in Late Imperial China*. Stanford, CA: Stanford University Press.

Emirbayer, Mustafa, and Ann Mische. 1998. "What Is Agency?" *American Journal of Sociology* 103 (4): 962–1023.

Enatsu, Yoshiki. 2004. *Banner Legacy: The Rise of the Fengtian Local Elite at the End of the Qing*. Ann Arbor: Center for Chinese Studies, University of Michigan.

Engels, Friedrich. 2001. *Origin of the Family, Private Property, and the State*. London: Electric Book Co. Originally published in 1884.

Esherick, Joseph. 1981. "Number Games: A Note on Land Distribution in Prerevolutionary China." *Modern China* 7 (4): 387–411.

Esherick, Joseph, and Mary Backus Rankin, eds. 1990. *Chinese Local Elites and Patterns of Dominance*. Berkeley: University of California Press.

Eshima, Hisao. 1999. "Sōjōhō" [Shuangchengpu]. In *Mindai Shinsho no Jochokushi kenkyu*, 547–54. Fukuoka shi: Chugoku Shoten.

Fan, Lijun. 2007. *Jindai guannei yimin yu Zhongguo Dongbei shehui bianqian (1860–1931)* [The immigration from inland and social changes in Northeast China in the modern period]. Beijing: Renmin chubanshe.

Faure, David. 1986. *The Structure of Chinese Rural Society: Lineage and Village in the Eastern New Territories, Hong Kong.* Hong Kong: Oxford University Press.

———. 1989. *The Rural Economy of Pre-Liberation China: Trade Increase and Peasant Livelihood in Jiangsu and Guangdong, 1870 to 1937.* Hong Kong: Oxford University Press.

———. 2007. *Emperor and Ancestor.* Stanford, CA: Stanford University Press.

Freedman, Maurice. 1965. *Lineage Organization in Southeastern China.* London: Athlone Press.

———, ed. 1966. *Chinese Lineage and Society: Fukien and Kwangtung.* London: Athlone Press.

Fukutake, Tadashi. 1951. *Chūgoku nōson shakai no kōzō* [The social structure of rural China]. Tokyo: Yūhikaku.

GJTJJ. 2005. "The List of Top 100 Grain Production Sites in China in 2005." National Bureau of Statistics of the People's Republic of China. Accessed on March 16, 2016. http://www.stats.gov.cn/ztjc/ztsj/bqx/200610/t20061009_54466.html.

Goffman, Erving. 1959. *The Presentation of Self in Everyday Life.* New York: Doubleday.

———. 1982. *Interaction Ritual: Essays on Face-to-Face Behavior.* New York: Pantheon Books.

Guggenheim, Scott E., and Michael M. Cernea, eds. 1993. "Anthropological Approaches to Involuntary Resettlement: Policy, Practice, and Theory." In *Anthropological Approaches to Involuntary Resettlement: Policy, Practice, and Theory*, 1–12. Boulder, CO: Westview Press.

Guo, Qitao. 2003. *Exorcism and Money: The Symbolic World of the Five-Fury Spirits in Late Imperial China.* Berkeley: Institute of East Asian Studies, University of California.

Guo, Songyi. 1997. *Zhongguo tunken shi* [The history of state-organized farming in China]. Taibei: Wenjin chubanshe.

Gupta, Akhil. 1995. "Blurred Boundaries: The Discourse of Corruption, the Culture of Politics, and the Imagined State." *American Ethnologist* 22 (2): 375–402.

Han, Guanghui. 1987. "Qingdai Beijing Baqi renkou de yanbian" [The change of the Eight Banner population in the Qing Beijing]. *Renkou yu jingji* 2: 51–56.

Han, Guopan. 1984. *Beichao Suitang juntian zhidu* [The equal-field system in the northern, Sui, and Tang dynasties]. Shanghai: Shanghai renmin chubanshe.

Harbury, Colin, and David Hitchins. 2012. *Inheritance and Wealth Inequality in Britain.* New York: Routledge.

Harrell, Stevan. 1985. "The Rich Get Children: Segmentation, Stratification, and Population in Three Chekiang Lineages, 1550–1850." In *Family and Population in East Asian History*, edited by Susan B. Hanley and Arthur P. Wolf, 81–109. Stanford, CA: Stanford University Press.

Hatada, Takashi. 1966. "Kyū chūgoku sonraku no kyōdōtaiteki seikaku ni tsuite no kentō mura no tochi to mura no hito" [Re-examination on the communal character of old Chinese village: On the boundary of a village and the qualification of the villager]. *Tokyo Toritsu Daigaku jinbun gakuho* 51 (5): 1–152.

HCDXTGZY. 1902. *Huangchao dao xian tong guang zouyi* [The imperial memorials from the reigns of Daoguang, Xianfeng, Tongzhi, and Guangxu]. 28 books, 64 juan. Edited by Wang, Yanxi and Wang, Shumin. Shanghai: Shanghai jiujing zhai.

HCJSWB. 1887. *Huangchao jingshi wenbian* [The imperial collection of statecraft writings]. 60 books, 120 juan. Edited by He, Changling. Sibu lou.

HCZDLZ. 1982. *Huangchao zhengdian leizuan* [Classified governmental institutes of the Qing]. 50 books, 500 juan. Edited by Xi, Yufu and Shen, Shixu. Taibei: Wenhai chubanshe.

He, Changqun. 1956. *Lun lianghan tudi zhanyou xingtai de fazhan* [On the development of the land ownership during the West and East Han dynasties]. Shanghai: Shanghai renmin chubanshe.

———. 1958. *Han Tang jian fengjian de guoyou tudi zhi yu juntian zhi* [The feudal state land ownership between Han and Tang and the Juntian system]. Shanghai: Shanghai renmin chubanshe.

He, Zhaohui. 2006. *Mingdai xianzheng yanjiu* [Research on the county administration in the Ming dynasty]. Beijing: Beijing daxue chubanshe.

Ho, Franklin Lian. 1931. *Population Movement to the Northeastern Frontier in China*. Shanghai: China Institute of Pacific Relations.

Ho, Ping-ti. 1959. *Studies on the Population of China, 1368–1953*. Cambridge, MA: Harvard University Press.

HS. 1962. *Hanshu* [The book of Han dynasty]. Edited by Ban Gu. 12 books, 100 juan. Beijing: Zhonghua shuju.

Hsiao, Kung-Chuan. 1960. *Rural China: Imperial Control in the Nineteenth Century*. Seattle: University of Washington Press.

Hu, Yingze. 2012. *Liudong de tudi: Mingqing yilai Huanghe xiaobeiganliu quyu shehui yanjiu* [Floating land: A study on the society in the middle Yellow River region in Ming and Qing dynasties]. Beijing: Beijing daxue chubanshe.

Huang, Philip C. 1985. *The Peasant Economy and Social Change in North China*. Stanford, CA: Stanford University Press.

———. 1990. *The Peasant Family and Rural Development in the Yangzi Delta, 1350–1988*. Stanford, CA: Stanford University Press.

———. 2001. *Code, Custom, and Legal Practice in China: The Qing and the Republic Compared, Law, Society, and Culture in China*. Stanford, CA: Stanford University Press.

Isett, Christopher M. 2004. "Village Regulation of Property and the Social Basis for the Transformation of Qing Manchuria." *Late Imperial China* 25 (1): 124.

———. 2007. *State, Peasant, and Merchant in Qing Manchuria, 1644–1862*. Stanford, CA: Stanford University Press.

Jing, Su, and Lun Luo. 1978. *Landlord and Labor in Late Imperial China: Case Studies from Shandong*. Cambridge, MA: Harvard University Asia Center / Harvard University Press.

Johnson, David. 1985. "The City-God Cults of T'ang and Sung China." *Harvard Journal of Asiatic Studies* 45 (2): 363–457.

Jones, Susan Mann, ed. 1979. *Select Papers from the Center for Far Eastern Studies. No. 3: Proceedings of the NEH Modern China Project, 1977–1978: Political Leadership and Social Change at the Local Level in China from 1850 to the Present*. Chicago: Center for Far Eastern Studies, University of Chicago.

JQCSYD. 2008. *Jiaqing chao shangyu dang* [The archives of the edicts of the Jiaqing reign]. Edited by the First Historical Archives. Beijing: Guangxi shifan daxue chubanshe.

Kato, Naoto. 1996. "Shindai Sōjōhō no tonkon ni tsuite" [Research on the Shuangcheng settlement in the Qing]. In *Shindai Chugoku no sho mondai*, edited by Hidekatsu Ishibashi, 141–58. Tokyo: Yamakawa shuppansha.

Kautsky, Karl. 1988. *The Agrarian Question*. Translated by Pete Burgess. London: Zwan Publications. Originally published in 1899.

Ke, Zhiming. 2001. *Fantou jia: Qingdai Taiwan zuqun zhengzhi yu shufan diquan*. Taibei: Zhangyang yanjiuyuan shehuixue yanjiusuo.

Keister, Lisa A. 2000. *Wealth in America: Trends in Wealth Inequality*. New York: Cambridge University Press.

Kertzer, David I., and Dominique Arel, eds. 2002. *Census and Identity: The Politics of Race, Ethnicity, and Language in National Censuses*. Cambridge: Cambridge University Press.

Khodarkovsky, Michael. 2002. *Russia's Steppe Frontier: The Making of a Colonial Empire, 1500–1800*. Bloomington: Indiana University Press.

Komekura, Jirou. 1941. "Shindai hokuman no tonkon—Sōjōhō tonden no yosatsu hōkoku wo chūshin toshite" [The state organized farming in northern Manchuria in the Qing dynasty: Taking the investigation report on the Shuangchengpu state farm as the center of study]. *Tōa jinbun gakuhō* 1 (3): 134–49.

Kong, Jingwei. 1963. "Qing chu zhi Jiawu zhanqian Dongbei guantian qidi de jingying he mindian yiji mindi de fazhan" [The management of state land

and banner land and the development of civilian tenants and private land in Northeast China from the early Qing to the first Sino-Japanese War]. *Lishi yanjiu* 4: 67–90.

———. 1986. *Dongbei jingji shi* [The economic history of Northeast China]. Chengdu: Sichuan renmin chubanshe.

Kuhn, Philip. 1975. "Local Self-Government Under the Republic: Problems of Control, Autonomy, and Mobilization." In *Conflict and Control in Late Imperial China*, edited by Frederic Wakeman Jr. and Carolyn Grant, 257–98. Berkeley: University of California Press.

———. 1980. *Rebellion and Its Enemies in Late Imperial China: Militarization and Social Structure, 1796–1864*. Harvard East Asian Series. Cambridge, MA: Harvard University Press.

Kurosu, Satomi. 2010. "Distribution of Land in Rural Communities in Northeastern Japan, 1716–1870." Paper presented at the Annual Meeting of the Social Science History Association, Chicago, November 18–21.

Lamont, Michèle, and Virág Molnár. 2002. "The Study of Boundaries in the Social Sciences." *Annual Review of Sociology* 281 (August): 167–95.

Lattimore, Owen. 1932. *Manchuria: Cradle of Conflict*. New York: Macmillan.

Lavely, William, and R. Bin Wong. 1992. "Family Division and Mobility in North China." *Comparative Studies in Society and History* 34 (3): 439–63.

Lee, James 1978. "Migration and Expansion in Chinese History." In *Human Migration: Patterns and Policies*, edited by William McNeill and Ruth Adams, 20–47. Bloomington: Indiana University Press.

———. 1982. "The Legacy of Immigration in Southwest China, 1250–1850." *Annales de Démographie Historique* 1: 279–304.

Lee, James, and Wang Feng. 1999. *One Quarter of Humanity: Malthusian Mythology and Chinese Realities, 1700–2000*. Cambridge, MA: Harvard University Press.

Lee, James, and Cameron Campbell. 1997. *Fate and Fortune in Rural China: Social Organization and Population Behavior in Liaoning 1774–1873*. Cambridge: Cambridge University Press.

Lee, James, Cameron Campbell, and Shuang Chen. 2010. China Multi-Generational Panel Dataset, Liaoning (CMGPD-LN) 1749–1909. User Guide. Ann Arbor, MI: Inter-university Consortium for Political and Social Research. doi.org/10.3886/ICPSR27063.v10.

Lee, Robert H. G. 1970. *The Manchurian Frontier in Ch'ing History*. Cambridge, MA: Harvard University Press.

Lenin, Vladimir Il'ich. 1964. *The Development of Capitalism in Russia: The Process of the Formation of a Home Market for Large-Scale Industry*. Vol. 3, V. I. Lenin Collected Works. Moscow: Progress Publishers Moscow.

Li, Dianrong. 2011. *Qingdai jingkong zhidu yanjiu* [A study of the Qing capital-appeal system]. Shanghai: Shanghai guji chubanshe.

Li, Haihong. 2011. "Preserving Manchu Tradition with Chinese Culture: The Banner People's Kinship Organizations (1644–1911)." PhD diss., Harvard University (Proquest, UMI no. 3462654).

Li, Huaiyin. 2005. *Village Governance in North China, 1875–1936*. Stanford, CA: Stanford University Press.

Li, Lilian M. 2007. *Fighting Famine in North China: State, Market, and Environmental Decline, 1690s-1990s*. Stanford, CA: Stanford University Press.

Li, Lin. 1992. *Manzu zongpu yanjiu* [Research on the genealogies of the Manchu people]. Shenyang: Liaoshen shushe.

Li, Zhongqing (James Lee). 2012. *Zhongguo xinan bianjiang de shehui jingji, 1250–1850* [Society and economy in Southwest China, 1250–1850]. Translated by Wenxun Lin and Shucai Qin. Beijing: Renmin chubanshe.

Li, Shi, and Chuliang Luo. 2010. "Re-estimating the Income Gap between Urban and Rural Households in China." In *One Country, Two Societies: Rural-Urban Inequality in Contemporary China*, edited by Martin King Whyte, 105–24. Cambridge, MA: Harvard University Press.

Li, Shi, and Renwei Zhao. 2007. "Changes in the Distribution of Wealth in China, 1995–2002." Research paper No. 2007/03. Helsinki: UNU-WIDER (United Nations University–World Institute for Development Economics Research).

Li, Wenzhi, and Taixin Jiang. 2005. *Zhongguo dizhu zhi jingjilun: Fengjian tudi guanxi de fazhan yu bianhua* [The landlord economy in China: Development and changes in the feudal land relations]. Beijing: Zhongguo shehui kexue chubanshe.

Liang, Fangzhong. 1957. *Mingdai liangzhang zhidu* [The institution of tax head in the Ming dynasty]. Shanghai: Shanghai renmin chubanshe.

———. 1980. *Zhongguo lidai hukou, tiandi, tianfu tongji* [Statistics of population, land, and land taxes of successive dynasties of China]. Shanghai: Shanghai renmin chubanshe.

Lindert, Peter H. 2000. "Three Centuries of Inequality in Britain and America." In *Handbook of Income Distribution*, Vol. 1, edited by Anthony Atkinson and Francois Bourguignon, 167–216. Amsterdam; New York: Elsevier.

Liu, Xiaomeng. 1998a. "Qian Jia nianjian jifu qiren de tudi jiaoyi: genju tudi qishu jingxing de kaocha" [Land transaction in Beijing surburbs during the Qianlong and Jiaqing periods: Examination based on land contracts]. In *Manzu de shehui yu shenghuo*, 244–61. Beijing: Beijing tushuguan chubanshe.

———. 1998b. "Qingdai Beijing neicheng jumin de fenbu geju yu bianqian" [The distribution and change of the residential pattern in the inner city of Qing Beijing]. In *Manzu de shehui yu shenghuo*, 322–46. Beijing: Beijing tushuguan chubanshe.

———. 1998c. "Qingdai Beijing qiren de fangwu maimai" [Housing transactions of the bannermen in Beijing during the Qing]. In *Manzu de shehui yu shenghuo*, 283–321. Beijing: Beijing tushuguan chubanshe.

———. 2001. *Manzu cong buluo dao guojia de fazhan* [The development of Manchu from tribes to a state]. 2nd ed. Shenyang: Liaoning minzu chubanshe.

———. 2008. *Qingdai Beijing qiren shehui* [The Banner society in Qing-dynasty Beijing]. Beijing: Zhongguo shehui kexue chubanshe.

Lishi yanjiu bianjibu ed. 1957. *Zhongguo lidai tudi zhidu wenti taolun ji* [The collection of discussions on the land system of all the dynasties in China]. Beijing: Dongfangxue chubanshe.

Liu, Xin. 2009. "Institutional Basis of Social Stratification in Transitional China." In *Creating Wealth and Poverty in Post-Socialist China*, edited by Deborah Davis and Feng Wang, 85–96. Stanford, CA: Stanford University Press.

Macauley, Melissa. 2001. "A World Made Simple: Law and Property in the Ottoman and Qing Empires." *Journal of Early Modern History* 5 (4): 331–52.

Menchik, Paul L. 1979. "Inter-generational Transmission of Inequality: An Empirical Study of Wealth Mobility." *Economica* 46 (181): 349–62.

Meng, Sen. 1936. "Baqi zhidu kaoshi" [Examination of the Eight Banners]. *Bulletin of the Institute of History and Philology, Academia Sinica* 6 (3): 343–412.

Migdal, Joel S. 2001. *State in Society: Studying How State and Societies Transform and Constitute One Another.* New York: Cambridge University Press.

Millward, James. 1998. *Beyond the Pass: Economy, Ethnicity, and Empire in Qing Central Asia, 1759–1864.* Stanford, CA: Stanford University Press.

Min, Tu-ki. 1989. *National Polity and Local Power: The Transformation of Late Imperial China.* Cambridge, MA: Council on East Asian Studies, Harvard University and Harvard-Yenching Institute.

MMTKK. 1909. *Kita Manshū keizai chōsa shiryō* [The investigation sources on northern Manchuria]. Dairen: Minami Manshū Tetsudō Kabushiki Kaisha.

MMTKK. 1911. *Zoku Kita Manshū keizai chōsa shiryō* [Sequel of the investigation sources on northern Manchuria]. Dairen: Minami Manshū Tetsudō Kabushiki Kaisha.

Mo, Dehui. 1968. *Shuangcheng Mo Dehui zi ding nian pu* [A self-compiled chronicle of the life of Mo Dehui of Shuangcheng]. Taibei: Taiwan shangwu yinshuguan.

Mullaney, Thomas. 2010. *Coming to Terms with the Nation: Ethnic Classification in Modern China.* Berkeley: University of California Press.

Myers, Ramon. 1970. *The Chinese Peasant Economy*. Cambridge, MA: Harvard University Press.

———. 1976. "Socioeconomic Change in Villages of Manchuria During the Ch'ing and Republican Periods: Some Preliminary Findings." *Modern Asian Studies*, 10 (4): 591–620.

———. 1991. "How Did the Modern Chinese Economy Develop?—A Review Article." *Journal of Asian Studies*, 50(3): 604–28.

Nakamura, Tetsuo. 1984. "Shin matsu kahoku ni okeru shijōken to shūkyōken" [The market and religion networks in North China in the late Qing]. In *Kindai Chūgoku shakaishi kenkyū josetsu*, 57–85. Kyoto: Hōritsu bunkasha.

Niu, Pinghan, ed. 1990. *Qingdai zhengqu yange zongbiao* [The synthesis of the development of administrative divisions of Qing dynasty]. Beijing: Zhongguo ditu chubanshe.

Noellert, Matthew. 2014. "New Perspectives on Communist Land Reform: Evidence from Northeast China, 1946–1948." PhD diss., Hong Kong University of Science and Technology.

Ocko, Jonathan K. 1988. "I'll Take It All the Way to Beijing: Capital Appeals in the Qing." *Journal of Asian Studies* 47 (2): 291–315.

Oi, Jean C. 1989. *State and Peasant in Contemporary China: The Political Economy of Village Government*. Berkeley: University of California Press.

Osborne, Anne. 2004. "Property, Taxes, and State Protection of Rights." In *Contract and Property in Early Modern China*, edited by Madeleine Zelin, Jonathan K. Ocko, and Robert Gardella, 120–58. Stanford, CA: Stanford University Press.

Oulton, Nicholas. 1976. "Inheritance and the Distribution of Wealth." *Oxford Economic Papers* 28 (1): 86–101.

Park, Nancy E. 1997. "Corruption in Eighteenth-Century China." *Journal of Asian Studies* 56 (4): 967–1005.

Pasternak, Burton. 1969. "The Role of the Frontier in Chinese Lineage Development." *Journal of Asian Studies* 28 (3): 551–61.

———. 1972. *Kinship and Community in Two Chinese Villages*. Stanford, CA: Stanford University Press.

Perdue, Peter C. 2005. *China Marches West: The Qing Conquest of Central Eurasia*. Cambridge, MA: Belknap Press of Harvard University Press.

Piketty, Thomas. 2000. "Theories of Persistent Inequality and Integenerational Mobility." In *Handbook of Income Distribution*, vol. 1, edited by Anthony B. Atkinson and François Bourguignon, 429–76. Amsterdam: North-Holland: Elvesier.

———. 2014. *Capital in the Twenty-first Century*. Cambridge, MA: Harvard University Press.

QDBQTZ. 2002. *Qinding baqi tong zhi* [Comprehensive history of the Eight Banners, imperially ordained]. 12 books, 342 + 12 juan. Original edition, 1796. Changchun: Jilin wenshi chubanshe.

QDHLJLSDAXB. 1986. *Qingdai Heilongjiang lishi dang'an xuanbian, 1875–1881* [Selected historical archival documents of Heilongjiang in the Qing dynasty]. Haerbin: Heilongjiang renmin chubanshe.

QDJLDASLXB. 1981. *Qingdai Jilin dang'an shiliao xuanbian* [Selected historical archival sources of Jilin in the Qing dynasty]. Changcun: Jilin sheng dang'an guan.

Qin, Hui, and Wen Su. 1996. *Tianyuanshi yu kuangxiangqu: Guanzhong moshi yu qian jindai shehui de zai renshi* [Pastorals and rhapsodies: A research for peasant societies and peasant culture]. Beijing: Zhongyang bianyi chubanshe.

Qiu, Yuanyuan. 2014. *Zhaoxun jingjiao qiren shehui: Koushu yu wenxian shuangchong shijiao xia de chengshi bianyuan qunti* [Search for the banner society in the suburbs of Beijing: The groups at the margins of the city]. Beijing: Beijing chubanshe.

QSG. 1976. *Qing shigao* [Draft standard history of the Qing]. 48 books. Beijing: Zhonghua shuju.

QSL. 1985. *Qing shilu* [Veritable records of the Qing), 60 books, Beijing: Zhonghua shuju, reprint.

Rankin, Mary Backus. 1986. *Elite Activism and Political Transformation in China: Zhejiang Province, 1865–1911*. Stanford, CA: Stanford University Press.

Reardon-Anderson, James. 2005. *Reluctant Pioneers: China's Expansion Northward, 1644–1937.* Stanford, CA: Stanford University Press.

Reed, Bradly. 2000. *Talons and Teeth: County Clerks and Runners in the Qing Dynasty.* Stanford, CA: Stanford University Press.

Ren, Yuxue. 2013. "Qingdai Jilin jiangjun Shuangcheng diqu de shenfen zhidu yu qijie, minjie (1815–1911)" [Banner and civilian sections in the status system of Shuangcheng, Jilin, during the late Qing dynasty]. *Zhongguo lishi dili luncong* 28 (3): 115–23.

Ren, Yuxue, Zhongqing Li, and Wenlin Kang. 2012. "Difang zhengfu de xingzheng shijian yu guojia zhidu zhijian de chongtu ji chongsu" [Conflict and reform in local government administrative practices and central government institutions: The emergence of the minjie in Shuangchengpu during the late Qing dynasty]. *Bulletin of the Institute of History and Philology Academia Sinica* 82 (3): 493–532.

Rhoads, Edward J. M. 2000. *Manchus and Han: Ethnic Relations and Political Power in Late Qing and Early Republican China, 1861–1928*. Seattle: University of Washington Press.

Rowe, William. 1984. *Hankow: Commerce and Society in China, 1796–1889.* Stanford, CA: Stanford University Press.

———. 1992. *Hankow: Conflict and Community in a Chinese City, 1796–1895*. Vol. 2: Stanford, CA: Stanford University Press.

———. 2001. *Saving the World: Chen Hongmou and Elite Consciousness in Eighteenth-Century China*. Stanford, CA: Stanford University Press.

Scogin, Hugh T., Jr. 1994. "Civil 'Law' in Traditional China: History and Theory." In *Civil Law in Qing and Republican China*, edited by Philip Huang and Kathryn Bernhardt, 13–41. Stanford, CA: Stanford University Press.

———. 2001. "Afterwords." In *Traditional Chinese Contracts and Related Documents from the Tian Collection (1408–1969)*, edited by Tao Tian, Hugh T. Scogin Jr., and Qin Zheng, vii–xviii. Beijing: Zhonghua shuju.

Scott, James C. 1998. *Seeing like a State: How Certain Schemes to Improve the Human Condition Have Failed*. New Haven, CT: Yale University Press.

SCPTTJL. 1990. *Shuangchengpu tuntian jilue* [The brief records of the history of Shuangcheng relocation]. Edited by Lütai Wang. Original edition 1823. Changchun: Jilin wenshi chubanshe.

Scudder, Thayer. 1985. "A Sociological Framework for the Analysis of New Land Settlements." In *Putting People First: Sociological Variables in Rural Development*, edited by Michael M. Cernea, 148–87. New York: Oxford University Press.

Scudder, Thayer, and Elizabeth Colson. 1982. "From Welfare to Development: A Conceptual Framework for the Analysis of Dislocated People." In *Involuntary Migration and Resettlement: The Problems and Responses of Dislocated People*, edited by Art Hansen and Anthony Oliver-Smith, 267–87. Boulder, CO: Westview Press.

SCXXTZ. 2006. *Minguo Shuangcheng Xian xiangtu zhi* [The local records of Shuangcheng County in the Republic of China], In *Zhongguo difang zhi jicheng: Heilongjiang Fu Xian zhi ji* (10 books), book 1, 555–718. Nanjing: Fenghuang chubanshe, originally published in 1916.

SCXZ. 1973. *Shuangcheng Xian zhi* [The gazetteer of Shuangcheng] edited by Gao Wenyuan and Zhang Ziming. Taibei: Chengwen chubanshe. Originally published in 1926.

SCXZ. 1990. *Shuangcheng xian zhi* [The gazetteer of Shuangcheng]. Beijing: Zhongguo zhan wang chu ban she.

Sewell, William H., Jr. 1992. "A Theory of Structure: Duality, Agency, and Transformation." *American Journal of Sociology* 98 (1): 1–29.

Shepherd, John Robert. 1993. *Statecraft and Political Economy on the Taiwan Frontier, 1600–1800*. Stanford, CA: Stanford University Press.

Shirokogorov, Sergeĭ Mikhaĭlovich. 1924. *Social Organization of the Manchus: A Study of the Manchu Clan Organization*. Vol. 3. New York: AMS Press.

Shiue, Carol H. 2008. "Human Capital and Fertility in Chinese Clans." Unpublished manuscript.

Sicular, Terry, Ximing Yue, Björn Gustafsson, and Shi Li. 2010. "How Large Is China's Rural-Urban Income Gap?" In *One Country, Two Societies:*

Rural-Urban Inequality in Contemporary China, edited by Martin King Whyte, 85–104. Cambridge, MA: Harvard University Press.

Sidanius, Jim, and Felicia Pratto. 1999. *Social Dominance: An Intergroup Theory of Social Hierarchy and Oppression*. Cambridge: Cambridge University Press.

Skinner, G. William. 1964. "Marketing and Social Structure in Rural China, Part I." *Journal of Asian Studies* 24 (1): 3–43.

———. 1971. "Chinese Peasants and the Closed Community: An Open and Shut Case." *Comparative Studies in Society and History* 13 (3): 270–81.

Solinger, Dorothy J. 1999. *Contesting Citizenship in Urban China*. Berkeley: University of California Press.

Song, Changbing. 1991. *Zhongguo gudai huji zhidu shigao* [Draft history of household registration in ancient China]. Xi'an: Sanqin chubanshe.

Song, Di, and Xiuhua Wang, eds. 1991. *Qingdai dongbei shenwu* [The ginseng affairs in the Qing dynasty Northeast China]. Changchun: Jilin wenshi chubanshe.

Song, Xi, Cameron Campbell, and James Lee. 2015. "Ancestry Matters: Patrilineage Growth and Extinction." *American Sociological Review* 80 (3): 574–602.

Sudo, Yoshiyuki. 1941. "Seichō chūki ni okeru hata chi no kosaku kankei no tobe jiku: satsu no shōkai o chūshin toshite" [About the land rental relationship on the banner land in the mid-Qing: With a focus on introducing the land registers in the archives of the Ministry of Revenue]. *Tō hō gakuhō* 12 (1): 1–25.

———. 1944. *Shindai Manshū tochi seisaku no kenkyū: toku ni kichi seisaku o chūshin to shite* [Research on the state policy toward land in Manchuria during the Qing]. Tokyo: Kawade shobō.

Szonyi, Michael. 2002. *Practicing Kinship: Lineage and Descent in Late Imperial China*. Stanford, CA: Stanford University Press.

Szreter, Simon, and Keith Breckenridge. 2012. "Recognition and Registration: The Infrastructure of Personhood in World History." In *Registration and Recognition: Documenting the Person in World History*, edited by Keith Breckenridge and Simon Szreter, 1–38. Oxford: Oxford University Press.

Tajfel, Henri, and John C Turner. 1986. "The Social Identity Theory of Intergroup Behavior." In *Psychology of Intergroup Relations*, edited by Stephen Worchel and William Austin, 7–24. Chicago: Nelson-Hall.

Tawney, R. H. 1932. *Land and Labour in China*. New York: Harcourt, Brace & Company.

Taylor, Verta, and Nancy Whittier. 1992. "Collective Identity in Social Movement Communities: Lesbian Feminist Mobilization." In *Frontiers in Social Movement Theory*, edited by Aldon D. Morris and Carol M. Mueller, 349–65. New Haven, CT: Yale University Press.

Tilly, Charles. 1975. "Reflections on the History of European State-Making." In *The Formation of National States in Western Europe*, edited by Charles Tilly, 3–83. Princeton, NJ: Princeton University Press.

———. 1998. *Durable Inequality*. Berkeley: University of California Press.

Tong, Jiajiang. 1994. "Qingdai Baqi zhidu xiaowang shijian xinyi" [New discussion on the death of the Qing Eight Banners system]. *Minzu yanjiu* 5: 101–8.

Treadgold, Donald W. 1957. *The Great Siberian Migration: Government and Peasant in Resettlement from Emancipation to the First World War*. Princeton, NJ: Princeton University Press.

Tsou, Tang. 1981a. Introduction to *Selected Papers from the Center for Far Eastern Studies. No. 4: Proceedings of the NEH Modern China Project, 1979–80: Political Leadership and Social Change at the Local Level in China from 1850 to the Present*, edited by Tang Tsou, v–xx. Chicago: Chicago University Press.

———, ed. 1981b. *Selected Papers from the Center for Far Eastern Studies. No. 4: Proceedings of the NEH Modern China Project, 1978–80: Political Leadership and Social Change at the Local Level in China from 1850 to the Present*. Chicago: Center for Far Eastern Studies, University of Chicago.

Tsuya, Noriko, Wang Feng, George Alter, and James Lee. 2010. *Prudence and Pressure: Reproduction in Europe and Asia, 1700–1900*. Cambridge, MA: MIT Press.

Twitchett, Denis. 1959. "The Fan Clan's Charitable Estate, 1050–1760." In *Confucianism in Action*, edited by David Nivison and Arthur Wright, 97–133. Stanford, CA: Stanford University Press.

UNICEF. 2005. *The "Rights" Start to Life: A Statistical Analysis of Birth Registration 2005*. New York: UNICEF.

Verdery, Katherine. 1994. "Ethnicity, Nationalism, and State-Making." In *The Anthropology of Ethnicity*, edited by Hans Vermeulen and Cora Govers, 33–58. Amsterdam: Het Spinhuis.

Von Glahn, Richard. 2012. "Household Registration, Property Rights, and Social Obligations in Imperial China: Principles and Practices." In *Registration and Recognition: Documenting the Person in World History*, edited by Keith Breckenridge and Simon Szreter, 39–66. Oxford: Oxford University Press.

Wang, Fang. 2004. "Chengwenfa, xiguanfa, yu chuantong Zhongguo shehui de tudi liuzhuan" [Official law, customary law, and land transactions in traditional Chinese society]. *Fazhi yu shehui fazhan* 4: 144–50.

Wang, Fei-ling. 2005. *Organizing Through Division and Exclusion: China's Hukou System*. Stanford: Stanford University Press.

Wang, Feng. 2008. *Boundaries and Categories: Rising Inequality in Post-Socialist Urban China*. Stanford, CA: Stanford University Press.

———. 2010. "Boundaries of Inequality: Perceptions of Distributive Justice among Urbanities, Migrants, and Peasants." In *One Country, Two Societies: Rural-Urban Inequality in Contemporary China*, edited by Martin King Whyte, 219–40. Cambridge, MA: Harvard University Press.

Wang, Guanwu. 1968. "Xu duhou ji" [Reflection on the chronicles of Mo Dehui's life]. In *Shuangcheng Mo Dehui ziding nianpu*, edited by Dehui Mo, 202–13. Taibei: Taiwan shangwu yin shu guan.

Wang, Hongbo, Shuang Chen, Hao Dong, Matthew Noellert, Cameron Campbell, and James Lee. 2016. China Multi-Generational Panel Dataset, Shuangcheng (CMGPD-SC) 1866–1913. User Guide. Ann Arbor: Inter-university Consortium for Political and Social Research.

Wang, Yuhai. 1999. "Qingdai Neimenggu dongbu mengqi kaiken zhong de lantou" [Contractors in the settlement and land cultivation in eastern Inner Mongolia by the Mongolian banners in the Qing]. *Qingshi yanjiu* 4: 33–39.

Wang, Yuquan. 1965. *Mingdai de juntun* [The military farms in Ming dynasty]. Beijing: Zhonghua shu ju.

Wang, Yuquan, Zhongri Liu, and Songyi Guo. 1991. *Zhongguo tunken shi* [The history of state organized farming in China]. Beijing: nongye chubanshe.

Watson, James. 1982. "Chinese Kinship Reconsidered: Anthropological Perspectives on Historical Research." *China Quarterly* 92 (December): 589–622.

Watson, Rubie S. 1982. "The Creation of a Chinese Lineage: The Teng of Ha Tsuen, 1669–1751." *Modern Asian Studies* 16 (1): 69–100.

———. 1985. *Inequality Among Brothers*. Cambridge: Cambridge University Press.

Wei, Guangqi. 2010. *Youfa yu wufa: Qingdai de zhouxian zhidu ji qi yunzuo* [With and without a law: The local government in the Qing and its operation]. Beijing: Shangwu yinshuguan.

Wei, Qingyuan. 1989. "Lun Qingdai renshi huibi zhidu" [On the avoidance system in official appointment in the Qing dynasty]. *Lishi dang'an* 2: 79–88.

———. 1995. "Lun baqi shengji" [On the livelihood of the Eight Banner people] In *Mingqing shi xin xi*, 412–31. Beijing: Zhongguo shehui kexue chubanshe.

Wei, Xiumei. 1992. *Qingdai zhi huibi zhidu* [The avoidance system of the Ch'ing dynasty]. Taibei: Institute of Modern History, Academia Sinica.

Wei, Ying. 2010. *Qingdai jingqi huitun wenti yanjiu* [Research on the rustication of metropolitan bannermen in the Qing]. Harbin: Heilongjiang daxue chubanshe.

———. 2011. "Qing Guangxu chao jingqi huitun Hulan shimo" [The whole story of the Qing rustication of metropolitan bannermen in Hulan in the Guangxu reign]. *Beifang wenwu* 4: 80–83.

White, Harrison C. 1992. *Identity and Control: A Structural Theory of Social Action*. Princeton, NJ: Princeton University Press.

Whyte, Martin King, ed. 2010. *One Country, Two Societies: Rural-Urban Inequality in Contemporary China*. Cambridge, MA: Harvard University Press.

Will, Pierre-Etienne, and R. Bin Wong. 1991. *Nourish the People: The State Civilian Granary System in China, 1650–1850*. Ann Arbor: Center for Chinese Studies, University of Michigan.

Wolf, Arthur P. 2001. "Is There Evidence of Birth Control in Late Imperial China?" *Population and Development Review* 27 (1): 133–54.

Wong, R. Bin, Theodore Huters, and Pauline Yu. 1997. "Introduction: Shifting Paradigms of Political and Social Order." In *Culture and State in Chinese History*, edited by Theodore Huters, R. Bin Wong, and Pauline Yu, 1–26. Stanford, CA: Stanford University Press.

Wu, Jieh-min. 2010. "Rural Migrant Workers and China's Differential Citizenship: A Comparative Institutional Analysis." In *One Country, Two Societies: Rural-Urban Inequality in Contemporary China*, edited by Martin King Whyte, 55–81. Cambridge, MA: Harvard University Press.

Wu, Xiaogang, and Donald J. Treiman. 2004. "The Household Registration System and Social Stratification in China: 1955–1996." *Demography* 41 (2): 363–84.

Xin, Tian. 2007. "Mingji, huji, bianhuqimin: shilun Chunqiu Zhanguo shiqi huji zhidu de qiyuan" [Name registration, household registration, and the state registered population: Tentative discussion on the origin of the household registration system in the Spring and Autumn and Warring State periods]. *Renkou yu jingji* 162 (3): 54–57.

Xu, Bing. 2010. *Mingqing E dong zongzu yu difang shehui* [Lineages in eastern Hubei and local society in the Ming and Qing dynasties]. Wuhan: Wuhan daxue chubanshe.

Xu, Yangjie. 1980. "Song-Ming yilai de fengjian jiazu zhidu shulun" [A discussion on the feudal family system since Song and Ming dynasties]. *Zhongguo shehui kexue* 4: 99–122.

Yan, Yunxiang. 2003. *Private Life Under Socialism: Love, Intimacy, and Family Change in a Chinese Village, 1949–1999*. Stanford, CA: Stanford University Press.

Yang, Guozhen. 2009. *Mingqing tudi qiyue wenshu yanjiu* [Research on land contracts in the Ming and Qing dynasties]. 2nd ed. Beijing: Zhongguo renmin daxue chubanshe.

Yang, Shengmin. 1990. "Handai tudi suoyou zhi liangchongxing zhu wenti shitan" [Tentative examination on the dual characteristics of land tenure in the Han]. *Zhongguo shi yanjiu* 4: 1–10.

Yi, Baozhong. 1990. *Dongbei nongye jindaihua yanjiu* [Study on the modernization of agriculture in Northeast China]. Jilin: Jilin wenshi chubanshe.

Young, Ernest P. 1977. *The Presidency of Yuan Shih-k'ai: Liberalism and Dictatorship in Early Republican China*. Ann Arbor: University of Michigan Press.

Zelin, Madeleine. 1984. *The Magistrate's Tael: Rationalizing Fiscal Reform in Eighteenth-century Ch'ing China*. Berkeley: University of California Press.

———. 2004. "A Critique of Rights of Property in Prewar China." In *Contract and Property in Early Modern China*, edited by Madeleine Zelin, Jonathan K. Ocko, and Robert Gardella, 17–36. Stanford, CA: Stanford University Press.

Zhang, Peiguo. 2002a. *Jindai jiangnan xiangcun diquan de lishirenleixue yanjiu* [A historical anthroplogical study on land tenure in the Yantzu River region in modern China]. Shanghai: Shanghai renmin chubanshe.

———. 2002b. "Zhidu yu huayu: Jindai Jiangnan xiangcun de fenjia xichan" [System and discourse: Household division in villages south of the Yangtze River]. *Fujian Tribune* [Humanities and social sciences] 2: 43–48.

Zhang, Xin. 2000. *Social Transformation in Modern China: The State and Local Elites in Henan, 1900–1937*. Cambridge: Cambridge University Press.

Zhao, Lingzhi. 1999. "Jingji zhufang qidi qiantan." [A survey on the banner land in suburban Beijing]. *Qingshi yanjiu* 3: 23–30.

———. 2001a. *Qing qianqi baqi tudi zhidu yanjiu* [Research on banner land system in the early Qing]. Beijing: Minzu chubanshe.

———. 2001b. "Qingdai zhisheng zhufang qidi qiantan" [A survey on the banner land in the provinces in the Qing]. *Minzu lishi* 2: 70–75.

Zhao, Liyan. 2000. "Qingdai Shuangchengpu diqu biancha baojia shulue" [A brief description of the establishment of the *baojia* system in Qing-dynasty Shuangchengpu]. *Manzu yanjiu* 3: 48–50.

Zhao, Zhongfu. 1972. "Yimin yu Dongsansheng beibu de nongye kaifa" [Migration and agricultural development in the northern part of the Three Northeastern Provinces]. *Jindaishi yanjiusuo jikan* 3, xia: 347–63.

Zheng, Zhenman. 2009. *Xiangzu yu guojia: Duoyuan shiye zhong de Mintai chuantong shehui* [Lineage and the state: The tradtional society in Fujian and Taiwan]. Beijing: Sanlian shudian.

Zhongyang dang'an guan, ed. 1992. *Zhonggong zhongyang wenjian xuanji* [The collection of the documents of the Central Committee of the Chinese Communist Party]. Vol. 16. Beijing: Zhonggong zhongyang dangxiao chubanshe.

Zhou, Feizhou. 2009. "Creating Wealth: Land Seizure, Local Government, and Farmers." In *Creating Wealth and Poverty in Post-Socialist China*, edited by Deborah Davis and Wang Feng, 112–25. Stanford, CA: Stanford University Press.

Zhu, Pengshou. 2002. *Gaoben qingdai renwu shiliao san bian* [Manuscript of biographical materials of Qing people, three books]. 10 volumes. Beijing: Beijing tushuguan chubanshe.

INDEX

Page numbers followed by "f" or "t" indicate material in figures or tables.